14 Arguments in Favour of Human Rights Institutions

14 Arguments *in Favour of* Human Rights Institutions

EDITED BY SHELAGH DAY,
LUCIE LAMARCHE, & KEN NORMAN

with the support of University of Ottawa Human Rights Research and Education Centre

IRWIN LAW

14 Arguments in Favour of Human Rights Institutions

Published in 2014 by

Irwin Law Inc.
14 Duncan Street
Suite 206
Toronto, ON
M5H 3G8

www.irwinlaw.com

ISBN: 978-1-55221-352-0
e-book ISBN: 978-1-55221-363-6

Library and Archives Canada Cataloguing in Publication

14 arguments in favour of human rights institutions / edited by Shelagh Day, Lucie Lamarche, & Ken Norman ; with the support of University of Ottawa Human Rights Research and Education Centre. Includes bibliographical references and index.

Issued in print and electronic formats.

ISBN 978-1-55221-352-0 (pbk.).—ISBN 978-1-55221-363-6 (pdf)

1. National human rights institutions—Canada. 2. Human rights advocacy—Government policy—Canada. 3. Human rights advocacy—Government policy—Canada—Provinces. I. Day, Shelagh, editor of Compilation II. Lamarche, Lucie, editor of compilation III. Norman, Ken, editor of compilation IV. Title: Fourteen arguments in favour of human rights institutions.

JC599.C3A14 2014 323.0971 C2013-908365-0
C2013-908366-9

The publisher acknowledges the financial support of the Government of Canada through the Canada Book Fund for its publishing activities.

We acknowledge the assistance of the OMDC Book Fund, an initiative of Ontario Media Development Corporation.

Printed and bound by CPI Group (UK) Ltd, Croydon, CR0 4YY

1 2 3 4 5 18 17 16 15 14

CONTENTS

ACKNOWLEDGEMENTS

The editors wish to acknowledge the professional and financial support of the Human Rights Research and Education Centre of the University of Ottawa as well as the support of the Social Sciences and Humanities Research Council Community-University Research Alliance through the Reconceiving Human Rights Practice project. In addition, the editors address their very special thanks to Audrey Corsi Caya, who patiently accompanied the editing process of this book.

EDITORS' INTRODUCTION

Shelagh Day, Lucie Lamarche, & Ken Norman

A. INTRODUCTION

Twenty years ago, the United Nations General Assembly adopted the widely known and well-celebrated *Paris Principles on National Institutions for the Promotion and Protection of Human Rights*.[1] The Paris Principles set standards for national human rights institutions. They specify that human rights institutions should be authorized to inquire into and report publicly on any violation of human rights; human rights institutions must also be independent from government, be appointed through inclusive and transparent procedures, and have adequate and stable funding. Subsequently the United Nations Human Rights Council has called on governments around the world to establish human rights institutions with broad mandates to protect and promote all human rights and, where they exist, to strengthen them.[2]

Today, over one hundred national human rights institutions exist in the world and are members of the International Coordinating Committee of the National Institutions for Promotion and Protection of Human Rights.[3] In Canada, the term *human rights institutions* refers to

---

1 *Principles Relating to the Status of National Institutions*, annex to *National Institutions for the Promotion and Protection of Human Rights*, CHR Res 54, UNESCOR, Supp No 2, UN Doc E/1992/22, (1992); GA Res 48/134, UNGAOR, 48th Sess, (1993) Annex.

2 *National Institutions for the Promotion and Protection of Human Rights*, UN Doc A/HRC/Res/20/14, 16 July 2012 and A/HRC/23/L.15, 7 June 2013.

3 See International Coordinating Committee of the National Institutions for Promotion and Protection of Human Rights (ICC), online: ICC http://nhri.

the human rights commissions and tribunals that have the capacity to promote and to protect human rights through receiving, screening, and adjudicating complaints, and through research, consultation, public education, guideline and policy development, inquiries, and the initiation of systemic complaints. In this volume, we extend the category of "human rights institutions" to include a new federal museum, the Canadian Museum for Human Rights, with its core mandate to promote human rights through public education.

Although only the Canadian Human Rights Commission has sought accreditation as a national human rights institution from the International Coordinating Committee, we believe that, because Canada is a federal state, the human rights commissions and tribunals in all jurisdictions should be considered collectively to be Canada's national human rights institution, and, additionally, each one should meet the standards of the Paris Principles.[4] Canada's human rights institutions are creatures of statute. Human rights laws in every jurisdiction delineate rights to be free from discrimination in employment, services, tenancy, and occupational and professional associations, and establish human rights institutions to administer and enforce the laws.

This book is not published to celebrate the Paris Principles, but to address serious concerns that Canada is not ensuring that its human rights institutions meet the standards of the Paris Principles and that it is not continuing to strengthen them. Many disturbing attacks have been made on human rights and human rights institutions over the last decade by governments themselves, by conservative activists, and by courts and tribunals when they deliver narrow and defeating interpretations of rights. After almost half a century of experience with human rights institutions in Canada, we believe that today there are troubling issues about the strength of some of our human rights institutions, and, because of that, about access to justice and to effective remedies for human rights violations in Canada.

So, the system of human rights institutions in Canada presents a contemporary challenge: can we say that human rights institutions in Canada satisfy the letter and spirit of the Paris Principles? As in all periods, some institutions are stronger than others, and some strategies for

---

ohchr.org/EN/Pages/default.aspx.

4 See, for example, Ontario Human Rights Commission, *Reviewing Ontario Human Rights System*, online: OHRC www.ohrc.on.ca/sites/default/files/discussion_paper_reviewing_ontario%27s_human_rights_system.pdf.

promoting human rights are ascendant, while others languish. This is why the editors invited writers from across the country to reflect upon the state of human rights institutions in Canada, and to speak candidly as litigators, advocates, human rights scholars, and former members and staff of commissions and tribunals.

We know that strong human rights institutions are essential. That said, we believe that a lively ongoing assessment and critique of how they are doing is necessary to make and keep them strong. So, while we have titled this book *14 Arguments in Favour of Human Rights Institutions*, this book is not a simple book of praise; it is also critical of human rights institutions and particularly of government treatment of them. It is a collection of reflections on what is happening to human rights and human rights institutions now — the good and the bad — reflections that arise from the genuine commitment of all of the authors to vital human rights institutions and a vigorous human rights culture.

As understandings of discrimination and equality have developed over time, so too have approaches for addressing and achieving them. Providing effective remedies to human rights complainants is an essential role of human rights institutions. However, human rights institutions now use more mixed methods, including larger public education projects and interinstitutional collaborations, to achieve the goals of human rights laws. As a result, this book takes a broad view of the roles of human rights institutions, examining the many different methods being used to foster recognition for human dignity and social solidarity.

As many authors explain in this book, it is the synergetic relationship between the different roles of human rights institutions — between research, public education, public policy design, and law enforcement — that truly promote and protect human rights and the right to live free from discrimination.

This book does not offer an exhaustive examination of what is happening in each jurisdiction. On the contrary, the book is structured thematically. We provide some background information on these themes so that the contributions of all those who generously gave their time and attention to this book can be fully appreciated.

B. EVOLUTION IN HUMAN RIGHTS SCHEMES IN CANADA

The evolution of human rights schemes in Canada is different from that envisioned by the Paris Principles. Of course, Canadian governments did not wait for the development of the Paris Principles, or for their adoption in 1993, to create human rights institutions. While Saskatchewan, in 1947, was the first Canadian government to pass a human rights act that prohibited discrimination in accommodation,[5] employment, and education, Ontario was the first in 1962[6] to adopt a comprehensive *Human Rights Code* that provided for the creation of a human rights commission.[7] The federal government and other provinces and territories soon followed, creating new human rights institutions in every jurisdiction to enforce anti-discrimination provisions and provide remedies. Everywhere in Canada, residents can seek a remedy for discrimination based on enumerated grounds by filing a complaint with a human rights institution, whether commission or tribunal.

Canada focused from the start on the role of human rights institutions as mechanisms for screening and resolving human rights complaints. However, as Maxwell Yalden points out in his chapter on the Paris Principles,[8] the Principles deal with this capability to process and adjudicate complaints as an optional role, while regarding a broad mandate to inquire into and report publicly on any human rights violations, and to advise governments regarding the conformity of legislation and practices with domestic and international human rights law, as mandatory roles for a national human rights institution. These monitoring, inquiry, and public reporting roles are still underdeveloped in Canada, but there is more interest in them now than before.

In Chapter 3, Ken Norman reminds us that early leaders in the human rights field, like Walter Tarnopolsky, envisioned the establishment of human rights commissions as a way to replace ineffective penal anti-discrimination statutes with administrative law institutions that would rely less on punishment of discriminators and more on "conciliation and settlement." This "velvet glove" model was seen as a step forward from court-based law enforcement, which was considered too adversarial and expensive, and which rarely helped the victim of the discrimination.

---

5 *The Saskatchewan Bill of Rights Act, 1947*, SS 1947, c 35.

6 *Human Rights Code*, RSO 1961–62, c 93.

7 See ch 6.

8 See ch 7.

The commission-based model would meet the needs of the most vulnerable and offer more flexibility.[9] It would foster expertise and guarantee to victims the required sensitivity to their experiences; it would be proactive and serve the broader public interest in the elimination of discrimination.

Since the creation of human rights institutions, the *Canadian Charter of Rights and Freedoms*[10] has been adopted and extensively interpreted, and interpretations of *Charter* equality rights and statutory anti-discrimination rights have become interwoven. At the beginning of *Charter* equality rights interpretation the Supreme Court of Canada carried the fundamental principles that had been established in human rights jurisprudence into interpretation of *Charter* equality guarantees. Perhaps most important of these was the understanding that discrimination is not defined by intent but by adverse effects. At the same time, the Supreme Court described human rights codes in Canada as "quasi-constitutional" in nature because of the importance of their subject matter, and confirmed that human rights legislation calls for large, purposive, and liberal interpretation in order to give effect to its remedial goals.[11]

Human rights institutions in Canada can wear Tarnopolsky's velvet glove sometimes, but to be transformative tools for equality and social justice, they need to exercise all of their powers — to conduct research, inquire, educate, consult, assist victims, design public policies, settle and adjudicate complaints, and initiate systemic complaints — including ones considered more confrontational. As this book demonstrates, there is still an ongoing discussion about just how "velvet" human rights institutions should be. What is the best combination of persuasion and enforcement? Does an emphasis on conciliation and settlement make

---

9 See John Dwyer, "Roles and Responsibilities in Implementing HR: Similarities and Differences in Approaches to Access to Justice" in Helena Birt, ed, *Access to a Specialized Human Rights Tribunal: an Urgent Need to Act in Quebec?* (Cowansville, QC: Yvon Blais, 2008) 277 at 292–93. Cited by Michelle Flaherty in ch 6.

10 *Canadian Charter of Rights and Freedoms*, Part I of the *Constitution Act, 1982*, being Schedule B to the *Canada Act 1982* (UK), 1982, c 11.

11 See, for example, *Insurance Corp of British Columbia v Heerspink*, [1982] 2 SCR 145 at 157–58; *Ontario (Human Rights Commission) v Simpsons Sears Ltd*, [1985] 2 SCR 536 at para 12; *Canadian National Railway Co v Canada (Canadian Human Rights Commission)*, [1987] 1 SCR 1114 at 1134–38; *Québec (Commission des droits de la personne et des droits de la jeunesse) v Montréal (City)*, 2000 SCC 27 at para 30.

institutions unwilling to address persistent and seemingly intransigent issues of discrimination?

Authors in this volume express deep regret about legislative changes that take away, weaken, or fail to enhance some of these powers: the lost opportunity to give the Saskatchewan Human Rights Commission a transformative regulatory role in the early 1980s;[12] the elimination in 2002 of the British Columbia Human Rights Commission and with it, the loss of public education, inquiry, and promotional roles;[13] and the 2011 return to court-based adjudication in Saskatchewan combined with the weakening of support for complainants.[14]

The nature of human rights complaints in Canada has also changed, and this has had an impact on government attitudes towards human rights institutions. In the beginning, many complaints addressed overt discrimination in private sector employment or services (access to taxis or restaurants). Over time, complaints have come to challenge more subtle or indirect forms of discrimination. But also, more complaints challenge discrimination or under-inclusiveness in benefit schemes and public services. This has had the effect of arousing government defensiveness because of their liability and given rise to a government respondent strategy of arguing for narrow interpretations of their own human rights statutes.

Another noticeable evolution is the globalization or universalization of human rights. Of course, human rights in Canada are rooted in the *Universal Declaration of Human Rights*,[15] and Canada holds out its human rights institutions as one of the means of fulfilling the human rights obligations it has signed on to under international human rights instruments that have been developed since the *Declaration*. Nonetheless, as explained in the chapters written by Shelagh Day and by Gwen Brodsky,[16] though Canada has supported and encouraged the drafting and adoption of many international human rights treaties, Canada currently appears to resent being monitored by the international agencies whose role is to assess the domestic compliance of signatories.

---

12 See ch 3.

13 See ch 1.

14 See ch 5 and 1.

15 *Universal Declaration of Human Rights*, GA Res 217(III), UNGAOR, 3d Sess, Supp No 13, UN Doc A/810, (1948) 71.

16 See ch 1 & 2.

The palpable resentment of human rights monitoring that the federal government currently expresses affects the climate in which all human rights institutions in Canada operate. It is a difficult time for them to take up the watchdog, monitoring role that the Paris Principles assign to them to ensure that their own governments comply with domestic and international human rights standards. Changes in the nature of complaints and the rapid development of international human rights instruments are positive and necessary developments in the human rights field, but they have exacerbated political tensions in Canada between governments and their human rights institutions.

C. HUMAN RIGHTS INSTITUTIONS AND COMPLAINT PROCEDURES

The classical journey of a human rights complaint looks a bit like a movie screenplay. In the beginning, there is a complainant or a group of complainants. With the complaint, comes a human rights commission, often described as the gatekeeper or the rainmaker. Most commissions have the power to assess the relevancy of the complaint, to conduct an investigation, to attempt mediation, and, if unsuccessful, to submit the case to adjudication and ask for appropriate remedies. All along, there is a respondent that some media commentators enjoy describing, wrongly, as "the accused."

"The End" of the movie is eliminating discrimination and compensating the victims. In some cases, remedies call upon respondents to implement systemic changes to alter discriminatory practices. Because the elimination of discrimination is understood to be in the public interest in Canada, one way this public interest can be satisfied is in the search for, and implementation of, remedies designed to ensure that the kind of discrimination addressed in a particular complaint does not recur.

In fact, the journey of a human rights complaint in Canada is legally and politically much more complex than it seems. First, the general conditions under which the system operates are worth noting: commissioners and *ad hoc* adjudicators or members of human rights tribunals

1 2 3 4 5 6 7 8 9 10 11 12 13 14

are politically appointed.[17] That raises the issue of the quality of appointments, how appointments are made, and the protections for the independence of human rights institutions that are in place, issues of central importance in the Paris Principles. Second, human rights institutions in Canada are notoriously underfunded. This means that among inquiry, research, consultation, and litigation, tough choices have to be made, which often end up being political choices. Third, complainants are desperately in need of legal advice and representation and look to human rights commissions to provide that support, which they do less often.

The rapid development of the expertise of non-governmental organizations (NGOs) in the field of human rights does not necessarily translate into a capacity to provide adequate legal support to human rights complainants in the absence of commissions playing that role. NGOs militate for change; they work at increasing awareness amongst the public and at building new consensus. But, they are still considered "outsiders," and in some cases threatening ones, by human rights institutions, of whom NGOs are sometimes critical, as they are of governments. This may be slowly changing. But still, NGOs do not have the capacity to answer all the needs for support and legal representation of victims of discrimination.

Concerns are raised that some private sector respondents (in particular, small business owners) are also in need of support and legal representation because discrimination complaints and complaint management are becoming more technical and complex. A careful examination of human rights commissions' annual reports shows that increasingly human rights complaints are directed against governments, governments' agencies, or other kinds of public authorities, such as municipalities or school boards. These respondents will have publicly funded counsel. Consequently, the fairness concerns regarding legal representation for respondents may arise in a smaller number of cases.[18]

---

17 Except in Québec: *Charter of human rights and freedoms*, RSQ 1975, c C-12, s 101:

> The Tribunal is composed of not fewer than 7 members, including a president and assessors, appointed by the Government. The president shall be chosen, after consultation with the chief judge of the Court of Québec, from among the judges of that court having notable experience and expertise in, sensitivity to and interest for matters of human rights and freedoms; . . .

18 See ch 4.

Finally, it is just a fact that human rights complaints are increasingly complex. The refinement of the standard of substantive equality, the requirement for accommodation, and the increased presence of public authorities as respondents command careful attention and, in certain cases, courage, from both human rights commissions and tribunals. As Gwen Brodsky notes in Chapter 2, governments are increasingly arguing aggressively against commissions and complainants and recommending to tribunals and courts interpretations that would defeat substantive and systemic claims. Recent research also suggests that a diverse society brings more complexity to the work of human rights institutions as rights protected both by the *Charter* and by human rights codes may conflict. In that regard, the chapter in this book written by Lesley Jacobs and Lorne Foster provides interesting examples as well as innovative solutions.[19]

As Genevieve Leslie puts it in Chapter 5, the gatekeeping function of a human rights commission (dismissing or investigating a complaint and bringing it in front of a tribunal) is governed by a set of rules: fairness, accessibility, transparency, accountability, and economy.[20] In other words, the screenplay of a discrimination complaint is governed by the rule of law and by the basic rules of administrative fairness. But commissions have been accused of taking too long in processing complaints, lacking transparency in their decision making process, providing limited access to adjudication, and not providing adequate support to complainants or, in the view of some, to respondents.

There is some truth to all that. Human rights complaints management has become a complex and sometimes cumbersome reality.

Accordingly, some provinces have made major changes in their human rights legislation. And some chapters in this book explain them in detail. In Saskatchewan, the 2011 legislation eliminated the human rights tribunal entirely and now all complaints will be adjudicated by the courts.[21] It also increased the discretion of the Chief Commissioner to dismiss a complaint. Quick mediation and settlement seem to be the goals of the reform. It may make the system quicker and more efficient,

---

19 See ch 13.

20 See Saskatchewan Human Rights Commission, *Renewing the Vision: Human Rights in Saskatchewan: Report of the Saskatchewan Human Rights Commission* (Saskatoon: SHRC, 1996), cited by Leslie in ch 5.

21 *An Act to amend* The Saskatchewan Human Rights Code *and to make consequential amendments to* The Labour Standards Act, SS 2011, c 17.

1 2 3 4 5 6 7 8 9 10 11 12 13 14

if the time it takes to open and close complaints is the measure. However, as Genevieve Leslie demonstrates, there are serious questions about whether this new scheme will better promote and protect human rights.

In Ontario, the adoption in 2008 of the amendments to the *Human Rights Code*[22] created a tripartite system: Commission, Tribunal, and Legal Support Centre, with the Commission entirely removed from the role of receiving and processing complaints. Because the Legal Support Centre is underfunded to handle the demand for its services, and many parties appear before the Tribunal unrepresented, Michelle Flaherty describes in Chapter 6 the Tribunal's efforts to develop effective mediation and active adjudication methods that will work for self-represented complainants and respondents.

The case of British Columbia is dramatic. The BC legislature simply abolished its human rights commission in 2002, leaving complainants to seek help from an underfunded community organization and public advocacy clinic, and the province with no human rights institution to carry out research, education, promotion, inquiries, consultations, or to initiate complaints.[23] When complaint processing is the only mandate of a human rights institution, the community feels the loss of the public voice, the public education, and guideline making roles — all of the work that is directed to preventing complaints and learning from them.

Some chapters of this book comment on the validity of the ostensible rationales for reforms of human rights institutions: efficiency, as measured by processing times; percentages of successful mediations; and "customer satisfaction" of complainants. Questions are raised about a "business" model that appears to conceptualize human rights institutions as little different from public agencies that inspect car emissions. A system that privileges mainly efficiency and settlements may produce good numbers. But this assessment neglects the public interest dimension of the work of human rights institutions. As well, it does not account for the fact that a complainant experiences a lot of frustration, pain, and isolation, and comes to a commission with a story that is socially rooted

---

22 *An Act to amend Human Rights Code*, RSO 2006, c 30.

23 These amendments were made in the *Human Rights Code Amendment Act, 2002*, by repealing or amending ss 5, 6, 19(1), 21(2) & 21(3) of the *Human Rights Code*, RSBC 1996, c 210. More detail can be found in Shelagh Day, *Bill 53: An Assessment of the Government of British Columbia's Draft Human Rights Legislation* (July 2002), online: Canadian Centre for Policy Alternatives, BC Office http://povertyandhumanrights.org/wp/wp-content/uploads/2009/08/bill53.pdf.

in exclusion, poverty, and inequalities. So, another way to frame the question is: how transformative, socially and economically speaking, is a version of human rights justice that mostly looks for "good numbers"?

D. HUMAN RIGHTS UNDER ATTACK

This book raises issues about the politics of human rights institutions in Canada today. Pearl Eliadis and Richard Moon's chapters[24] discuss the orchestrated attack on human rights institutions by Ezra Levant and Mark Steyn, who used section 13 of the *Canadian Human Rights Act*,[25] the hate speech provision, as a platform. Although Eliadis and Moon disagree about whether an anti-discriminatory restriction on speech belongs in human rights legislation, they agree that the real target of Levant and Steyn was human rights commissions and tribunals, which were dubbed "kangaroo courts." Eliadis explains that the attack of the "free speechers" was an attack on normal administrative law procedures, which are necessarily different from criminal law procedures. While Levant and Steyn claim criminal law procedures are those that define "real law," Eliadis notes that administrative law institutions, like workers' compensation and residential tenancy boards, are where most dispute resolution in Canada occurs; they are closer to citizens than courts, and they are essential to the effective exercise of citizenship. Moon demonstrates eloquently that there has never been a "section 13 driven obsession" on the part of the Canadian Human Rights Commission or any other human rights commission in Canada. However, as noted earlier, human rights protections are also under attack from governments when they are respondents in human rights cases. As Gwen Brodsky notes, this attack on statutory human rights protections is being made at a moment when the equality guarantees of the *Charter* have become virtually inaccessible to disadvantaged groups in Canada because of the abolition of the Court Challenges Program.[26]

1 2 3 4 5 6 7 8 9 10 11 12 13 14

---

24 See ch 4 and 10.

25 RSC 1985, c H-6.

26 From 1985 to 2006, the Court Challenges Program of Canada (CCP) provided modest funds to applicants who wished to bring forward test cases under section 15, the equality guarantee of the *Charter*. Over its twenty years in operation, the CCP provided genuine access to the use of *Charter*

Human rights litigation is, by its nature, public interest litigation. With the public interest comes the need for remedies that look to the future. Public interest remedies go beyond a single complaint and are designed to transform the entities that practice discrimination: workplaces, schools, benefit programs, or police services. Such remedies appear in numerous decisions from the Supreme Court of Canada, including those regarding the duty to accommodate.

Sadly, however, the recent Supreme Court decision in *Moore v British Columbia (Ministry of Education)*[27] sends a discouraging message about remedies that would hold provincial ministries and school districts accountable for eliminating discrimination against children with severe learning disabilities. The Supreme Court declined to order systemic remedies against either the provincial Ministry of Education or the North Vancouver School District, permitting only individual remedies for Jeffrey Moore to stand. The BC Human Rights Tribunal had crafted a detailed order including components addressed to both the province and the school district.[28] But Justice Abella agreed with government lawyers that such remedies should not be ordered and scolded the Tribunal, reminding it that it is "not a Royal Commission." Both Gwen Brodsky and Shelagh Day comment on this decision in their respective chapters.

In the same vein, the Québec Court of Appeal, in *Québec (Commission des droits de la personne et des droits de la jeunesse) c Commission scolaire des Phares*,[29] invalidated the part of the Québec Human Rights Tribunal decision[30] ordering the school board to revisit its policies for autistic children. Both these decisions clearly isolate the families of disabled children who are struggling for accommodation at school and multiply the number of cases and the cost of litigation.

Gwen Brodsky examines in detail what is happening in the litigation regarding the right to non-discriminatory services. According to Brodsky, governments as litigators are currently attempting to create a "human rights free zone" when services are challenged. Because of

---

equality rights for members of marginalized groups. Funding for the program was cancelled by the Government of Canada in September 2006.

27 *Moore v British Columbia (Ministry of Education)*, 2010 BCCA 478, aff'g 2008 BCSC 264, rev'd 2012 SCC 61.

28 *Moore v North Vancouver School Dist No 44*, 2005 BCHRT 580.

29 *Québec (Commission des droits de la personne et des droits de la jeunesse) c Commission scolaire des Phares*, 2008 QCCA 2320.

30 *Québec (Commission des droits de la personne et des droits de la jeunesse) c Commission scolaire des Phares*, 2009 CanLII 19 (QC TDP).

this, governments' conduct when litigating in human rights cases, says Brodsky, does not conform with their positive duty to uphold the *Charter* value of equality.

The weakening of human rights can also come through the unexpected results of well-intentioned legislative amendment. Rachel Cox offers a fascinating case study of "human rights reframing" by exploring the Québec statutory prohibition of psychological harassment at work.[31] Her chapter makes an excellent companion piece to Constance Backhouse's moving piece about her personal crusade for the inclusion of sexual harassment at work as discrimination based on sex.[32] Reading Cox and Backhouse together teaches us that a well-intentioned law reform initiative, in this case one promoted by Québec unions, can make sex discrimination invisible once more by subsuming it under a broader, de-gendered harm — psychological harassment — and placing it in labour standards legislation. Cox explains that since the introduction of protection from psychological harassment, complaints of sexual harassment filed with the Québec Human Rights Commission have dwindled, while, at the same time, the sexual harassment that is inherent in many psychological harassment complaints is not being addressed. In Québec, the courts, and particularly the Québec Court of Appeal in the devastating decision in *Ménard c Rivet*,[33] added to the problem by deciding that complainants must use either labour legislation or human rights legislation, but not both. Of course, damages for psychological harassment are not the same as damages for sexual harassment. Further, Cox demonstrates that when psychological harassment at work is set outside the human rights framework, the victim, who is often a non-unionized working woman, becomes "medicalized."

Rights face threats from many directions — from governments and government litigators, from conservative anti-rights activists, from courts that weaken rights through timid interpretation, and from well-intentioned initiatives that broaden but de-gender protections.

---

31 See ch 9.
32 See ch 8.
33 *Ménard c Rivet*, [1997] RJQ 2108 (QC CA).

E. THE FUTURE OF HUMAN RIGHTS INSTITUTIONS IN CANADA

Where does that leave human rights institutions, which are not, as we have said, sufficiently independent or adequately and stably funded? They shy away from tackling larger issues of systemic discrimination, says Shelagh Day in Chapter 1, in part because they are not receiving encouragement from governments or reinforcement from the courts. In some cases, the business model adopted by some commissions inclines them to privilege quick and simple solutions reached by mediation. In other cases, commissions seem to be convinced that "softer" strategies can be more effective than those, like litigation, that are seen to be more confrontational. However, the problem seems to lie in treating the complaint handling or litigation powers and the research, inquiry, and education powers as though human rights institutions must choose between them. In practice, the powers of research, guideline writing, consultation, and litigation are mutually reinforcing, and importantly so.

Shaheen Azmi[34] (Ontario Human Rights Commission) and Paul Eid[35] (formerly with the Québec Human Rights Commission) demonstrate this in their chapters on the development and application of the concepts of racial and social profiling. These are important case studies because the institutions, particularly in Ontario, have combined litigating complaints against police agencies with research, consultation, policy formulation, and collaboration with police forces to create a larger, interconnected group of anti-discrimination strategies. In both jurisdictions, research and legal policy formulation have been central to developing sophisticated methods of addressing racial and social profiling, including through well-supported complaints.

Lorne Foster and Lesley Jacobs in Chapter 13 describe the *Policy on Competing Human Rights*[36] recently adopted by the Ontario Human Rights Commission. For Foster and Jacobs, recognizing that rights may conflict can foster transformative social justice practices. They note that a "problem solving" method can be more empowering for some vulnerable citizens than a formal adversarial process. Interested parties in a conflict of

---

34 See ch 11.

35 See ch 12.

36 Ontario Human Rights Commission, *Policy on Competing Human Rights* (Toronto: OHRC, 2012), online: OHRC www.ohrc.on.ca/sites/default/files/policy%20on%20competing%20human%20rights_accessible_2.pdf.

rights, if treated with respect and invited to engage in dialogue, may be able to craft remedies that are acceptable and practical in a complex and diverse society. This proactive and multi-stakeholder approach, according to Foster and Jacobs, can prevent leaping too swiftly to complaint-filing. Foster and Jacobs do not claim that using the Competing Rights Policy should always come first. But they do suggest that sometimes it may help human rights law deliver social inclusion.

Jennifer Carter and Jennifer A Orange are also interested in innovative ways of promoting human rights.[37] They suggest in their chapter that museums can be human rights educators and should be seen as new forms of human rights institutions. Their survey of different initiatives around the world, including the Museo de la Memoria y los Derechos Humanos in Santiago, Chile, and the Osaka Human Rights Museum in Japan, as well as the new Canadian Museum for Human Rights in Winnipeg, is challenging for those who still consider human rights to be the exclusive purview of courts and tribunals. For Carter and Orange, museums are experts at disseminating knowledge, promoting informal learning, and politicizing public interest issues, such as human rights. They consider human rights museums to be human rights activists, ideally positioned to broaden and enliven the understanding of human rights in Canada.

In a time of adversity, human rights institutions struggle. The crisis of human rights institutions in Canada is multi-faceted, and our institutions are fragile. Nonetheless, there is a lot of vital work going on. Crisis is a time for new strategies and for renewal. We believe that Canada's human rights institutions can be strengthened, especially if those who know the value of human rights institutions become more active in their defence.

We hope this book will foster discussion about human rights institutions — their strengths and weaknesses, their roles, and their future directions. We also hope this book promotes a sense of shared ownership of human rights and human rights institutions, and fosters wider support for a robust and sturdy human rights system in Canada.

1 2 3 4 5 6 7 8 9 10 11 12 13 14

37 See ch 14.

PART 1

Human Rights Institutions in Canada: Manoeuvring in a Context of Hostility and Political Tension

CHAPTER 1

REFLECTIONS ON GOVERNMENT HOSTILITY, SYSTEMIC DISCRIMINATION, AND HUMAN RIGHTS INSTITUTIONS

Shelagh Day[1]

A. INTRODUCTION

Governments create and fund human rights commissions and tribunals, but they often treat them with ambivalence and sometimes outright hostility.[2] The last decade has been particularly bad. When government hostility makes human rights commissions — the institutions that are the public voice for human rights — "risk-averse" and soft-spoken, there is a public silence about some of the toughest human rights problems and a shrinking understanding of human rights.

This institutional fright is understandable, warranted. Nonetheless, I believe that "lying low" is neither a legitimate response for commissions, given their mandate, nor strategic. When human rights commissions do not engage with the key human rights issues of the day, two things happen. First, the broad public understanding of what is a human rights issue in Canada is diminished. The lie that equality exists is more easily accepted if human rights institutions, whose business it is to address inequality, are mainly silent on larger, persistent patterns. Second, human rights commissions can be seen to be unimportant and unnecessary, making

---

1 Shelagh Day is an expert on human rights with many years of experience working with governments and non-governmental organizations. She is the President and Senior Editor of the *Canadian Human Rights Reporter*, as well as a Director of the Poverty and Human Rights Centre in Vancouver.

2 By human rights institutions, I mean both statutory human rights commissions and tribunals, although this chapter is principally about commissions.

them vulnerable to being abolished, *because* they are not taking on the toughest human rights challenges. In short, silence is dangerous.

Virtually every human rights law in Canada provides a mandate to its commission to be a public voice to foster an understanding of human rights. For example, the *Canadian Human Rights Act*[3] (CHRA) gives the Canadian Human Rights Commission (Canadian Commission) a mandate to foster public recognition of the principle of non-discrimination, and to "try by persuasion, publicity or any other means that it considers appropriate to discourage and reduce discriminatory practices."[4]

In human-rights-denying moments, this is a key responsibility of human rights commissions: to keep alive a public narrative about human rights — what they mean, where they are being violated, which groups experience violations, and what is the nature of the harm. Human rights commissions need to provide a continuing and detailed commentary on the state of human rights compliance in Canada in order to provide a realistic picture and to sustain a culture of expectation that human rights will be fulfilled.

Commissions have diverse tools for addressing larger patterns of inequality and discrimination, including legal advocacy, research, annual and special reports, inquiries, and consultations. They can also combine processes to develop strategic approaches to particular systemic issues.

My contention is that counteracting government hostility and attempts to ignore, diminish, or dismiss systemic human rights problems requires the full engagement of all of the capacities of human rights institutions, some of which are currently underused.

These reflections address the extent and nature of government hostility to human rights and human rights institutions, and the capacities that human rights commissions, in particular, have to address systemic discrimination and to counteract chill and denial.

B. GOVERNMENT HOSTILITY TO HUMAN RIGHTS AND HUMAN RIGHTS INSTITUTIONS

Government hostility to human rights has taken many forms over the last decade. But it appears to be rooted in an unwillingness to acknow-

3 RSC 1985, c H-6, ss 2 and 27 (1)(a) [*CHRA*].
4 *Ibid*, s 27(1)(h).

ledge the seriousness of discrimination and inequality in Canada and, in particular, governmental responsibility for it. It posits that human rights violations in Canada are aberrant incidents and that members of disadvantaged groups are mainly responsible for their own marginality.[5] It asserts that there is neither history nor context for discrimination.

The Harper administration has a particularly bad case of denial. A tour of the Status of Women Canada website, for example, reveals that the policy issue that most concerns the Harper government about women is discrimination in corporate boardrooms.[6] Speeches of Rona Ambrose, the federal Minister for the Status of Women, are perfunctory: on the question of women's equality, she has little to say.[7]

The refusal to admit that there is any serious discrimination or inequality in Canada is also manifest in Canada's response to critical commentary on its human rights record from United Nations treaty bodies and rapporteurs. Olivier De Schutter, the United Nations Special Rapporteur on the Right to Food, was subjected to unprecedented personal attacks by the federal government when he came to Canada on an official

---

5 A recent example of this victim-blaming can be seen in the remarks of Kelowna-Mission NDP candidate Dayleen van Ryswyk. She was ousted from her candidacy after the NDP learned that she had posted these comments about Aboriginal people on the Internet:

> It's not the status cards, it's the fact that we have been paying out of the nose for generations for something that isn't our doing. If their ancestors sold out too cheap it's not my fault and I shouldn't have to be paying for any mistake or whatever you want to call it from MY hard earned money.
>
> It's time our generation stopped paying for the mistakes of the past . . . let us all be one people . . . THE SAME . . . race, creed colour or gender shouldn't matter anymore in this day and age . . . enough is enough already . . . .
>
> In my opinion, we have paid our debt . . . a thousand fold . . . it's time to move on, heal, and grow. If the native people are to be the proud nation they keep talking about, then stand on your two feet and hold your heads high. There are a lot of things to be proud of, stop dwelling on the past . . . .

See Jonathan Fowlie, "NDP Dumps Candidate over 'Unacceptable' Comments" *The Vancouver Sun* (16 April 2013), online: The Vancouver Sun http://blogs.vancouversun.com/2013/04/16/ndp-dumps-candidate-over-unacceptable-comments/.

6 Status of Women Canada, *Women on Boards*, online: SWC www.swc-cfc.gc.ca/pol/wob-fca/index-eng.html.

7 Status of Women Canada, *Speeches*, online: SWC www.swc-cfc.gc.ca/med/spe-dis/index-eng.html.

visit. Despite the well-known and documented problem of hunger among low-income people in Canada, Mr De Schutter's mission was described by the Minister of Citizenship and Immigration as "completely ridiculous." He was told that he should not get involved in "political exercises in developed democracies like Canada" and the fact that he made reference to the food security issues of Aboriginal people was called "insulting."[8] Unfortunately, Mr De Schutter is not the only international human rights expert or agency to receive dismissive and insulting treatment by the Harper government.[9] There is a pattern of hostility to human rights scrutiny, which includes not responding to requests for visits to Canada from the United Nations Committee on the Elimination of Discrimination Against Women and the Inter-American Commission to investigate murders and disappearances of Aboriginal women and girls.[10] This pattern of hostility obtains whether the monitoring human rights institutions are domestic or international.

---

8 See Letter to Prime Minister Stephen Harper (30 May 2012) endorsed by over 100 organizations, online: Food Secure Canada http://foodsecurecanada.org/sites/foodsecurecanada.org/files/ENGLISH-LETTER-FINAL,JUNE10-1.pdf; Food Security Canada, *Canada's Politicians and the Right to Food Report*, online: Food Secure Canada http://foodsecurecanada.org/sites/foodsecurecanada.org/files/CanadasPoliticiansandtheRight-toFoodreport.pdf; Human Rights Council, *Report of the Special Rapporteur on the Right to Food, Olivier De Schutter*, UNGAOR, 22nd Sess, Supp No 50, Addendum No 1, UN Doc A/HRC/22/50/Add.1, (2012), online: UN Special Rapporteur on the Right to Food www.srfood.org/images/stories/pdf/officialreports/20121224_canadafinal_en.pdf.

9 *Empty Words and Double Standards: Canada's Failure to Respect and Uphold International Human Rights: Joint Submission to the United Nations Human Rights Council in relation to the May 2013 Universal Periodic Review of Canada* (October 2012), online: Social Rights in Canada http://socialrightscura.ca/documents/international/UPR%202013%20NGO%20Coalition%20submission.pdf.

10 Requests for visits from James Anaya, the Special Rapporteur on the Rights of Indigenous Peoples, the CEDAW Committee, and the Inter-American Commission on Human Rights were not responded to by Canada for more than a year. The requests were finally granted at the time of Canada's second Universal Periodic Review by the Human Rights Council because it had become known that the requests had been made, and Canada's poor record on indigenous women was a concern for many countries during the review. See Adrian Humphreys, "Three UN Rapporteurs on their Way to Probe Canada's Human Rights Record" *National Post* (26 April 2013), online: National Post http://news.nationalpost.com/2013/04/26/harper-government-grants-un-rapporteurs-permission-to-probe-canadas-human-rights-record about breaking this logjam.

Government hostility has not just been expressed in rhetoric, but also in action, and not just by Harper, but by other governments in Canada as well. Perhaps most extreme was the 2002 elimination of the BC Human Rights Commission (BC Commission) by the provincial government.[11] The Attorney General of the time, Geoff Plant, claimed that moving to a "direct access" model, with only a tribunal and no commission, was an advance.[12] There were legitimate concerns about delays at the screening stage, caused by the BC Commission's discharge of its gatekeeping role — that is, by the investigation and decision making entailed in deciding whether a complaint should be dismissed, settled, or go to a hearing on its merits — but the abolition of the BC Commission had implications and effects far beyond the correction of this problem.

The rationale proffered by the government for eliminating the BC Commission was to get rid of the time-consuming screening and to ensure that claimants got "directly" to a hearing of the merits of their complaints. In fact, the gatekeeping role was not eliminated. It was transferred, in part, to the BC Human Rights Tribunal (BC Tribunal), where (mostly unrepresented) claimants now deal with the same gatekeeping issues through technical and often disputatious pre-hearing procedures that are respondent-driven.[13] It was also transferred, in part, to the BC Human Rights Coalition, which is funded by the Government of British Columbia to provide initial advice to complainants and to refer complainants to the Community Legal Assistance Society, which provides some legal services.[14]

---

11 *Human Rights Code Amendment Act, 2002*, SBC 2002, c 62 [*Amendment Act, 2002*], amending *Human Rights Code*, RSBC 1996, c 210 [BC *Code*].

12 For an assessment of British Columbia's post-2002 human rights system, see Shelagh Day, *Rolling Back Human Rights in BC: An Assessment of Bill 53 — the Government of British Columbia's Draft Human Rights Legislation* (September 2002), online: Canadian Centre for Policy Alternatives BC Office www.policyalternatives.ca/sites/default/files/uploads/publications/BC_Office_Pubs/human_rights_code_brief.pdf.

13 BC Human Rights Tribunal, *Annual Report 2011–2012* (Vancouver: BCHRT, 2012) at 11, online: BCHRT www.bchrt.bc.ca/annual_reports/info/Annual_Report_2011-2012.pdf; BC Human Rights Tribunal, *Annual Report 2010–2011* (Vancouver: BCHRT, 2011) at 12 & 13, online: BCHRT www.bchrt.bc.ca/annual_reports/info/Annual_Report_2010-2011.pdf; BC Human Rights Tribunal, *Annual Report 2009–2010* (Vancouver: BCHRT, 2010) at 19, online: BCHR www.bchrt.bc.ca/annual_reports/info/Annual_Report_2009-2010.pdf.

14 See BC Human Rights Coalition, *Annual Report 2011–2012* (Vancouver: BC HR Coalition, 2012) at 17, online: BC HR Coalition www.bchrcoalition.org/files/documents/11-12AnnualReport.pdf.

Two things were lost with the abolition of the BC Commission: first, the understanding that the enforcement of human rights laws and the elimination of discrimination is in the public interest; and second, the roles of the BC Commission that support the public interest in the elimination of discrimination that are not specifically related to complaint handling.

When comprehensive human rights legislation was designed in the 1960s and 1970s, a fundamental principle underlying human rights laws was that the elimination of discrimination is in the public interest. Discrimination was understood to be an offence against shared public values of equality and fairness for all individuals and groups. Because of this, for many years, complaints of discrimination were not viewed merely as disputes between private parties, but rather as matters in which the community as a whole has a stake. Among other things, commissions were seen to be stewards of the development of human rights jurisprudence with an inherent interest in its robustness and sensitivity to the forms of discrimination experienced by different groups.

Through the 1980s and 1990s human rights commissions, through carriage of complaints before adjudicators and courts, articulated and ultimately secured recognition from the Supreme Court of Canada of fundamental principles for the interpretation of human rights law. These principles include: that human rights legislation sets out comprehensive procedures for the vindication of the public policy of non-discrimination;[15] that human rights legislation is fundamental public policy intended to benefit the community as a whole as well as individual victims of discrimination;[16] that human rights laws are quasi-constitutional, have primacy, and cannot be waived or varied by private contract;[17] that human rights are remedial and directed to the removal of anti-social conditions without regard to the intention of those who

---

15 *Seneca College of Applied Arts and Technology v Bhadauria*, [1981] 2 SCR 181 at 183 and 195 [*Bhadauria*].

16 *Ontario (Human Rights Commission) v Borough of Etobicoke*, [1982] 1 SCR 202 at 213 & 214 [*Etobicoke*]; *O'Malley v Simpsons-Sears Ltd*, [1985] 2 SCR 536 at 547 [*O'Malley*].

17 *O'Malley, ibid* at 547; *Winnipeg School Division No 1 v Craton*, [1985] 2 SCR 150 at 156; *Insurance Corporation of British Columbia v Heerspink*, [1982] 2 SCR 145 at 158; *Action travail des femmes v Canadian National Railway Company*, [1987] 1 SCR 1114 at 1136 [*Action travail*]; *Etobicoke*, above note 16 at 213 & 214.

cause them.[18] Commissions, as legal advocates for complainants, have been the builders of human rights jurisprudence in Canada; the major cases that are considered the pillars of human rights law were mounted and argued by them.[19]

However, in British Columbia with the BC Tribunal alone and no commission, the character of human rights legislation has changed dramatically. The BC Tribunal is an adjudicator and must be seen to be impartial. The BC Tribunal can only deal with the arguments made by the parties to a complaint, and schematically, with no commission, there is no advocate for the public interest in the elimination of discrimination; there are only the individual or group claimants who bring their particular cases forward, and those who are alleged to have discriminated against them. Human rights complaints become disputes between these private parties.[20]

One might argue that the public interest remains sufficiently protected because of the established character of the rights. But when that public interest has no institutional means of expression, it is hard to hold on to. It is not just that with the elimination of the commission, there is no steward of the jurisprudence, but also that a number of the other functions that are necessary to protect the broad public interest in the elimination of discrimination have vanished.

In the BC *Human Rights Code*[21] (BC *Code*) now, there is no public body with a mandate:

- to provide education and information programs designed to promote an understanding and acceptance of human rights;[22]

---

18 *Action travail*, above note 17 at 1136 & 1137; *Robichaud v Canada (Treasury Board)*, [1987] 2 SCR 84 at 90–95 [*Robichaud*]; *Brooks v Canada Safeway Ltd*, [1989] 1 SCR 1219 at 1239 [*Brooks*].

19 *Brooks, ibid*; *Janzen v Platy Enterprises Ltd*, [1989] 1 SCR 1252; *Robichaud*, above note 18.

20 The BC *Code* and the BC Tribunal's rules permit intervenors who could have a broader public interest in an issue raised in a particular case. But in practice, such interventions are rare. BC *Code*, above note 11, s 22.1; British Columbia, Human Rights Tribunal, *Rules of Practice and Procedure*, r 28.

21 BC *Code*, above note 11.

22 *Ibid*, s 5, before being repealed by *Amendment Act*, 2002, above note 11, s 3. The Government of British Columbia may argue that it provides information regarding human rights on the Attorney General's web page and that it funds the BC Human Rights Coalition to provide public information and education on human rights. However, these offerings are very limited, because, in the main, they only describe established law. Since the meaning

- to conduct and encourage research on matters relevant to human rights;[23]
- to hold public hearings and consultations regarding matters relevant to the BC *Code*;[24]
- to make special reports to the Legislative Assembly concerning urgent human rights matters;[25]
- to deal with systemic discrimination, to initiate complaints, or to join complaints as a party in order to argue — on behalf of the broader public interest — for interpretations of law that will eliminate discrimination;[26] or
- to ensure that complainants receive legal representation at hearings and appeals, and assistance during pre-hearing procedures.[27]

The current BC *Code* states that among the purposes of the *Code* are:

- to foster a society in British Columbia in which there are no impediments to full and free participation in the economic, social, political, and cultural life of British Columbia;[28]
- to promote a climate of understanding and mutual respect where all are equal in dignity and rights;[29] and
- to identify and eliminate persistent patterns of inequality associated with discrimination prohibited by this *Code*.[30]

---

and parameters of human rights are, by definition, always shifting and expanding, human rights education by commissions has to be forward-looking and foster thinking about the application of human rights to as yet unadjudicated circumstances.

23 *Ibid*, s 6(1).

24 *Ibid*, s 6(2).

25 BC *Code*, above note 11, s 19(1), before being repealed by *Amendment Act*, 2002, above note 11, s 5.

26 *Ibid*, ss 21(2) & 21(3), before being repealed by *Amendment Act*, 2002, above note 11, s 5.

27 For further information, see Community Legal Assistance Society, *BC Human Rights Clinic*, online: CLAS www.clasbc.net/human_rights_clinic.php; The BC Human Rights Coalition, *Human Rights Clinic*, online: BC Human Rights Coalition www.bchrcoalition.org/files/services_a.html; Judith Doulis & Susan O'Donnell, "The BC Human Rights Clinic" in Continuing Legal Education Society of BC, *Human Rights - 2003* (Vancouver: Benwell-Atkins Ltd, 2003) 2.1 at 2.1.01–2.1.04.

28 BC *Code*, above note 11, s 3(a).

29 *Ibid*, s 3(b).

30 *Ibid*, s 3(d).

But without a commission, there is no one to do this. The only part of the human rights system that is left is individual complaint-processing by the BC Tribunal. This diminishment matters. Governments narrow the meaning of rights by diminishing the means of their realization.[31] In British Columbia now, the human rights system has been reduced to a mechanism for resolving private disputes between complainants and respondents.

The decision of the government to abolish the BC Commission was not merely intended to address delays in gatekeeping, which could have been done in other ways, it was intended to reduce the capacities of the province's human rights system to deal with systemic issues. That this was the case is demonstrated by the fact that at the same time it abolished the BC Commission, the Government of British Columbia also repealed the section of the BC *Code* that prohibited paying women less than men for work of equal value,[32] and it dismantled the government's internal employment equity program.[33]

---

31 This insight belongs to Roberto Mangabeira Unger.

32 The BC *Code* was amended by the *Human Rights Code Amendment Act, 2001*, SBC 2001, c 15, s 1, to require equal pay for work of equal value. This provision was repealed almost immediately, after a change in government, by *Miscellaneous Statutes Amendment Act, 2001*, SBC 2001, c 32, s 11.

33 Abigail B Bakan & Audrey Kobayashi, "Backlash against Employment Equity: The British Columbia Experience" (2004) 29:1 Atlantis 61 at 62. Subsequent attacks have been directed at the BC Tribunal. The Government of British Columbia decided not to re-appoint Heather MacNaughton, the Chair of the BC Tribunal, and member of the Tribunal Judy Parrack. This discontent was articulated by Peter A Gall, Kate Bayne, & Susan Chapman in "Human Rights in the Workplace: The Case for a Specialized Workplace Tribunal," online: CBA www.cba.org/cba/cle/pdf/Gall_Peter.pdf. In this paper, Peter Gall, who is the Government of British Columbia's most senior employment lawyer, expresses explicit disapproval of decisions of the BC Tribunal made by MacNaughton, Lindsay Lyster, and Parrack on the grounds that: "In more recent decisions . . . the Tribunal has demonstrated an unduly protectionist and overly broad view of its own jurisdiction, a procedurally rigid and formal approach to decision-making, and a lack of appreciation for the realities and exigencies of the organized workplace" (*ibid* at 3). This paper and its principal argument — that complaints regarding employment should be taken away from the BC Tribunal and adjudicated instead by a "super workplace tribunal" — was referred by the Government of British Columbia to the BC Law Institute for study. The Law Institute recommended against pursuing Peter Gall's recommendations. See British Columbia Law Institute, *Workplace Dispute Resolution Project: Report to the Ministry of Labour and the Ministry for the Attorney General* (31 October 2010), online: BCLI www.bcli.org/sites/default/

The brutal approach to human rights and its human rights commission taken by the Government of British Columbia sent a signal to the public that little importance need be attached to the rights or to the institutions that enforce them. Understandably, what the British Columbia government did makes commissions in other jurisdictions feel threatened. If British Columbia can abolish its human rights commission, other governments may feel at liberty to do the same.[34]

The attacks of the past decade on human rights institutions have not been directed to human rights commissions alone. Saskatchewan has also gutted its human rights system, although in a different way.[35] The Government of Saskatchewan abolished the Saskatchewan Human Rights Tribunal and now requires complainants to take their cases to court.[36] Under amended legislation, the Saskatchewan Human Rights Commission (Saskatchewan Commission) still receives all complaints and the Chief Commissioner is the sole gatekeeper. He has complete discretion to determine which complaints can go forward to court. Now he need only decide that "having regard to all the circumstances of the complaint, a hearing of the complaint is not warranted." The only recourse for those whose complaints are dismissed is judicial review of the Chief Commissioner's decision at the complainant's own expense;

---

files/BCLI_Workplace_Dispute_Resolution_Report.pdf. Nevertheless, five of the nine members of the Tribunal were replaced between 2010 and 2012.

34 British Columbia's assertion that all that is needed is a direct access tribunal, that is, a procedure and an arena for disputes between parties to be resolved, influenced the Territory of Nunavut when it introduced its first human rights legislation in 2008. Instead of establishing both a commission and a tribunal, the Government of Nunavut eliminated the commission from its legislation at the last minute and established only a "direct access" tribunal. Many Nunavuumi have come to understand, from experience, that the Territory would have been better off with only a commission, rather than with only a tribunal, since there has been no institution to support and guide those trying to use their rights, and no public advocate or educator in a jurisdiction where anti-discrimination legislation is completely new. See Gwen Brodsky & Shelagh Day, *Strengthening the Nunavut Human Rights System: A Report for the Government of Nunavut* (February 2012), online: Legislative Assembly of Nunavut http://assembly.nu.ca/library/GNedocs/2012/000707-e.pdf.

35 For full discussion of the Saskatchewan amendments, see ch 5.

36 *Saskatchewan Human Rights Code*, SS 1979, c S-24.1, ss 29–31, repealed by SS 2000, c 26, ss 25–27 and SS 2011, c 17, ss 12–17.

the courts are likely to defer to the Chief Commissioner's administrative decisions.[37]

Following closely on amendment of the legislation came the firing of senior staff of the Saskatchewan Commission,[38] among them the supervisor of investigations. There is no clarity now about how complainants, who are permitted to proceed to court because the Chief Commissioner has opened the gate, will be represented or assisted.

The firings were accompanied by statements from the Chief Commissioner that there would be a new emphasis on "directed mediation."[39] "Directed mediation" is not a credible option unless there is an enforcement process that is accessible if mediation fails. Ken Norman, Mary Eberts, and Alex Neve noted in their commentary on these changes that:

> The recent departures have left the Commission with no lawyers on staff to advise investigators on a daily basis, to carry cases forward to the Court of Queen's Bench and beyond, or to serve the Commission in any other capacity. For a complainant with no hope of having his or her case taken forward vigorously and effectively, "mediation" may be simply another term for "give up now rather than later."[40]

---

37 See *Bateman v Canada (Attorney General)*, 2008 FC 393 at para 27, citing *Slattery v Canada (Human Rights Commission)*, [1994] 2 FC 574 at para 49, aff'd (1996), 205 NR 383 (FCA).

38 Six employees were terminated without cause on 25 January 2012. See "Union Miffed over Layoffs at Human Rights Agency" *Canadian Press* (1 March 2012), online: CBC News www.cbc.ca/news/canada/saskatchewan/story/2012/03/01/sk-human-rights-union-120301.html.

39 Angela Hall, "Gov't Set to Dissolve Tribunal" *The Star Phoenix [Saskatoon]* (30 October 2010), online: The Star Phoenix www2.canada.com/saskatoonstarphoenix/news/third_page/story.html?id=9557fb53-f15a-4fbd-9614-95821fc88c96. Judge David Arnot, the Chief Commissioner of the Saskatchewan Human Rights Commission, has been a principal architect of this change, demonstrating that appointments to human rights leadership positions are crucial, as a carefully chosen Chief Commissioner can assist a hostile government to diminish the institution which he leads. Justice Minister Don Morgan said that the new system "will both strengthen confidence in the process and help reduce the lengthy timelines within the current process." See Government of Saskatchewan, News Release, "Government Moves to Update Human Rights Code" (29 November 2010), online: Government of Saskatchewan www.gov.sk.ca/news?newsId=00190364-b11c-4c5e-8fbc-f34695bc27e6.

40 Ken Norman, Mary Eberts, & Alex Neve, "The Wrong Moves for Saskatchewan Human Rights" *Human Rights Digest* 13–4 (June 2012), online: CHRR http://cdn-hr-reporter.ca/new/viewpoints.

Mediation and education seem to be only the two roles of human rights institutions which Saskatchewan currently supports. These are not enough, especially when mediation is an endgame, and education does not include the educative role that a vital development of jurisprudence can play in teaching the public what human rights mean.

The antipathy to opening the gate to adjudication is palpable in the Saskatchewan Commission's response to the Supreme Court of Canada's decision in *Saskatchewan (Human Rights Commission) v Whatcott*[41] (*Whatcott*). The Saskatchewan Commission's press release claims the decision is a victory, but goes on to say:

> The SHRC has prosecuted only five cases relating to the dissemination of hate in the last 32 years and considers prosecution a tool to be used sparingly and judiciously and only in the most extreme cases.[42]

Like British Columbia's 2002 amendments, the Saskatchewan changes are designed to narrow the capacity of the province's human rights institutions. The Government of Saskatchewan has dealt with the adjudication of human rights complaints as a suspect activity, particularly if conducted by a specialized human rights tribunal, and has turned it over to the courts, without apparent supports for complainants or commitment on the part of the Saskatchewan Commission to appear or intervene. It is clear that the goal of this amendment is not to improve the quality of adjudication, but to stop human rights complaints from going forward. Although the legislative redesign in Saskatchewan is very different, one aspect of the result is similar to that in British Columbia: complaints become a matter of private dispute resolution and mediation, not public interest and concern.[43]

Further, the fact that the current Chief Commissioner in Saskatchewan, David Arnot, advocated for these changes and fired the senior staff, makes it unlikely that the Saskatchewan Commission will turn to using its reporting or inquiry powers to address systemic issues of inequality in the province, particularly with respect to issues where the

---

41 *Saskatchewan (Human Rights Commission) v Whatcott*, 2013 SCC 11.

42 Saskatchewan Human Rights Commission, Media Release, "Saskatchewan Human Rights Commission Calls Supreme Court Decision a Victory for Minorities" (27 February 2013), online: SHRC www.shrc.gov.sk.ca/pdfs/news/SHRC_MEDIARELEASE_FEB27.pdf.

43 As can be seen from the response to *Whatcott*, this is a position not only of the Government of Saskatchewan but also of the current Saskatchewan Commission.

government has a role in maintaining a systemic or structural inequity or could provide the remedy for it.

Frequently, there is a connection between hostility to human rights institutions and hostility to the substantive content of human rights protection. Consequently, it is not surprising that Ezra Levant has been a cheerleader for the Saskatchewan amendments. Since three human rights complaints were made regarding Mark Steyn's article on the "rising influence of Islam," and one complaint was made about Ezra Levant's republication of the Danish cartoons of Mohammed, Steyn, Levant, and others have been engaged in a furious anti-human rights campaign against human rights institutions — both commissions and tribunals — and against the substantive protections from speech that promotes hatred.[44] Steyn and Levant have characterized human rights commissions as "kangaroo courts" and jackbooted oppressors. It is not surprising that Levant applauds the Saskatchewan amendments for "taking human rights matters out of the hands of their human rights commission, and giving it to real courts."[45]

Steyn and Levant have campaigned with some success against the provisions in human rights laws, like the Saskatchewan provision at issue in *Whatcott*, that prohibit publishing or distributing material that exposes a person or group to hatred or contempt on the basis of a prohibited ground of discrimination.[46] Because of the Steyn-Levant campaign, the Harper Government supported a private member's bill introduced by Conservative backbencher Brian Storseth,[47] which had the effect of repealing section 13 of the *CHRA*.[48]

---

44 For full discussion of the attacks on section 13 of the *Canadian Human Rights Act*, see ch 4 and 10.

45 Kendall Anderson, "Ezra Levant's Human Rights Crusade" *The Mark* (20 July 2011), online: The Mark www.themarknews.com/articles/6190-ezra-levants-human-rights-crusade/#.UFNWxa7qs6F. Of course this is a mischaracterization of what the amendments actually do, because they have taken adjudication away from the Saskatchewan Tribunal, not "out of the hands of their human rights commission." Accuracy is not Mr Levant's strong suit.

46 The first version of this discussion of the repeal of section 13 appeared in Shelagh Day, "Freedom of Expression Harper Style" (2012) 13:5 Human Rights Digest, online: Human Rights Digest www.cdn-hr-reporter.ca/new/viewpoints. (Authorship of columns in the Digest is unattributed, but they are written by Shelagh Day, the President and Senior Editor of the *Canadian Human Rights Reporter*, except where guest authorship is identified.)

47 Bill C-304, *An Act to amend the Canadian Human Rights Act (protecting freedom)*, 1st Sess, 41st Parl, 2011 (first reading by the Senate 7 June 2012).

48 Mr Storseth's bill received Senate approval on 26 June 2013.

This section, since 1977, has been used mainly against prominent white supremacists, such as John Ross Taylor and Ernst Zündel, who have made careers of promoting hatred against Jews and non-whites.[49] The human rights complaints regarding Mark Steyn's political commentary on Islam, and Ezra Levant's republication of the Danish cartoons of Mohammed, which were offensive but not hate-promoting, broke the pattern.[50] The media reaction, fired by Steyn and Levant, has been unmeasured. Canada's modest and carefully enforced anti-hate provisions have been depicted inaccurately as gigantic threats to freedom of speech. The fact that the complaints against Steyn's article were dismissed at an early stage[51] and the complaint against Levant to the Alberta Human Rights Commission was withdrawn was ignored.[52]

I agree with the Supreme Court of Canada's finding in *Whatcott* that the purpose of hate speech provisions in human rights law is to eliminate systemic discrimination against vulnerable groups. I do not believe that the repeal of section 13 is a legitimate effort to improve the law.[53] Rather, it is a signal from the federal government that restraints on public speech about racialized minorities, gays and lesbians, and women —

---

49 *Canada (Human Rights Commission) v Taylor*, [1990] 3 SCR 892.

50 Ontario Human Rights Commission, "Commission Statement Concerning Issues Raised by Complaints against Maclean's Magazine" (9 April 2008), online: OHRC www.ohrc.on.ca/en/news_centre/commission-statement-concerning-issues-raised-complaints-against-macleans-magazine; "Human Rights Complaint Dismissed against Maclean's" *Canadian Press* (29 June 2008), online: Toronto Star www.thestar.com/news/canada/2008/06/29/human_rights_complaint_dismissed_against_macleans.html; *Elmasry and Habib v Roger's Publishing and MacQueen (No 4)*, 2008 BCHRT 378.

51 *Ibid* at para 6.

52 Graeme Morton, "Muslim Leader Drops Complaint against Levant; Printed Cartoon" *National Post* (13 February 2008) A2.

53 It is particularly hard to justify the repeal of section 13 after the suicide of Rehteah Parsons, who was harassed on the Internet by the public display of photographs of her rape by four boys. The *Criminal Code*, RSC 1985, c C-46 hate speech provisions, which are offered as a substitute for the *CHRA*'s protection from the dissemination of hate-promoting material, do not provide any answer to this sexualized and sexist Internet harassment. Sections 318 & 319 of the *Criminal Code* prohibit incitement to hatred based on colour, race, ethnicity, religion, and sexual orientation, but not sex. Further, what was done to Rehteah Parsons might not be recognized by prosecutors as incitement to hatred within the meaning of the *Criminal Code*, even if sex were a ground.

whether in law or in social practice — are not consonant with the Harper Government's libertarianism or with its tolerance for harshness.[54]

The Harper Government's hostility to the content of protections that are designed to address entrenched patterns of discrimination was also obvious in the 2009 decision to, in effect, take away the right of female federal public servants to equal pay for work of equal value. The Government claimed that it recognizes that pay equity is a right of women and, by taking their right to pay equity out of the *CHRA* and setting it out in the *Public Sector Equitable Compensation Act*[55] (*Equitable Compensation Act*), it merely introduced efficiency and speed to the process of obtaining pay equity in the public service. In fact, as women wrote to Harper at the time, this legislation "empties the right to pay equity of its meaning" for female federal public servants.[56]

The new criteria for evaluating "equitable compensation" for female public servants legitimizes sex discrimination in pay practices, rather than eliminating it. The *Equitable Compensation Act* stipulates that the assessment of the value of work performed will now take into account not just skill, effort, and responsibility, but also "the qualifications required to perform the work and *the market forces operating* in respect of employees with those qualifications" [emphasis added].[57] This permits any evaluation to take into account that male-dominated jobs are valued more highly in the market, requiring the employer to pay more to attract or retain employees, even if the value of the work when it is assessed based on skill, effort, and responsibility is no greater than that of female-dominated jobs.

---

54 I owe this phrase to Hugo Young writing for *The Guardian* about the legacy of Margaret Thatcher. See Hugo Young, "Margaret Thatcher Left a Dark Legacy that Has Still Not Disappeared" *The Guardian* (11 April 2013), online: The Guardian www.guardian.co.uk/politics/interactive/2013/apr/11/margaret-thatcher-legacy-best-writing.

55 RSC 2009, c 2, s 394 [*Equitable Compensation Act*]. The *Equitable Compensation Act* was assented to 12 March 2009. It will come into force after regulations are developed and approved by the Governor in Council; see Treasury Board of Canada Secretariat, "FAQ: The *Public Sector Equitable Compensation Act*," online: TBS www.tbs-sct.gc.ca/lrco-rtor/relations/faq/pseca-lersp-eng.asp#faqq4. Regulations are expected in the spring of 2014.

56 Letter from Shelagh Day et al to Prime Minister Stephen Harper (23 February 2009), online: Law of Work http://lawofwork.ca/wp-content/uploads/2009/02/payequityletterfinal2009.htm.

57 *Equitable Compensation Act*, above note 55, s 4(2)(b).

Under the new scheme, employers and unions are jointly responsible for "equitable compensation," even though federal public sector unions do not have any control over the federal purse. "Equitable compensation" for female federal public servants is a matter to be negotiated between employers and unions at the same time as other collective bargaining issues, not separately and distinctly. This puts female federal public servants at risk of having their right to be free from sex discrimination in pay bargained away because other issues are of more importance to the employer or the union, or both.

Individual women are permitted to make complaints to the Public Service Labour Relations Board if they believe that their compensation is not "equitable." However, there is no investigatory body or legal assistance available. Previously, if women filed complaints with the Canadian Commission, the Commission would investigate. Under the *Equitable Compensation Act*, not only is there no support provided, there is a bar against unionized women having the assistance of their unions to make pay equity complaints. Unions will be fined $50,000 if they assist any woman to make a complaint.[58]

Complaints about pay equity are, by definition, systemic group-based complaints. Individual female public servants, without help from the Canadian Commission or their unions, will not have access to the information about pay rates and job descriptions that is necessary to make an "equitable compensation" complaint.

There have been many problems with the current federal pay equity system. At the moment, there is no proactive legislation that requires federal sector employers, including the Government of Canada, to review their compensation schemes and ensure that women are paid equal pay for work of equal value. The complaint system under the *CHRA* has proven notoriously slow and unwieldy.[59]

---

58 As the letter to Harper notes, this imposition of a fine contravenes article 9(3)(c) of the *Declaration on the Rights of Human Rights Defenders* which states that "everyone has the right, individually and in association with others, . . . to offer and provide professionally qualified legal assistance or other relevant advice and assistance in defending human rights and fundamental freedoms." See *Declaration on the Right and Responsibility of Individuals, Groups and Organs of Society to Promote and Protect Universally Recognized Human Rights and Fundamental Freedoms*, GA Res 53/144, UNGAOR, 53d Sess, (1999) 1 at 5, online: OHCHR www.ohchr.org/Documents/Issues/Defenders/Declaration/declaration.pdf.

59 For example, in *Public Services Alliance of Canada v Canada Post Corp*, 2011 SCC 57, the Supreme Court of Canada made a final ruling on a complaint

For some years, there has been a broad consensus among employers, unions, and women's organizations that this system needs fixing. In 2004, a Pay Equity Task Force was appointed, which, after thorough review and consultation, made recommendations for a new proactive pay equity system, with a Pay Equity Commission and Tribunal. These recommendations had widespread support, and, if they had been implemented, female workers in the federal sector would have had access, for the first time, to an efficient and effective mechanism for realizing their right to non-discrimination in pay.

The *Equitable Compensation Act* is a dismaying alternative and reveals the stark unwillingness of the Harper Government to address systemic discrimination in pay structures for women.

This is a considerable pile of wreckage. The elimination of a commission and a tribunal, the loss of pay equity provisions in British Columbia, and, *de facto*, in the federal public service, the repeal of the prohibition against spreading hatred on the Internet — these have chilled the climate for human rights in Canada, particularly as they have occurred along with the erosion of access to the use of rights in the *Canadian Charter of Rights and Freedoms*[60] (*Charter*) rights due to the cancellation of the Court Challenges Programme, reduced legal representation for human rights complainants, cuts to civil legal aid, de-funding of non-governmental organizations that advocate for the realization of human rights,[61] and a government practice of making anti-equality arguments before courts and tribunals.[62]

It appears that some governments have concluded that Canada's statutory human rights system should have little, if any, applicability to larger, persistent patterns of inequality that Aboriginal peoples, women, members of racial minorities, people with disabilities, and others experience in Canada, and that it should deal only with individual, narrowly

---

filed by female employees of Canada Post in 1983.

60 Part I of the *Constitution Act, 1982*, being Schedule B to the *Canada Act 1982* (UK), 1982, c 11.

61 For commentary on reduced access to the use of rights, see Voices-Voix, "The Court Challenges Program," online: Voices-Voix http://voices-voix.ca/en/facts/profile/court-challenges-program; Shelagh Day, *Rolling Back Human Rights in BC*, above note 12; "Harper Government Steps Up Attacks against Women's Human Rights — Several Key Feminists Groups Lose Funding" *Canada Newswire* (6 May 2010), online: CNW www.newswire.ca/en/story/687923/harper-government-steps-up-attacks-against-women-s-human-rights-several-key-feminists-groups-lose-funding.

62 For full discussion of government anti-equality arguments, see ch 2.

defined instances of discrimination. The statutory human rights system is not capable, on its own, of eliminating systemic discrimination in Canada. But the human rights system does need to be, and be seen to be, a central mechanism for challenging it.

What should human rights institutions do? My contention is that at this moment they should engage with systemic discrimination more vigorously and more publicly because passivity has its own greater hazards. What follows is a discussion of the capacities of human rights commissions and how those capacities can be used now.

C. SYSTEMIC DISCRIMINATION AND INSTITUTIONAL CAPACITY: LITIGATION, RESEARCH, REPORTING

Canada's human rights commissions have a number of powers. They can be legal advocates through carriage of complaints, appearances, interventions, and initiation of complaints. They can develop policy guidelines; conduct research; undertake inquiries, studies, or reviews; engage in consultations; review laws and regulations for their compliance with human rights legislation and, in some jurisdictions, with international human rights treaties; and provide reports or special reports to Parliament or a minister. These all provide key ways to address systemic discrimination and they can be used in integrated and strategic ways that are mutually reinforcing. Some of these powers are overlooked or underused.

The role of human rights commissions is to foster a human rights culture, a culture in which human rights are well understood and fulfilment of them is expected. This requires a lively public discourse and constant attention to a narrative thread, a public storytelling about what is happening to various groups in our communities, how human rights violations occur, and what remedies are needed.

The litigation of systemic issues is an essential part of this storytelling. But the public narrative can also be carried and strengthened, and important groundwork for litigation of systemic issues can be laid, through reports, research, studies, and consultations, which paint a larger picture of an issue and develop public understanding.

1) Providing the Systemic Backdrop for Individual Complaints

A focus on systemic discrimination matters because the goal of human rights schemes is to eliminate discrimination, not merely to provide a mechanism for processing complaints from individuals. Providing remedies to individuals whose rights have been violated is essential, and, in theory, it should lead to not needing to do so, as a particular form of conduct becomes widely understood as discriminatory and falls into disuse.

However, commissions and tribunals deal every year with a plethora of complaints about the same forms of discrimination — firings because of pregnancy,[63] for example, because women are still too often treated by employers as though they have transgressed reasonable expectations when they need time away from work in order to give birth. The resolution of each individual complaint matters; it has a systemic dimension since it is about an act that happens to a person because of their membership in a group, and because the complaints and the resolution of them give effect to the public policy that there will be no sex discrimination in employment. Pregnancy complaints are systemic in the sense that the complaints arise because of deeply entrenched, lasting models of "the worker" as male, unencumbered by the exigencies of reproductive labour. However, the resolution of each pregnant woman's complaint does not, in itself, prevent any other woman from being discriminated against in a similar way.

Similarly, sexual harassment complaints and complaints about racial profiling arise because of embedded assumptions about women's sexual availability and about the innate dangerousness and criminality of Black and Aboriginal men. But while pregnancy discrimination, sexual harassment, and racial profiling are systemic in the sense that they are based on entrenched assumptions, and affect women and members of racialized minorities broadly, they cannot be adjudicated on a group basis, because each incident of racial profiling or sexual harassment is idiosyncratic, and confirmation of the presence of profiling or harassment depends on scrutiny of the conduct of individual respondents.[64]

---

63 *Wang v Rick Hansen Institute*, 2013 BCHRT 93.

64 Probably the most effective means of combating sexual harassment in the workplace has been the inclusion of anti-harassment protocols in union contracts. This has provided unionized women with readily available procedures, which are agreed to by their co-workers, for addressing this form of sex discrimination.

1 2 3 4 5 6 7 8 9 10 11 12 13 14

It is important to acknowledge, however, that individual complaints about racial profiling or sexual harassment have become viable and comprehensible to adjudicators, respondents, and the public, because of broader investigations, consultations, and reports that have been prepared by human rights commissions and experts.[65] These reports and consultations have explored the discriminatory practice and revealed the systemic pattern which is the backdrop for both individual complaints and the development of policy guidelines. Reports and consultations can also be vehicles for taking public awareness another step forward on a particular issue, when the law is evolving, or because the energy of new insight and incentive is needed to move employers and service providers out of a discriminatory rut.

For example, the reports and guidelines produced by the Ontario Human Rights Commission (Ontario Commission) regarding racial profiling by the police have been important to raising the profile of this issue. In 2003, the Ontario Commission initiated an inquiry into "the effects of racial profiling on individuals, families, communities, and society as a whole." The Ontario Commission produced an inquiry report entitled *Paying the Price: The Human Cost of Racial Profiling* based on over 400 personal accounts.[66] The Ontario Commission hoped ultimately to "bridge the divide between those who deny the existence of profiling and communities that have long felt that they are being targeted." Since that time,

---

65 See Québec, Commission des droits de la personne et des droits de la jeunesse, *Racial Profiling and Systemic Discrimination of Racialized Youth: Report of the Consultation on Racial Profiling and its Consequences* (2011), online: CDPDJ www.cdpdj.qc.ca/publications/Profiling_final_EN.pdf; Manitoba, Manitoba Human Rights Commission, *Racialized Communities and Police Services Project 2005–2012* (2012), online: The Manitoba Human Rights Commission www.manitobahumanrights.ca/publications/reportsandsubmissions/rcaps_final_report_2005-2012.pdf; Nova Scotia, Nova Scotia Human Rights Commission, *Working Together to Better Serve All Nova Scotians: A Report on Consumer Racial Profiling in Nova Scotia* (2013), online: Nova Scotia Human Rights Commission http://humanrights.gov.ns.ca/sites/default/files/files/crp-report.pdf.

66 Ontario Human Rights Commission, *Paying the Price: The Human Cost of Racial Profiling* (21 October 2003), online: OHRC www.ohrc.on.ca/sites/default/files/attachments/Paying_the_price%3A_The_human_cost_of_racial_profiling.pdf. See also Ontario Human Rights Commission, "Paying the Price: the Human Cost of Racial Profiling: Human Rights Commission Releases Report" (9 December 2003), online: OHRC www.ohrc.on.ca/en/news_centre/paying-price-human-cost-racial-profiling-ontario-human-rights-commission-releases-report. For full discussion of the Ontario Commission's work on racial profiling, see ch 11.

the Ontario Commission has produced *Policy and Guidelines on Racism and Racial Discrimination*[67] and a guide for organizational change in police institutions — *Human Rights and Policing: Creating and sustaining organizational change*[68] — which is the result of a three-year collaborative project with the Toronto Police Services and the Toronto Police Services Board. This report sets out strategies that police organizations can use to disrupt discriminatory practices and foster a human rights culture in their own institutions. There is also a new commission-mandated study on racial profiling in traffic stops in Ottawa which is now underway.[69]

The stream of consultations, reports, guides, and studies has increased public awareness in Ontario of racial profiling by the police, particularly of African-Canadian men, and, along with the pressure of a significant number of complaints, has encouraged some police organizations to begin to try to eliminate it from their practices.

My contention is that the research, study, inquiry, and policy guideline powers of commissions can be used in two ways: first, they can be used to lay a groundwork of systemic analysis that assists adjudicators and the public to understand how the particular circumstances of individual complaints fit into a broader pattern; second, they can be used to build on the adjudicative outcomes of individual complaints to foster a broader search for systemic solutions.

On the issue of racial profiling, this combining of litigation with studies, inquiries, the development of policy guidelines, and strategies for institutional change has proved useful. The guidelines assist tribunals when they are analyzing fact patterns in individual cases because they provide a description of the multiple ways in which racial profiling can occur and set out analytical principles.[70] Reports and studies which identify racial profiling by the police as an important human rights issue in Ontario, and the publicity surrounding them, have made

67 Ontario Human Rights Commission, *Policy and Guidelines on Racism and Racial Discrimination* (9 June 2005), online: OHRC www.ohrc.on.ca/en/book/export/html/2475.

68 Ontario Human Rights Commission, *Human Rights and Policing: Creating and Sustaining Organizational Change* (2011), online: OHRC www.ohrc.on.ca/sites/default/files/attachments/Human_rights_and_policing%3A_Creating_and_sustaining_organizational_change.pdf.

69 Ottawa Police Service, online: www.ottawapolice.ca/en/community/diversitymatters/racialprofiling.aspx.

70 See, for example, *McKay v Toronto Police Services Board*, 2011 HRTO 499 at paras 119 and 156.

those from the Black community who experience police abuse feel safer making complaints about it. Conversely, complaint fact patterns and a developing jurisprudence inform the studies and guides and lead to an understanding of the urgent need for reform of police practices on a system-wide basis.

Over the last decade, Ontario tribunals have adjudicated numerous complaints against police forces and have wrestled with cases where there were no overtly racist comments made by police officers, but where non-white race was a factor in a decision to stop or investigate.

In Ontario in 2012, the Ontario Court of Appeal upheld the decisions of the Ontario Human Rights Tribunal and the Divisional Court in *Shaw v Phipps*.[71] Phipps is an African-Canadian postal worker who was stopped and questioned by police while he was working in a well-to-do, mainly white, neighbourhood in Toronto. Chief of Police William Blair argued that the test under the Ontario *Human Rights Code*[72] (Ontario *Code*) for race discrimination in policing should be the same as the test for racial profiling in the criminal law context, that is, "whether an officer has an 'articulable cause' to stop or detain." But the court rejected this argument. The test under the Ontario *Code* is whether race was a factor in a decision to put a person under surveillance, stop, or arrest.[73] The Court of Appeal quoted with approval the finding of the Divisional Court that: "Police officers . . . have a statutory duty to uphold the *Code* . . . ."[74]

This statement seems patently obvious in a society that claims to be based on the rule of law. Yet it matters to have the Ontario Court of Appeal articulate the obvious — police officers in Canada have a legal duty to provide non-discriminatory policing — because non-discriminatory policing is still not the norm in Canada.

This is an issue, like others, where individual complaints combined with the strategic use of reports, guidelines, and collaborative studies are all needed to make progress towards systemic change.

By themselves, some individual complaints can result in a remedy that affects a whole group because the rule complained of affects many others in the same way, and individual differences between those affected do not determine whether there is discriminatory impact. In *Ontario*

---

71 *Shaw v Phipps*, 2010 ONSC 3884 [*Phipps*, ONSC], aff'd 2012 ONCA 155 [*Phipps*, ONCA].

72 RSO 1990, c H.19 [Ontario *Code*].

73 *Phipps*, ONSC, above note 71 at paras 54 and 60.

74 *Phipps*, ONCA, above note 71 at para 42.

(Disability Support Program) v Tranchemontagne, for example, the two claimants, Robert Tranchemontagne and Norman Werbeski, were alcoholics and were disqualified, because of the nature of their disability, from receiving disability benefits in Ontario.[75] Tranchemontagne and Werbeski belonged to a group of persons who were all disqualified from disability benefits by section 5(2) of the *Ontario Disability Support Program Act, 1997*, which disqualified from eligibility for disability benefits "those who are disabled solely because of dependence on alcohol, drugs . . . ."[76] They made a complaint alleging that the law was discriminatory. Finding the challenged provisions discriminatory and refusing to apply it — as the Social Benefits Tribunal did in a decision upheld by the Ontario Court of Appeal — the court provided a remedy to all persons in Ontario who qualify for benefits and whose sole disability is reliance on alcohol or drugs.

However, in complaints where it is not an overt policy or a law that is challenged, or where there may be variations in the way a policy or practice affects the members of the group, adjudicators can fail to order systemic remedies even when they find that more than one person is affected.

The Supreme Court of Canada's recent decision in *Moore v British Columbia (Ministry of Education)* (*Moore*) is a case in point.[77] The BC Tribunal found that Jeffrey Moore, who has severe dyslexia, was discriminated against by the BC Ministry of Education and the North Vancouver School District because they failed to provide him with the supports necessary to learn to read.[78] The BC Tribunal also found that both the ministry and the school district discriminated against all students with severe learning disabilities by closing the district's Diagnostic Centre, where students with severe learning disabilities had been given specialized assistance, without putting any alternative plan in place.

The BC Tribunal ordered systemic remedies against both the district and the province that would ensure that funding was available for students with severe learning disabilities at actual incidence levels, and to ensure that all districts have in place early intervention programs and the range of services necessary to meet the needs of students with

---

75 *Ontario (Disability Support Program) v Tranchemontagne*, 2010 ONCA 593.
76 *Ibid* at para 2.
77 *Moore v British Columbia (Ministry of Education)*, 2012 SCC 61 [*Moore*].
78 *Moore v North Vancouver School Dist No 44 (No 2)*, 2005 BCHRT 580 at paras 1015–18.

severe learning disabilities. However, when the case reached the Supreme Court of Canada, it ruled that these systemic remedies should not stand.[79] Justice Abella, writing for a unanimous Court, found that the remedies were "remote" from the factual circumstances of Jeffrey Moore.

This is an extremely unfortunate ruling, and it lacks logic in light of the Court's resounding endorsement of the right of all children with learning disabilities to enjoy equal access to education. Despite clear evidence that Jeffrey's severe dyslexia is not a learning problem for him alone but for many children in the province, the Court's ruling on remedies may force more parents to resolve accommodation issues through individual complaints.

Making her point that the remedies were "remote" from the factual circumstances of Jeffrey Moore, Abella J wrote: "The Tribunal, with great respect, is an adjudicator of the particular claim that is before it, not a Royal Commission."[80] Given the result in *Moore* — the broad endorsement of the right of equal access to education for children with learning disabilities, accompanied by the refusal to require the province and the school district to put systemic remedies in place — this is an excellent occasion for the use of a commission's other powers, to inquire, to study, to consult, to be something, in fact, like a Royal Commission. Although the province claims that "since [the 1990s when Moore's complaint was filed] BC's education system has changed significantly, . . . [and there are] many improvements to services and supports available for students with special needs,"[81] another British Columbia parent of a child with severe dyslexia recently filed a complaint with the Tribunal about inadequate accommodation of her child's needs.[82]

If British Columbia had a human rights commission, it could study, inquire, consult widely, and issue findings on the state of education for children with severe learning disabilities in the province today, including recommendations directed to the province and school boards that

79 For a full discussion of the *Moore* case and its implications for disability jurisprudence, see Gwen Brodsky, Shelagh Day, & Yvonne Peters, *Accommodation in the 21st Century* (March 2012), online: desLibris www.canadianopenlibrary.ca/SwfDocs/232/232141.pdf.

80 *Moore*, above note 77 at para 64.

81 Janet Steffenhagen, "Delta Mom Says School Discriminated against Disabled Son" *Vancouver Sun* (15 February 2013), online: Vancouver Sun http://blogs.vancouversun.com/2013/02/15/delta-mom-says-schools-discriminated-against-learning-disabled-son/.

82 *Ibid.*

could help to preclude more parents from having to file complaints in order to obtain a *Moore*-type ruling for their own child. If, according to Abella J, the *Moore* Tribunal should not have done this, a commission could and should. Since the *Moore* decision has legal implications outside British Columbia, human rights commissions in other jurisdictions can legitimately inquire into whether the rights of children with severe dyslexia, as defined in that judgment, are being fully implemented in their jurisdictions.

In short, a commission's "other powers" can be used before and after complaint adjudication in order to work with, reinforce, and strengthen the impact of complaints.

2) Systemic Discrimination against Groups

The common understanding of systemic discrimination grew out of Abella's report on employment equity in the 1980s and influenced the Supreme Court of Canada's decision in *Action travail des femmes v Canadian National Railway Company*[83] (*Action travail*). Dickson wrote in *Action travail*:

> . . . systemic discrimination in an employment context is discrimination that results from the simple operation of established procedures of recruitment, hiring and promotion, none of which is necessarily designed to promote discrimination. The discrimination is then reinforced by the very exclusion of the disadvantaged group because the exclusion fosters the belief, both within and outside the group, that the exclusion is the result of "natural" forces, for example, that women "just can't do the job."[84]

Unfortunately, complaints that challenge a complex of practices and policies are still few in number. They are difficult to mount without the assistance of a union or a non-governmental organization. For example, Action travail des femmes could bring forward the systemic challenge to CN Rail's sexist employment practices because they were a women's organization whose purpose was to assist women to find non-traditional jobs. They referred women to CN for work and had detailed knowledge, and personal accounts, of the discriminatory policies and practices

---

83 *Action travail*, above note 17.
84 *Ibid* at 1139.

which the women encountered. The Canadian Human Rights Tribunal (Canadian Tribunal) in a decision that was subsequently upheld by the Supreme Court of Canada ruled that CN Rail discriminated against women in recruitment, testing, interviewing, hiring, and on the job. The Canadian Tribunal imposed on CN a "special temporary measure" in the form of an order that it hire one woman in four until the percentage of women in non-traditional jobs reached 13 percent.[85]

Similarly, the complaint against SELI Canada Inc et al. regarding discrimination against Latin American workers on temporary work visas who were engaged in construction of the Canada Line in Vancouver was filed by the Construction and Specialized Workers' Union, Local 1611 (CSWU).[86] The complaint alleged that foreign workers were discriminated against in pay, housing, meal arrangements, and expenses by the respondent corporations. CSWU had been granted a certificate by the Labour Relations Board to represent these workers, and it had direct knowledge of the work and the workers.

In these cases, an individual complaint would simply not work because the evidence of one complainant regarding his pay rate, meal arrangements, housing, and expenses, or her experience of intimidation and exclusion would not necessarily indicate that foreign workers, or women as a group, were being treated in a discriminatory way. Also, both the applicants for work at CN Rail and the foreign workers who were in Canada for a short period on temporary visas, were too vulnerable to make the complaint for themselves, and they lacked the necessary knowledge that there was a pattern of discriminatory treatment. Action travail des femmes and CSWU were essential to bringing these cases forward.[87]

However, this is a time when non-governmental organizations, like Action travail des femmes, are losing ground, and trade unions are increasingly beleaguered. It is important that commissions step in, as they have never done so far, to fill this vacuum.

Andrew Pinto, in his recent report which assesses the effectiveness of the 2008 amendments to human rights legislation in Ontario — includ-

---

85 *Ibid* at 1140 & 1141.

86 *CSWU Local 1611 v SELI Canada Inc (No 8)*, 2008 BCHRT 436.

87 Keven Drews, "Foreign Workers Who Helped Build Vancouver's Canada Line Win Wage Fight" *The Globe and Mail* (2 April 2013), online: The Globe and Mail www.theglobeandmail.com/newsbritish-columbia/foreign-workers-who-helped-build-vancouvers-canada-line-win-wage-fight/article10701631/.

ing a direct access tribunal system and a revised mandate for the Ontario Commission — finds that the Commission should "engage in more strategic litigation . . . ."[88] Pinto makes two recommendations:

> The Commission should develop a litigation strategy at the Tribunal focused on cases where applicants would have difficulty advancing and proving a systemic deprivation of rights. The Commission should initiate applications and intervene at the Tribunal consistent with this strategy.
>
> The Commission should have a process based on established criteria whereby community organizations can request the Commission to initiate a public interest application [to the Tribunal].[89]

These are particularly pertinent recommendations, useful not just in Ontario, but in all jurisdictions.

Pinto recounts that since the Bill 107 reforms in Ontario, the Ontario Commission has focused its efforts on achieving organizational change through partnerships and strategies designed to achieve "buy-in," and has wanted to cast off its old role as the (often-resented) "human rights police." Given this approach, "litigation is seen as a last resort that, if used unwisely, could result in the Commission setting the clock back on much of the progress it has achieved."[90]

Pinto's conclusion is that this strikes the wrong balance and that the Ontario Commission's engagement in strategic litigation is essential to fulfilling its mandate to address systemic human rights issues.[91]

I agree. Commissions have been wary of appearing to be heavy-handed law enforcers if they initiate complaints themselves, even though legislatures and Parliament have authorized them to do so. This is a misplaced desire to be seen to be only a velvet glove and not an iron hand.[92]

But there is also a process problem. Commissions have not had solid, planned strategies for gathering the threshold evidence to ground a

---

88 Andrew Pinto, *Report of the Ontario Human Rights Review 2012* (Toronto: OAG, 2012), online: OAG www.attorneygeneral.jus.gov.on.ca/english/about/pubs/human_rights/Pinto_human_rights_report_2012-ENG.pdf at 189.

89 *Ibid* at 200.

90 *Ibid* at 129.

91 *Ibid* at 123.

92 See Walter S Tarnopolsky, "The Iron Hand in the Velvet Glove: Administration and Enforcement of Human Rights Legislation in Canada" (1968) 46 Can Bar Rev 565.

1 2 3 4 5 6 7 8 9 10 11 12 13 14

credible systemic complaint. As Pinto points out, there should be a publicly known process that non-governmental organizations can use to request that a commission initiate a complaint. In addition, however, commissions can use their research, study, and consultation functions to lay down the evidentiary and analytical groundwork for systemic litigation. When Canada is a "chilly climate" for human rights, it is particularly important that commissions connect with civil society organizations in a goal-oriented way and use all of the functions they have to address systemic issues.

Apart from the vital companionship that research, study, and reporting provide to legal advocacy on systemic issues, they are an essential tool in their own right. In my view, there are some issues that are ripe for study and reporting, whether they eventually result in initiation and adjudication of systemic cases or not. One is the treatment of Aboriginal women and girls by police. While racial profiling by police has received considerable attention from commissions, particularly in Ontario and Québec, but also in Manitoba and Nova Scotia, no similar attention has been paid by commissions to the intersecting race and sex discrimination in the police treatment of Aboriginal women and girls.

Over the last five years, the much-ignored issue of police failures to protect Aboriginal women and girls from violence has been exposed through the excellent work of the Native Women's Association of Canada and others.[93] Human Rights Watch recently documented direct abuse of Aboriginal women and girls by police in northern British Columbia; abuse that is verbal, physical, and sexual.[94]

But the public narrative about policing and Aboriginal women is mainly still not a narrative about human rights violations. It is a victim-

93 For documentation of police failures, see Native Women's Association of Canada, *What Their Stories Tell Us: Research Findings from the Sisters in Spirit Initiative* (2010), online: NWAC www.nwac.ca/sites/default/files/reports/2010_NWAC_SIS_Report_EN.pdf at 3, 32, & 33; Amnesty International, *Matching International Commitments with National Action: A Human Rights Agenda for Canada* (December 2012), online: Amnesty International Canada www.amnesty.ca/sites/default/files/canadaaihra19december12.pdf at 12; Missing Women Commission Inquiry, *Forsaken: The Report of the Missing Women Commission of Inquiry*, vol IIB (Victoria: Service BC Distribution Centre, 2012) at 2.

94 Human Rights Watch, *Those Who Take Us Away: Abusive Policing and Failures in Protection of Indigenous Women and Girls in Northern British Columbia, Canada* (February 2013) at 8, online: HRW www.hrw.org/sites/default/files/reports/canada0213webwcover_0.pdf.

blaming narrative about Aboriginal women with alcohol or addiction problems who live "risky lifestyles." Nor is there a mainstream human rights narrative about discrimination against women in policing generally. Although women's non-governmental organizations have worked hard since the 1970s to bring violence against women into the open, and there are multiple public education strategies and a sophisticated academic literature on the subject, women do not file human rights complaints about the still deeply entrenched sexist practices of police. This is, at least in part, because there is no encouragement from human rights commissions to do so.[95] Sexist practices by police have been identified as an ongoing issue for the criminal justice system, but not, as racial profiling has been, also a violation of statutory human rights law.

Human rights commissions could make a contribution to promoting a broader public understanding that serious human rights violations occur when police fail to respond promptly and effectively to reports of murders, disappearances, and violence against Aboriginal women and girls, and when they are themselves the perpetrators of violence against them.

Aboriginal women and girls have effectively been abandoned, or worse, by the police, but also by other public institutions whose role it is to protect them and defend their rights. Mechanisms for holding police accountable are notoriously ineffective in Canada, principally because they are not independent, and police are often investigating complaints against themselves.[96] Human rights commissions and human rights procedures could be an important means of holding police to a standard of non-discrimination. Human rights commissions could also help to flesh out what non-discrimination or equal protection of the law means with respect to the provision of police services to women and

---

95 It is noteworthy that the case of Rehteah Parsons is mainly not being discussed publicly as a problem of sex discrimination on the part of the police and her peers. Instead, it is called "cyberbullying."

96 David MacAlister, *Police-Involved Deaths: The Failure of Self-Investigation Final Report* (BC Civil Liberties Association, November 2010), online: BCCLA http://bccla.org/our_work/police-involved-deaths-the-failure-of-self-investigation/; Kent Roach, Nathalie Des Rosiers, & Abby Deshman, *Brief to the Standing Committee on Public Safety and National Security Regarding Bill C-42, An act to amend the Royal Canadian Mounted Police Act and to make related and consequential amendments to other Acts* (30 October 2012), online: CCLA http://ccla.org/wordpress/wp-content/uploads/2012/10/2012-10-30-CCLA-Submissions-RCMP-oversight.pdf.

1 2 3 4 5 6 7 8 9 10 11 12 13 14

to Aboriginal women and girls specifically. Commissions could use their powers to inquire, study, consult, and report publicly to legislatures and Parliament.

Canada is not coming to grips with this problem, even though it has now been identified as a serious human rights concern for the country by United Nations Committees and Rapporteurs, by the Inter-American Commission on Human Rights, and by a majority of countries participating in the second Universal Periodic Review of Canada at the United Nations Human Rights Council.[97] So far, the contribution to this issue made by commissions has been to pass a resolution through their collective body, the Canadian Association of Statutory Human Rights Agencies, supporting the widespread call for a national public inquiry into the murders and disappearances of Aboriginal women and girls.[98] The resolution is timely and appropriate, but it is not enough. When human rights commissions are silent on nationwide human rights issues of this kind, they diminish the trust of the groups that need their protection and foster a narrowed understanding of what commissions do.

---

97 Human Rights Committee, *Concluding Observations: Canada*, UN Doc CCPR/C /CAN/CO/5, (2006) at 23 & 24, online: UNHCHR www.unhchr.ch/tbs/doc.nsf/%28Symbol%29/CCPR.C.CAN.CO.5.En?Opendocument; Committee on Economic, Social and Cultural Rights, *Concluding Observations: Canada*, UN Doc E/C.12/CAN/CO/4, E/C.12/CAN/CO/5, (2006) at 11(d), 15, and 26, online: UNHCHR www.unhchr.ch/tbs/doc.nsf/%28Symbol%29/E.C.12.CAN.CO.4,%20E.C.12.CAN.CO.5.En?Opendocument; Committee on the Elimination of Racial Discrimination, *Concluding Observations: Canada*, UN Doc CERD/C/CAN/CO/18, (2007) at 20 & 21, online: OHCHR www2.ohchr.org/english/bodies/cerd/cerds70.htm; Committee on the Elimination of Discrimination against Women, *Concluding Observations: Canada*, UN Doc CEDAW/C/CAN/CO/7, (2008) at 30–32 and 43–46, online: OHCHR www2.ohchr.org/english/bodies/cedaw/docs/co/CEDAW-C-CAN-CO-7.pdf; Committee on the Elimination of Racial Discrimination, *Concluding Observations: Canada*, UN Doc CERD/C/CAN/1920, (2012) at 17, online: OHCHR www2.ohchr.org/english/bodies/cerd/docs/CERD.C.CAN.CO.19-20.pdf; Committee against Torture, *Concluding Observations: Canada*, UN Doc CAT/C/CAN/CO/6, (2012) at 20, online: OHCHR www2.ohchr.org/english/bodies/cat/cats48.htm; Committee on the Rights of the Child, *Concluding Observations: Canada*, UN Doc CRC/C/CAN/CO/34, (2012) at 48, online: OHCHR www2.ohchr.org/english/bodies/crc/docs/co/CRC-C-CAN-CO-3-4_en.pdf.

98 Canadian Association of Statutory Human Rights Agencies, "CASHRA Motion on Missing and Murdered Aboriginal Women and Girls" (21 February 2013), online: CASHRA http://cashra.ca/news/cashra-motion-on-missing-and-murdered-aboriginal-women-and-girls.html.

The second issue that is ripe for study, reporting, and guideline making is the accommodation of caregiving responsibilities. For women workers, the conflict between work requirements and childcare responsibilities has always been a key equality issue, and women have been penalized as workers because they are the primary caregivers for children and other family members. They find it necessary to leave paid work, cut back hours, step aside from promotions, or avoid assignments that require travel, in order to care for their family members.

However, today about 60 percent of women work for pay in Canada. They are almost half the workforce, and two-thirds of them have children under six.[99] Some of them are also responsible for older parents — they are known as members of the "sandwich generation." Women (and some men too) are increasingly in conflict with employers who want them as workers, but want them to function as though they do not have family responsibilities.[100]

In two recent decisions — *Canadian National Railway Co v Seeley*[101] and *Canada (Attorney General) v Johnstone*[102] — the Federal Court ruled that the conflict between workplace rules and caregiving responsibilities resulted in discrimination based on "family status." The two women complainants worked for employers with rotating or unpredictable schedules. When Denise Seeley, a freight train conductor whose home depot was Jasper, AB, did not report to Vancouver to cover a shortage because she could not arrange adequate childcare, she was fired by CN Rail. When Fiona Johnstone, a border services agent, requested a static shift so that she could make stable childcare arrangements instead of working fifty-six-day rotating shifts, the Canadian Border Services Agency offered her only part-time hours.

Now that failure to recognize caregiving responsibilities is finally gaining ground as a human rights issue, valuable groundwork can be laid by commissions through studies, commentary, consultation, and the development of guidelines. It is a huge societal issue, so far unsolved: how to make work, and all its benefits, truly accessible for women, who are still the principal caregivers. Men are taking on increasing responsibility

---

99 Statistics Canada, *Women in Canada: A Gender-based Statistical Report, Paid Work* (Ottawa: StatCan, December 2010) at 5 and 9.

100 Shelagh Day, "Accommodation of Caregiving Responsibilities: A Key Employment Issue" (2013) 14:3 Human Rights Digest 11.

101 *Canadian National Railway Co v Seeley*, 2013 FC 117.

102 *Canada (Attorney General) v Johnstone*, 2013 FC 113.

1 2 3 4 5 6 7 8 9 10 11 12 13 14

for caregiving, and it needs to be possible for all workers, women and men, to work *and* care for family members without making unnecessary sacrifices.

However, there is a danger if the issue is de-gendered and addressed only as an issue of "family status" discrimination rather than as deeply entrenched sex discrimination, which affects some men too as they take on women's traditional roles. There is a danger in de-gendering the issue because in addressing every form of discrimination it is essential to understand its character in order to find the effective solutions. Caregiving responsibilities are still not evenly shared between women and men, and the search for solutions must recognize, not obscure, this fact.[103]

The answers to the conflict between caregiving responsibilities and work requirements cannot come only from employers. Greater employer willingness to accommodate caregiving responsibilities needs to be accompanied by social programs that support caregiving — including the long-called-for national childcare program and a national home care strategy.[104] Nor should workers be consigned to trying to solve this one complaint at a time. Commissions could use their reporting and study powers to excellent effect here, to identify both government and employer responsibilities for addressing this issue, to put it into a larger context than is provided by any individual complaint, and to provide guidance from a human rights perspective.

3) Commissions as Watchdogs

Finally, some of the powers of human rights commissions are akin to those provided to Canada's "watchdogs." Human rights commissions can monitor and assess the implementation of the public policy to elim-

---

103 Health Canada, *National Profile of Family Caregivers in Canada — 2002: Final Report* (September 2002), online: Health Canada www.hc-sc.gc.ca/hcs-sss/alt_formats/hpb-dgps/pdf/pubs/2002-caregiv-interven/2002-caregiv-interven-eng.pdf at 9; Linda Duxbury & Christopher Higgins, *Revisiting Work-Live Issues in Canada: The 2012 National Study on Balancing Work and Caregiving in Canada* (2012) at 3, online: Carleton Newsroom http://newsroom.carleton.ca/wp-content/files/2012-National-Work-Long-Summary.pdf.

104 See Commission on the Future of Health Care in Canada, *Building on Values: The Future of Health Care in Canada: Final Report* (November 2002) at 171, online: Government of Canada Publications http://publications.gc.ca/collections/Collection/CP32-85-2002E.pdf?

inate discrimination. For example, the Ontario Commission is authorized to:

> examine and review any statute or regulation, and any program or policy made by or under a statute, and make recommendations on any provision, program or policy that in its opinion is inconsistent with the intent of this Act; [and]
>
> . . .
>
> report to the people of Ontario on the state of human rights in Ontario and on its affairs . . . .[105]

The Ontario Commission is required to make an annual report and can make any other reports it considers warranted.[106]

Not all jurisdictions articulate the powers of commissions as fully as the Ontario legislation does. But in every jurisdiction, the commission is authorized to provide public education and information to foster recognition and respect for human rights[107] and to further the purpose of the legislation.[108] In my view, commissions should consider their public education and reporting roles to include a "watchdog" and accountability function as a part of fostering public understanding and compliance

---

105 Ontario *Code*, above note 72, ss 29(d) and (j).

106 *Ibid*, ss 31.6 & 31.7.

107 *CHRA*, above note 3, s 27(1)(a).

108 Purpose clauses also vary in their articulation, but nonetheless strongly resemble each other. They affirm that all people are equal in dignity and rights, and have the right to live free from discrimination. Nova Scotia's purpose clause is typical. The Nova Scotia *Human Rights* Act, RSNS 1989, c 214 says:

> The purpose of this Act is to
> (a) recognize the inherent dignity and the equal and inalienable rights of all members of the human family;
> (b) proclaim a common standard for achievement of basic human rights by all Nova Scotians;
> (c) recognize that human rights must be protected by the rule of law;
> (d) affirm the principle that every person is free and equal in dignity and rights;
> (e) recognize that the government, all public agencies and all persons in the Province have the responsibility to ensure that every individual in the Province is afforded an equal opportunity to enjoy a full and productive life and that failure to provide equality of opportunity threatens the status of all persons; and
> (f) extend the statute law relating to human rights and provide for its effective administration.

with human rights law.[109] Watchdogs typically have mandates to review government services and practices; commissions arguably have a mandate to review and report on any discriminatory conduct, public or private, that has to do with services, employment, housing, or union or professional membership. As a part of annual reports, or as freestanding reports, commissions could be contributing to a public narrative about human rights by providing critical commentary on human rights compliance.

An example is provided by a line of reports prepared for the Canadian Commission on national security and human rights. Starting with a 2006 report on the human rights concerns, including discrimination based on ethnicity and religion, raised by the implementation of new security measures after 9/11,[110] the Canadian Commission issued a set of guidelines for national security agencies and an assessment in 2011. The assessment found that there have been decisions and reports that reveal the use of "unreliable data and intelligence; bias; and improper information-sharing practices."[111] It concluded that there is not sufficient oversight of national security agencies to safeguard human rights:

> There have been many well-publicized examples of situations in which people within national security institutions fell well short of the appropriate balance between the legitimate protection of national security and respect for human rights. While there is evidence that those institutions have responded to the need for a more consistent commitment to human rights and anti-discrimination in their work, there is still an absence of accountability, backed up by transparency and data to demonstrate the results that Canadians deserve to expect.

---

109 For example, the mandate of the British Columbia Representative for Children and Youth is described, in part, as follows:

> Review: The Representative holds the system of care [for children] to account by conducting independent audits, and monitoring and reviewing government services.

See Representation for Children and Youth, "Mandate and Scope," online: RCYBC www.rcybc.ca/Content/AboutRCY/MandateAndScope.asp.

110 See Wesley K Wark, *National Security and Human Rights Concerns in Canada: A Survey of Eight Critical Issues in the Post-9/11 Environment* (October 2006), online: CHRC www.chrc-cdp.ca/sites/default/files/ns_sn_en.pdf.

111 Pearl Eliadis, *National Security and Human Rights* (November 2011) at 2, online: CHRC www.chrc-ccdp.ca/sites/default/files/eliadis-eng.pdf.

> Accountability is fundamental to democracy and the rule of law. In the national security context, the particular impacts on human rights are such that accountability is critical to demonstrating compliance with human rights standards, including those in the *Canadian Human Rights Act*.[112]

Providing critical assessments of compliance with human rights, and whether there are sufficient accountability mechanisms in place to ensure compliance, is an essential function for human rights commissions. Fostering a public understanding of human rights requires this.

D. CONCLUSION

There is strength in the "other functions" of human rights commissions — research, inquiry, study, consultation, reporting — the ones that have been, in my view, underused. They are sturdy tools for sustaining an essential public discourse about human rights that can also strengthen and broaden the impact of legal advocacy and adjudication. They provide a key way to address emerging issues, critical incidents, and systemic issues which are not being addressed through complaints, or not yet, or only partially. They permit commissions to play a monitoring and accountability role and report on human rights implementation, broadly or very specifically.

Although this is a particularly hostile moment for human rights, there may not be a better one coming. Governments of every political stripe are ambivalent about the institutions which they create to challenge and monitor their own conduct, among which human rights institutions count.

I believe that the best strategy for human rights institutions is to use all the powers they have to enforce the law, educate the public, and monitor human rights compliance in the most vigorous ways possible. In the face of hostility, a sophisticated human rights culture and an expectant public are the best protectors of rights and rights institutions.

---

112 *Ibid* at 7.

1 2 3 4 5 6 7 8 9 10 11 12 13 14

CHAPTER 2

GOVERNMENTS AS INTERPRETERS AND SHAPERS OF HUMAN RIGHTS

Gwen Brodsky[1]

A. INTRODUCTION

Human rights legislation in every jurisdiction in Canada is intended to apply to services customarily provided to the public.[2] In this time of neo-liberalism, governments have been attempting increasingly to privatize responsibilities for the provision of public services. However, it remains the case that governments are primary providers of services, from child welfare services to education. Such services should conform to the norm of equality. However, increasingly, when confronted with a formal allegation of discrimination regarding a social program, governments are arguing, in effect, that human rights legislation does not apply to them.

My claim is a simple one. Canada has committed itself to the norm of equality. Therefore, governments should not be campaigning in the courts to undermine the capacity of human rights legislation to deal with allegations of governmental discrimination. It is contrary to the commitment to equality, and it has insidious effects on the public trust. Usually we talk about the interpretation of legislation as the task of courts and tribunals. And there is a discourse about the interpretive obligations that attend judging. For example, it has been argued that

1 Gwen Brodsky is an equality rights and human rights litigator, and a founder and Director of the Poverty and Human Rights Centre in Vancouver.

2 There are minor variations in the wording of various human rights statutes, but all provide protection against discrimination with regard to services that are provided to the public.

adjudicators and judges have an obligation to take Canada's international human rights obligations seriously when interpreting domestic law.[3] What I want to address is different but related. I believe it is time to talk about the role and obligations of governments, and by necessary implication, legal representatives of government, as interpreters and shapers of human rights law, when they are engaged in litigation.

This is a subject I have written about previously, with regard to the problematic role and detrimental influence of governments as interpreters and shapers of the *Canadian Charter of Rights and Freedoms*[4] (*Charter*) equality rights through positions advanced in *Charter* litigation and through control of funding for access to the courts.[5] In this paper, I wish to focus on the role of governments in statutory human rights litigation. I remain steadfast in my belief that it is crucial to hold governments to account for interpreting and shaping *Charter* jurisprudence. In that regard, my perspective has not changed. However, my sense of the importance of human rights legislation as a means of giving effect to Canada's equality commitments has intensified. The cancellation of the Court Challenges Program, combined with drastic cuts to civil legal aid in places like British Columbia, have greatly reduced opportunities for access to *Charter* litigation by everyone except governments, the wealthy, and criminally accused.[6] Furthermore, self-exempting arguments that

3 Armand de Mestral & Evan Fox-Decent, "Rethinking the Relationship Between International and Domestic Law" (2008) 53 McGill LJ 573; Bruce Porter, "Judging Poverty: Using International Human Rights Law to Redefine the Scope of Charter Rights" (2000) 15 J L & Soc Pol'y 117; The Poverty and Human Rights Centre, "The Role of International Social and Economic Rights in the Interpretation of Domestic Law in Canada" (2008), online: The Poverty and Human Rights Centre http://povertyandhuman rights.org/wp/wp-content/uploads/2009/07/domesticlaw_v6-1.pdf.

4 Part I of the *Constitution Act, 1982*, being Schedule B to the *Canada Act 1982* (UK), 1982, c 11 [*Charter*].

5 Gwen Brodsky, "The Subversion of Human Rights by Governments in Canada" in Margot Young et al, eds, *Poverty: Rights, Social Citizenship, and Legal Activism* (Vancouver: UBC Press, 2007) 355.

6 Some jurisdictions, British Columbia among them, have also experienced cuts in criminal legal aid. However, the cuts to civil legal aid are even more extreme. See Leonard T Doust, QC, *Foundation for Change: Report of the Public Commission on Legal Aid in British Columbia* (Vancouver: Public Commission on Legal Aid, 2011), online: Canadian Bar Association www.cba.org/bc/Practice_Resources/PDF/pcla_report_03_08_11.pdf. Additional reports may be viewed online: Canadian Bar Association www.cba.org/bc/public_media/legal_aid/research.aspx.

governments have long been making in the *Charter* equality litigation context have leaked into statutory human rights litigation.

The first part of this chapter highlights and exposes some of the rhetorical manoeuvres that governments make, through their lawyers in human rights litigation, to attempt to immunize governments and their services from scrutiny for compliance with human rights legislation.

In the second part of the chapter, I develop my thesis that governments should not be making arguments in the courts intended to diminish the capacity of human rights legislation to provide effective remedies for governmental discrimination.

B. THE SELF-IMMUNIZING ARGUMENTS THAT GOVERNMENTS MAKE

1) Arguments Routinely Made by Governments

There are some self-immunizing arguments that governments have been making repeatedly in statutory human rights litigation. One is about "services." Efforts have been made repeatedly to exempt social programs from the ambit of what counts as a service under human rights legislation. Another is the attempt to impose a "comparator group" requirement on a rights claimant, the effect of which can be to pre-empt a discrimination analysis. These manoeuvres, which governments first utilized in section 15 *Charter* equality cases,[7] tend to be interrelated.

---

7 Courts have come under intense scholarly criticism for formalistic comparator group analysis in section 15 *Charter* equality cases: Sophia Reibetanz Moreau, "Equality Rights and the Relevance of Comparator Groups" (2006) 5 JL & Equality 81; Daphne Gilbert & Diana Majury, "Critical Comparisons: The Supreme Court of Canada Dooms Section 15" (2006) 24 Windsor YB Access Just 111; Beverley Baines, "Equality, Comparison, Discrimination, Status" in Fay Faraday, Margaret Denike, & M Kate Stephenson, eds, *Making Equality Rights Real: Securing Substantive Equality under the Charter* (Toronto: Irwin Law, 2006) 73; Dianne Pothier, "Equality as a Comparative Concept: Mirror, Mirror, on the Wall, What's the Fairest of Them All?" in Sheila McIntyre & Sanda Rodgers, eds, *Diminishing Returns: Inequality and the Canadian Charter of Rights and Freedoms* (Markham, ON: LexisNexis Butterworths, 2006) [McIntyre & Rodgers] 135. See also Dianne Pothier, "Connecting Grounds of Discrimination to Real People's Real Experiences" (2001) 13 CJWL 37; Bruce Ryder, Cidalia C Faria, & Emily Lawrence, "What's *Law* Good For? An Empirical Overview of *Charter* Equality Rights Deci-

2) Recalling First Principles

Before turning to the cases it is useful to recall first principles for the interpretation of human rights legislation. Human rights legislation has been described as "the final refuge of the disadvantaged and the disenfranchised."[8] It is well established that the special nature of human rights legislation requires that it be given a large, purposive, and liberal interpretation in a manner consistent with its overarching objectives, so as to ensure that the remedial goals of the legislation are best achieved.[9] The Supreme Court of Canada has repeatedly warned of the dangers of formalistic interpretive approaches that would restrict or defeat the remedial purpose of such a quasi-constitutional document, and explained that the task is to "breathe life, and generously so, into the particular statutory provisions [in issue]."[10] So well established are these interpretive principles that they are routinely acknowledged in government factums. The problem is that the acknowledgement often appears to be lip service only. Governments routinely make arguments in litigation that precisely are designed to render human rights protections meaningless, particularly in their application to them.

3) Cases that Exemplify the Pattern of Problematic Argumentation

Two statutory human rights cases that lend themselves particularly well to a consideration of this troubling government conduct are *First Nations*

---

sions" (2004) 24 Sup Ct L Rev (2d) 103; Mayo Moran, "Protesting Too Much: Rational Basis Review Under Canada's Equality Guarantee" in McIntyre & Rodgers, above note 7 at 71; Sheila McIntyre, "Deference and Dominance: Equality without Substance" in McIntyre & Rodgers, above note 7 at 95; Margot Young, "Blissed Out: Section 15 at Twenty" (2006) 33 Sup Ct L Rev (2d) 45.

8 *Zurich Insurance Co v Ontario (Human Rights Commission)*, [1992] 2 SCR 321 at para 18.

9 See, for example, *Canada (Attorney General) v Mossop*, [1993] 1 SCR 554 at para 94. See also *Insurance Corp of British Columbia v Heerspink*, [1982] 2 SCR 145 at 157–58 [*Heerspink*]; *Ontario (Human Rights Commission) v Simpsons Sears Ltd*, [1985] 2 SCR 536 at para 12; *Canadian National Railway Co v Canada (Canadian Human Rights Commission)*, [1987] 1 SCR 1114 at 1134–38; *New Brunswick (Human Rights Commission) v Potash Corporation of Saskatchewan Inc*, 2008 SCC 45 at para 67; *Québec (Commission des droits de la personne et des droits de la jeunesse) v Montréal (City)*, 2000 SCC 27 at para 30.

10 *Gould v Yukon Order of Pioneers*, [1996] 1 SCR 571 at para 7.

Child and Family Caring Society of Canada v Canada (Attorney General)[11] (*First Nations Child Welfare Challenge*), a highly contested complaint under the *Canadian Human Rights Act*[12] (*CHRA*), about discrimination in the provision of child welfare services to children living on Indian reserves, and *Moore v British Columbia (Ministry of Education)*[13] (*Moore*), a case about the rights of children with disabilities to an accessible education in the public school system.

a) *First Nations Child and Family Caring Society of Canada v Canada (Attorney General)*

i) The Complaint

In 2007, the First Nations Child and Family Caring Society and the Assembly of First Nations filed a complaint with the Canadian Human Rights Commission in which they alleged that the Government of Canada underfunds child welfare services for on-reserve First Nations children. The Government of Canada is the sole funder of child welfare services for First Nations children living on reserves. The provinces fund child welfare services for other Aboriginal and non-Aboriginal children. The complainants say that the result of this underfunding is that the level of some of the services provided for on-reserve First Nations children is inadequate, and that child welfare services otherwise available to Canadian children are not available to these children. The complainants allege that this amounts to discrimination in the provision of services customarily available to the public on the grounds of race and national or ethnic origin.[14] They say that the complaint concerns over 160,000 First Nations children, including at least 8,000 children in child welfare

---

11 *Canada (Attorney General) v First Nations Child and Family Caring Society of Canada*, 2010 FC 343, aff'g (24 November 2009), Ottawa T-1753-08 (FC) (Proth) [*First Nations Child Welfare Challenge*, FC 2010]; *First Nations Child and Family Caring Society of Canada v Canada (Attorney General)*, 2011 CHRT 4 [*First Nations Child Welfare Challenge*, CHRT]; *Canada (Human Rights Commission) v Canada (Attorney General)*, 2012 FC 445 [*First Nations Child Welfare Challenge*, FC 2012]; *Canada (Human Rights Commission) and First Nations Child and Family Caring Society v Canada (Attorney General)*, 2013 FCA 75 [*First Nations Child Welfare Challenge*, FCA]; *First Nations Child and Family Caring Society of Canada v Canada (Attorney General) (No 11)*, 2013 CHRT 16 [CHRT Decision on Document Disclosure].

12 RSC 1985, c H-6 [*CHRA*].

13 *Moore v North Vancouver School Dist No 44*, 2005 BCHRT 580 [*Moore*, BCHRT], rev'd *Moore v British Columbia (Ministry of Education)*, 2008 BCSC 264 [*Moore*, BCSC], aff'd 2010 BCCA 478 [*Moore*, BCCA], rev'd 2012 SCC 61 [*Moore*, SCC].

14 *CHRA*, above note 12, s 5.

1 2 3 4 5 6 7 8 9 10 11 12 13 14

care, who are denied the equal benefit of child protection services due to their race and ethnic origin.[15]

ii) Canada's Efforts to Avoid a Hearing on the Merits

The issues are complex, novel, and without doubt very significant. However, repeatedly, since 2007 when the case started, the Government of Canada has attempted to avoid a hearing on the merits, first by opposing the referral of the complaint for hearing, and then by filing a succession of motions and appeals before the Canadian Human Rights Tribunal (Tribunal) and both levels of the Federal Court. In 2013, Canada was rebuked by the Tribunal for its failure to disclose documents.[16]

---

15 *First Nations Child Welfare Challenge*, CHRT, above note 11 (submissions of the Complainant).

16 When the human rights complaint was filed with the Canadian Human Rights Commission (Commission), the government wrote to the Commission asking that it decline to deal with the complaint on the basis that it was outside the Commission's jurisdiction and there was no *prima facie* case of discrimination. The assessor appointed by the Commission recommended that the complaint be referred to the Canadian Human Rights Tribunal (Tribunal). The Commission refused Canada's request and referred the complaint to the Tribunal for a hearing.

Canada sought judicial review of the Commission's decision to refer the complaint to the Tribunal and the complainants brought a motion to strike the government's Notice of Application or, alternatively, to stay the application until the Tribunal could hear the complaint. Prothonotary Aronovitch refused the complainants' motion to strike but stayed the government's application for judicial review pending the Tribunal's decision. This decision was upheld by O'Reilly J. See *First Nations Child Welfare Challenge*, FC 2010, above note 11.

At the first case management conference at the Tribunal, the government asked the Tribunal to make a preliminary decision on both the services and the comparator group issues. The chairperson, Grant Sinclair, refused to make a preliminary decision and scheduled thirteen weeks of hearing. The new chairperson, Shirish Chotalia, vacated all the scheduled hearing dates. In December 2009, the government filed a motion to dismiss the complaint, arguing that the Tribunal did not have jurisdiction to hear the complaint based on the services and the comparator group issues. After significant delay, the Tribunal released its decision dismissing the complaint in February 2011. See *First Nations Child Welfare Challenge*, CHRT, above note 11.

The complainants and the Commission applied to the Federal Court for judicial review of the Tribunal's decision. Justice Mactavish granted the application, set aside the Tribunal's decision, and remitted it to the Tribunal for re-determination in accordance with its reasons. See *First Nations Child Welfare Challenge*, FC 2012, above note 11. The government was unsuccessful in appealing the decision of Mactavish J. See *First Nations Child*

iii) Canada's Services Argument in the First Nations Child Welfare Challenge

Canada persistently argues that the First Nations Child and Family Services Program should be insulated from review under the *CHRA*. Canada's first argument is that the federal government does not provide child welfare services within the meaning of the *CHRA*; it is merely a funder. It funds the First Nations child protection agencies that deliver the services, but it is not the direct deliverer of the services. And funding is not a service, says Canada. This is known as the services issue. Canada's second argument is that since Canada does not fund child welfare for anyone but First Nations, discrimination is an impossibility. This is referred to as the comparator group issue. There are serious problems with both these positions.

With regard to the services issue, to begin with, characterizing the Government of Canada as merely a funder of the First Nations Child and Family Services Program seems disingenuous. The complainants have provided compelling evidence showing that the Government of Canada exercises substantial control over the First Nations Child and Family Services Program. The evidence of the complainants, which they were forced to tender on a preliminary basis, is that the Government of Canada exercises control in various ways: indirectly, through funding formulas and the imposition of funding agreements that determine what services are eligible for reimbursement; and directly, through monitoring and overseeing the First Nations agencies and the services delivered to children and their families, and dictating how the First Nations agencies are governed, for example, by setting specific requirements regarding the bylaws of the agencies and their board members.[17]

The evidence of the complainants shows further that the manner in which Indian and Northern Affairs Canada controls child protection services affects *de facto* access to child welfare services, notwithstanding the greater needs of First Nations children living on reserve. They emphasize that children and families on reserve have access to fewer preventative child protection services and resources resulting in status Indian children being placed out of the care of their families at significantly greater

---

Welfare Challenge, FCA, above note 11. A newly constituted Tribunal panel rebuked the government for failure to disclose documents. See CHRT Decision on Document Disclosure, above note 11 at para 59.

17 *First Nations Child Welfare Challenge*, CHRT, above note 11 (submissions of the Complainant) at paras 11–14.

frequency than non-Aboriginal children in provincial and territorial jurisdictions.[18] The complainants also emphasize that the federal government has always been involved in the provision of Aboriginal child welfare services, in different ways over time, and they argue that the federal government is responsible for remedying the alleged discrimination, regardless of the mode of delivery.[19] Although the proper characterization of the degree of ongoing supervision and control exercised by Canada in the current model of service provision is a matter of dispute between the parties, the evidence of the complainants is largely uncontradicted.

Given the seriousness of the issues raised by the *First Nations Child Welfare Challenge*, it seems unreasonable that the complainants should be confronted by so much governmental resistance to even getting a hearing. Among other things, the cost to the complainants whose case is not being carried by a human rights commission[20] will have been very substantial. On 1 October 2012, *The Globe and Mail* reported that invoices obtained through the *Access to Information Act* show that the Justice Department, acting on behalf of Aboriginal Affairs, paid out at least $3.1 million for its efforts to prevent this case from going to a hearing on the merits, between 2007 and June 2012.[21] It is a testament to the endurance and courage of the complainants that they have not simply been snowed under by the government's preliminary motions and appeals.

Even more disturbing than the question of whether it is in any way reasonable for Canada to oppose this case going to hearing are the doc-

18 *First Nations Child Welfare Challenge*, FC 2012, above note 11 at paras 56 & 57.

19 In support of their claim of federal government responsibility for remedying the alleged discrimination, the complainants make several arguments, including arguments that are grounded in *Robichaud v Canada (Treasury Board)*, [1987] 2 SCR 84 and other human rights cases holding that when a party exercises a considerable degree of control or influence over a discriminatory practice, this party may be held responsible for breaches of human rights legislation. See *First Nations Child Welfare Challenge*, CHRT, above note 11 (submissions of the Complainant) at paras 37–44. See also *First Nations Child Welfare Challenge*, FC 2012, above note 11 (submissions of the Intervenor the Chiefs of Ontario) at paras 35 and 41, arguing that the federal government has a fiduciary obligation to Aboriginal children and their families.

20 The Canadian Human Rights Commission is a supportive intervenor in the case, but this role does not entail covering the complainants' expenses or providing legal representation to them.

21 RSC 1985, c. A-1; Heather Scoffield, "Ottawa Spends $3-Million to Battle First Nations Child Welfare Case" *The Globe and Mail* (2 October 2012) A9.

trinal implications of Canada's position on the non-application of human rights legislation to a government-funded social program. The doctrinal implications of Canada's position that government funding for a social program falls outside the scope of human rights legislation are deeply disturbing. The potential effect of the government's position is to make discriminatory government underfunding of a social program always untouchable.

We must ask ourselves shouldn't funding alone by a government be considered a service within the meaning of human rights legislation? Ignore the factual dispute in the *First Nations Child Welfare Challenge*, and consider a hypothetical: a federal government (but university-delivered) program of financial assistance for post-secondary education that is restricted to males. For the sake of discussion, assume that the only activity the federal government is engaged in is funding of the program. If the activity of government funding alone can never constitute a service within the meaning of human rights legislation, the government's role would be immune from review. It might be that a complaint could be brought against a university for delivering a discriminatory program. But if the restriction is built into the government funding, and yet the government cannot be sued, practically speaking, a university's only recourse may be to decline to deliver the program, which is a pyrrhic victory for human rights. Even if the discriminatory eligibility criteria are imposed by the universities rather than the government, letting the government off the hook poses various problems including that female students may be left in the position of having to bring multiple complaints against one university at a time.

Similarly, if the federal government cannot be sued for discriminatory underfunding of Aboriginal child welfare services, in theory, that leaves the bands and band agencies to be sued. However, a suit against those entities would be futile because only the federal government controls the means to resolve the problem. Canada's attempt to place government funding off-limits for judicial review has implication for all government-funded social programs and all human rights grounds.

iv) *Canada's Comparator Group Argument in the* First Nations Child Welfare Challenge

Canada's second argument in the *First Nations Child Welfare Challenge* is that the Tribunal lacks jurisdiction to hear the complaint because Canada does not fund child welfare for anyone but First Nations. Therefore, there is no comparator group. This interpretation of the *CHRA*'s protections against discrimination in the provision of services rests on a rigid and formulaic approach that is inconsistent with Canada's commitments to equality. It also flies in the face of the scheme and purpose of the *CHRA* and leads to absurd results.

The evidence in the *First Nations Child Welfare Challenge* shows there is a potentially relevant comparator group: off-reserve children and families for whom services are provided by the provinces.[22] The Government of Canada disputes the validity of cross-jurisdictional comparisons. However, as noted by Mactavish J, the Government of Canada has itself chosen to hold its child welfare programming for First Nations children living on reserves to provincial child welfare standards.[23] The Government's National Program Manual for the First Nations Child and Family Services Program provides that the "primary objective" of the First Nations Child and Family Services Program is to support culturally-appropriate child welfare services to First Nations children living on reserves "in the best interest of the child, *in accordance with the legislation and standards of the reference province*."[24] There is also a directive which provides that "the department . . . is committed to expanding First Nations Child and Family Services on reserve *to a level comparable to the services provided off reserve in similar circumstances* . . . ."[25] Similar language appears in a 1965 *Indian Welfare Agreement*.[26]

But once again, even more disturbing than the government's approach to the evidence are the implications of Canada's doctrinal position. On the government's comparator group analysis, with which the Tribunal sadly agreed[27] but the Federal Court did not,[28] the employer who decides to pay his or her only employee less because she is a woman, or black, or Muslim, would not have committed a discriminatory practice within the meaning of the *CHRA*'s prohibition against discrimination in employment because there is no other employee to whom the disadvantaged employee could be compared. Similarly, the shopkeeper who forces his or her employee to work in the back of the shop after discovering that

---

22 Finding of fact made by Mactavish J in *First Nations Child Welfare Challenge*, FC 2012, above note 11 at paras 373–79.

23 *Ibid* at para 374.

24 *Ibid* at paras 33, 374, & 375 [emphasis in original].

25 *Ibid* at para 376 [emphasis in original].

26 *Ibid*.

27 *First Nations Child Welfare Challenge*, CHRT, above note 11.

28 *First Nations Child Welfare Challenge*, FC 2012, above note 11.

the employee is gay would not have committed a discriminatory practice if no one else was employed in the store. These are situations in which a direct comparator will not be available to prove discrimination.[29] Although reference to a comparator group may sometimes assist in identifying whether there has been discrimination in some cases, there are many human rights cases in which no comparator group analysis is or should be required.[30]

v) *The Negative Implications of Canada's Positions in the* First Nations Child Welfare Challenge

A ruling in favour of Canada on either the service issue or the comparator group issue would have the effect of permanently insulating much of the federal programming for First Nations from review under human rights legislation. This is deeply problematic itself, and it nullifies the repeal of section 67 of the *CHRA*. Section 67 of the *CHRA* notoriously provided that "[n]othing in this Act affects any provision of the *Indian Act* or any provision made under or pursuant to that Act."[31] In the course of committee hearings leading up to the passage of the bill repealing section 67, Jim Prentice (Minister of Indian and Northern Affairs) discussed the significance of the repeal. Minister Prentice testified that the *CHRA* would now provide a basis for reviewing federal actions, including the quality of services provided by the Government of Canada. In this regard, the minister stated that:

> The repeal of section 67 will provide [F]irst [N]ation citizens, in particular [F]irst [N]ation women, with the ability to do something that they cannot do right now, and that is to file a grievance in respect of an action either by their [F]irst [N]ation government, or frankly by the Government of Canada, relative to decisions that affect them. This could include access to programs, access to services, *the quality of services that they've accessed*, in addition to other issues . . . .[32] [emphasis added]

---

29 These examples are drawn from the decision of Mactavish J in *First Nations Child Welfare Challenge*, FC 2012, above note 11 at para 256.

30 As was held by Mactavish J, *ibid* at para 291.

31 *CHRA*, above note 12, s 67 (as repealed by *An Act to Amend the Canadian Human Rights Act*, RSC 2008, c 30, s 1).

32 Canada, Standing Committee on Aboriginal Affairs and Northern Development, *Minutes of Proceedings and Evidence*, 39th Parl, 1st Sess (22 March 2007), as referred to by Mactavish J in *First Nations Child Welfare Challenge*, FC 2012, above note 11 at para 344.

Yet, in the *First Nations Child Welfare Challenge*, the Government of Canada is urging an interpretation of the *CHRA* on the Tribunal which assumes that the repeal of section 67 has not occurred.

As the Chiefs of Ontario and Amnesty International submitted to the Federal Court in the *First Nations Child Welfare Challenge*, the bottom line of the government's position appears to be that there is really no comparison or baseline for the federal government's on-reserve child welfare program. It is a program that is offered only to one segment of the Canadian population, defined by race. As long as all individuals within the unique program are treated more or less the same, no matter how poorly, there is no discrimination.[33] This is a shocking position for Canada to take. It deprives members of First Nations of the protection of human rights legislation in relation to matters of fundamental importance. It is absurd and extremely offensive to require Aboriginal people living on reserve, to whom the federal government has unique responsibilities, to demonstrate, as a precondition to advancing a discrimination claim, that they are similarly situated to any other group.

The government's comparator group analysis in the *First Nations Child Welfare Challenge* recalls to mind long-discredited positions advanced in cases under the *Canadian Bill of Rights*:[34] a criminal prohibition making it an offence for an Indian to be intoxicated off-reserve is not discrimination;[35] discrimination against pregnant women is not discrimination if all pregnant persons are treated the same.[36] The similarly situated analysis in these cases was expressly and rightly rejected and deplored by the Supreme Court of Canada and intervenor groups in *Law Society British Columbia v Andrews*[37] because it lacks substantive content and can easily be reduced to a categorization game.

---

33 *Ibid* (submissions of the Intervenor the Chiefs of Ontario) at para 37.

34 SC 1960, c 44.

35 *R v Gonzales* (1962), 32 DLR (2d) 290 (BCCA).

36 *Bliss v Canada (Attorney General)*, [1979] 1 SCR 183.

37 *Law Society British Columbia v Andrews*, [1989] 1 SCR 143 at paras 28 & 29. See also the factums of the intervenors Women's Legal Education and Action Fund and the Coalition of Provincial Organizations of the Handicapped, which emphasize the positive content of the right to equality. Factums are on file with the author.

b) *Moore v British Columbia (Ministry of Education)*

i) *The Respondents' Comparator Group Argument in* Moore

With only slight variation, the government's arguments in the *First Nations Child Welfare Challenge* mirror the arguments of governmental respondents in the disability rights case of *Moore*. At issue in the *Moore* case was a claim that the British Columbia Ministry of Education and North Vancouver School District No 44 discriminated against Jeffrey Patrick Moore and other students with severe learning disabilities by failing to accommodate their needs in the public school system.[38] While at elementary school, Jeffrey Moore was diagnosed as having a severe learning disability, in the form of dyslexia, which interfered with his ability to learn to read and to comprehend words. In the wake of funding cuts by the province for education, the school board closed the facility that provided the intensive remediation required by Jeffrey and other students with severe dyslexia. On the advice of district officials, Jeffrey's parents removed him from the public school system and, at significant and unaffordable personal expense, sent him to private schools that provide special assistance to students with severe learning disabilities.

In a complaint to the British Columbia Human Rights Tribunal, the Moores alleged that the ministry and the district discriminated against Jeffrey Moore individually and that they also discriminated on a systemic basis against students with severe learning disabilities in the provision of general education. As in the *First Nations Child Welfare Challenge*, the respondents repeatedly sought to defeat the claim by making arguments with regard to the service in issue and the comparator group analysis. In the *Moore* case the services arguments and the comparator group analysis are inextricably connected and firmly grounded in the template established by the Attorney General of British Columbia in *Auton (Guardian ad litem of) v British Columbia (Attorney General)*[39] (*Auton*), a section 15 *Charter* case. Comparator group analysis, as understood and applied by the lower courts in *Moore* and the Supreme Court of Canada in *Auton*,[40] requires the claimant to establish differential treatment in

38 *Moore*, above note 13.

39 *Auton (Guardian ad litem of) v British Columbia (Attorney General)*, 2004 SCC 78 [*Auton*].

40 The same understanding emerges in *Hodge v Canada (Minister of Human Resources Development)*, 2004 SCC 65.

comparison with a mirror comparator group to whom a sought-after benefit is already provided.

In *Auton*, the plaintiffs alleged that their section 15 right to equality was violated because the British Columbia health care system failed to provide applied behavioural therapy for young autistic children. Adopting the argument of the government, the Court ruled that the health care system did not provide "funding for all medically required treatment."[41] Rather, it provided core funding for services delivered by medical practitioners and funding, or partial funding, for some non-core services. Applied behavioural therapy for autistic children was not a listed non-core therapy provided by health practitioners. The Court concluded that the exclusion of a particular non-core service cannot be viewed as an adverse distinction based on disability that amounts to discrimination. In short, applied behavioural therapy was not a part of the pre-existing service, and therefore there could be no discrimination in the failure to provide it.

In *Moore*, the argument entails redefining the service in issue not as general education, including the opportunity to learn to read, but narrowly as the special education services that were provided by the school district. Jeffrey Moore was not discriminated against, the argument goes, because he received the special education services that were available, although they did not include the particular remediation he required in order to become literate. According to this analysis, the comparator group is other students with disabilities, and the service is only the special education that is already provided to other students with disabilities, and the duty to accommodate requires nothing more than providing the same special education services to Jeffrey Moore as were provided to other students with disabilities.

In *Moore*, the respondents successfully argued in two levels of court that the *Moore* case is just like *Auton*. The Moores were successful before the British Columbia Human Rights Tribunal (BC Tribunal).[42] However, the well-reasoned judgment of the BC Tribunal was overturned on judicial review by the British Columbia Supreme Court, based on the arguments advanced by the respondents, the Government of British Columbia, and the North Vancouver School Board.[43] On appeal, a majority of the British Columbia Court of Appeal upheld the British Columbia

41 *Auton*, above note 39 at para 35.
42 *Moore*, BCHRT, above note 13.
43 *Moore*, BCSC, above note 13.

Supreme Court's decision, with one judge, Rowles JA, dissenting.[44] On further appeal to the Supreme Court of Canada,[45] a unanimous Court confirmed the BC Tribunal's central finding of discrimination, and roundly rejected the lower courts' tortured discrimination analysis. This is an advance, but it does not ensure that respondents will desist from arguing that future cases are "just like *Auton*."[46]

Requiring a person seeking an accommodation to compare him or herself to other "similarly situated" persons with disabilities, who, incidentally, may also be suffering from a lack of accommodation, is offensive in itself. This approach to equality analysis risks reducing the duty to accommodate to a race to the bottom. It perpetuates the very exclusion from the mainstream that is at the heart of an accommodation claim.

Such arguments, even when unsuccessful in the end, can result in justice being delayed, not to mention the huge expenditure of civil society resources that is required to pursue a claim all the way to the Supreme Court of Canada. By conceptually circumscribing the kind of education that children with disabilities are entitled to, for years, the governmental respondents in *Moore* successfully shielded themselves from the BC *Human Rights Code*[47] and the legal consequences of the probing inquiry conducted by the BC Tribunal.

Another way of manipulating the definition of the service is to conflate the sought-after accommodation with the "service customarily available to the public." In *Moore*, the way the school board put it in the Supreme Court of Canada was that the accommodation sought by the Moore family was not "customarily available."[48] On this version of the rhetorical manipulation, the service is the accommodation, but since it is not customarily available it does not count as a service. This is just another way of saying the sought-after benefit is not a pre-existing benefit of the law, as in *Auton*.

---

44 *Moore*, BCCA, above note 13.

45 *Moore*, SCC, above note 13.

46 For further discussion of the Supreme Court of Canada decision in *Moore*, see Gwen Brodsky, "*Moore v British Columbia*: Supreme Court of Canada Keeps the Duty to Accommodate Strong," Case Comment (2013) 10 JL & Equality 85; see also Joanna Birenbaum, "From Equal Access to Individual Exit: The Invisibility of Systemic Discrimination in *Moore*" (2013) 10 JL & Equality 93.

47 RSBC 1996, c 210.

48 *Moore*, SCC, above note 13 (Factum of the Respondent The Board of Education of School District No 44) at paras 13, 65–81, and 103.

For people with disabilities, the *Auton* analysis of the benefit or service in issue, applied by two levels of court in *Moore*, can present an absolute wall. If the duty to accommodate is only a duty to provide accommodations that are already provided, human rights protections cannot be used to compel governments to design or implement different or additional accommodations that may be necessary for persons with disabilities.[49] The enthusiasm of both government respondents and courts for this line of analysis threatens to gut the meaning of the duty to accommodate because it is a way of relieving governments of any obligation to alter the substance of the services they already provide in order to make a more inclusive, functioning society for people with disabilities.

It is critical to understand that at its heart the *Auton* model of comparator group analysis advanced by the respondents in *Moore* is designed to determine nothing more than whether an existing benefit scheme *treats* similarly situated people *differently*. This differential treatment approach, or, in other words, formal equality approach, is another way to make the duty to accommodate meaningless. In the Supreme Court of Canada, the government of British Columbia emphasized that the complainant must show that she or he has been adversely *treated* in comparison with another group.[50] The government argued that regardless of whether the service in *Moore* is defined as special education or general education, the claim must fail because there is no evidence that Jeffrey Moore was treated differently from the members of any comparator group.

However, the claim of Jeffrey Moore, and of disability accommodation claimants generally, is not that the complainant was treated differently from members of another group based on disability, but rather that

---

49 As Isabel Grant and Judith Mosoff have written:

> A true understanding of participation and access to the social world will require some accommodations that are individualized and may make persons with disabilities much like the able-bodied norm, or "like us" [as in *Eldridge* where the plaintiffs required only a modicum of accommodation to access health services on the same bases as the "able" consumer]. However, other accommodations may require more far reaching modifications to the mainstream physical and social world in order to enable a person with a disability to participate fully.

See Isabel Grant & Judith Mosoff, "Hearing Claims of Inequality: *Eldridge v British Columbia (Attorney General)*," Case Comment (1998) 10:1 CJWL 229 at 231.

50 *Moore*, SCC, above note 13 (Factum of the Respondent The Ministry of Education) at paras 47–83.

there was a failure to take disability into account with the result that the complainant's access to a service was compromised. The fact that some groups may have received the same or similar treatment is irrelevant. From a claimant perspective, the issue is not differential treatment at all. The issue is that services designed for persons without disabilities are exclusive. They have adverse effects on persons with disabilities.

It is wrong-headed and unfairly defeating to require a person seeking accommodation because of disability to demonstrate that they have been treated differently from anyone else. Governments should not be trying to escape from accounting for their duty to accommodate by pretending that accommodation claims are claims for same treatment, and imposing a model of comparator group analysis on discrimination claims that, in effect, immunizes governments and their services from review, but does not do anything towards remedying the long-standing exclusion of people with disabilities from the mainstream.

ii) The Province's Mere Bystander Argument in Moore

It bears mentioning that in *Moore*, the Government of British Columbia, like the federal government in the *First Nations Child Welfare Challenge*, argued that it does not "provide" a service; it is merely a funder. The government's argument did not prevail before the BC Tribunal or in the courts of British Columbia.[51] However, the Government of British Columbia made the argument again in the Supreme Court of Canada and, in the end, it worked. The Supreme Court of Canada, going along with the argument advanced by the province, excused the provincial government from liability. Even though the Court agreed that the province's funding cuts had created a crisis for the school district, it laid the blame for the discrimination solely at the feet of the district.

In so doing, the Court completely ignored the province's statutorily mandated responsibilities for the system as a whole, its power to control and direct the school districts, and remedy discrimination on a province-wide basis.[52] The Court, turning its back on its own earlier articulation of the principle that the party that has the ability to prevent and remedy discrimination will be held responsible,[53] said that it is "entirely legitim-

51 *British Columbia (Ministry of Education) v Moore*, 2001 BCSC 336; *Moore*, BCHRT, above note 42 at paras 682 & 683.

52 For the Tribunal's discussion of the province's powers. see *Moore*, BCHRT, above note 13 at paras 679–83 and 713–18.

53 *Robichaud v Canada (Treasury Board)*, [1987] 2 SCR 84.

1 2 3 4 5 6 7 8 9 10 11 12 13 14

ate" for the province to choose a block funding mechanism so long as it also complies with human rights legislation. This seems to suggest that the province has no responsibility to prevent human rights violations at the level of the school district. This aspect of the decision is profoundly worrisome, especially when we live in an era during which senior governments are keen to download responsibilities for the delivery of social programs to a multiplicity of lower level governments and private sector organizations that do not necessarily have strong internal accountability mechanisms.

Even though the individual aspect of the *Moore* complaint was successful, and that family was granted a remedy, the Court's catch and release approach to the big fish — the province — does not auger well for the effective enforcement of human rights. To derive the benefit of *Moore*, other families of children with disabilities are now having to bring complaints, one school board at a time. That is not an approach that one would expect to commend itself to a provincial government that was concerned to promote human rights in the school system. However, for governments, like that of British Columbia, that are looking for a way to slip off the hook, *Moore* makes it easy.

iii) Governments' Quest for a Human Rights-Free Zone

Although the *First Nations Child Welfare Challenge* and *Moore* are two particularly high profile cases, they are not alone. There are other service cases in which governments have had their way with adjudicators and judges by arguing that: the complainant has misidentified the service; the impugned service is not a service; government funding is not a service; the sought-after accommodation is not "customarily available" to the public; there is no comparator group; the complainant has misidentified the comparator group; and if there is a comparator group, the complainant is treated the same as other members of the comparator group.[54] The Government of Québec has been successful in persuading the Québec Court of Appeal that the Québec *Charter of Human Rights and Freedoms* does not apply to legislation, and that acts of a public authority must be valid if carried out in conformity with legislation.[55] Formalis-

---

54 Gwen Brodsky, Shelagh Day, & Yvonne Peters, *Accommodation in the 21st Century* (Ottawa: CHRC, March, 2012) [Brodsky, *Accommodation*], online: CHRC www.chrc-ccdp.ca/sites/default/files/accommodation_eng.pdf.

55 RSQ 1975, c C-12. In *Québec (Commission des droits de la personne et des droits de la jeunesse) c Québec (Procureur Général)*, 2006 QCCA 1506, the court stated at para 38:

tic interpretive approaches to key doctrinal issues, such as what counts as a service and comparator group analysis, threaten to create a human rights-free zone for governments and their services, with consequences that are particularly threatening to disadvantaged groups such as Aboriginal people and people with disabilities. These are groups that have distinct needs for government-funded services that are targeted and tailored to their needs, and which may not always be directly delivered by civil servants.

C. BREACH OF PUBLIC TRUST BY GOVERNMENTS

1) Public Services Should Not Be Immune from Review for Human Rights Compliance

Canada should not be campaigning in the courts to immunize itself and its services from review for compliance with human rights legislation. It is contrary to the commitments to equality that Canada has made, and it has insidious effects on the public trust. It is to these concerns that I now turn.

> I share the view of the trial judge that a statute adopted by the National Assembly, does not come within the meaning of the words "... refusal to make a juridical act concerning goods or services ordinarily offered to the public" and neither does the refusal of the public authority who follows the requirement set out in the statute. The evaluation of the comportment of the public official who acts in conformity with the statute is subsumed by the decision regarding the validity of the statutory provision. In other words if the statute is valid, the action of the public authority who correctly acts in conformity with the statute must also be valid. It appears to me to be clear that neither the statute itself, nor the public authority who correctly applies the statute comes within the scope of s 12 of the Quebec Charter.

To a similar effect, the Human Rights Tribunal has agreed with the federal government that the *CHRA* does not apply to a complaint of discrimination with regard to the status registration provisions of the *Indian Act*. See *Matson v Canada (Indian and Northern Affairs)*, 2013 CHRT 13. For a discussion of *Matson*, see Gwen Brodsky, "Giving with One Hand, Taking with the Other" *Canadian Human Rights Reporter* (May/June 2013), online: CHRR www.cdn-hr-reporter.ca/new/viewpoints.

a) Government Is Not an Ordinary Litigant

In our adversarial system, the notion that a party, including his or her legal representative, should be able to try out any argument at hand is pervasive.[56] However, there are sound reasons for refusing to extend that notion to government as an interpreter and shaper of human rights. Governments are not ordinary litigants. Governments are bound by the equality guarantees of the *Charter*, international human rights treaties, the rule of law, and the honour of the Crown.

In other areas of law, it has long been recognized that government litigants are not ordinary litigants. For example, it is well established that Crown prosecutors are not allowed to seek a conviction at all costs. They are understood to have a special status distinct from mere opposition, and to have broad duties to the public interest that are much more extensive than the obligations of other litigants and their legal counsel. The Crown in its prosecutorial role is bound by the value of fairness, in the conduct of prosecutions and in the exercise of discretion about whether to initiate or continue a prosecution.[57]

The critique I advance in this paper is mainly focused on government. However, it also has implications for the lawyers who represent governments in litigation. It must be recognized that governments' litigation positions are advanced by lawyers. I agree with Christine Boyle and Marilyn MacCrimmon, who have argued persuasively that lawyers are guardians of equality, and that attention to the value of equality is at the very heart of what it means to analyze issues within the discipline of law.[58] Boyle and MacCrimmon explain that "to engage in legal reasoning is to be attentive to human rights, in the broadest sense — that legally-trained people, that those who understand and are committed to the concept of the rule of law, reflect the investment that society makes in insurance against tyranny and injustice," and that the very essence of lawyering requires attention to human rights values. As a helpful illustration of inattention to human rights values leading to conduct that is perhaps legalistic but not law, they offer the spectre of the lawyer acting

---

56 Allan C Hutchinson, *Legal Ethics and Professional Responsibility*, 2d ed (Toronto: Irwin Law, 2006) at 20–24.

57 Hon Michel Proulx & David Layton, *Ethics and Canadian Criminal Law* (Toronto: Irwin Law, 2001) at 643–44.

58 Christine Boyle & Marilyn MacCrimmon, "To Serve the Cause of Justice: Disciplining Fact Determination" (2001) 20 Windsor YB Access Just 55 at 59–60. See also AC Hutchinson, "Calgary and Everything After: A Post-modern Re-vision of Lawyering" (1995) 33 Alberta L Rev 768 at 772.

for the Crown who asks: "How can I use the technical tools of law to avoid my client's obligation to act honourably towards Aboriginal people?" rather than "How can I advise my client to act honourably toward Aboriginal peoples?" or "How are my ethical obligations as a lawyer affected by my client's obligation to act honourably to another party in litigation?" The notion that parties in litigation and the lawyers who represent them are free to make any argument that might succeed is badly outdated.

b) Human Rights Legislation Is Not Ordinary Legislation

Governments are clearly bound by the value of equality and should always conduct themselves in accordance with the value of equality. It is particularly important that in human rights litigation governments are understood to have responsibilities to promote the public interest in advancing equality. When thinking about the nature of the obligations governments have when they are parties to human rights litigation, we should not neglect to consider the special status and character of human rights legislation. Human rights legislation has the status of being quasi-constitutional and enjoying primacy[59] over ordinary domestic legislation. It has that special status because of the fundamentality of the values articulated and embodied by human rights legislation. When governments are participants in human rights litigation, their obligation to conduct themselves in accordance with the norm of equality should be understood to extend to the arguments they advance about the interpretation of statutory human rights guarantees and their application to governments.

c) Human Rights Legislation Has a Special Relationship to the Norm of Equality and to Canada's Obligations under International Human Rights Law

Human rights legislation is a primary means for giving effect to Canada's equality commitments. At a practical level this is obvious, because statutory human rights law is the most accessible mechanism for holding Canada to account legally for its equality commitments. In addition, there is a special relationship between international human rights law and domestic human rights legislation. International human rights law is the inspiration for domestic human rights legislation.[60] Canada's

---

59 *Heerspink*, above note 9 at 157–58.

60 See, for example, *Québec (Commission des droits de la personne et des droits de la jeunesse) c Maison des jeunes À-Ma-Baie Inc (No 2)* (1998), 33 CHRR D/263

obligations under international human rights law both preclude Canada from arguing against equality and mandate the provision of effective human rights remedies.

Canada has signed every major human rights treaty, and in so doing has committed itself repeatedly to respecting, protecting, and promoting equality; prohibiting discrimination; and, significantly, to ensuring that there are effective remedies for rights violations. Regard may be had to the *International Covenant on Civil and Political Rights*[61] (ICCPR), which is a foundational guarantee of equality and non-discrimination. Pursuant to the *ICCPR*, Canada is bound to: give effect to, respect, and ensure the rights guaranteed by the Covenant; and to ensure that any person whose Covenant rights are violated has access to an effective remedy.[62] The essential obligation is to give effect to the rights contained in the Covenant. The duty of state parties to ensure that effective remedies are available, including that there are available and appropriate means of ensuring government accountability for equality violations, is reinforced by *General Comment 13 on the Nature of the General Legal Obligation Imposed on States Parties to the Convenant. General Comment 13* explains that Covenant rights must be recognized within the domestic legal order and that

---

(QC TDP) wherein the Tribunal acknowledged international human rights law as a relevant and persuasive source of interpretation in relation to Québec's human rights legislation. See also *Canadian Odeon Theatres Ltd v Saskatchewan (Human Rights Commission) and Huck* (1985), 6 CHRR D/2682 (SK CA) wherein the court acknowledged international human rights law as the backdrop to the inclusion of the disability ground in Saskatchewan's *Human Rights Code*. The court states at para 22175:

> At the international level the *International Covenant on Civil and Political Rights* and the *Optional Protocol to the International Covenants* was adopted by the General Assembly of the United Nations on December 16, 1966, and became effective March 23, 1976. On May 16, 1976, Canada became a party to the Covenant and its Optional Protocol. Saskatchewan legislation, for the most part, gives effect to the rights protected in the International Covenant.

61 16 December 1966, 999 UNTS 171, arts 3, 12, 26, Can TS 1976 No 47 [*ICCPR*].

> Article 26
> All persons are equal before the law and are entitled without any discrimination to the equal protection of the law. In this respect, the law shall prohibit any discrimination and guarantee to all persons equal and effective protection against discrimination on any ground such as race, colour, sex, language, religion, political or other opinion, national or social origin, property, birth or other status.

62 *Ibid*, arts 3 and 26.

appropriate means of redress, or remedies, must be available; and that appropriate means of ensuring governmental accountability must be put in place.[63]

It is generally understood by Canada and by the treaty bodies that the primary means of providing effective remedies and of ensuring government accountability for rights violations is human rights legislation. In successive periodic reports submitted by Canada under the *ICCPR*, federal, provincial, and territorial governments have held out domestic human rights legislation and the *Charter* as the primary means by which Canada's compliance with the *ICCPR* commitments to equality and effective remedies for equality rights violations is achieved.

The following reports are illustrative. In Canada's May 1997 periodic report to the Human Rights Committee, the federal government explained " . . . Canada's federal, provincial and territorial human rights codes primarily implement the requirement in article 26 of the Covenant that the law prohibit discrimination."[64] Similarly, in 2004

---

63 Human Rights Committee, General Comment 31 [80], *The Nature of the General Legal Obligation Imposed on State Parties to the Covenant*, CCPR/C/21/Rev.1/Add.13, 26, May 2004 at paras 15–19.

64 Human Rights Committee, *Fourth Periodic Reports of States Parties under Article 40 of the Covenant: Canada*, UN Doc CCPR/C/103/Add.5 (1997) at paras 21–28 and 277–78 [*Fourth Periodic Report*, 1997].

> 22. The Canadian Charter of Rights and Freedoms, which is part of the Constitution of Canada and applies to all governments in Canada, is not a direct incorporation of the Covenant into domestic Canadian law . . . [h]owever, the rights recognized in the Covenant are protected in Canada by a combination of constitutional, legislative and other measures. As Canada is a federal State, different aspects of human rights fall within the jurisdiction of the different levels of government (federal, provincial, territorial).
>
> 277. The following factors serve to ensure that the division of responsibility in Canada in the human rights area does not impede protection against discrimination in Canada: the basic similarities between federal, provincial and territorial human rights codes; the role of the Supreme Court of Canada in interpreting them, thus contributing to their consistent application across Canada; and the application of the Canadian Charter of Rights and Freedoms to all human rights codes.
>
> 278. In practice, there has been little conflict between the Charter and Canada's human rights codes. There have been cases where the Charter has been invoked to broaden the scope of human rights code protection . . . and also cases dealing with the relationship between freedom of expression and the right not to be subjected to discrimination . . . . For the most part, the Charter and human

the governments of New Brunswick and Yukon reported the addition of newly protected grounds of discrimination, such as source of income, as evidence of Canada's fulfillment of Canada's obligation to respect and ensure equal rights, take measures to give effect to rights, and ensure there are adequate remedies for rights breaches.[65] In turn, the Human Rights Committee, taking Canada at its word, has directed Canada to ensure that human rights legislation operates in such a way that all victims of discrimination have full and effective access to a tribunal and to an effective remedy.[66]

> rights codes have worked together to promote the protection of human rights in Canada.

Human Rights Committee, *Fifth Periodic Reports of States Parties under Article 40 of the Covenant: Canada*, UN Doc CCPR/C/CAN/2004/5 (2004) at paras 11 and 302–5 [*Fifth Periodic Report*, 2004]

> 11. . . . The Government of Canada emphasizes that the Canadian Human Rights Commission and Tribunal have a broad mandate with respect to complaints alleging discrimination. The *Canadian Human Rights Act* (CHRA) also provides for a range of remedies at the tribunal disposal.

Most provinces and territories reported how amendments to their human rights legislation, education initiatives of their human rights commissions, and the quantitative and qualitative composition of complaints in their human rights systems fulfil their obligations under the Covenant. See, for example, Québec's report in *Fifth Periodic Report*, 2004 from paras 302–5.

65 *Ibid* at paras 267–75 and 294–300 for New Brunswick and paras 756–61 for Yukon.

> 756. In 1998 the *Yukon Human Rights Act*, was amended to add source of income as a prohibited ground of discrimination.

66 Human Rights Committee, *Concluding Observations: Canada*, UN Doc CCPR/C/79/Add.105 (1999) at paras 9 & 10:

> 9. The Committee is concerned with the inadequacy of remedies for violations of articles 2, 3 and 26 of the Covenant. The Committee recommends that the relevant human rights legislation be amended so as to guarantee access to a competent tribunal and to an effective remedy in all cases of discrimination.
> 10. The Committee is concerned that gaps remain between the protection of rights under the Canadian charter and other federal and provincial laws and the protection required under the Covenant, and recommends measures to ensure full implementation of Covenant rights. In this regard the Committee recommends that consideration be given to the establishment of a public body

Similarly, with regard to sex equality, under the *International Convention on the Elimination of All Forms of Discrimination Against Women*[67] (*CEDAW*), Canada has assumed broad responsibilities to promote equality for women and to protect women against discrimination. The *CEDAW* commits Canada to pursue through all appropriate means a policy of eliminating discrimination against women. Pursuant to article 2 of the *CEDAW*, Canada has "undertaken" to: prohibit discrimination against women;[68] establish protection for the rights of women to equality and non-discrimination;[69] refrain from engaging in any act or practice of discrimination and ensure that public authorities and institutions act in conformity with this obligation;[70] take all appropriate measures to eliminate discrimination by a person, organization or enterprise;[71] and modify laws and practices that discriminate against women.[72]

With regard to race equality, the language of the *International Convention on the Elimination of All Forms of Racial Discrimination*[73] (*CERD*) is similar to that of the *ICCPR* and the *CEDAW*. The *CERD* requires Canada to pursue, by all appropriate means, a policy of eliminating race discrimination, and to assure effective protection and remedies against acts of race discrimination. In Canada's periodic reports on its progress in implementing its treaty obligations under the *CEDAW* and the *CERD*,

---

> responsible for overseeing implementation of the Covenant and for reporting on any deficiencies.

Human Rights Committee, *Concluding Observations: Canada*, UN Doc CCPR/C/CAN/CO/5 (2006) at para 11:

> 11. The Committee regrets that its previously expressed concern relating to the inadequacy of remedies for violations of articles 2, 3 and 26 of the Covenant remains unaddressed. It is concerned the human rights commissions still have the power to refuse referral of a human rights complaint for adjudication and that legal aid for access to courts may not be available.
>
> The State party should ensure that the relevant human rights legislation is amended at federal, provincial and territorial levels and its legal system enhanced, so that all victims of discrimination have full and effective access to a competent tribunal and to an effective remedy.

67 18 December 1979, 1249 UNTS 13, art 2, Can TS 1982 No 31 [*CEDAW*].

68 *Ibid*, art 2(b).

69 *Ibid*, art 2(c).

70 *Ibid*, art 2(d).

71 *Ibid*, art 2(e).

72 *Ibid*, art 2(f).

73 7 March 1966, 660 UNTS 195, art 2, Can TS 1970 No 2.

references to the existence of human rights legislation, and the promulgation of human rights decisions by tribunal cases figure very prominently.[74] A similar analysis could be done for other human rights treaties to which Canada is a signatory.[75]

The Committee on Economic, Social, and Cultural Rights has been highly critical of positions that Canada has adopted in litigation, which, in the view of the Committee, are contrary to Canada's obligations under the *International Covenant on Economic, Social and Cultural Rights*[76] (*ICESCR*).

---

74 See, for example, Committee on the Elimination of Discrimination against Women, *Fifth Periodic Report of State Parties: Canada*, UN Doc CEDAW/C/CAN/5 (2002); Committee on the Elimination of Discrimination against Women, *Combined Sixth and Seventh Periodic Reports of State Parties: Canada*, UN Doc CEDAW/C/CAN/7 (2007); Committee on the Elimination of Racial Discrimination, *Fourteenth Periodic Reports of States Parties due in 1997, Addendum: Canada*, UN Doc CERD/C/320/Add.5 (2001); Committee on the Elimination of Racial Discrimination, *Nineteenth and Twentieth Periodic Reports of States Parties Due in 2009: Canada*, UN Doc CERD/C/CAN/19-20 (2011).

75 Examples of such treaties include the *International Covenant on Economic, Social and Cultural Rights*, 16 December 1966, 993 UNTS 3, Can TS 1976 No 46; and the *Convention on the Rights of the Child*, 20 November 1989, 1577 UNTS 3, Can TS 1992 No 3.

76 Committee on Economic, Social and Cultural Rights, *Concluding Observations: Canada*, UN Doc E/C.12/1993/5 (1993) at paras 21, 24, and 30:

> 21. The Committee is concerned that in some court decisions and in recent constitutional discussions, social and economic rights have been described as mere "policy objectives" of governments rather than as fundamental human rights. The Committee was also concerned to receive evidence that some provincial governments in Canada appear to take the position in courts that the rights in article 11 of the Covenant are not protected, or only minimally protected, by the Charter of Rights and Freedoms. The Committee would like to have heard of some measures being undertaken by provincial governments in Canada to provide for more effective legal remedies against violations of each of the rights contained in the Covenant.
> 24. The Committee is concerned that provincial human rights legislation has not always been applied in a manner which would provide improved remedies against violations of social and economic rights, particularly concerning the rights of families with children, and the right to an adequate standard of living, including food and housing.
> 30. The Committee encourages the Canadian courts to continue to adopt a broad and purposive approach to the interpretation of the Charter of Rights and Freedoms and of human rights legislation so as to provide appropriate remedies against violations of social and economic rights in Canada.

It also may be noted that the *Montréal Principles on Women's Economic, Social, and Cultural Rights*[77] (Montréal Principles) which were developed by an international group of experts on women's rights as an aid to the interpretation of the *ICESCR*, provide support for the proposition that interpretive positions advanced by governments in litigation should reflect Canada's equality commitments. The Montréal Principles explain that the legal obligations of signatories to the *ICESCR* extend to the doctrinal positions taken by governments in litigation, and in particular that when appearing before judicial and quasi-judicial bodies, governments must advocate for the interpretation and application of rights that will ensure women's substantive equality and enjoyment of economic, social, and cultural rights.[78]

Any consideration of the relationship between domestic human rights legislation and Canada's international human rights obligations

---

Committee on Economic, Social and Cultural Rights, *Concluding Observations: Canada*, UN Doc E/C.2/1/Add.31 (1998) at paras 15 and 50:

> 15. The Committee is deeply concerned at the information that provincial courts in Canada have routinely opted for an interpretation of the Charter which excludes protection of the right to an adequate standard of living and other Covenant rights. The Committee notes with concern that the courts have taken this position despite the fact that the Supreme Court of Canada has stated, as has the Government of Canada before this Committee, that the Charter can be interpreted so as to protect these rights.
>
> 50. The Committee urges the federal, provincial and territorial governments to adopt positions in litigation which are consistent with their obligation to uphold the rights recognized in the Covenant.

Committee on Economic, Social and Cultural Rights, *Concluding Observations: Canada*, UN Doc E/C.12/CAN/CO/4 (2006) at para 11(b):

> 11.(b) The lack of legal redress available to individuals when governments fail to implement the Covenant, resulting from the insufficient coverage in domestic legislation of economic, social, and cultural rights, as spelled out in the Covenant; the lack of effective enforcement mechanisms for these rights; the practice of governments of urging upon their courts an interpretation of the Canadian Charter of Rights and Freedoms denying protection of Covenant rights, and the inadequate availability of civil legal aid, particularly for economic, social, and cultural rights.

77 "Montréal Principles on Women's Economic, Social and Cultural Rights" (2004) 26:3 Hum Rts Q 760.

78 *Ibid* at paras 17, 18, and 32:

must also include the *Vienna Convention on the Law of Treaties*.[79] Pursuant to this Convention, a signatory to a treaty assumes obligations to refrain from acts which would defeat the object and purpose of the treaty, and to perform the treaty in good faith.[80]

It can be seen from the foregoing brief review of international human rights that when governments advance arguments calculated to create a human rights-free zone for themselves, they contravene their obligations to give effect to and respect rights to equality and to ensure effective protection and remedies for equality rights violations.

---

17. Rights-claiming mechanisms
States must ensure that women's rights to non-discrimination and to the equal exercise and enjoyment of economic, social, and cultural rights can be effectively interpreted and applied by judicial and quasi-judicial bodies that are independent from government. Further, states must ensure that the right to be free from discrimination and the right to equality are interpreted substantively, rather than formally, by judicial and quasi-judicial bodies, so as to foster the equal enjoyment by women of economic, social, and cultural rights. States, when appearing as parties or intervenors before judicial or quasi-judicial bodies, must advocate for the interpretation and application of rights that will ensure women's substantive enjoyment of them.

18. Maximum Available Resources
States must use the maximum available resources to respect, protect, fulfill, and promote economic, social, and cultural rights. The maximum available resources must be distributed in a manner that provides substantively equal exercise and enjoyment of economic, social, and cultural rights by women.

32. Policy Mechanisms
States are required to ensure that there is a national system of institutions and mechanisms, including national human rights institutions, commissions, and ombuds offices, which will support the development of strategies, plans, and policies specifically designed to guarantee women's equal exercise and enjoyment of their economic, social, and cultural rights. This system must guarantee the effective inclusion of women's perspectives in the design and application of public policies in economic, social, and cultural areas.

79 23 May 1969, 1155 UNTS 331, Can TS 1980 No 37.

80 *Ibid*, arts 18 and 26.

D. CONCLUSION

As we have seen, governments in Canada have held out human rights legislation as a primary vehicle for giving effect to rights to equality and of ensuring effective protection and remedies against discrimination. Seeking to establish a human-rights-free zone for governments is the opposite of giving effect to equality rights, and ensuring effective protection and remedies against discrimination. Even if the shell of human rights legislation remains, seeking a human-rights-free zone in which governments can operate without complying with human rights legislation risks removing any meaningful protections or remedy against discrimination by governments.

The practice of advancing arguments to establish a human-rights-free zone for governments can also be viewed as discriminatory in and of itself, contrary to all of Canada's commitments to equality, because its effect is to deprive disadvantaged and disenfranchised groups of the final refuge or last protection that human rights legislation often represents. The problem is not a theoretical one. Governments have a disproportionate opportunity to influence tribunals and courts, by virtue of their access to resources and the frequency of their presence as parties to human rights litigation. No matter what governments may say about how limited their resources are, in reality the resources at their disposal to oppose human rights complainants are virtually unlimited. Furthermore, a very significant volume of complaints about services are complaints against government. Government litigants therefore frequently have the ear of human rights tribunals. In addition, governments have the advantage of being in a position to advance very similar doctrinal arguments in *Charter* cases, which also have an influence on adjudicators in statutory human rights cases.[81]

The hostile arguments that governments have been making repeatedly in human rights litigation have had an influence on adjudicators. This should not be surprising. Arguments to the effect that the complainant has misidentified the service; the alleged service is not a service; government funding is not a service; the sought after accommodation is not "customarily available" to the public; there is no comparator group; the complainant has misidentified the comparator group; and if

81 I have discussed the example of *Auton*, above note 39, which is a constitutional template for governmental defences to challenges to discrimination in social programs.

there is a comparator group, the complainant is treated the same as other members of the comparator group, can all be seen in the jurisprudence.[82]

Although, thankfully, government arguments do not always prevail, it is clear that they have had a detrimental influence. The effect is similar to repealing human rights protections, but more insidious because it is creeping, and results in the gradual insulation of government conduct from challenge. Repeal by means of litigation is also invisible to most Canadians because tracking trends in jurisprudence requires time, expertise, and access to materials, such as factums and transcripts, which are not always easy to obtain.

Ultimately, when governments argue for a human-rights-free zone for themselves they undermine the public trust. They undermine the public trust of the citizenry that when Canada espouses equality as public policy, and expressly assumes legal obligations to promote equality in human rights treaties and the *Charter*, it will perform its obligations in good faith.

The honour of the Crown is implicated when governments espouse and enshrine equality as public policy but advance positions that are antithetical to the enjoyment of equality rights by Aboriginal people and seek to excuse governments from accountability, as in the *First Nations Child Welfare Challenge*. When I refer to the honour of the Crown, I mean that in a very broad sense as a bedrock of principles of fundamental justice that lie beyond persons and beyond politics and not merely that which can be justified technically. When governments act in ways that do not bring honour to the Crown this frays the public trust.

Attempts by governments to exempt themselves from human rights legislation also undermine the public trust because the overall endeavour smacks of disregard for the rule of law. The principle of legality, which is central to the rule of law, requires that all governmental activities conform to the legal norm of equality, and that there be practical and effective ways to challenge the legality of governmental conduct.[83] By attempting to immunize themselves and their services from judicial review for compliance with human rights legislation, governments remove the most practical and effective way to challenge discrimination.

---

82 See Brodsky, *Accommodation*, above note 54.

83 For a discussion of the principle that rights against government must be susceptible to judicial review, see authorities on standing, beginning with *Thorson v Canada (Attorney General)*, [1975] 1 SCR 138 and *Finlay v Canada (Minister of Finance)*, [1986] 2 SCR 607.

Government efforts at self-immunization signal that there is a double standard that is contrary to the equality component of the rule of law: on the face of it, human rights legislation applies to all providers of public services, but it is not enforceable against government.

As I write, a senior federal government lawyer has courageously blown the whistle and sued the government in Federal Court for inadequately evaluating whether bills violate the *Charter*.[84] Edgar Schmidt, general counsel and special adviser in the Department of Justice's Legislative Services Branch, has set a new standard of principled conduct for government lawyers who believe that their clients' instructions are not consistent with the public interest. The day after Mr Schmidt filed suit, his employer accused him of violating his duties as a lawyer and public servant and has suspended him without pay.

Though Mr Schmidt and the government agree that the Minister of Justice has a duty to report to the House of Commons if proposed legislation or regulations are inconsistent with the *Charter*, they disagree about the standard. Mr Schmidt argues that Parliament originally expected the evaluative test would be whether, on balance, a measure is likely not in compliance. However Mr Schmidt says that since as far back as 1993,

---

84 *Edgar Schmidt v Canada (Attorney General)*, Federal Court File no T-2225-12 (Statement of Claim), online: CharterDefence.ca http://charterdefence.ca/uploads/3/2/1/7/3217767/statement_of_claim_2012-12-14.pdf (Schmidt sues the Attorney General claiming that the standard by which new legislation is examined for *Charter* compliance is not consistent with statutory requirements); *Schmidt v Canada (Attorney General)*, [2013] FCJ No 289, Ottawa T-2225-12 (FC) (Justice Noël orders the Attorney General to pay Schmidt's legal fees); Bill Curry, "Judge Raps Justice Officials for Treatment of Whistle-Blower" *The Globe and Mail* (16 January 2013), online: The Globe and Mail www.theglobeandmail.com/news/politics/judge-raps-justice-officials-for-treatment-of-whistle-blower/article7394559/?cmpid=rss1; Kirk Makin, "Justice Department Whistleblower on a Crusade to Sustain the Rule of Law" *The Globe and Mail* (23 February 2013), online: The Globe and Mail www.theglobeandmail.com/news/national/justice-department-whistleblower-on-a-crusade-to-sustain-the-rule-of-law/article9001991/?cmpid=rss1; Douglas Quan, "Staffer Suing Justice Gets Legal Costs Covered" *Postmedia News* (9 March 2013), online: Canadian Justice Review Board www.canadianjusticereviewboard.ca/charter-novel_lawsuit.htm; Cristin Schmitz, "Legislative Vetting Process Called into Question by Lawyer for Feds" (1 February 2013) 32:36 *The Lawyers Weekly* 1; Cristin Schmitz, "Conservatives Stymie Probe of DOJ Vetting Practices" (1 March 2013) 32:40 *The Lawyers Weekly* 3; Cristin Schmitz, "Suit over DOJ Policy Goes Ahead, Fed Drops Bid to Have Case Tossed" (8 March 2013) 32:41 *The Lawyers Weekly* 2; Cristin Schmitz, "State Must Pay Costs for Schmidt Case" (22 March 2013) 32:43 *The Lawyers Weekly* 1.

government lawyers have been directed to approve all measures as long as they can imagine an argument in favour of compliance that would have a 5 percent chance of success.

I am filled with admiration for Schmidt and any lawyer who is willing to examine whether their practice of law lives up to the values of the *Charter*, and to take a risk by speaking out when situations arise that are not consistent with a lawyer's duty to serve the cause of justice. I call on all government lawyers to examine their practice of law to ask whether their legal reasoning is attentive to human rights.

Respect for the public trust demands that governments in Canada exercise their role as interpreters and shapers of human rights in ways that give effect to the value of equality, and the promise of access to effective remedies and government accountability. It is time for governments, and the lawyers who represent them in litigation, to take a good hard look in the mirror.

CHAPTER 3

SASKATCHEWAN'S ONE BRIGHT SHINING MOMENT, AT LEAST IT SEEMED SO AT THE TIME

Ken Norman[1]

A. INTRODUCTION

In August of 1979, *The Saskatchewan Human Rights Code*[2] (*Code*) came into force. Its ambition was to be comprehensive and transformative in novel ways. I propose to discuss this in some detail. But first, a little background might be helpful.

On the twentieth anniversary of the *Universal Declaration of Human Rights*[3] (*UDHR*), the *Canadian Bar Review* (Review) dedicated its December 1968 issue to *The International Year for Human Rights 1968*.[4] In his introduction, editor JG Castel referred to the range of penal statutory anti-discrimination provisions across the country in the areas of employment and accommodation as being "often narrow and quite ineffectual."[5] Further along in that same number of the Review, Walter Tarnopolosky advanced arguments in favour of the shift, lead by Ontario,[6] to replace these penal statutes with "the velvet glove" on the hand of a human rights commission whose primary tools were to be "conciliation and

1 Ken Norman is a professor of Law at the University of Saskatchewan. This chapter draws in part on Ken Norman, "Promoting and Protecting Human Rights: Snakes and Ladders" (Spring 2013) Canadian Issues 55.

2 SS 1978, c S-24.1 [*SHR Code*].

3 GA Res 217A (III), UNGAOR, 3d Sess, Supp No 13, UN Doc. A/810, (1948) 71. Adopted 10 December 1948.

4 (1968) 46 Can Bar Rev.

5 JG Castel, "International Year for Human Rights 1968" (1968) 46 Can Bar Rev 545.

6 *Human Rights Code*, RSO 1961-62, c 93.

settlement."[7] Tarnopolsky's metaphor of "the velvet glove" leaves litigation of human rights complaints as a tool to be utilized by a human rights commission if and only if the softer techniques come to impasse. In short, the emphasis for human rights commissions was to be on persuasion. Daniel Hill, first Director of the Ontario commission elaborated:

> Modern day human rights legislation is predicated on the theory that the actions of prejudiced people and their attitudes can be changed and influenced by the process of re-education, discussion, and the presentation of dispassionate socio-scientific materials that are used to challenge popular myths and stereotypes about people.[8]

As Brian Howe and Malcolm Andrade put it:

> The dominant thinking behind the legislation [in Ontario and elsewhere until the mid-1970s] was that discrimination is caused primarily by misguided persons in need of education, persuasion, and enlightenment . . . . Every effort is made by commission officers to bring the disputing parties together, encourage negotiation and compromise, and achieve a settlement. If conciliation should happen to fail, then the iron hand of law enforcement and adjudication through tribunals and the courts is used, but *only* as a last resort.[9]

B. A CHANCE TO DRAFT A TRANSFORMATIVE TEMPLATE

Near the end of the 1970s I had occasion to think long and hard about this state of things in terms of the role of a human rights commission. In the early summer of 1978, I was appointed "chairman" of the Saskatchewan Human Rights Commission. This position was attractive to me because it seemed to offer a way forward in terms of promoting a culture of human rights as envisaged by the *UDHR*. A review of the "velvet glove," the underlying assumption and a decade's experience in its use by human

7 Walter Surma Tarnopolsky, "The Iron Hand in the Velvet Glove" (1968) 46 Can Bar Rev 565.

8 Daniel Hill, "Merchants of Hate" in *Human Relations* (Toronto: Ontario Human Rights Commission, June 1965), cited in Walter Surma Tarnopolsky, *Discrimination and the Law in Canada* (Toronto: Richard De Boo, 1982) at 32 [Tarnopolsky].

9 R Brian Howe & Malcolm J Andrade, "The Reputations of Human Rights Commissions in Canada" (Fall/automne 1994) 9:2 CJLS/RCDS 1.

rights commissions in Ontario and several other provinces, left me with no confidence that Saskatchewan should have *that* as its main idea as to what a human rights commission was about. To my eye, marginalization and exclusion of disadvantaged minorities and women was a continuing story left pretty much untouched by the "velvet glove" elsewhere in Canada.

And, Saskatchewan hadn't even reached *that* stage. The commission in Saskatchewan had been established six years earlier.[10] However, it was given a quite limited role, captured by Attorney General Romanow's comment, on moving the second reading of the bill establishing the commission that, "this Bill is another step forward to the guaranteeing of civil liberties in the province."[11] The concept of "civil liberties" does not, on its face, attend to the challenge of redress for historically marginalized groups. Though the Attorney General made much in his speech[12] about the new commission's mandate "to forward the principle that cultural diversity is a basic human right and a fundamental human value,"[13] *The Saskatchewan Human Rights Commission Act* (*SHRC Act*) created no new substantive law in this or any other regard. Rather, it simply gave to the commission responsibility to administer *The Saskatchewan Bill of Rights*[14] (*Bill of Rights*), *The Fair Accommodation Practices Act*,[15] and *The Fair Employment Practices Act*.[16] Strangely, and of concern to me, the *SHRC Act* made the commission both the investigator of complaints under these three statutes and the adjudicator of formal inquiries into these complaints. There is nothing in the *SHRC Act* to indicate that "the velvet glove" was to be the commission's primary tool, as was the case elsewhere in the country. All that meets the eye is a threshold comment that where the commission "is unable to effect a settlement" it "may direct a formal inquiry into the complaint to hear and decide the matter."[17]

---

10 *The Saskatchewan Human Rights Commission Act*, SS 1972, c C-108 [*SHRC Act*].

11 Saskatchewan, Legislative Assembly, *Hansard* (9 March 1972) at 502, Saskatoon, University of Saskatchewan Archives (Ken Norman fonds, MG 79) [Archives], (box 6), online: SAIN Collections http://sain.scaa.sk.ca/collections/index.php/ken-norman-fonds;rad.

12 *Ibid* at 500.

13 *SHRC Act*, above note 10, s 7(e).

14 SS 1947, c 35 [*Bill of Rights*].

15 SS 1965, c 379.

16 SS 1965, c 293.

17 *SHRC Act*, above note 10, s 10(1).

By early fall I announced that I would "be proposing several fundamental changes to [the] structure, function and inquiry procedure [of the commission] at the next sitting of the Saskatchewan legislature."[18] The proposals would equip the commission with new proactive regulatory agency roles; with a robust law enforcement capacity to redress individual acts of discrimination, including a provision enabling the commission to initiate a complaint on its own motion, and with public education and community liaison mandates to prevent discrimination from occurring. As well, save for Québec, no other human rights statutes went beyond the field of anti-discrimination law. The proposal envisaged was to incorporate the fundamental freedoms set out in the *Bill of Rights* in order to make the *Code* comprehensive and thus to justify a proposal that it be given paramountcy over all other legislation.

Additional protected grounds of discrimination would be recommended including "handicap, age, marital status, and sexual orientation."[19] In the Saskatchewan context, there was a reason for proposing that sexual orientation be listed flowing from a dismissive analysis from the Court of Queen's Bench a couple of years earlier in *Re Board of Governors of the University of Saskatchewan et al and Saskatchewan (Human Rights Commission)*[20] (*Wilson*). This was an application by the University of Saskatchewan to the court for an order prohibiting the Saskatchewan Human Rights Commission, in its role as adjudicator of complaints under *The Fair Employment Practices Act*, from holding a hearing into a complaint on the listed ground of "sex" by Doug Wilson, a sessional lecturer at the College of Education. The College had removed him from

18 Marcel Guay, "Provincial Human Rights Commission to Propose Changes" *The Leader Post [Regina]* (13 September 1978) 61, Archives, above note 11 (box 7).

19 *Ibid*. I wish to acknowledge the work of commission vice-chair, Louise Simard, for her careful advocacy in guiding the proposed text of the *Code* though every governmental and legislative scrutiny stage over the course of the next half year. See below note 46 as an example of a response from the Crown Solicitor in charge of the ministry's file on a specific proposal concerning the adjudication forum. Louise Simard was present at every such key moment. And, save for "sexual orientation" and its related category of "analogous grounds," it is very much thanks to her stewardship of the text that the *Code* emerged unscathed from the legislature. That it was fully endorsed, in its final form, by both parties in the assembly is another story that I am in the midst of telling.

20 *Re Board of Governors of the University of Saskatchewan et al and Saskatchewan (Human Rights Commission)* (1976), 66 DLR (3d) 561 (SKQB) [*Wilson*].

supervising practicums in Saskatoon public schools on the ground that he was a homosexual.

Judge Johnson granted the university's application on the ground that "if the Legislature had intended the word 'sex' . . . to cover homosexuality or lesbianism, it ought to have said so in express language, and its failure so to do confirms my view that it did not so intend."[21] Judge Johnson also noted, in passing, that "sex" had to do with immutable characteristics whereas, " . . . *if* a homosexual has certain characteristics related to his condition I am unable to say that they are 'immutable' or even 'sex' characteristics."[22] [emphasis added]

The *Wilson* case had very much put the question of the lack of protection of gays and lesbians from discrimination on the public's agenda.[23] So, it seemed to me that it was appropriate to ask the Legislature to do what Johnson J had declined to take on by way of an expansive interpretation of the ground of "sex." In 1977, Québec had added "sexual orientation" to its *Charter of Human Rights and Freedoms*.[24] As well, that same year, the Ontario Human Rights Commission had recommended in its *Life Together* report[25] that "sexual orientation" be added to the Ontario *Human Rights Code* (Ontario *Code*).[26]

In terms of "structure," I aimed first to elevate the purposes of the *Code* above the current understanding of a human rights commission being just about protecting individual civil liberties violations to the level of the grand purposes of the *UDHR*. Therefore, I proposed that the *Code* set out, in the body of its text, an "objects" clause mirroring the *UDHR*'s vision of a world where the inherent dignity and the equal inalienable rights of all members of the human family would be recognized. This was novel. The Ontario *Code* had made such linkage in its preamble. However, preambles just weren't given the same weight as statutory text:

21 *Ibid* at 565.

22 *Ibid* at 566.

23 For a rich account of this, see Valerie Korinek, "The Most Openly Gay Person for at least a Thousand Miles: Doug Wilson and the Politicization of a Province" (2003) 84:4 Canadian Historical Review 517 [Korinek].

24 RSQ 1975, c C-12.

25 Ontario Human Rights Commission, *Life Together: A Report on Human Rights in Ontario* (Toronto: Ontario Human Rights Commission, 1977–78) at 81–82.

26 RSO 1970, c 318.

> The preamble is not . . . of the same weight as an aid to construction of a section of the Act as are other relevant enacting words to be found elsewhere in the Act or even in related Acts.[27]

In addition, I was aware that, no doubt for this reason, preambles were "rarely used these days."[28]

In the hope that this "objects clause" would illuminate the specific prohibitions to be set forth in the *Code*. I proposed language expanding on the "notice, sign, symbol" prohibition against hate propaganda in the *Bill of Rights*.[29] The new text extended to any "representation . . . which exposes, or tends to expose, to hatred, ridicules, belittles, or otherwise affronts the dignity of, any person . . . or group" protected by the *Code*. By using the word "dignity," this clause linked with the "inherent dignity" language of the objects clause.[30] No human rights code had reached this far[31] to fashion a shield against free speech absolutists.[32]

In the same vein, new ground was meant to be broken by the combined proposals to equip the commission with administrative/regulatory agency capacity to move forward in building a culture of human rights by overcoming systemic barriers to the full participation in society of marginalized groups.[33] This proactive role for the commission

---

27 *Attorney General v Prince Ernest Augustus of Hanover* (1957), [1957] AC 436 at 467 (HL), Lord Normand, discussed in EA Driedger, *The Construction of Statutes* (Toronto: Butterworths, 1974) at 120 [Driedger] and Sir Rupert Cross, *Statutory Interpretation* (London: Butterworths, 1974) at 109.

28 Driedger, above note 27 at 120.

29 *Bill of Rights*, above note 14, s 14.

30 *Ibid*, s 3.

31 Tarnopolsky, above note 8 at 330 refers to this language as being "the most extensive."

32 I was influenced by the *Cohen Report* (Canada Parliament House of Commons Special Committee on Hate Propaganda in Canada. *Report to the Minister of Justice* (Ottawa: Roger Duhamel, 1966)) which lead to the 1969 hate crime provision of the *Criminal Code*, RSC 1985, c 25. The first sentence of the *Cohen Report* stated: "This Report is a study in the power of words to maim, and what it is that a civilized society can do about it." It seemed to me that the transformative capacity of a human rights code had a better chance of moving towards a civil society based on respect for the inherent dignity of every human being than did the *Criminal Code*, with its narrow language requiring proven intent wilfully to promote hatred against an identifiable group.

33 In this I had a kindred spirit in Carole Geller, the director of the commission. She and my predecessor, Judge Tillie Taylor, first chair of the commission, had stretched the commission's limited statutory mandate in doing a study of the Department of Northern Saskatchewan's hiring practices.

included a "rule-making" function to set standards for overcoming systemic barriers as well as an approval and monitoring function to ensure that change actually took place. In support of this transformative vision, I proposed that the *Code* be elevated to a quasi-constitutional level, as paramount legislation in the hands of the commission. This was accomplished by section 44 of the *Code*:

> Every law of Saskatchewan is inoperative to the extent that it authorizes or requires the doing of anything prohibited by this Act unless it falls within an exemption provided by this Act or unless it is expressly declared by an Act of the Legislature to operate notwithstanding this Act.[34]

Related to the first exception set out in this clause was a power given to the commission in section 48 either on the application of a person or class of persons or on its own motion to grant, to review, and revoke an exemption from "any or all of the provisions of this Act." Vesting authority in the commission, in this way, seemed to me to signal that the commission could temporize in a progressive way, in circumstances where the institution involved might be granted a temporary exemption on the ground that it was taking steps to overcome systemic barriers, to bring itself into compliance with the values of the *Code*.

As it turned out, shortly after the *Code* was proclaimed the following August, the commission engaged in just such an exemption exercise with regard to provincial jails. After an extensive hearing process, on 27 February 1980, the commission granted an order, for a period of two years, allowing women to continue to be excluded from being guards in aging male jails in Regina, Prince Albert, the Battlefords, and Saskatoon.

Thus, Carole Geller was very keen on the *Code* providing a clear mandate for changing systemic barriers to disadvantaged groups. The Northern Saskatchewan Study's conclusion that the department was discriminating against Native peoples in its hiring practices had raised the ire of the minister, the Hon GR Bowerman, and of Premier Blakeney in 1977. Both ". . . repeatedly denied that the finding was well-grounded." WH McConnell, *Prairie Justice* (Toronto: Carswell, 1980) at 246 [McConnell]. In the aftermath of this squabble, Judge Taylor had resigned as chair.

34 *Ibid* at 243. A year after the *Code*'s proclamation, Howard McConnell wrote that:

> It is patent that considerable publicity would attend the infrequent employment of such a *non obstante* clause, and that for political and other reasons it would not be invoked by the Legislature without the most anxious forethought and canvassing of alternatives.

By the same order, with the plans of the Department of Corrections for two new jails in Prince Albert and Saskatoon in hand, the commission ordered that women be excluded from holding just a few specific custodial duties in the new facilities. By the same order, the commission excluded men from living and admitting positions in the women's jail in Prince Albert. On 7 July 1982, following another set of hearings, the commission narrowed its blanket exclusions as they applied to the three remaining old jails, allowing the exclusion of women from 44 of 151 positions at the Regina Correctional Centre and from four of seven positions at the Battlefords Correctional Centre. As well, the exclusion of men from positions at the women's Pine Grove Correctional Centre in Prince Albert was reduced to six of nine positions.[35]

With regard to "function," there were two areas, in addition to this exemption power, where it seemed to me that the commission needed to be mandated to enable it to go beyond being responsive to investigate individual complaints of discrimination. Barriers denying access to protected groups needed to be brought down. And, if fostering a human rights culture was the objective, then the classroom was an obvious site of activity for the commission. As to barriers, the two urgent fields of interest, for me, were the underrepresentation of disadvantaged groups both in the workforce and in educational institutions *and* the physical barriers found everywhere in the built environment barring access for people with disabilities. To me, neither of these vast systemic challenges seemed likely to be transformable by means of a case-by-case litigation process.

So, I drew from the work of KC Davis,[36] who had argued that rule making by administrative agencies "was one of the greatest inventions of modern government":[37]

> Affected parties who know facts that the agency may not know or who have ideas or understanding that the agency may not share have opportunity by quick and easy means to transmit the facts, ideas, or understanding to the agency at the crucial time when the

---

35 Saskatchewan Human Rights Commission, *Annual Report* (Saskatoon: SHRC, 14 March 1983), Archives, above note 11 (box 14) at 15 [SHRC, *Annual Report* 1983].
36 KC Davis, *Administrative Law Text* (St Paul: West Publishing, 1972) [Davis].
37 *Ibid* at 142.

> agency's positions are still fluid. The procedure is both democratic and efficient.[38]

Ralph Nader's Center for Study of Responsive Law had recently published a manual for citizen access to such processes.[39] This book discusses a number of US federal agencies and the opportunities their mandates afforded to concerned citizens to make their voices heard with regard to regulatory policy development.[40] Thus, on democratic grounds, I thought it quite appropriate, albeit "unCanadian," for a human rights commission to be proactive in policy development in this very public "rule making" way.

Section 47 of the proposed legislation gave the commission authority to "approve or order any program to be undertaken by any person if the program is designed to prevent disadvantages . . . that are suffered by" disadvantaged groups protected by the *Code*. The commission was to have the power to "make inquiries concerning the program, vary the program, impose conditions on the program or withdraw approval of the program." Finally, as an incentive for employers and educational institutions to come forward with such "affirmative action" programs, section 47 ended with "nothing done in accordance with a program approved pursuant to this section is a violation of the provisions of this Act."[41] To my eye, section 47's reference to the commission's authority envisaged for the commission an open and democratic "rule making" responsibility for the working out of regulations governing affirmative action to be submitted to the cabinet for adoption and proclamation.

---

38 *Ibid.*

39 James R Michael & Ruth C Fort, eds, *Working on the System: A Comprehensive Manual for Citizen Access to Federal Agencies* (New York: Basic Books, 1974).

40 *Ibid* at 6ff.

41 This language was largely drawn from section 19 of the Nova Scotia *Human Rights Act*, SNS 1969, c 11 and section 13 of the New Brunswick *Human Rights Act*, RSNB 1973, c H-11 with one significant difference. Both of the maritime provisions had vested the commissions with power to approve programs "to promote the welfare of any class of individuals" whereas the Saskatchewan power was more clearly directed to overcoming systemic barriers to disadvantaged groups protected by the *Code*. The language used to achieve this was drawn from section 15 of the *Canadian Human Rights Act*, SC 1976–77, c 33, though there is no approval and monitoring role given by section 15 to the new Canadian Human Rights Commission. Ontario had amended its code in 1972, by section 6(a), to give the commission power to approve employment programs for the benefit of disadvantaged groups protected by the code. Manitoba had done something similar in section 9, in 1974.

Concerning physical barriers in the built environment faced by people with disabilities, no specific legislative proposal was made. Rather, I drew from KC Davis' assertion that "power to make rules always accompanies discretionary power and need not be separately conferred."[42] Should the legislature accept the recommendation to add "handicap" to the list of protected grounds in the *Code*, then the commission would be free to launch a public consultation process with a view to framing accessibility standards for the built environment. In the short run, the hope was to persuade municipalities to amend their building codes and streetscaping practices so as to make the built environment accessible to people with mobility limitations. In the long run, the objective was to persuade the Blakeney government to bring forward a new uniform accessibility standard statute.

On the educational front, the commission was mandated by the proposed *Code* to "develop and conduct educational programs designed to eliminate discriminatory practices related to" protected disadvantaged groups.[43] With this in hand, the commission proposed that a budget be developed to enable a director of education to move forward not only on the sort of materials published by other commissions in Canada but also to work with the Ministry of Education on curriculum reform to bring human rights education into the classroom.[44] In an interview with a reporter from the *Star Phoenix*, I stated that I will recommend that the commission be given "a broader mandate so it can get involved in public education in the area of human rights. If young people in the classroom for example, could be taught to understand tolerance and the dignity of the individual, we would have the battle won."[45]

---

42 Davis, above note 36 at 143.

43 *SHR Code*, above note 2, s 25(c).

44 McConnell, above note 33 at 246:

> Since the publication of the reports, *Sex Bias in Primary Readers* and *Prejudice in Social Studies Textbooks*, [the commission] has brought to the attention of educators the danger of propagating in textbooks negative images of women and members of visible minority groups. Such images could, it was contended, foster prejudicial attitudes about vulnerable social groups on grounds of race, colour or sex. Valuable discussions were also held with teachers on how to deal with prejudice and stereotypes in material currently in general use in schools.

45 Tom Loran, "Human Rights Group Function Split Urged" *The Star Phoenix [Saskatoon]* (15 December 1978) 61, Archives, above note 11 (box 7).

With regard to the formal inquiry procedure, in order to promote expedition, expertise, and independence, I proposed that an end be put to the commission's dual role as both the investigator and the adjudicator of complaints; that adjudication of complaints be done by a member of an appointed panel of inquirers — a tribunal system. Though the ministry was open to the creation of an adjudication process at arm's length from the commission, by letter of 19 December 1978, the Crown solicitor in charge of the file on the human rights commission's legislative change project advised that this proposal had been rejected in favour of *ad hoc* appointments of a single inquirer by the Attorney General on application to him from the commission.[46]

C. THE LOBBY

During the process of ministerial review of the recommended text of the *Code*, efforts were made to press the government to respond favourably to the two proposals that seemed likely to be lightning rods: sexual orientation and affirmative action.[47] The Saskatchewan Association on Human Rights submitted a brief to the cabinet in December 1978, urging:

---

46 Letter from the Crown Solicitor to Ken Norman (chairperson of the Saskatchewan Human Rights Commission) (19 December 1978), Archives, above note 11 (box 14).

47 With regard to "affirmative action," I well knew how controversial these words were in American politics heightened by the Supreme Court's decision in *Regents of the University of California v Bakke*, 438 US 265 (1978). This case was handed down in June 1978, at the very time that I took up my appointment to the chair of the commission. However, my law school had been engaging in affirmative action, in our summer program of legal studies for Native people and our admissions policy, for five years. I had defended this program against those who wanted to equate "affirmative action" with "reverse discrimination" and to use the word "quota" with distaste. I had dealt with these critics three years earlier in a paper entitled, "Admissions Policies, Quotas and Civil Rights" in HN Janisch, ed, *The University and the Law: Proceedings of a Conference Held at the Faculty of Law, Dalhousie University, February 28–March 1, 1975* (Halifax: Dalhousie University, 1975) 73. And, in light of our successes in persuading all other Canadian law schools to accept student achievement records from our summer program as a valid element for consideration in their admissions policies, I was excited by the prospect of winning support for affirmative action in Saskatchewan's public discourse.

> No person, and certainly no Canadian, should have to live in fear, have to hide, and have to deny his or her true feelings. The fact that our society and governments do not offer gay men and women equal rights and thereby force them to live double lives is perhaps the worst oppression of all.[48]
>
> . . . the government [should] exercise the strong mandate given by the general population on October 18 and the even stronger endorsation given by the N.D.P. Convention on November 19 for the addition of sexual orientation, age, physical handicap, and marital status as prohibited grounds of discrimination to the existing human rights legislation.[49]

The brief explains that:

> Affirmative action programs can take many forms. They may be quota systems, special training programs, special recruitment programs, etc. It may be that different situations will require different combinations of plans and policies. The Human Rights Commission should be left with the job of advising and working with the agencies and companies setting up the plans. Despite the difficulties inherent in affirmative action programs, it is obvious from the experience in this country that such plans are absolutely necessary if we are going to succeed in granting native people, women, the physically handicapped and the economically and socially disadvantaged access to the labour force as equals having any realistic expectation of being able to take an equal position in society.[50]

On 1 February 1979, I met with Attorney General Roy Romanow and his officials over the question of whether the listed grounds should be left open-ended. I had recommended that this be done so that, over time, an understanding of "analogous grounds" could be developed by the commission and the inquiry system. In a follow-up letter of 5 February 1979, I advised the Attorney General that "a judgment must always be made as to what can effectively be done today to take us a step closer to an egalitarian society."[51] This statement was of a piece with the new proactive

48 Brief from the Saskatchewan Association on Human Rights to the Cabinet (December 1978), Archives, above note 11 (box 14) at 2–3.

49 *Ibid* at 9.

50 *Ibid* at 8.

51 Letter from Ken Norman (chairperson of the Saskatchewan Human Rights Commission) to Roy Romanow (Attorney General) (5 February 1979), Ar-

rule-making, regulatory/educational agency functions of the commission under the proposed *Code*; with the mission of moving Saskatchewan in the direction of being more inclusive as a matter of growing a culture of respect for human rights. In effect, this proposal aimed to plant "a living tree"[52] of human rights enabling understandings of the reach of the *Code* to expand over time without the need for legislative amendments.[53]

D. CLOUDS ROLL IN

This juncture in the run-up to the bill reaching the floor of the legislature was a rhetorical high point. Then, things began to go south, with what struck me as a sobering moment in prairie political life. The stage was set by a newspaper story of 24 February 1979, wherein the Attorney General " . . . gave no indication whether sexual orientation would be part of the government's final list of inclusions in human rights prohibitions."[54]

---

chives, above note 11 (box 7) [Letter from Norman to Romanow].

52 *Human Rights Code of British Columbia*, SBC 1973 (2d Sess), c 119 and the Manitoba *Human Rights Act*, SM 1974, c 65, as amended by SM 1976, c 48, had such an open-ended list of grounds by means of a general provision that there was to be no discrimination "unless reasonable cause exists" followed by way of illustration by enumerated grounds. This non-exclusive approach to protected grounds seemed to me to make a very good fit with Lord Sankey's "living tree" assertion about the nature of Canada's constitutional order in the *Persons' Case* (*Edwards v Canada (Attorney General)*, [1929] UKPC 86, where in the course of acknowledging that women had the same political rights as men, Lord Sankey asserted that our constitution was organic and needed to be read in a broad and liberal manner so as to adapt to changing times.

53 Of influence was *Wilson*, above note 20, where the court's plain reading of the statute's protected ground of "sex" shut the door to a claim by a gay victim of discrimination. For me, this case served as a cautionary tale with regard to the problem of having the *Code* provide a closed list of protected grounds. Hence, I argued for what have now come to be known as "analogous grounds" under section 15 of the *Charter* so as to facilitate the addition of additional protected grounds being added as an exercise in adjudicative reasoning, in adaptation to changing times, rather than having to await the will of the legislature.

54 Marsha Erb, "Judicial, Policing Functions Split in Human Rights Code" *The Star Phoenix [Saskatoon]* (24 February 1979), Archives, above note 11 (box 7). Though dismayed by this evasive comment, I tried to take comfort from the fact that the Attorney General hadn't actually rejected the proposal. And, I hoped that he was advocating for it within the cabinet and caucus as he

1 2 3 4 5 6 7 8 9 10 11 12 13 14

Three days later, the Leader of the Opposition, Dick Collver, rose in the legislature with a statement apparently taken by the Attorney General in the spirit of good fun.

> MR COLLVER: The other day in the city of Saskatoon a member of the press (not ourselves) revealed to the people of Saskatchewan that a cabinet minister was a member of the homosexual community in Saskatchewan . . . . The fact is Mr Speaker, unless we are prepared to show the leadership necessary to ensure that total honesty is put before the people of Saskatchewan, unless we are absolutely certain to present this to the people, then we stand the chance of every cabinet minister being called into question, we stand the chance of every cabinet minister being subjected to blackmail . . . (inaudible interjection) . . . Mr Speaker, I notice the Attorney General makes jokes. I notice he thinks that this is a funny situation . . . .
>
> AN HON MEMBER: . . . said they were hidden in the PC caucus.
>
> MR COLLVER: . . . (inaudible) . . .
>
> MR ROMANOW: That's what he said.
>
> AN HON MEMBER: He did not.
>
> MR ROMANOW: He did so. Have you tested your boys?[55]

Brian Currie, president of the Gay Community Centre in Saskatoon responded to this exchange in the legislature in a letter to Premier Allan Blakeney explaining that " . . . what he said on the program was that because 10 percent of the population is homosexual, it would stand to reason that one member of the cabinet would be homosexual."[56] This

might have felt some remorse for the stance that he had taken at the NDP convention in November when he elected not to support the motion calling for the addition of sexual orientation to the *Code*. By letter to Attorney General Romanow, John McConnell expressed concern "that the resolution has been deferred for further study, especially as the means by which the resolution is to be studied is not clear. Also, we were keenly disappointed by your personal opposition to the bill." Letter from John McConnell (chairperson of the Gay Academic Union, University of Saskatchewan) to the Attorney General (Roy Romanow) (6 December 1978), Archives, above note 11 (box 7).

55 Saskatchewan, Legislative Assembly, *Hansard*, 19th Leg, 1st Sess, Vol XXI, No 4A (27 February 1979) at 81–82.

56 Larry Johnsrude, "Homosexuality Charge May Effect Passage of Human Rights Code" *The Star Phoenix [Saskatoon]* (6 March 1979), Archives, above,

explanation apparently did not move the Attorney General to alter his understanding of what was in/at "play." He told a reporter that this "accusation" by Mr Collver was likely to make the government's decision whether to include sexual orientation in the *Code* "more difficult": "The question really is that if cabinet was to include sexual orientation, would the next allegation be that we did it to protect a cabinet minister?"[57]

A few weeks later, during the debate on second reading of Bill 94, *An Act Respecting The Saskatchewan Human Rights Code and its Administration*, now stripped of sexual orientation as a protected ground,[58] the Leader of the Opposition took the occasion to pat himself on the back while justifying his stance on purely homophobic grounds.

> MR COLLVER: As a matter of fact, the Attorney General himself said on CBC television on Friday evening that one of the major reasons they didn't proceed with the NDP resolution on gay rights, and they didn't proceed on Mr Norman's recommendations on gay rights, was the fact I had raised at the start of this session, a question that had been raised outside this Assembly by a leading gay rights spokesman pertaining to the government . . . . Thank goodness, it was raised at the start of the session and raised enough of a furor at the start of the session that the Attorney General and the cabinet and the whole caucus of members opposite had to listen to the people of the province of Saskatchewan. They had to listen to the people of the province who refused to accept that kind of lowering of the moral standards and the moral fibre of our province . . . . there are the rights of children to be free from this kind of moral degradation. There are rights of schools to determine whether or not that kind of degradation is to be taught to their children.[59]

---

note 11 (box 7).

57 *Ibid.*

58 Larry Johnsrude, "Gays Claimed Not Protected" *The Star Phoenix [Saskatoon]* (23 April 1979), Archives, above note 11 (box 7).

> Attorney-General Roy Romanow last week tabled the Saskatchewan Code of Human Rights in the legislature which was missing a section dealing with sexual orientation, despite its recommendation by Saskatchewan Human Rights Commission chairman, Prof. Ken Norman . . . . Norman said he expects the question of sexual orientation protection to be an ongoing issue and legislation will eventually be passed.

59 Saskatchewan, Legislative Assembly, *Hansard*, 19th Leg, 1st Sess, Vol 85 (23 April 1979) at 1953–55.

1 2 3 4 5 6 7 8 9 10 11 12 13 14

Apparently thus satiated, the opposition was content to lend their voting support to *Bill 94*. The commission's new proactive mandates were not called into question in the debate. Come the proclamation of the *Code* and its regulations in August, I sought to make the most of the unanimous support given to it by the assembly.

> *New human rights code now law* — Norman was instrumental in designing the new code and feels it is an accomplishment that it gained unanimous approval of both parties in the legislature this spring . . . . In fact, the cabinet accepted his proposals in full, except for one section which dealt with anti-discrimination protection for homosexuals.[60]

The central point that I wanted to make about the unanimous support given to the *Code* by the legislature had everything to do with the major new systemic change mechanisms assigned to the commission, especially the affirmative action promotion/approval/monitoring/ordering processes with their planned launch in Prince Albert two weeks later.

> Affirmative action is a major component of the recently-proclaimed Saskatchewan Human Rights Code, Shelagh Day, assistant director of the commission, said today at a Prince Albert news conference. The new code gives the commission the power to approve or order comprehensive affirmative action programs which are designed to assist groups protected by the code to gain equality in employment and education . . . . [I]t is the policy of the Saskatchewan Human Rights Commission that programs designed to assist those of Indian ancestry, women and the disabled will be a first priority.[61]

---

60 Larry Johnsrude, "New Human Rights Code Now Law" *The Star Phoenix [Saskatoon]* (8 August 1979) D3, Archives, above note 11 (box 7). For the record, the recommendation that I had pressed in a meeting with the Attorney General on 1 February 1979 (Letter from Norman to Romanow, above note 51) — to leave room for analogous grounds — also bit the dust. However, I assumed that it went down because it was seen to be a way to overcome *Wilson* (which it was!) should sexual orientation not make the cabinet cut. See *Wilson*, above notes 20 and 53.

61 Government of Saskatchewan, News Release (20 August 1979) and Heather Macdonald, "New Human Rights Code Means Affirmative Action" *The Prince Albert Daily Herald* (20 August 1979) 9, Archives, above note 11 (box 7). In June 1979, in the aftermath of the passage of the new *Code*, I had spoken in Vancouver on a panel at a Canadian Association of Statutory Human Rights Conference about Saskatchewan's new affirmative action thrust. Another panellist, Shelagh Day, also spoke about affirmative

With the informal approval of my colleagues on the commission, I spoke to a reporter about where the commission intended to go with its new proactive mandates.

> The Saskatchewan Human Rights Commission plans to hold public hearings on two aspects of the province's new human rights code — affirmative action and access for the handicapped to public buildings. Hearings will be held Nov 1 in Regina and Nov 29 in Saskatoon into the implications of the law guaranteeing people restricted to wheelchairs access to public buildings for services, housing, employment or education, chief commissioner Ken Norman said Wednesday. Norman said, "on the face of it" the law entitles a chair-bound person to insist on being able to enter any building open to the public. However, the commission has the power to exempt certain buildings if the necessary renovations would place undue hardship on the owner, Norman said. He suggested a first step may be to ensure that municipalities set minimum standards for new buildings to avoid any conflict with the human rights code. The other set of public hearings will begin in Saskatoon on Nov 14 and continue the next day in La Ronge. They will focus on what affirmative action programs should be in this province. La Ronge was chosen as the site for one hearing because resource development and employment opportunities in that area offer obvious chances for affirmative action.[62]

---

action. Shelagh had served as the first human rights investigator for the British Columbia Human Rights Commission. Latterly, as equal employment officer for the City of Vancouver, she had shepherded a study before city council proposing to open the then "males only" hiring gate for the Vancouver Fire Department. As these things go, shortly thereafter she became the city's "ex-equal employment officer." I left Vancouver determined to persuade her to drop her job search and come to Saskatchewan to assume leadership of the *Code*'s transformative mission of bringing down systemic barriers to disadvantaged groups. With the hiring of Shelagh Day as Assistant Director, with a primary responsibility for affirmative action, the Saskatchewan Commission began a reconfiguration of positions such that, within months, half of our staff was devoted to promotional activities in the fields of education, affirmative action, and exemptions. This is noted in Tarnopolsky, above note 8 at 437, as constituting "the largest emphasis" of any Canadian human rights commission on "the education/promotion function."

62 Laurence Thoner, "Public Meetings Planned on Human Rights Code" *The Star Phoenix [Saskatoon]* (20 September 1979), Archives, above note 11 (box 7).

At the commission's meeting of 27 September 1979, we received a report from Shelagh Day on behalf of the affirmative action subcommittee.[63] Further to this report, the commission formally resolved to " . . . hold a public hearing for the purposes of rule-making with respect to Affirmative Action Programs which may be approved or ordered pursuant to Section 47 . . . ."[64] As well, the commission resolved to " . . . hold public investigatory hearings on the matter of building accessibility as it affects public accommodation and services, rental accommodations, housing, employment and, education for persons with disabilities."[65] Finally, the commission agreed that proposed affirmative action regulations " . . . be sent out to persons wishing to comment on them at the hearings."[66]

E. A RELUCTANT PREMIER

And so we sallied forth spending the month of November holding public hearings to prepare the ground for systemic changes for persons of Aboriginal ancestry, women, and the disabled as a first priority. In December, we occupied ourselves with analysis of what we had learned and turned our minds to what the next steps needed to be in the new year. Then Premier Blakeney took the occasion of his year-end press conference to take the wind out of our sails. The transcribed tape of this segment of the conference is as follows:

> Q. Are you going full bore ahead with an enforcement of the affirmative action legislation through the Human Rights Commission?
>
> A. Well, if you don't mind, I don't like the term "affirmative action" so I don't want to use it.
>
> Q. But it is your program, that's the Government, that the Human Rights Commission has been holding hearings around the province about affirmative action.

---

63 Meeting of the Saskatchewan Human Rights Commission, Saskatoon (27 September 1979), Archives, above note 11 (box 7), Item #7514/79.

64 *Ibid*, Resolution #1.

65 *Ibid*, Resolution #2.

66 *Ibid*, Item #7515/79.

> A. That's a colloquial term, you know, it's not, I don't think it's a descriptive term, so it's not in the legislation, for example. Just happened to bring along the legislation, just in case . . . . I don't know the pace at which the Human Rights Commission would proceed, but my guess is that they would proceed with some caution.[67]

It struck me that the "fog of war"[68] around "sexual orientation" leading up to and throughout the passage of the *Code* through the legislative process had not only left the leader of the opposition with just one target to shoot at, apparently it had also obscured the implications of the proposed text of section 47 from the premier's scrutiny. Professor Howard McConnell mirrored Premier Blakeney's tone in the new year, though, as a scholar, the term "affirmative action" didn't seem to stick in his throat:

> The Code . . . provides a powerful instrument for the purpose of affirmative action in s 47. By invoking this section the Commission may approve any program designed to prevent disadvantages experienced by groups of individuals on the basis of their various indicia of discrimination. Where systematic [sic] discrimination is perpetrated on groups through unjust policies, or is experienced by groups for virtually any reason, the Commission may, on the application of any person, or on its own initiative, approve or order a program to be undertaken to eliminate or reduce such discrimination. The Code, accordingly, is here progressing from the protection of individual to group or collective rights, and the Commission is acquiring as [sic] strong mandate and a sweeping sanction which it will no doubt use circumspectly.[69]

The commission took Premier Blakeney's advice to "proceed with some caution" and Professor McConnell's assumption that we would be circumspect under advisement, but opted to stay the course, and to stand by our statutory mandate. To this end, on 9 April 1980, as a culmination of our rule-making exercise, the commission published a set

---

67 Transcript of Premier Blakeney's press conference, Regina (27 December 1979), Archives, above note 11 (box 7).

68 See Korinek, above note 23. At 547 of this article there is a reference to "the overtly hateful comments of the provincial Progressive Conservatives, both as the official opposition and, later during the government of Grant Devine." A footnote to this assertion cites Leslie Biggs & Mark Stoble, eds, *Devine Rule in Saskatchewan: A Decade of Hope and Hardship* (Saskatoon: Fifth House Publishers, 1991).

69 McConnell, above note 33 at 244.

of proposed regulations governing the process by which the commission would exercise its authority under section 47. By letter on that date, I wrote to Attorney General Romanow tendering regulations made by the commission " . . . that they may be 'approved' by the Lieutenant Governor in Council, on your recommendation."[70] My letter explained that the regulations represented my best efforts at reflecting the spirit of what I understood had been accomplished at a meeting with "certain of your Cabinet colleagues" on 5 March 1980. I noted that no legal impediment to the promulgation of the regulations had been raised by law officers of the ministry. I then drew a line in the sand:

> [The regulations] are the furthest that I am prepared to go in the direction of flexibility, and they go some considerable distance in that regard. To take another step would be for me to abandon any emphasis on the special needs of the target groups [persons of Indian ancestry, women, and disabled persons]. I must say that, if such a step is to be taken, it will have to be with someone else in the chair of the Human Rights Commission.[71]

What ensued was a continuing exchange of letters between the Crown solicitor on the file and the commission. In the end, the issue slipped from the table as the commission proceeded to be guided by the regulations in any case as part of our discretionary authority buoyed by the democratic exercise in rule making that we had undertaken in November 1979.[72] The process we followed and the criteria we looked to were on the table at every hearing and *were* public knowledge. And we heard no further discouraging words from the Attorney General's of-

70 Letter from Ken Norman (chairperson of the Saskatchewan Human Rights Commission) to Roy Romanow (Attorney General) (9 April 1980), Archives, above note 11 (box 16), File "Affirmative Action Regulations."

71 *Ibid.*

72 SHRC, *Annual Report 1983*, above note 35 at 13. In this report to the new Devine government's Attorney General, Gary Lane, the commission explains that seven affirmative action programs were granted full or provisional approval by the commission in the preceding year " . . . pursuant to the proposed regulations of 9 April 1980, which the commission incorporated by reference into each of its published decisions." The approved programs were (1) Potash Corporation of Saskatchewan, (2) Saskatchewan Housing Corporation, (3) The Co-operators, (4) Pre-Employment Trades Exploration for Women, Prince Albert Natonum Community College, (5) Saskoil Affirmative Action Program, (6) Key Lake Mining Corporation, Construction Phase, (7) Sask Tel Affirmative Action Program.

fice. The commission promoted the affirmative action process in various media in the following months.[73] By year's end, then director of the commission, Shelagh Day, was reported as saying:

> Major progress was made in human rights in the province in 1980 . . . Day said, 1980 saw the adoption of accessibility standard to buildings for the handicapped,[74] the establishment of affirmative action programs and increasing awareness of the provisions in the human rights code.[75]

Early in the following year, the commission was in a position to begin hearings on applications for approval of affirmative action programs. We announced that public hearings would be held with regard to two applications. The first was from the Saskatchewan Piping Industry, Joint Training Board seeking approval for an apprenticeship-training program for Native people. The second was from the Department of Northern Saskatchewan with regard to an affirmative action hiring program.[76] By October 1981, the commission had approved half a dozen affirmative action programs.[77] November saw the intense first ministers' negotiations around the proposed language of the Constitution[78] and *Charter*.[79] At a certain point around the reach of the "override clause," Premier Blakeney made some positive comments about the Saskatchewan *Code*'s

---

73 For a discussion of this, see Saskatchewan Human Rights Commission, *Newsletter*, Vol 9, No 5 (Saskatoon: SHRC, Nov/Dec, 1980), Archives, above note 11 (box 7) [SHRC, *Newsletter*].

74 Accessibility Standards Adopted by the Commission (14 August 1980), Archives, above note 11 (box 7).

75 Donna Sherman, "Accessibility Standards Further Human Rights" *The Star Phoenix [Saskatoon]* (30 December 1980), Archives, above note 11 (box 7).

76 "Affirmative Action Hearings Scheduled" *The Prince Albert Daily Herald* (4 May 1981), Archives, above note 11 (box 7). Given the sorry history of the rejection by the Department of Northern Saskatchewan and the government of the report done in 1977, (see McConnell, above note 33) this was good news indeed.

77 Vern Greenshields, "Implementing Affirmative Action Programs Takes Time" *The Star Phoenix [Saskatoon]* (9 October 1981), Archives, above note 11 (box 7). In the commission's next Annual Report, filed on 11 March 1982, they are listed: (1) Saskatchewan Piping Industry Joint Training Board, (2) St Andrews College, (3) Northern Teacher Education Program, (4) Pre-Trades Training Program for Women, (5) Sask Power, (6) Potash Corporation of Saskatchewan: Saskatchewan Human Rights Commission, *Annual Report* (Saskatoon: SHRC, 11 March 1982).

78 *Constitution Act, 1982*, being Schedule B to the *Canada Act 1982* (UK), 1982, c 11.

79 *Canadian Charter of Rights and Freedoms*, *ibid*, Part I.

affirmative action provisions and how they would fit with the *Charter*. I commented in the press:

> . . . the commission is pleased by Premier Allan Blakeney's support for affirmative action programs in Saskatchewan. The recent public debate over removing the override clause from Section 28 of the constitutional proposal has brought the Premier's commitment to affirmative action out very strongly.[80]

So, the way ahead looked like clear sailing to me. Premier Blakeney had come to be persuaded that affirmative action *was* a good Saskatchewan idea. And that his cabinet had not taken the step of approving the affirmative action regulations "made" by the commission in April 1980, didn't seem to be any kind of problem as the commission was carrying on regardless, fettering its statutory discretion by these standards to no one's apparent dismay. In a speech at *A Practitioners' Workshop on Affirmative Action* in Toronto, on 15 April 1983,[81] I noted, "at least in the Province of Saskatchewan, there is no longer any doubt about the definition of what amounts to an acceptable affirmative action plan. It must entail: (1) a systematic analysis of an employer's current workforce; (2) a comparison of the make-up of that workforce with that of the larger surrounding community; (3) establishment of management policies which will move in the direction of overcoming those imbalances which have been identified, with a certain time frame; (4) a monitoring system in order that the goals not slip out of sight and the timetables not be ignored."[82] This amounted to my "swan song" given what the Devine Government, elected on 26 April 1982, had in mind for my tenure as Chief Commissioner.

However, before jumping to that end point for me, there are two other significant loose ends that I wish to discuss. First, there is the story of what was done and not done in light of the accessibility hearings held by the commission in November 1979. In the immediate aftermath of the hearings, a nine-member Provincial Accessibility Committee was established at the commission's call. This committee concluded its deliberations by authoring an eighty-one-page *Accessibility Standard*, "taking

80 "Commission Pleased with Action Programs" *Weyburn Review Weekly* (9 December 1981), Archives, above note 11 (box 7).

81 Ken Norman, Chief Commissioner, Saskatchewan Human Rights Commission, "The Future for Affirmative Action Practitioners" (Notes for an address delivered at the Ontario Institute for Studies in Education, Toronto, 15 April 1983), Archives, above note 11 (box 7).

82 *Ibid*.

into account persons with mobility issues as well as persons with visual and hearing impairments. This standard applies not only to buildings but also to the entire 'built environment,' indoors and out."[83] Following further consultations and approaches to government, Bill 33, *The Uniform Building and Accessibility Standards Act*[84] was tabled in the legislature on 19 March 1982. A month later, the Devine Government arrived on the scene with no interest in pursuing this path. A year after that, in my covering letter to the commission's Annual Report to Attorney General Gary Lane,[85] I noted "there is the outstanding issue of built environment accessibility for persons with physical disabilities. We very much hope that this coming year will see legislated accessibility standards along the line proposed and adopted by the Commission."[86]

Second, there is the issue of independence, of the need for human rights commissions to be at arm's length from the government of the day. Though I was concerned about this in 1978 during the drafting process, I went no further than to recommend five-year appointments by order-in-council. This step put Saskatchewan in the lead as the only commission in the country where commissioners enjoyed a fixed term of office.[87] What I did not recommend at the time was to follow the lead shown in Québec in 1975 and promised federally, of having the commission answerable to the legislature, rather than to a minister of the government. Four years later, with the Devine government showing no interest in the systemic work of the commission,[88] in June 1982, I was elected as president of the Canadian Association of Statutory Human Rights Agencies. At that conference I presented a paper, "Independence for Human Rights Commissions: An Idea Whose Time Has Come."[89]

---

83 SHRC, *Newsletter*, above note 73.

84 Bill 33, first reading on 19 March 1982. "New Building Standards Bill Tabled in Legislature" *The Star Phoenix [Saskatoon]*, (20 March 1982) A14, Archives, above note 11 (box 7).

85 Covering letter from Ken Norman to Gary Lane (14 March 1983), SHRC, *Annual Report 1983*, above note 35.

86 *Ibid.*

87 Tarnopolsky, above note 8 at 435.

88 Covering letter from Ken Norman to Gary Lane (14 March 1983), SHRC, *Annual Report 1983*, above note 35, noting the passage of a year with no action by the government on the matter of accessibility standards for the built environment.

89 Ken Norman, "Independence for Human Rights Commission: An Idea Whose Time Has Come" (Paper delivered at the CASHRA Conference, Montebello, QC, 31 May to 2 June 1982), (1982) 3 CHRR C/82-1.

> . . . with regard to the crucial matter of tenure of office, only Quebec and federal commissions have the security of knowing that nothing short of an act of the legislative body will see them thrown out of their offices . . . . In other provinces, the "new broom" of a newly elected government can and does sweep clean an entire commission.[90]

F. A NEW BROOM

Unaware that my commission was about to be swept clean, a few months later I expressed grave concern about Premier Bennett's proposal not just to houseclean, but to abolish the British Columbia Human Rights Commission. In a letter to Premier Bennett I said, " . . . tearing apart the institutional fabric of the human rights commission and human rights branch is a very regressive step."[91] The next notable event spelling the end of my time with the commission and the beginning of a good deal of backsliding on the systemic discrimination fronts that we had opened up was a courteous letter to me from Attorney General Lane thanking me for my services during my tenure as Chief Commissioner, commending me for my dedication to human rights, and wishing me well in the future.[92]

---

90 *Ibid* at C/82-2. See "Proposed Manitoba Code of Human Rights Summary," [1985] CHRR C/85-1 for a similar point made a couple of years later. "Members of the public would be understandably skeptical of a body like ours if they believed that it was our obligation to 'take orders' from the government of the day, rather than to apply consistent principles and exercise independent judgment" cited in Ken Norman, "Problems in Human Rights Legislation and Administration" in Mahoney & Martin, eds, *Equality and Judicial Neutrality* (Toronto: Carswell, 1987) at 398.

91 Letter from Ken Norman to William Bennett, Vancouver, University of British Columbia, Rare Books and Special Collections (Solidarity Coalition Papers, file 19-1) cited in Dominique Clement, "Human Rights Law and Sexual Discrimination in British Columbia, 1953–84" in Alvin Finkel, Sarah Carter, & Peter Fortna, eds, *The West and Beyond: New Perspectives on an Imagined Region* (Edmonton: Athabasca University Press, 2010) 297 at 309.

92 Letter from Gary Lane (Attorney General) to Ken Norman (chairperson of the Saskatchewan Human Rights Commission) (19 October 1983), Archives, above note 11 (box 7).

CHAPTER 4

HUMAN RIGHTS SYSTEMS: ARE THEY FAIR?[1]

Pearl Eliadis[2]

> *"Just because commissions and tribunals don't follow the same rules as the courts does not mean that they are illegitimate."*
>
> — *Alan Borovoy*[3]

A. INTRODUCTION

Human rights systems[4] in Canada have never been popular institutions.[5] Frequently, they have been highly controversial. In recent years, criticisms

---

1 This chapter is an adaptation of Pearl Eliadis, *Speaking Out on Human Rights: Debating Canada's Human Rights System* (Montréal & Kingston: McGill-Queen's University Press) [forthcoming, 2014] [Eliadis]. All interviews referenced in this chapter are drawn from the book. Interviewee affiliations are based on the date of the interview.

2 Pearl Eliadis is a lawyer, lecturer, and author. Her Montréal-based law practice focuses on human rights, national institutions, and democratic governance.

3 Interview of Alan Borovoy, former General Counsel, Canadian Civil Liberties Association (14 September 2009) in Eliadis, above note 1.

4 The term "human rights system" refers compendiously to commissions, tribunals, and other public institutions established by law to protect and promote human rights.

5 See R Brian Howe & David Johnson, *Restraining Equality: Human Rights Commissions in Canada* (Toronto: University of Toronto Press, 2000). See also Rosanna L Langer, *Defining Rights and Wrongs: Bureaucracy, Human Rights and Public Accountability* (Vancouver: UBC Press, 2007).

have escalated and become more prevalent and pervasive, to the point where public discourse has become highly biased and even corrupted.[6] The proximate cause of the media storm was a concerted attack on the hate speech jurisdiction of human rights systems by the media, led by conservative pundit Ezra Levant and writer Mark Steyn. Neither individual took up the mantle of anti-commission crusaders randomly. Both were targets of human rights complaints, either directly or indirectly. The result of the hate speech debates was a campaign to "denormalize" human rights commissions, leaving a clear impression among many Canadians that the human rights system is unfair and flawed.[7]

Human rights commissions and tribunals are part of a large family of administrative agencies, boards, and commissions (administrative systems). They are part of the executive branch of government and subject to principles of administrative law. Administrative systems touch every aspect of our lives: we are much more likely to encounter them than the courts. According to a Canadian expert, administrative systems decide the bulk of rights disputes of our citizens.[8] They deal not only with human rights claims, but also with refugee claims, national security oversight, health and safety standards, access to public health insurance, employment standards, food safety, housing standards and building codes, and the regulation of transportation and broadcasting, to name but a few. The list goes on.

Human rights commissions and tribunals are based on well-developed principles of procedural fairness and natural justice. Although they have an adjudicative role, they are not courts and do not operate identically to courts. This does not make them illegal, rogue, or arbitrary dispensers of justice. Administrative agencies are not "junior, imitation or quasi-courts. They are instrumentalities of government policy which are, nonetheless, required to act fairly."[9]

---

6 Richard Moon, "The Attack on Human Rights Commissions and the Corruption of Public Discourse" (2010) 73 Sask L Rev 93.

7 Eliadis, above note 1, Introduction.

8 Ron Ellis, "Current Issues in Tribunal Independence" (Paper delivered at The Future of Administrative Justice Symposium, Faculty of Law, University of Toronto, 17 & 18 January 2008) [Ellis], online: University of Toronto Library www.law-lib.utoronto.ca/Conferences/Administrative_Justice_Bibliography/ajb.htm#papers.

9 J Sprague, "*Ocean Port Hotel v British Columbia (General Manager, Liquor Control and Licensing Branch)*," Case comment (2000) 12 Can J Admin L & Prac 349 at 356.

This article addresses two main areas of criticism that are responsible for most of the myths and misunderstandings about human rights systems in Canada. The first is the confusion between human rights and criminal justice systems and the belief that the rules of the criminal justice system should apply to human rights systems. This has led to a good deal of misunderstanding, especially about objectives of the two systems, the types of remedies that human rights systems offer, and allegations that human rights systems expose people to *Canadian Charter of Rights and Freedoms*[10] (*Charter*) violations like "double jeopardy."

The second area of critique is the accusation that human rights commissions and tribunals are unfair "kangaroo courts," a critique that has thrived largely because of the way that human rights law deals with issues like truth, intent, hearsay, settlements and mediation, and support for human rights claimants.

B. COMPENSATION, CRIME, AND PUNISHMENT

The idea that human rights commissions and tribunals spend their time dispensing a diluted or deficient form of criminal justice is in part the result of a perception that human rights systems are criminal or quasi-criminal in nature. Conflating human rights and criminal law is encouraged by language commonly found in the Canadian media like "100 percent conviction rates,"[11] by the tendency of some writers to use language like "prosecution" and "accused," or to denounce the risk of incarceration for contempt of court related to human rights tribunal orders.[12]

---

10 Part I of the *Constitution Act, 1982*, being Schedule B to the *Canada Act 1982* (UK), 1982, c 11 [*Charter*].

11 "100 percent conviction rates" is an accusation that was levelled by some in the media: for example, a *National Post* editorial stated that "the CHRC has a 100 percent conviction rate on hate speech." See "A Bit Late for Introspection," Editorial, *National Post* (19 June 2008) A20. The reality is that 90 percent of all cases filed with human rights commissions in Canada do not succeed. Some writers then shifted to saying that 100 percent of *hate speech* cases were accepted (see, for example, "Muzzling the Human Rights Debate," Editorial, *National Post* (18 June 2009) A14). As it turned out, that too was inaccurate. See Joseph Brean, "Hate Speech Cases 2% of Complaints" *National Post* (5 April 2008) A8.

12 Interview of Philippe Dufresne, Senior Counsel, Canadian Human Rights Commission (13 May 2009) in Eliadis, above note 1. Dufresne noted that

1 2 3 4 5 6 7 8 9 10 11 12 13 14

Such language reinforces the image of crypto-criminal processes that expose people to penal sanctions and "double jeopardy" with none of the usual legal rights and defences.

The reality is that human rights systems are not part of the criminal justice system. They are subject to administrative law and their main objective is to compensate claimants, and eradicate discrimination. It is true that there are provisions in human rights laws that include sanctions and serve different functions and these merit some analysis to understand their role. Their existence does not alter the fundamental nature of human rights systems as mainly compensatory and not criminal in nature. They are discussed in the following section.

1) Compensation, Punishment, and Penalties

The main objective of human rights law is not to prosecute people or to even to punish them:

> In contrast to the criminal realm, the filing of a human rights complaint implies no suspicion of wrongdoing on the part of the state. The investigation by the Commission is aimed solely at determining what took place and ultimately to settle the matter in a non-adversarial manner. The purpose of human rights proceedings is not to punish but to eradicate discrimination. Tribunal orders are compensatory rather than punitive. The investigation period in the human rights process is not one where the Commission "prosecutes" the respondent.[13]

The vast majority of remedial provisions in human rights statutes do aim to compensate claimants for human rights violations and to eradicate discrimination. The idea of compensation can encompass direct pecuniary losses and non-pecuniary losses, or go beyond the claimant's own situation and offer systemic remedies, which are orders aimed at eliminating discriminatory rules and practices.[14] While individual com-

---

these are common themes in general interest writing about human rights systems.

13 *Blencoe v British Columbia (Human Rights Commission)*, [2000] 2 SCR 307 at para 94 [*Blencoe*].

14 The classic case on systemic discrimination is *CN v Canada (Canadian Human Rights Commission)*, [1987] 1 SCR 1114. This case is frequently referred to as *Action Travail des Femmes*, the name of the plaintiff organization. The original complaint was about a longstanding series of hiring and promotion policies

plainants remain at the centre of how courts and tribunals deal with complaints, human rights law has a long-standing role in targeting systemic or strategic cases that have implications beyond the individual complainant. Certain statutes in Canada also provide for exemplary or punitive damages, designed to punish respondents for egregious behaviour. Such damages are intended for exceptional cases where the behaviour is such that a more deterrent or punitive approach is needed. They are not criminal sanctions and are consistent with the aim of eradicating discrimination.

There are exceptions to the principle of compensation that do engage with criminal law. First are the criminal sanctions that are still on the books for human rights statutes in relation to acts of discrimination.[15] Second, all human rights statutes contain some form of penal or criminal sanction for violating orders, obstructing justice, or for reprisals against complainants or witnesses. For example, section 60 of the *Canadian Human Rights Act*[16] (*CHRA*) creates a summary conviction offence for obstruction and reprisal. Virtually every human rights statute in Canada contains similar provisions as a consequence for the failure to respect a valid legal order and not for the discrimination itself. The role of these provisions is ancillary and peripheral to the overall objective of human rights systems, which, again, is focused on eradicating discrimination, compensating the victim and making the victim "whole." Fines and criminal sanctions are rarely, if ever, used and their existence does not transform the human rights system into a criminal regime. Rather, such sanctions are typical of most administrative and regulatory systems. According to Gordon McKinnon, a senior lawyer in Manitoba who has practiced before many administrative tribunals:

---

that operated to exclude women from blue-collar jobs. The Court upheld the employment equity program that the Tribunal had imposed on CN.

15 For example, any violation of the Manitoba *Human Rights Code*, CCSM c H175, including discrimination, can proceed by way of civil or criminal proceedings. The Newfoundland and Labrador *Human Rights Act*, SNL 2010, c H-13.1 contains a similar provision. These statutes are exceptional and are something of a throwback to quasi-criminal fair practices legislation. Other statutes in Canada, such as the *Saskatchewan Human Rights Code*, SS 1979, c S-24.1, as amended by SS 2011, c 17, do not provide for summary conviction offences, precisely because the drafters sought to emphasize the compensatory role of human rights laws and move away from quasi-criminal enforcement. Email communication with Ken Norman (12 November 2012) [email on file].

16 RSC 1985, c H-6 [*CHRA*].

> All the professional discipline bodies I deal with have a component that would contain some sort of a fine. Medical, legal, and nursing disciplinary bodies, for example, would all have some sort of fine or sanction attached to them. So do taxi board companies and liquor licensing boards. This does not make them criminal in nature in this sense; they are a standard part of the administrative regulatory scheme.[17]

Most of the concerns about sanctions are not the result of any of the above-mentioned types of remedies, but rather because of a public interest penalty clause in the *CHRA*, which imposed a fine for hate speech.[18] It came under fire in a 2009 case before the Canadian Human Rights Tribunal (Tribunal) called *Warman v Lemire*[19] (*Lemire*). Mark Lemire was alleged to be a webmaster for online sites containing racist material and hate speech. The Tribunal found that Lemire had posted an article that was "likely to expose homosexuals and Blacks to hatred or contempt"[20] under section 13 of the *CHRA*, a finding that was upheld by the Federal Court of Canada on judicial review.[21] However, Lemire had challenged section 13 of the *CHRA*, arguing that the penalty clause was unconstitutional and inconsistent with the overall purpose of human rights legislation. The penalty clause is contained in section 54(1)(c) of the *CHRA*. The penalty clause was said to divert the *CHRA* from its compensatory objectives, rendering section 13 unconstitutional. The Tribunal agreed. Prior to the enactment of that clause in 1998, the hate speech prohibition, section 13, was said to have only played

> a minimal role in the imposition of moral, financial or incarcerating sanctions, the primary goal being to act directly for the benefit

---

17 Interview of Gordon McKinnon, Partner, Thompson Dorfman Sweatman LLP (5 March 2010) in Eliadis, above note 1.

18 Section 54(1)(c) of the *CHRA* permits the Tribunal to order the respondent to pay a penalty of not more than $10,000. Bill C-304, *An Act to amend the Canadian Human Rights Act (protecting freedom)*, 1st Sess, 41th Parl, 2011 (assented to 26 June 2013). Among other things, the effect of the bill will be to repeal ss 13 and 54(1)(c). The bill will take effect one year after receiving Royal Assent.

19 *Warman c Lemire*, 2009 TCDP 26 at para 292 [*Lemire*].

20 *Ibid* at para 292.

21 *Ibid* at para 26. The Tribunal decision was overturned by the Federal Court of Canada in *Canada (Human Rights Commission) v Warman*, 2012 FC 1162 [*Warman*].

> of those likely to be exposed to the harms caused by hate propaganda.[22]

However, after the amendment, Tribunal Member Hadjis thought it could no longer be characterized as "minimal."

No matter that the penalty did not result in a criminal record, or that it did not proceed by way of summary conviction offence, or that there are many provisions in human rights laws across the country that constitute "moral, financial or incarcerating sanctions" without being unconstitutional. The Tribunal decided to not apply the Supreme Court of Canada's 1990 decision in *Taylor* which had affirmed the constitutionality of section 13 more than two decades earlier.[23] The Tribunal had been persuaded by the respondents in the *Lemire* case to admit large swaths of evidence about how the Commission investigated hate speech cases. The media, which was hostile to the Canadian human rights system, largely because of free speech concerns, celebrated the Tribunal decision as a definitive victory.[24]

On judicial review, the Federal Court overturned the Tribunal decision with respect to the constitutionality of section 13.[25] First, it decided that the Tribunal had exceeded its jurisdiction when it admitted evidence about the Commission's statutory role in handling section 13 investigations, which was a duty conferred on it by Parliament. Second, the Tribunal had failed to take the proper route that was available to it, namely severing the penalty clause from the rest of the statute. This would have permitted the Tribunal to uphold section 13 of the *CHRA*, while respecting the Supreme Court of Canada's decision in *Taylor*.

The Commission did not contest the penalty clause's unconstitutionality before the Federal Court of Canada in *Warman*. Throwing the penalty clause under the bus may have averted a difficult argument for the Commission before the Federal Court in *Warman*, but it exposed other parts of its own law and, indeed, other human rights laws across Canada to attacks on similar grounds. It also proved a pyrrhic victory since section 13 was on the way to repeal because of Bill C-304.

---

22 *Lemire*, above note 19.

23 *Canada (Human Rights Commission) v Taylor*, [1990] 3 SCR 892 [*Taylor*].

24 Joseph Brean, "Hate Speech Law Unconstitutional: Rights Tribunal" *National Post* (2 September 2009), online: National Post www.nationalpost.com/news/story.html?id=1954734.

25 *Warman*, above note 21.

The *Lemire* case has troubling implications for human rights systems that extend beyond the little-used penalty clause in the *CHRA*. In the aftermath of the Tribunal's decision in *Lemire*, the Canadian Human Rights Commission released a report that proposed the repeal of section 54(1)(c) because it did not "fit easily" within the human rights system.[26] The vulnerability of remedial provisions that are not strictly compensatory in nature also applies to exemplary and punitive damages, which are at least to some degree aimed at punishing conduct and not at compensating victims. The Supreme Court of Canada has described the conduct that attracts such damages as conduct that is "malicious, oppressive, and high-handed."[27] In *Québec (Commission des droits de la personne et des droits de la jeunesse) c Calego international inc*,[28] the Tribunal cited a decision of the Québec Court of Appeal describing the role of such damages in the human rights context:

> The preventive function of punitive damages is fundamental; punitive damages have a dual objective of punishment and deterrence, but cannot exceed what is sufficient to achieve those objectives . . . . It is not a question of compensating the plaintiff but of punishing the defendant as the defendant deserves, of discouraging both the defendant and others from acting in that manner in the future and expressing disapproval of such events in all respects.[29]

The Northwest Territories and Manitoba also permit punitive or exemplary damages.[30] In Ontario, wilful and reckless behaviour can result in damages awards for mental anguish to the complainant.[31] These are but a few examples of sanctions and punitive provisions that go beyond the

---

26 Canadian Human Rights Commission, *Special Report to Parliament: Freedom of Expression and Freedom from Hate in the Internet Age* (Ottawa: Canadian Human Rights Commission, June 2009) at 37 [Canadian Human Rights Commission], online: CHRC www.chrc-ccdp.gc.ca. The Canadian Bar Association also agreed with this recommendation.

27 *Hill v Church of Scientology of Toronto*, [1995] 2 SCR 1130 at para 196.

28 *Québec (Commission des droits de la personne et des droits de la jeunesse) c Calego international inc*, 2011 QCTDP 4.

29 *Ibid* at para 478. See Québec *Charter of Human Rights and Freedoms*, RSQ 1975, c C-12, art 49.

30 Manitoba *Human Rights Code*, CCSM c H175, s 43(2); Northwest Territories *Human Rights Act*, SNWT 2002, c 18, s 62.

31 See, for example, *Heintz v Christian Horizons*, 2008 HRTO 22 at paras 241ff. The damages award was upheld on appeal to the Divisional Court. See *Ontario (Human Rights Commission) v Christian Horizons*, 2010 ONSC 2105.

individual complainant's direct damages. They do not, for all that, invalidate the broad principles set out in *Blencoe v British Columbia (Human Rights Commission)*,[32] let alone transform human rights systems into unconstitutional regimes.

2) Double Jeopardy and Forum Shopping

The prohibition against double jeopardy is a *Charter* right in the criminal context, designed to prevent people from being charged twice for the same crime. The criticism that human rights systems subject people to "double jeopardy" is the direct result of the *Maclean's* hate speech cases. Three complaints were filed: one with the Canadian Human Rights Commission, one with the Ontario Human Rights Commission, and the third with the British Columbia Human Rights Tribunal. The background of the cases is well known. Osgoode Hall law students prepared and filed the human rights complaints against the media company Rogers.[33] They argued that its magazine, *Maclean's*, had published more than twenty articles, starting in 2005, that the students felt had discriminated against Muslims and "went well beyond simply being offensive and became dangerous."[34] The students singled out writer Mark Steyn's October 2006 article "The Future Belongs to Islam" in *Maclean's*, for its prediction of an imminent, "bloody" Muslim global takeover.[35]

None of the three complaints involved a criminal charge of hate speech, and thus the use of the term "double jeopardy" is inaccurate. While double jeopardy may not have been the correct term, however, it is true that multiple claims about the same issue can prompt concerns about "forum shopping" and about the cost and risk of litigating in multiple jurisdictions.

---

32 *Blencoe*, above note 13.

33 The students appeared as the complainants in the Ontario case, but asked other individuals and organizations to act as complainants in the other two.

34 Naseem Mithoowani, Khurrum Awan, & Muneeza Sheikh, "Rights Complainants Want Only Reasonable Access to Media" *The [Montreal] Gazette* (24 February 2008) at A15.

35 Mark Steyn, "The Future Belongs to Islam" *Maclean's* (20 October 2006) [Steyn], online: Macleans.ca www.macleans.ca/culture/books/article.jsp?content=20061023_134898_134898. The online version of the article is an excerpt from the book, *America Alone* (Washington DC: Regnery Publishing, 2006).

In theory, the same or similar human rights claims can be filed in each of the fourteen human rights jurisdictions in Canada. Situations like the ones in the *Maclean's* hate speech cases are very rare, but they do occur. However, the reason is straightforward and has nothing to do with human rights commissions or abuse of process. It is the result of how the constitutional division of powers operates. There is no national human rights commission in Canada that has the authority to bundle up cases in multiple jurisdictions into a single proceeding. While it may be unfair to respondents to have to fight multiple but identical human rights complaints across the country, it is also unfair to complainants to have to file and litigate complaints in multiple jurisdictions about the same case, simply because our constitutional division of powers imposes such a result. The use of legal systems as strategic and public policy vehicles to communicate a message at a national level is hardly novel, nor is it a tactic reserved for human rights activists.

That said, there is merit in the idea of a more coordinated national approach, so that in the very rare cases where multiple proceedings occur, procedures can be simplified and made less fraught with cost and uncertainty for all parties. The *CHRA* does contain a provision that addresses the issue of potentially conflicting decisions, but it does not deal with forum shopping directly. The Canadian Human Rights Commission has said that it will work with other jurisdictions on this matter, but the status of these negotiations is unclear.[36]

C. KANGAROO COURTS AND STAR CHAMBERS

Fear and mistrust of human rights systems are based in part on widespread accusations that commissions are "star chambers" and "kangaroo courts." Some of the evidence marshalled in support of these accusations includes concerns about existence or non-existence of rules related to truth, hearsay, and intent. They are summarized as follows:

- Someone can be telling the truth, and yet found "guilty" of hate speech (or any other discriminatory practice, presumably) simply because a claimant is "offended";

---

36 Canadian Human Rights Commission, above note 26.

- The usual defence of lack of intent cannot be pleaded before human rights institutions;
- Human rights tribunals and boards use informal proceedings that breach "normal" court rules, such as hearsay;
- Mediation proceedings are a "shakedown," forcing innocent respondents to pay up; and
- Human rights commissions offer support for claimants, which is unfair to respondents.

None of these concerns turns out to have much substance. Each one is dealt with in turn.

1) Truth

Critics have denounced human rights proceedings because truth is irrelevant and people can be found "guilty" merely if someone is offended. Due to the media's greater familiarity with criminal procedure and defamation cases, the lack of a truth defence would appear problematic if human rights proceedings were criminal (which they aren't) or based on defamation proceedings (which they aren't).

Truth matters, but being offended is not enough to make out a claim of discrimination. Claimants must prove their allegations on the balance of probabilities. It must be more likely than not that the allegations are true. This standard applies to all discrimination cases, including those where speech and speech alone is the basis of the discriminatory act.

In a British Columbia case called *McIntosh v Metro Aluminum Products*[37] (*McIntosh*), Lisa McIntosh sued her boss and former boyfriend for repeatedly and aggressively "sexting" her at work. The messages contained lewd insinuations and invitations to both McIntosh and her daughter. The ex-boyfriend sent the messages long after his relationship with McIntosh had ended, and McIntosh made it clear that his messages were completely unwelcome. McIntosh was not fired or demoted and he instigated no discriminatory "act" other than the texting, which is expressive behaviour.

McIntosh had to prove the truth of her allegations, namely that the messages were received and who had sent them. The British Columbia Human Rights Tribunal (BC Tribunal) found that McIntosh had been

37 *McIntosh v Metro Aluminum Products*, 2011 BCHRT 34.

harassed and her rights had been violated under the British Columbia *Human Rights Code*.[38]

In addition to damages for lost wages and expenses, the BC Tribunal ordered $12,500 in damages for injury to dignity, feelings, and self-respect. (British Columbia's human rights law does not provide for punitive damages, but the aggressive and provocative nature of the "sext" messages was clearly a factor in the damages award.)

Critics of the "truth defence" do have a point in the following sense: the BC Tribunal did not examine whether the content of the messages was accurate. For example, the BC Tribunal did not examine whether McIntosh's boss really "needed a nooner" or whether he had indeed wanted to date the complainant's daughter. Proving these "facts" would have been absurd. Indeed, they are at the heart of the human rights claim, namely the sexist denigration of a woman based on stereotypes or impressions about her sexual availability or that of her daughter.

Articles and commentary of the kind that concern free-speech defenders differ from discrimination cases in employment, schools, or services. Unlike the articles penned by Mark Steyn, the *McIntosh* case was about a specific person in the relational context of employment, which imposes power relationships. In the *McIntosh* case, the employee could not easily walk away from the situation without risk to her own job. Discrimination cases like this bring expressive behaviour much closer to equality law and further from free speech rights because of the relational context and the direct attack on a single or identifiable person.

Hate speech cases, such as hate on the Internet, work differently. They more strongly engage core speech interests, in part because they are not attacks on specific people in relational contexts like employment that are protected by human rights legislation. However, even in this context, speech loses its constitutional protection when it provokes unusually strong and deep-felt emotions of detestation and vilification.[39] This is a very high standard and requires evidence of discriminatory effects. The assertion that entire groups of people are inherently criminal, inferior, diseased, or dangerous simply because of their race, gender, religion, ethnicity, or similar characteristics have long been established as evidence *in se* of the likelihood that the targeted groups will be exposed

---

38 RSBC 1996, c 210.

39 *Taylor*, above note 23; *Saskatchewan (Human Rights Commission) v Whatcott*, 2013 SCC 11.

to hatred.[40] Simply put, there should no longer be any question as to whether some people, by virtue of personal attributes that are protected by law, are considered less human than others.

Here is where the relevance of truth is quite different: John Ross Taylor, the respondent in the 1990 *Taylor* decision, described his anti-Semitism and racism as "truth literature."[41] Should we, as a society, seriously engage with the so-called "truth" of his assertion that Jews deserve to be deported en masse to Madagascar? (Truth is not a defence either, incidentally, when it comes to public incitement of hatred under section 319(1) of the *Criminal Code*,[42] although it is a defence to wilfully promoting hatred where incitement has not occurred.)

There is another reason to be careful about insisting on truth as a defence in human rights cases involving hate speech. By focusing on truth, writers and journalists can be exposed to hate speech complaints if their assertions turn out to be false. Mark Steyn's article "The Future Belongs to Islam" predicted a Muslim takeover and suggested that the only remaining question was "how bloody the transfer of real estate will be."[43] Steyn's anti-Muslim writings may have danced on the edge of what a national magazine should have been publishing, but they were at least within the realm of a widely debated theory about the implications of immigration and demographic data about Muslims in Western society. In that respect, they were no better or worse than what is commonly seen in Western Europe, for example, in the National Front's aspirations for France or in writings predicting a violent and extremist "Eurabia."

One source of these dire predictions was a 2004 study from the US National Intelligence Council that proposed demographic scenarios, including a major population increase of Muslims in Europe by 2025.[44] What the study did not say was that when one actually did the math, even assuming the highest level of reproductive rates, the Muslim population

---

40 *Ibid*. See also *Payzant v Mcaleer* (1994), 26 CHRR 271 (ON HRT).

41 Interview of John Ross Taylor by Tom Koch (17 January 1965) on *This Hour Has Seven Days*, CBC Television, Toronto, CBC Digital Archives at time code 47:05, online: CBC www.cbc.ca/archives/discover/programs/t/this-hour-has-seven-days/this-hour-has-seven-days-january-17-1965.html. I thank Dominique Clément for bringing this episode to my attention.

42 RSC 1985, c C-46.

43 Steyn, above note 35.

44 National Intelligence Council, *Mapping the Global Future: Report of the National Intelligence Council's 2020 Project Based on Consultations with Non-governmental Experts around The World* (Pittsburgh: Government Printing Office, 2004).

would reach a total of 8 percent in Europe by 2025 — hardly a demographic takeover. The 2004 study was reportedly based on "consultations" and meetings with "futurists" as well as non-governmental organizations, "academic and other sources."[45] As *Newsweek* writer William Underhill observed, the figures were "speculation based on speculation."[46] Underhill cited Grace Davie of the University of Exeter, Jytte Klaussen at Boston's Brandeis University, and Carl Haub, a senior Washington-based demographer, who described the predictions as "scaremongering," "a quite deliberate exaggeration," and "absolutely absurd," respectively. A year later, Eric Kaufmann's *Shall the Religious Inherit the Earth?* demolished the Eurabia myth, but received scant attention.[47] Had the focus been on the truth of the demographic predictions, it is not inconceivable that the outcome of the BC Tribunal's decision in the *Maclean's* hate speech might have been in favour of the plaintiffs.

But the real issue from a human rights perspective was how to characterize the message that Muslims are menaces who are looming on the edges of our property lines to carry out bloody transfers of real estate and the like. The repetition of such claims, especially in a respectable national magazine, gave them a degree of authenticity and reliability that they did not deserve and served to amplify damaging and unfair stereotypes.[48] The Steyn articles (there was more than one article that the students had identified) made the obligatory exculpatory mentions: there are, no doubt, moderate Muslims in existence somewhere, but the overall impression that Muslims are dangerous as a group and associated directly or indirectly with extremism is a clear conclusion.

Law professor Richard Moon had this to say about the so-called truth defence:

---

45 *Ibid* at 83.

46 William Underhill, "Why Fears of a Muslim Takeover Are All Wrong" *Newsweek* (20 July 2009) 33.

47 Eric Kaufmann, *Shall the Religious Inherit the Earth? Demography and Politics in the Twenty-First Century* (London: Profile Books, 2010) at 118ff. The term "Eurabia" was popularized by Bat Ye'or [Gisèle Littman], author of *Eurabia: The Euro-Arab Axis* (Madison, NJ: Fairleigh Dickinson University Press, 2005).

48 Ontario Human Rights Commission, News Release, "Commission Issues Statement on Decision in Maclean's Cases" (9 April 2008), online: OHRC www.ohrc.on.ca/en/news_centre/commission-issues-statement-decision-maclean%E2%80%99s-cases.

> In my view, a truth defence is not required because hate speech is necessarily untrue. Hate speech makes the claim that the members of an identifiable group share a dangerous or undesirable trait – that they are by nature violent or corrupt or dishonest — and must be stopped by violent means if necessary. Our commitment to equality entails a rejection of any view that the members of a racial or other identifiable group are inherently inferior or dangerous.[49]

Researchers and writers should have the right to be wrong, and that is why truth is not as much of an issue in the hate speech context. The line is drawn at inciting hatred against entire groups of people as inherently inferior, dangerous, or diseased, based on their race, religion, or other personal characteristics that have historically been the domain of human rights law. There is a long and sad history of these kinds of tactics, their effects, and their success.

2) Intent

A common criticism about human rights systems is that they do not take the intent of the respondent into consideration as a potential "defence" to a human rights claim.

Again, the sleight of hand that conflates human rights law with criminal law is what allows this argument to bear the weight that it does. The requirement to prove state of mind or intent is a general requirement in criminal law. The general rule in discrimination cases is that *effects*, not intent, are central to discrimination claims. The rule was established in 1985 by a unanimous decision of the Supreme Court of Canada (and not, incidentally, by human rights commissions):

> . . . we are dealing here with consequences of conduct rather than with punishment for misbehaviour. In other words, we are considering what are essentially civil remedies. The proof of intent, a necessary requirement in our approach to criminal and punitive legislation, should not be a governing factor in construing human rights legislation aimed at the elimination of discrimination. It is

49 Canadian Human Rights Commission, Report to the Canadian Human Rights Commission Concerning Section 13 of the Canadian Human Rights Act and the Regulation of Hate Speech on the Internet by Richard Moon (Ottawa: CHRC, 2008) at 37, online: CHRC www.chrc-ccdp.ca/pdf/moon_report_en.pdf.

> my view that the courts below were in error in finding an intent to discriminate to be a necessary element of proof.[50]

The Court observed that "intent" in the human rights context has had insidious consequences, noting its influence on the notorious "separate but equal" doctrine in the US, which helped to reinforce the segregation of African-Americans.

In 1987, the Supreme Court of Canada examined the intent issue again in a case involving recruitment, hiring, and promotion policies at Canadian National Railways. The policies had the practical effect of preventing or discouraging women from getting blue-collar jobs.[51] The policies may not have been *intended* to discriminate against women, but they did. Such cases helped to change the way discrimination is both understood and litigated.

Three years later, the Supreme Court of Canada applied the same reasoning to the act of exposing people to hatred under section 13 of the *CHRA*:

> Intent to discriminate is not a precondition of a finding of discrimination under human rights codes . . . . The preoccupation with effects, and not with intent, is readily explicable when one considers that systemic discrimination is much more widespread in our society than is intentional discrimination. To import a subjective intent requirement into human rights provisions, rather than allowing tribunals to focus solely upon effects, would thus defeat one of the primary goals of anti-discrimination statutes.[52]

Intent does have a limited role under the Alberta statute in hate speech cases. Section 3 of the *Alberta Human Rights Act*[53] says:

> 3(1). No person shall publish, issue or display or cause to be published, issued or displayed before the public any statement, publication, notice, sign, symbol, emblem or other representation that

---

50 *Ontario (Human Rights Commission) v Simpsons-Sears*, [1985] 2 SCR 536 at para 14. The Court also distinguished between direct and indirect discrimination, a distinction in law that was overturned in *British Columbia (Public Service Employee Relations Commission) v BCGSEU*, [1999] 3 SCR 3.

51 *CN v Canada (Canadian Human Rights Commission)*, [1987] 1 SCR 1114.

52 *Taylor*, above note 23, Dickson CJ.

53 RSA 2000, c A-25.5.

(a) indicates discrimination *or an intention to discriminate* against a person or a class of persons, or

(b) is likely to expose a person or a class of persons to hatred or contempt. . . . [emphasis added]

Section 3(1)(a) deals with discriminatory speech and requires *either* intent to discriminate *or* evidence of a publication that indicates discrimination on its face. A publication, notice, sign, symbol, or emblem that urges people not to rent apartments to, say, Blacks or Jews, is discriminatory on its face, because it clearly and publicly signals intent to discriminate, regardless of whether or not potential complainants have actually been refused an apartment.

Much has been made about the fact that section 3 refers to inciting discrimination as opposed to violence, but prohibiting incitement to discrimination is consistent with Canada's international human rights obligations under the *International Covenant on Civil and Political Rights*:[54] article 20 prohibits "[a]ny advocacy of national, racial or religious hatred that constitutes *incitement to discrimination*, hostility or violence shall be prohibited by law." [emphasis added]

The absence of a requirement for intent is also the source of criticism of human rights systems in Canada because it allows the possibility of a contempt order. If a tribunal issues an order after a person has been found liable for discrimination, and if that order is not respected, the person can be found to be in contempt. A person who is cited for contempt can end up in prison. The result, it is argued, is that a non-criminal provision in human rights laws can result in incarceration, without the usual defence of intent. Philippe Dufresne, a lawyer at the Canadian Human Rights Commission, observed that such views reflect a "complete lack of understanding of contempt proceedings" in the public commentary about human rights commissions and in their connection to contempt proceedings.[55]

Contempt proceedings are designed to ensure respect for the justice system: a person can be cited for contempt in any type of case that is before the courts, criminal or non-criminal. The Federal Courts rules, for example, provide that "contempt of court" occurs when a person dis-

54 19 December 1966, 999 UNTS 171, Can TS 1976 No 47, 6 ILM 368 (entered into force 23 March 1976).

55 Interview of Philippe Dufresne, Senior Counsel, Canadian Human Rights Commission (13 May 2009), in Eliadis, above note 1.

obeys any process or order of the court or a judge, interferes with the orderly administration of justice, or impairs the authority or dignity of the court.[56] In order to be cited for contempt, at least in the context of human rights proceedings before the federal jurisdiction, the person must have acted intentionally.

In the *Taylor* case,[57] John Ross Taylor had failed to respect a cease and desist order relating to hate messages under section 13 of the *CHRA*.[58] The order was then filed by the Canadian Human Rights Commission in the Federal Court, resulting in a contempt order:

> A term of imprisonment is only possible where the respondent *intentionally* communicates messages which he or she knows have been found likely to cause the harm described in s 13(1), and I therefore cannot agree that the possibility of a contempt order issuing against an individual unduly chills the freedom of expression.[59] [emphasis added]

In short, an individual must wilfully engage in actions prohibited by a court order.[60] Attempts to attack collaterally human rights tribunal orders using contempt proceedings failed in 1990, and two decades later they rightly failed again.[61]

3) Hearsay

Administrative tribunals differ from courts in important ways. They use more relaxed rules of evidence and procedure. Because human rights courts and tribunals make decisions about fundamental issues like rights, it is reasonable to expect that on the spectrum of formality, human rights tribunals should look more like courts. Even so, human rights decision makers do operate with less formality and one of the most criticized differences is the absence of the hearsay rule.

---

56 *Federal Courts Rules*, r 466ff.

57 *Taylor*, above note 23.

58 Section 13 makes it a discriminatory practice to communicate telephonically any matter likely to expose a person or a group to hatred or contempt on the basis, *inter alia*, of race or religion.

59 *Taylor*, above note 23 at 934.

60 *Re Sheppard and Sheppard* (1976), 12 OR (2d) 4 at 595–96 (ON CA). See also *Prescott-Russell Services for Children and Adults v G(N)* (2006), 82 OR (3d) 686 at para 27 (ON CA).

61 *Warman v Tremaine*, 2010 FC 1198.

Hearsay evidence is excluded in courts because the truth of what someone said is most reliably presented by the speaker. There are well-established exceptions to the hearsay rule. The application of the rule and its exceptions is a difficult area of law. Many people appear unrepresented before human rights tribunals and a strict application of the hearsay rules would operate unfairly for those who cannot afford lawyers.[62] This includes respondents.

As well, a more relaxed approach to rules allows parties to get to the nub of issues more efficiently. Gordon McKinnon has appeared before several kinds of administrative decision makers outside the human rights context and notes that:

> In most administrative hearings, what you are looking at is hearsay evidence. Workers' compensation decisions will often be based on hearsay evidence cases, including medical reports and other documentary reports that are admissible at the hearing, but are still hearsay. They would not generally be admitted in court without calling in the actual doctor or author who wrote the document. In an administrative hearing, however, the rules are relaxed to permit the evidence without this type of expense and additional time.[63]

In administrative hearings, a requirement to bring in fifty witnesses to establish fifty separate statements in connection with one set of facts would cripple the system. According to litigator David Baker, very few cases actually turn on hearsay, and, when they do, tribunals have tools to deal with the evidence in a way that is fair to both parties.[64] Most administrative tribunals can admit hearsay evidence, but they can assess its reliability and relevance. Evidence that is found to be unfair or unreliable will be excluded or discarded, although the route for doing this will be different than the one used by courts.

62 Interview of David Baker, Partner, Bakerlaw (30 July 2009) in Eliadis, above note 1.

63 Interview of Gordon McKinnon, Partner, Thompson Dorfman Sweatman LLP (5 March 2010) in Eliadis, above note 1.

64 Interview of David Baker, Partner, Bakerlaw (30 July 2009) in Eliadis, above note 1.

4) Conciliation or Capitulation?

Over the last two decades, most human rights system in Canada have been using alternative dispute resolution (ADR), and especially mediation, to encourage the early resolution of cases. The ADR movement that began in the 1980s sought to push cases out of the courts, reduce delays, and put an end to deals wrangled at the last minute by lawyers seemingly more interested in settling a case quickly than in justice.

Most human rights statutes require that commissions attempt to settle complaints, but there is generally no obligation on the parties to participate in settlement discussions.

Mediation has been criticized by litigants in the human rights system for strong-arm tactics like threats of long delays (up to three or even four years) as a way to pressure them into accepting settlement terms. Mediation was also accused of failing to serve the public interest because mediated agreements were frequently confidential.[65] Critics further alleged that by taking into consideration the interests of the parties in addition to their rights, there was a risk that principles of human rights law would be overlooked.

Mediation became sufficiently controversial at the Ontario Human Rights Commission that when Bill 107 took effect in 2008,[66] the mediation service was scrapped entirely, despite its early successes. Nonetheless, it is useful to look at a 1998 statistical report on Ontario's mediation services because it offered insights into how parties saw mediation during the experimental period for the Ontario Human Rights Commission in the late 1990s:

- Respondents showed stronger general satisfaction with mediation as compared to complainants, suggesting that criticisms of mediation as being complainant-friendly are misplaced;
- About 75 percent of complainants and respondents strongly agreed that mediation officers were fair and neutral;
- Respondents were more likely than complainants to say that they felt their concerns had been heard;

---

65 Most human rights commissions actually do seek some form of publicity for settlements that establish important principles, or that resolve long-standing disputes on high-profile issues.

66 *An Act to amend the Human Rights Code*, 2d Sess, 38th Leg, Ontario, 2006 (assented to 20 December 2006), SO 2006, c 30.

- Between 70 and 80 percent of complainants and respondents felt that they were equal participants in mediation; and
- Both parties said they would choose mediation if they were confronted with future cases, and 92 percent of respondent's representatives reported that they would do so.[67]

More than a decade after that study, Keith Norton remained a supporter of mediation:

> I've never understood the accusation that the myriad people who have gone through the system and managed to reach a successful resolution of their cases, to their mutual satisfaction, could reasonably describe themselves as having been coerced.[68]

In the 1998 Ontario study, about 70 percent of complainants and respondents said that they had not experienced any pressure to settle, although twice as many complainants (22 percent) as respondents (11 percent) felt they were pressured to settle.[69]

In 2012, the Pinto Report, which provided an assessment of the new direct access human rights system in Ontario, reported high levels of satisfaction with the mediation process. The main improvement appears to be that the interest-based component of mediation had significantly diminished to address concerns about fairness and respect for the principles of human rights.

> Most participants were generally satisfied with the mediation process. Mediation occurs relatively early in the process and the mediators are helpful in resolving complaints. Tribunal members conduct mediations that are guided by a rights-based orientation and which are informed by the member's adjudicative experience and many mediations result in public interest remedies.[70]

---

67 Ontario Human Rights Commission, *Mediation Services: Participant Satisfaction Report (for the period May 8, 1998 to September 22, 1998)* (Toronto: OHRC, 1998) [Ontario Human Rights Commission]. Evaluation results for mediation services in British Columbia's system can be found in Phil Bryden & William Black, "Mediation as a Tool for Resolving Human Rights Disputes: An Evaluation of the B.C. Human Rights Commission's Early Mediation Project" (2004) 37 UBC L Rev 73.

68 Interview of Keith Norton, former Chief Commissioner, Ontario Human Rights Commission (21 April 2009) in Eliadis, above note 1.

69 Ontario Human Rights Commission, above note 67.

70 Ministry of the Attorney General, Report of the Ontario Human Rights Review 2012 by Andrew Pinto (Toronto: Ministry of the Attorney General,

Another critique of mediation, from the right this time, accused commissions of engaging in "shakedowns."[71] The author, Ezra Levant, argued that human rights claimants demand "large cash payments" and that human rights commissions are a "a tool for hustlers to shake down their enemies for cash."[72] Such accusations carry a whiff of extortion about them, but in human rights law, as in most legal situations, parties are invited to resolve their cases without going to court. Complainants seek financial settlements and respondents are entitled to refuse, for a variety of motives that can be perfectly legitimate. Levant himself sought a cash settlement for his client, Stephen Boissoin, in a defamation case linked to a hate speech claim against Boissoin in Alberta.[73]

Most rights systems in Canada favour voluntary mediation processes where both parties come to the table and can make offers. Still, there are principled objections to mediation and to ADR more generally, notably along the lines raised by Owen Fiss in his celebrated article, "Against Settlement."[74] Settlements can purchase peace without securing justice, but this critique also assumes that rights are ignored in favor of expediency. Mediators in human rights systems are not (and should not be) in the business of crafting settlements that look only at payoffs and what the parties want. They should weigh the respective rights of all parties, as well as the broader public interest.

The Manitoba system, which features different mediation options, has led to a high level of success. Several factors are at play. First, the mediators are highly qualified. Byron Williams, a Manitoba practitioner, noted that the Manitoba Human Rights Commission uses high-level subcontracted mediators for complex and high-profile cases. Second, where mediation is abused, for example when one party uses it to drag the process out, time limits are set and then used to push parties towards resolution and to avoid undue delays.[75] Williams said: "I do not see a

---

2012) at 16 [Pinto Report].

71 Ezra Levant, *Shakedown: How Our Government Is Undermining Democracy in the Name of Human Rights* (Toronto: McClelland & Stewart, 2009).

72 The remarks are from Levant's written exchange with this author in 2008. See "Ezra Levant responds" *Maisonneuve* (Winter, 2008) at 8–9.

73 The offer to settle is signed by Levant for his client, for $20,000. The offer was refused, and the defamation case went to trial. Mr Boissoin consented to drop the case.

74 Owen M Fiss, "Against Settlement" (1984) 94 Yale LJ 1073.

75 Interview of Byron Williams, Executive Director, Public Interest Law Centre (9 February 2010) in Eliadis, above note 1.

problem with the trade-offs inherent in mediation. This has been one of the things that saved us in Manitoba: investigations do not take forever anymore."[76] The success of the Manitoba system, which includes early and directed forms of mediation, influenced the recent restructuring of the Saskatchewan Human Rights Commission in 2012.[77]

Mediation has been a highly successful way of settling complaints in a way that is generally seen as fair and balanced. The allegation that settlement efforts are inherently corrupt or extortionate in nature ignores major developments in all legal systems over the last thirty years, and is a gross distortion of the current practice.

5) Lopsided Justice?

Human rights systems provide support to people who file complaints. Human rights institutions that accept complaints and investigate claims do so free of charge everywhere in the world. However, this has led to the allegation in Canada that respondents are disadvantaged both legally and financially. From the respondents' perspective, it does not seem clear why human rights systems support complainants when, in contrast to the criminal regime, the alleged perpetrator receives a lawyer.

Implicit in this criticism is the belief that human rights commissions represent the claimant during the investigation process. They don't. During the process of receiving, screening, and investigating complaints, commissions remain completely neutral. However, once a decision has been made to take a matter forward to a tribunal, human rights commissions in most jurisdictions do take sides and will take carriage of the complaint before the tribunal or court and take the side of the complainant or the interests of the complainant.

Offering legal assistance to claimants before a tribunal is consistent with our international law obligations as part of the state's duty to "respect, protect, and fulfil human rights." Human rights treaties require states to provide legal mechanisms that can secure remedies for victims. People whose jobs, homes, and access to basic services are at stake need support and guidance and protection from reprisal. Human rights activists like Shelagh Day contend that victims of discrimination are sup-

---

76 *Ibid.*

77 See Saskatchewan Human Rights Commission, *Mediation – Pillar – Strategic Focus* (May, 2011), online: SHRC www.shrc.gov.sk.ca/bill-160.html.

ported "simply because we, as a society, have made a collective decision that discrimination is unacceptable."[78] Keith Norton put it another way:

> I would argue that it is a fundamental role of the state to protect the most vulnerable. The problem with the way in which human rights commissions are being seen now, at least in some circles, is that the critiques are coming from people who have never met a vulnerable person in their lives.[79]

There is, moreover, a positive impact for both complainants and respondents when the public system pays to provide legal information to complainants. Having good counsel early on averts weak cases from flooding the Tribunal. A 2010 study by the Human Rights Legal Support Centre over a ten month period showed that about 85 percent of applicants who successfully proved discrimination at the Tribunal had received legal services or representation from the Centre. Only 10 percent of unsuccessful claimants were represented at the Tribunal by the Centre.[80] This says a lot about the importance of identifying genuine cases of discrimination, screening out non-meritorious ones, and moving meritorious cases forward.[81]

For those cases that do go forward, respondents experience considerable stress and anxiety when they receive a complaint. "Will the commission be competent and reasonable? People do not know." As counsel to respondents, Gordon McKinnon had sympathy for people who receive complaint letters. In most cases, they take it very hard and very personally:

> A lot of my job is to be a support for these people, and they need a lot of personal support. They receive these letters and they are very upset, even if it really is just a formality before the case is dismissed. It is very difficult to make people understand that there is a process

---

78 Interview of Shelagh Day, activist, former Director, Saskatchewan Human Rights Commission (9 March 2011) in Eliadis, above note 1.

79 Interview of Keith Norton, former Chief Commissioner, Ontario Human Rights Commission (21 April 2009) in Eliadis, above note 1.

80 Human Rights Legal Support Centre, *Human Rights Legal Support Centre Information for the Human Rights Review*, online: HRLSC www.hrlsc.on.ca/en/HumanRightsReview.aspx.

81 Interview of Kathy Laird, Executive Director, Human Rights Legal Support Centre (2 October 2011) in Eliadis, above note 1.

> to go through, even if the complaint is likely to be dismissed. People take this sort of thing very personally.[82]

Underneath the bluster of attacks by commission critics lies the insecurity and fear of being confronted with legal procedures about which little is known or understood and the sense that the process is one-sided. While neither party actually needs a lawyer before human rights tribunals, the fact that a complainant may be supported by free legal counsel while individual respondents, small businesses, and non-profit organizations may not, places respondents at a disadvantage. That imbalance may not be overwhelming enough in individual cases to change the broad social consensus about the importance of support for claimants, but it can wreak havoc on the lives of respondents in individual cases and we should not be insensitive to these issues here or elsewhere in the legal system.

Human rights systems should offer information to both respondents and complainants at the investigation stage. Human rights commissions in Canada do provide extensive information and guidance to respondent communities, but this type of support is completely gone in direct access jurisdictions like British Columbia, and is mostly gone in Ontario. This should be remedied.[83]

D. CONCLUSION

Canadian human rights institutions have come in for a lot of criticism, most of which, on closer examination, does not withstand scrutiny. Human rights tribunals offer a range of remedies to victims, mainly focused on compensation, but there are many and perfectly valid provisions in human rights laws that go well beyond compensation but are not criminal in nature. That said, provisions in human rights laws that do permit commissions to proceed on discrimination cases by way of summary conviction offence should be repealed.[84]

There is a possibility of complaints in multiple jurisdictions, and although the nomenclature of "double jeopardy" is inaccurate, there is no

---

82 Interview of Gordon McKinnon, Partner, Thompson Dorfman Sweatman LLP (5 March 2010) in Eliadis, above note 1.

83 Pinto Report, above note 70.

84 See above note 14.

1 2 3 4 5 6 7 8 9 10 11 12 13 14

doubt that our constitutional structure permits such scenarios. The only way of dealing with this, barring a constitutional amendment, would be through cooperative efforts among commissions to develop national strategies to eliminate duplication and minimize uncertainty.

Allegations that human rights systems are inherently unfair because they lack key features of courts are based primarily on controversies that arose as a result of the hate speech debates starting in 2007, and raise particular problems that are unique to the investigation of hate speech complaints. These include the roles of truth, intent, hearsay, settlements, and support for complainants.

Human rights systems are subject to basic rules of natural justice and procedural fairness and, as noted in this article, they have more leeway when it comes to admitting evidence. However, the general standard for admitting evidence is relevance. Moreover, as the Federal Court of Canada noted in the *Lemire* case, the Tribunal's decision to admit virtually everything that the respondents wanted to use to justify a full-on attack on human rights commissions turned out to be not only irrelevant to the case but an inappropriate exercise of the Tribunal's authority.[85] And contrary to popular reports, mediation and settlement discussions are neither extortionate nor inappropriate strategies to address human rights complaints.

Finally, the decision to support complainants in cases where there is evidence to show that discrimination has occurred is a social policy choice that is reflected not only in Canadian human rights systems but also in human rights systems around the world. It is important to note, however, that only a tiny percentage of complainants receive such support. These figures put the lie to the generalized concern that complainants are supported regardless of the merits of their case.

What is true, however, is that in direct access systems in Canada, such as Ontario and British Columbia, where there is no longer any commission at all, and respondents are cut off from receiving valuable information that they might need to navigate the human rights system, many respondents, especially small business owners or non-profits, might not have the wherewithal to hire counsel. In direct access jurisdictions, some form of support and guidance to respondents is necessary to ensure that they have adequate information and are able to speak to commission staff or a specialized advisor.

---

85 *Warman*, above note 21.

In closing, there are areas where change is required: improvements to human rights systems would make them more responsive to the needs of Canadians, more consistent with human rights standards, and more legitimate in the public eye.

PART 2

The Evolution of Human Rights Complaints Management in Canada:
Transformative Justice or Efficient Justice?

CHAPTER 5

SASKATCHEWAN AND THE GATEKEEPING DEBATE

Genevieve Leslie[1]

A. INTRODUCTION

The public institutions set up to defend human rights can also, paradoxically, be the biggest obstacles faced by individuals seeking protection from discrimination. Typically, human rights statutes across Canada give human rights commissions (HRCs) the responsibility of protecting human rights by means of complaint systems which can address individual acts of discrimination. At the same time, these statutes require commissions to act as gatekeepers, to decide when complaints should be accepted and how they should be processed.[2]

HRCs do not have the authority to decide on the merits of complaints or award remedies, and findings of fact and law can only be made by the tribunals or courts to which HRCs may refer complaints if they do not dispose of them in other ways. HRCs make many discretionary screening

1 Genevieve Leslie is a former employee of the Saskatchewan Human Rights Commission (1983–2012). She has occupied a variety of positions, including investigator/facilitator, supervisor of Public & Special Programs, and staff solicitor.

2 This chapter is restricted to the gatekeeping role played by human rights commissions (HRCs), the government agencies responsible for processing human rights complaints prior to a possible hearing by a court or tribunal. In jurisdictions with a "direct access" model, HRCs either do not exist or do not routinely deal with individual complaints; people who believe they have experienced discrimination take their complaints directly to a human rights tribunal. Human rights statutes in those jurisdictions therefore differ from the conventional human rights statutes being considered in this chapter.

decisions as they filter, divert, resolve, forward, or dismiss complaints. Such decisions may be difficult because they involve complex facts, new questions of law, or novel scenarios to which existing law has not yet been applied. Because screening decisions are made at many points, gatekeeping occurs at all steps in the complaint process from initial intake through investigation or mediation up to settlement, dismissal, or referral to a hearing.

The way in which the gatekeeping role is expressed in legislation and then interpreted and implemented can have a profound effect on the nature, extent, and availability of human rights protections. Moreover, courts typically show great deference to commissions' gatekeeping decisions unless they are incorrect in law, procedurally unfair, or clearly unreasonable. It is therefore important that decisions which can affect or even end human rights claims be made in ways which are consistent with the basic nature and purposes of human rights.

This chapter proposes that the gatekeeping function of HRCs be guided by the principles of fairness, accessibility, transparency, accountability, efficiency, and economy. It will use as a case study the 2011 amendments to *The Saskatchewan Human Rights Code*[3] (*Code*) which fortified the gatekeeping function of the Saskatchewan Human Rights Commission (SHRC). Due to limited space, this chapter will address only the most significant changes. Few of the specific provisions discussed below are completely unique in Canada. Where similar provisions exist in other human rights statutes, this chapter's comments may be applied to them as well.

B. THE GOALS OF HUMAN RIGHTS LEGISLATION

Modern human rights statutes are grounded in the *Universal Declaration of Human Rights*[4] (*UDHR*), which was adopted and proclaimed by the General Assembly of the United Nations on 10 December 1948. The *UDHR* is both an aspirational and pragmatic document. It proclaims the rights and freedoms of all human beings, and articulates a vision which has

---

3 *The Saskatchewan Human Rights Code*, SS 1979, c S-24.1, as amended by SS 2011, c 17 [*Code*].

4 *Universal Declaration of Human Rights*, GA Res 217(III), UNGAOR, 3d Sess, Supp No 13, UN Doc A/180, (1948) 71.

been the model for human rights statutes in Canada. It opens with the words "WHEREAS recognition of the inherent dignity and of the equal and inalienable rights of all members of the human family is the foundation of freedom, justice and peace in the world," and goes on to state in article 1: "All human beings are born free and equal in dignity and rights." Many human rights statutes contain similar wording in their statements of purpose.

The *UDHR* commits its signatories to a broad plan of action which requires both public education and enforcement. The preamble states that the *UDHR* expresses "a common standard of achievement" which all peoples and all nations should strive to make a reality through teaching and education. It also states, " . . . it is essential, if man is not to be compelled to have recourse, as a last resort, to rebellion against tyranny and oppression, that human rights should be protected by the rule of law." Article 1 of the Paris Principles reinforces this dual obligation "to promote and protect human rights."[5]

In keeping with the *UDHR*, human rights statutes like the *Code* require HRCs to act as both enforcers and educators in the creation of common standards of behaviour that respect and protect human rights. HRCs are asked to seek redress for persons who have experienced discrimination and to promote human rights through public education and broad, proactive initiatives. This chapter focuses on the enforcement role of HRCs but, as will be argued below, effective enforcement is essential if the overarching aspirations of human rights statutes are to be realized. It has also been said that human rights enforcement is itself an extension of human rights education, insofar as both education and enforcement progressively seek to refine the "fit" between human rights legislation and "the way Canadians think and act in everyday life."[6]

---

5 *Principles Relating to the Status of National Institutions*, annex to *National Institutions for the Promotion and Protection of Human Rights*, CHR Res 54, UNESCOR, Supp No 2, UN Doc E/1992/22, (1992); GA Res 48/134, UNGAOR, 48th Sess, (1993) Annex [Paris Principles].

6 Walter Surma Tarnopolsky, William F Pentney, & John D Gardner, eds, *Discrimination and the Law* (Scarborough, ON: Thomson Professional, 2004) at 14/18 [Tarnopolsky].

C. THE GATEKEEPING ROLE OF HUMAN RIGHTS COMMISSIONS

In broad terms, gatekeeping can be seen as a means of limiting accessibility to the human rights enforcement process. Through this lens, legislative change to the gatekeeping role may be viewed as a decision about how much access individuals should have to the enforcement process on a spectrum ranging from narrowly limited to wide open.

The task of defining the gatekeeping role can also be viewed as an effort to meet a variety of goals, needs, and public interests. When attempting to reconcile these interests, however, it is important to remember that human rights are fundamental values in Canadian society. Human rights statutes recognize that whole groups of people experience damaging and unfair treatment because of irrelevant personal characteristics, and that the problem of discrimination is one which should be ameliorated by law. In this sense, a human rights statute is not "neutral"; it has a remedial and transformative purpose. The crafting of the gatekeeper role should therefore begin with the premise that human rights and freedoms should be protected to the greatest extent possible and circumscribed only as necessary on the basis of certain defined principles. It was suggested above that these principles should be fairness, access to justice, transparency, accountability, efficiency, and the responsible use of public resources.

Within the framework of the overall purposive nature of human rights legislation, HRCs must be scrupulous about meeting all the requirements of administrative fairness when processing individual complaints. For example, commissions must act in a neutral manner until and unless they "change hats" and begin to argue on behalf of a complaint after concluding it has merit. The rules and standards of fairness followed by commissions must of course be those established by law. The complaint process is evidence based, and fairness does not involve a subjective evaluation of circumstances or a sympathetic reaction to one party or another. Similarly, HRCs should process complaints as efficiently as possible, regardless of how the gatekeeping role is envisioned. A process which values accessibility and transparency, for example, can also be efficient.

Administrative fairness and efficiency are goals which should be achievable in any gatekeeping system, but the goals of accessibility and fiscal prudence may sometimes appear difficult to reconcile. The genuine accessibility of human rights protections must be a primary goal of human rights statutes and agencies — not only because "there can be no right without a remedy," but also because the very universality of the human rights declared by the *UDHR* demands that they be genuinely accessible to all individuals. Until the establishment of modern human rights commissions between the late 1950s and the late 1970s, however, this goal was not met in Canada in any meaningful way.[7]

Saskatchewan enacted the first detailed human rights statute in Canada, *The Saskatchewan Bill of Rights Act, 1947*,[8] but this quasi-criminal statute left individuals on their own to seek sanctions and there is no recorded case of an individual successfully achieving a remedy under it.[9] The fair accommodation and fair employment practice statutes later enacted in Saskatchewan and elsewhere were an improvement insofar as they created administrative processes for filing, investigating, conciliating, and settling complaints. However, as noted by the authors of *Discrimination and the Law*:

> . . . this legislation continued to place the whole emphasis of promoting human rights upon the individual who had suffered most, and who was therefore in the least advantageous position to help himself. It placed the administrative machinery of the state at the disposal of the victim of discrimination, but it approached the whole problem as if it were solely his problem and his responsibility. The result was that very few complaints were made, and very little enforcement was achieved.[10]

Human rights commissions were eventually established to make human rights protections accessible to the groups and individuals most frequently in need of them.

Despite the passage of time, accessibility of the complaint process continues to be a major concern. During public consultations in the 1990s, the SHRC was repeatedly told that its services were inaccessible to many groups. In its subsequent report, the commission said:

> Some participants — including Aboriginal people, seniors, immigrants, people with disabilities and people from northern Saskatchewan — said the commission's services are inaccessible. To begin

---

7 *Ibid* at 2/6–2/12.
8 SS 1947, c 35.
9 Tarnopolsky, above note 6 at 2/4–2/5.
10 *Ibid* at 2/7.

> with, the commission is physically inaccessible to people in northern or rural communities . . . . But participants also identified language and cultural barriers to commission services, and noted that people are unlikely to make complaints if they are vulnerable, isolated, or "don't want to make waves." Some groups recommended outreach activities tailored to the needs of their communities, such as visits to friendship centres, information about the *Code*'s anti-retaliation measures, or translations of commission materials into non-English languages, Braille and other formats.[11]

Ensuring accessibility will always be a challenge, because the persons who experience discrimination are frequently those with relatively little power, money, or other resources. They experience barriers and obstacles which other people do not. Nevertheless, the desire to make human rights protections genuinely available to the people who need them does not justify a completely open process.

Human rights commissions are defenders and advocates of human rights and equality, but they must also play a gatekeeping role in order to ensure fairness to the parties and the responsible, efficient use of public resources. To quote again from *Discrimination and the Law*:

> In the matters of administering and enforcing human rights codes, commissions are first and foremost gatekeepers. Theirs is the task of winnowing down the masses of incoming complaints into a manageable docket of cases which ought, according to legislative fiat and common sense, to proceed to hearing.[12]

Typically, commissions are required by their governing statutes to screen out inquiries and complaints which fail to meet statutory and jurisdictional requirements, which have no reasonable prospect of success at a hearing, or which fall into a category of complaints which the statute says should be dismissed.

One goal of gatekeeping is simply to conserve the financial resources of HRCs, courts, and tribunals, and the prudent use of public resources is an important interest. However, a note of caution must be sounded. Although the Supreme Court of Canada has frequently said human rights statutes are quasi-constitutional because they express fundamen-

---

11 Saskatchewan Human Rights Commission, *Renewing the Vision: Human Rights in Saskatchewan: Report of the Saskatchewan Human Rights Commission* (Saskatoon: SHRC, 1996) at 85 [SHRC, 1996].

12 Tarnopolsky, above note 6 at 14/19.

tal Canadian values, human rights commissions have historically been chronically underfunded. This has had a detrimental impact on all the interlocking roles they are asked to play in the areas of enforcement, prevention, and systemic change. HRCs must fulfill their legislated mandate with inadequate budgets, and this has obliged them to undertake endless "streamlining" of the complaint process in order to make ends meet. Told to do the best they can with the resources they have and to process complaints in a timely manner, HRCs can find themselves under great pressure to dispose of complaints as quickly as possible. The work of "winnowing down the masses of incoming cases into a manageable docket" must be done efficiently, but the work of HRCs should also be based on adequate funding and on statutes which reflect a principled approach to gatekeeping. Fundamental rights should not be discarded or downgraded because enforcing them costs money.

Given the discretionary nature of many gatekeeping decisions, transparency and accountability should also be required of the gatekeeping process. Decisions should not be or appear to be arbitrary, unfair, or inconsistent. Parties should know from the outset what to expect, and they should receive accurate, comprehensible information about processes and decisions affecting their rights and responsibilities. Because legislation is a statement of public policy, transparency and accountability are also necessary in the process through which human rights legislation is changed to either expand or decrease access to the complaint process.

D. A TALE OF TWO *CODE* REVIEWS

The Saskatchewan Human Rights Code (1979)[13] was an amalgamation and improvement upon an assortment of human rights statutes enacted to address specific forms of discrimination. It underwent two major revisions, one in 2000[14] and another in 2011. The two sets of amendments were the products of very different processes.[15] The first flowed from

---

13 *Code*, above note 3.

14 *Ibid*, as amended by SS 2000, c 26.

15 As an employee of the Saskatchewan Human Rights Commission, the author was very involved in the first review process and participated in the second review process to a lesser extent.

extensive public consultation, but the second suffered from a lack of public input.

1) 2000 Amendments

Under the leadership of Chief Commissioner Donna Greschner, the SHRC obtained funding to undertake a comprehensive review of the *Code* in the 1990s. The commission engaged in extensive public consultations in 1993 and 1994, developed its proposals over the next two years, and released its recommendations in the 1996 report entitled *Renewing the Vision: Human Rights in Saskatchewan*.[16] Chief Commissioner Donna Scott continued the *Code* review project, and in 2000, many of the amendments proposed in the report became law.

The commission described the public consultations as "critical to our review."[17] It held twenty round table discussions throughout the province, and public meetings in Prince Albert, La Ronge, North Battleford, Regina, Estevan, Swift Current, Yorkton, and Saskatoon. The SHRC received written submissions, and individuals could further participate by means of telephone conversations or one-on-one meetings with review staff. The SHRC also undertook research, met with human rights professionals, and consulted former commissioners as well as individuals who had served as boards of inquiry.

The review process led the commission to identify the following features of an effective human rights system: fairness, effectiveness, efficiency, flexibility, and accessibility. It stated that " . . . a system must be available to as many people as possible."[18] The goals of the SHRC's proposals included improving access to human rights protections; enhancing and strengthening those protections; establishing an expert human rights tribunal to replace the *ad hoc* board of inquiry system of adjudicating complaints; and providing complainants with a degree of autonomy by giving them the right to ask the tribunal to review SHRC dismissal decisions.

16 SHRC, 1996, above note 11 at 6–7.

17 *Ibid* at i.

18 *Ibid* at 9–10.

2) 2011 Amendments

The 2010–11 review of the *Code* led by Chief Commissioner David Arnot was a much faster and very different process.

The Minister of Justice described the *Code* amendments as necessary to fulfil the SHRC's "four pillar strategic business plan" which focused on "gatekeeping and investigation, directed mediation, systemic advocacy, and civics education."[19] The 2011 amendments increased threshold requirements for accepting complaints and added a broad new basis for dismissing them; namely, that "having regard to all the circumstances of the complaint, a hearing of the complaint is not warranted." They abolished the Saskatchewan Human Rights Tribunal, made the Court of Queen's Bench responsible for the initial adjudication of complaints, and eliminated the statutory right to a review of dismissal decisions. In cases where there was otherwise no statutory basis for dismissing a complaint, the amendments gave the Chief Commissioner the authority to require the parties to enter mediation and to dismiss a complaint if the respondent made a settlement offer which the Chief Commissioner considered fair and reasonable but the complainant rejected. In addition, the amendments eliminated the commission's public reporting requirements with regard to complaints.

There is no public record of community consultations soliciting input on the content of the amendments prior to the drafting of Bill 160, the amending bill. In contrast to the 1990s process, in which the SHRC conducted an independent review that included extensive consultation and then presented its proposals to government and the public at the same time, Bill 160 was the first public document indicating what the actual changes to the *Code* would be. At second reading of Bill 160, the day after first reading, Opposition Member of the Legislative Assembly (MLA) John Nilson stated, ". . . Mr Speaker, we've only seen this legislation since yesterday."[20] The Chief Commissioner had meetings with community-based groups before and after Bill 160 was presented to the legislative

19 Saskatchewan, Legislative Assembly, *Hansard*, 26th Leg, 4th Sess, No 53 (30 November 2010) at 6291 (Hon Don Morgan) [Morgan, *Hansard*]. It may be noted that, although the amendments inserted a general reference to systemic advocacy in the SHRC's "duties" section (section 25), the amendments added nothing to the commission's already existing powers to pursue systemic advocacy or public education.

20 Saskatchewan, Legislative Assembly, *Hansard*, 26th Leg, 4th Sess, No 53 (30 November 2010) at 6295 (John Nilson) [Nilson, *Hansard*].

assembly, but they were described by Opposition MLA Frank Quennell as "marketing" of the four pillars rather than consultation on the amendments' actual content.[21]

At best, the review process was marked by a lack of transparency. The lack of public consultation sparked considerable criticism from human rights experts, academics, Opposition MLAs, groups, and individuals who included the Secretary General of Amnesty International Canada.[22] By the time the amendments were passed, MLA Frank Quennell was tabling daily petitions in the legislative assembly asking that public consultations be held prior to any changes to the *Code*.[23]

---

21 Saskatchewan, Legislative Assembly, *Hansard*, 26th Leg, 4th Sess, No 53 (10 May 2011) at 7580 (Frank Quennell) [Quennell, *Hansard*]. Mr Quennell stated:

> . . . there was no consultation with the public before this Bill was drafted and introduced, and there's been no consultation with the public or listening to the public since then, only a repetition of the four pillars because . . . the government doesn't want to actually talk about Bill 160 . . . . And so I think, Mr. Speaker, we see how the Bill has been marketed as if it actually enables the four pillars when in fact it is the . . . current Human Rights Code that enables those four pillars . . . . The legislative authority exists and has existed for some period of time.

22 These included Alex Neve, Secretary General of Amnesty International Canada; Professors Ken Norman and Mary Eberts of the College of Law, University of Saskatchewan; Professor Ailsa Watkinson of the Faculty of Social Work, University of Regina; and the Saskatchewan Federation of Labour. For two examples of ongoing criticism of the 2011 amendments, see Ailsa Watkinson, "Commission Changes Weaken Protections" *The Star Phoenix [Saskatoon]* (8 March 2012) A7; Ken Norman, Mary Eberts, & Alex Neve, "The Wrong Moves for Sask. Human Rights" *The Leader Post [Regina]* (24 April 2012) A6.

23 Quennell, *Hansard*, above note 21. Mr Quennell stated:

> And the Speaker will know, and members of the Assembly will know, that almost every day of this sitting, I have risen and presented petitions, today from, I think, over 70 communities of people who want the Bill withdrawn and it become public consultations on human rights legislation.

E. 2011 AMENDMENTS TO THE COMPLAINT PROCESS IN SASKATCHEWAN

1) Elimination of Statutory Right of Review

The 2011 amendments increased the discretionary authority of the Chief Commissioner in several respects but, for the first time in the *Code*'s history, omitted any legislated process for reviewing dismissal decisions. The Chief Commissioner can now make rights-determining decisions without any kind of review or "second look" provided by the *Code*. The caselaw is unclear about the extent of the common law duty of an administrative decision maker to give reasons for dismissal decisions.[24] Since human rights are fundamental rights, it is arguable that an individual is entitled to know in clear and intelligible terms why his or her claim has been extinguished. A statutory provision can require this.

Between the enactment of the *Code* and its regulations[25] in 1979 and the amendment of the *Code* and its regulations in 2000[26] and 2001[27] respectively, complaints determined to be without merit could be dismissed by either the director or assistant director, who was obliged to provide complainants with notice of and written reasons for the decisions and to advise complainants of their right to apply to the commission (the board of commissioners) for reconsideration. The commission would then decide either to dismiss the complaint or direct the director or assistant director to proceed with it. In either case, the commission was required to provide the complainant with written reasons.[28] In addition, the *Code* provided complainants with a further, external avenue of appeal. Section 29(1) stated that the minister responsible for administering the *Code* could direct a formal hearing into a complaint even if the commission did not.[29]

---

24 See, for example, *Green v Nova Scotia (Human Rights Commission)*, 2011 NSCA 47, in which the Nova Scotia Court of Appeal upheld the right of the Nova Scotia Human Rights Commission to give "terse" reasons for dismissing a complaint.

25 Sask Reg 216/79, 258/79 [Sask Reg 79].

26 *Code*, above note 3, as amended by SS 2000, c 26, s 25 [2000 Amendments].

27 RRS, c S-24.1, Reg 1 [2001 Amendments].

28 Sask Reg 79, above note 25, s 7.

29 *Code*, above note 3, s 29(1). This provision was repealed in the 2000 amendments.

The 2000 amendments eliminated the statutory position of director and made the Chief Commissioner the chief executive officer of the SHRC as well as head of the board of commissioners. To speed up the complaint process, the amendments made the Chief Commissioner rather than the board responsible for decisions on individual complaints. Because the Chief Commissioner was now the sole decision maker with regard to complaints, an internal appeal process no longer made sense. Instead, the 2000 amendments provided a strong, external appeal mechanism by giving complainants the right to ask the Saskatchewan Human Rights Tribunal (SHRT) to review a dismissal decision and order a formal hearing into a complaint.[30] Regulations under the *Code* continued to require written notification of a dismissal decision, but not written reasons for dismissal.[31] In effect, however, the statutory right of review obliged the Chief Commissioner to provide written reasons which could withstand scrutiny by the SHRT. In practice, there were some problems with the new review process. It was slow and rarely led to the hearing of a complaint which had been dismissed by the SHRC. Nevertheless, the statutory right of review made the entire complaint process more transparent. It required the SHRC to give defensible reasons for dismissal decisions and acted as a check on the discretionary authority of the Chief Commissioner.

One of the SHRC's arguments for abolishing the SHRT was the length of time the tribunal took to make decisions.[32] By implication, the tribunal was similarly slow in its review of dismissal decisions. Though such delays are clearly undesirable, there were other possible ways of addressing them: adequate funding for SHRT, legislated time limits on decision making, and restrictions on the materials considered during a review, to name a few. In any event, it should have been possible for the amendments to establish a different mechanism for reviewing dismissal decisions — preferably by an external agency in order to promote public confidence in its independence.

The only recourse now available to a complainant who disagrees with a decision of the Chief Commissioner is an application to court for

30 2000 Amendments, above note 26, s 29.4.

31 2001 Amendments, above note 27, s 7.

32 Saskatchewan Human Rights Commission, "Frequently Asked Questions: Bill 160 — Proposed Amendments to the Human Rights Code," Question 4 (8 February 2011) [SHRC, "FAQ"], online: SHRC www.shrc.gov.sk.ca/pdfs/bill_160/FAQs-Bill160_February8-2011.pdf.

judicial review at the complainant's own expense. This is a costly process which few complainants can afford. Moreover, judicial review is limited in its scope. Courts will typically defer to the decisions of administrative officials unless they are wrong in law or outside the range of reasonableness. If the human rights statute does not explicitly require written reasons for the Chief Commissioner's decisions, the Chief Commissioner can decline to provide them unless and until a court directs otherwise. This is a situation which offends the principles of fairness, accessibility, transparency, and accountability.

2) The Threshold Decision

Before a person can file a formal complaint, he or she must show a reasonable possibility that the actions complained of could constitute a *Code* violation. Screening at the intake stage is critically important to complainants, respondents, the commission, and the public interest. The acceptance of complaints outside the commission's jurisdiction or with no reasonable possibility of success is a waste of public resources and unfair to respondents. On the other hand, decisions to turn away complaints that do have a reasonable prospect of success can deprive complainants of remedies and the public of guidance in groundbreaking cases or new fact patterns. Assessments at the intake stage are therefore among the commission's most important decisions.[33]

The 2011 amendments made a change to the kind of information individuals must give the SHRC before their complaints are accepted. Previously, section 27(1) read:

> 27(1) *Any person who has reasonable grounds for believing* that any person has contravened a provision of this Act . . . in respect of a person

33 In "Mediation of Settlements — Pillar 2" (May 2011) [SHRC, "Mediation"], online: SHRC http://saskatchewanhumanrights.ca/+pub/documents/bill_160/DirectedMediation-Manitoba-Model-May-2011.pdf, the SHRC indicates its intention to engage in "pre-complaint mediation" prior to formalizing complaints. The 2011 amendments are not relevant to such a strategy. Pre-complaint interventions could be beneficial, so long as respondents do not object to actions taken before the SHRC has determined that the requirements of section 27(1) have been met. One concern (discussed later in this chapter) is the possible "trickle-down" effect of the new section 29.5, which will create pressures on complainants to accept low offers of settlement. Another concern is that respondents who have not violated the *Code* may feel pressured to make a settlement offer in order to avoid a complaint.

> or class of persons, may file with the commission a complaint in the form prescribed by the commission. [emphasis added]

The "reasonable grounds" requirement is a useful one. It means a complainant cannot file a complaint simply because he or she has experienced a negative act and belongs to a group protected by the *Code*. For example, it is not enough for a complainant to say "I am a woman, and I was fired; therefore, I was fired because of my gender." For her complaint to be accepted, the complainant must point to evidence indicating a possible nexus between gender and termination, such as a discriminatory remark or practices suggesting a discriminatory motive.

The 2011 amendments changed section 27(1) to read:

> 27(1) A person may file with the commission a complaint in the form prescribed by the commission if:
> (a) the complaint falls within the jurisdiction of the commission; and
> (b) *the person provides sufficient evidence that reasonable grounds exist for believing* that any person has contravened a provision of this Act . . . with respect to a person or class of persons. [emphasis added]

The minister described this change as moving the threshold requirement from a subjective standard (the complainant's perspective) to an objective one (the commission's assessment),[34] but this goal could have been achieved by drafting section 27(1)(b) to read, "reasonable grounds exist for believing . . . . " The additional words "sufficient evidence" are difficult to interpret. It cannot be that a complainant must prove something akin to a *prima facie* case of discrimination at the intake stage, prior to any investigation; a *prima facie* case is in some circumstances sufficient to establish discrimination at a formal hearing. Perhaps the words "sufficient evidence" add nothing to the former "reasonable grounds" requirement. However, they suggest an intention to raise the bar, and this is troubling given the high degree of judicial deference to the decisions of administrative officials and the inability of most complainants to amass evidence on their own. It would be unfortunate if the additional words are interpreted as requiring more information than a complainant can typically provide. Complainants do not have the investigative powers of a human rights commission and rarely have manag-

34 Morgan, *Hansard*, above note 19.

erial positions, "inside" information, or the resources to hire lawyers or private investigators. This matter may ultimately require clarification by the courts. Until that time, an expansive interpretation of "sufficient evidence" would run counter to the principles of fairness and accessibility. Although very restrictive practices at the front end serve the principle of fiscal prudence, they are not justified where there is a reasonable possibility that discrimination occurred and could be substantiated by investigation.

3) New Basis for Dismissal

Prior to 2011, section 27.1(2) gave the Chief Commissioner the authority to dismiss complaints for the following seven reasons:

> 27.1(2) At any time after a complaint is filed or initiated pursuant to section 27, the Chief Commissioner may dismiss the complaint where he or she is of the opinion that:
>
> (a) the best interests of the person or class of persons on whose behalf the complaint was made will not be served by continuing with the complaint;
>
> (b) the complaint is without merit;
>
> (c) the complaint raises no significant issue of discrimination;
>
> (d) the substance of the complaint has been appropriately dealt with pursuant to another Act or proceeding;
>
> (e) the complaint is made in bad faith or for improper motives or is frivolous or vexatious;
>
> (f) there is no reasonable likelihood that an investigation or further investigation will reveal evidence of a contravention of this Act; or
>
> (g) the complaint arises out of circumstances for which an exemption order has been made pursuant to section 48.

The 2011 amendments eliminated the old section 27.1(2)(g) (because the SHRC's authority to issue exemption orders had been eliminated), and replaced it with the following, broad basis for dismissal:

> (g) having regard to all the circumstances of the complaint, a hearing of the complaint is not warranted.

The new section 27.1(2)(g) is almost identical to section 44(3)(b)(i) of the *Canadian Human Rights Act*[35] (*CHRA*), which requires the Canadian Human Rights Commission (CHRC) to dismiss a complaint if it is satisfied that "having regard to all the circumstances of the complaint, an inquiry into the complaint is not warranted." However, the *CHRA* does not contain any bases for dismissal comparable to those provided in sections 27.1(2)(a)(b)(c) and (f) of the Saskatchewan *Code*. In particular, it lacks a provision stating that the CHRC may dismiss a complaint because it is "without merit"; the CHRC must rely on section 44(3)(b)(i) in such cases. The different legislative contexts of the Saskatchewan and federal provisions may suggest that the SHRC should only apply section 27.1(2)(g) in truly exceptional circumstances; for example, where parties cannot be located. It remains to be seen how the SHRC will use this section and how courts will assess SHRC dismissal decisions based on it, should they be challenged by way of judicial review.

4) Directed Mediation and Dismissal

Another new provision enables the Chief Commissioner to require parties to participate in mediation after an investigation shows a complaint has sufficient merit for referral to a hearing, and to dismiss the complaint if the complainant then rejects a settlement offer which the Chief Commissioner considers to be fair and reasonable. Section 29.5 states:

> 29.5(1) If the Chief Commissioner determines that there are no grounds to dismiss a complaint pursuant to subsection 27.1(2), he or she may, before making an application to the court pursuant to section 29.6, require the parties to enter into mediation.
>
> (2) If the parties reach a settlement during the mediation entered into pursuant to subsection (1), the complaint shall be considered settled for the purposes of this Act.
>
> (3) If, during the mediation entered into pursuant to subsection (1), the person against whom the complaint is made proposes an offer of settlement that the Chief Commissioner considers fair and reasonable but that the complainant rejects, the Chief Commissioner may dismiss the complaint.

---

35 RSC 1985, c H-6 [*CHRA*].

The SHRC describes section 29.5 as being based on the "Manitoba Model."[36] At the time of the 2011 amendments, section 29(2) of Manitoba's *Human Rights Code*[37] stated:

> 29(2) Where the Commission does not dismiss a complaint under subsection (1), it may cause mediation to be undertaken between the complainant and respondent in an attempt to settle the complaint, and . . .
>
> (b) if the respondent proposes an offer of settlement that the Commission considers reasonable but the complainant rejects, the Commission shall terminate its proceedings in respect of the complaint.

The SHRC gives the following explanation of why it wanted a similar section in the *Code*.

> We . . . want to see an increased focus on early resolution using mediation, collaboration, talking circles and other forms of alternative dispute resolution . . . .
>
> We are placing the emphasis on case resolution through restorative justice and away from the punitive approach of retributive justice. We expect to provide several dispute resolution alternatives as a means of settlement of the majority of complaints, resorting to prosecution only when necessary. We are particularly interested in a best practice from Manitoba called directed mediation. It is hard to argue with its success. They settle 98 percent of their complaints by resolution and settlement without litigation, prosecution and tribunals. In the last two years they have conducted only three prosecutions.[38]

These statements invite scrutiny. First, the SHRC's focus on mediation is nothing new. In 2003, for example, Chief Commissioner Scott stated:

> A goal for 2002–2003 was to increase the proportion of complaints resolved through mediation, focusing on resolution rather than adjudication. The Commission allocated resources to this area and

36 SHRC, "Mediation," above note 33.
37 CCSM c H175.
38 SHRC, "FAQ," above note 32.

adopted a flexible process to provide complainants access to mediation at all stages.[39]

The statement that the Manitoba Human Rights Commission (MHRC) settles 98 percent of its complaints by "resolution and settlement" is also surprising, if it is meant to suggest that the MHRC resolves 98 percent of all complaints through negotiated settlements. The MHRC's 2010 annual report (containing the statistics relevant to the SHRC's above statement in February 2011) indicates that 97.6 percent of complaint files were closed that year for reasons other than referral to adjudication. However, over half of those files were closed because complaints had been dismissed (41.5 percent) or withdrawn or abandoned (11.6 percent). Of the remainder, 2.4 percent were closed by referral to adjudication and 8.5 percent were settled following directed mediation.[40] The 98 percent figure only makes sense if the phrase "by resolution and settlement" refers to files closed in any other way than by referral to a hearing. If this is the meaning of the phrase, the SHRC has a comparable record. In 2010–11, without the assistance of directed mediation, the SHRC closed 95.2 percent of complaint files for reasons other than referral to a hearing; in 2009–10, this percentage was 97.5 percent,[41] almost identical to Manitoba's 97.6 percent figure in 2010.

More importantly, the substance of the directed mediation section creates significant disadvantages for complainants but virtually none for respondents. Directed mediation compels complainants to participate in a process they may find intimidating because of power imbalances, the discrimination they have experienced, and the threat that their complaints will be terminated if they reject an offer the Chief Commissioner considers fair and reasonable — a vague, discretionary standard which may shift over time. However, the provision contains no penalties for respondents who fail to make a fair and reasonable offer of settlement. If this happens, the complaint simply proceeds to a hear-

39 Saskatchewan Human Rights Commission, *2002–2003 Annual Report* (Saskatoon: SHRC, 2003) at 12, online: SHRC www.shrc.gov.sk.ca/pdfs/publications/SKHR_AnnualReport_2002-2003.pdf.

40 Manitoba Human Rights Commission, *2010 Annual Report* (Winnipeg: MHRC, 2012) at 13, online: MHRC www.manitobahumanrights.ca/publications/annual_reports/annual_report_2010.pdf.

41 Saskatchewan Human Rights Commission, *2010–2011 Annual Report* (Saskatoon: SHRC, 2011) at 23, Table 4, online: SHRC www.shrc.gov.sk.ca/pdfs/news/SHRC_2010_Annual_Report.pdf.

ing as it would have if the directed mediation provision had not been added to the *Code*.

Another concern is the meaning of "fair and reasonable." A decision from the Manitoba Court of Queen's Bench provides some guidance. In *Korsch v Manitoba (Human Rights Commission)*[42] (*Korsch*) the court said the MHRC's assessment of the reasonableness of a respondent's offer must rely on caselaw precedents regarding two main factors: the strengths and weaknesses of a complaint (its likelihood of success at a hearing), and the remedies and quantum of damages a complainant would likely receive through a hearing and adjudication process.

Typically, compensation is considered appropriate if it is comparable to that awarded by adjudicators in cases from the same jurisdiction involving similar facts and issues. Unfortunately, comparable cases are scarce in Saskatchewan, where there is a relatively small body of decisions under the *Code*. Moreover, the current commission has signalled its desire to avoid litigation in "the vast majority of cases."[43] This means the database of comparable awards for specific categories of complaints will grow slowly if at all. There may be a tendency to fall back on previous settlements as a basis for comparison, and some of these will simply reflect what past complainants were willing to accept, not what they might have been awarded in court. In this way, a downward spiral of comparable ranges of compensation can develop.

An additional problem in Saskatchewan is the $10,000 statutory limit in section 31.4 of the *Code* on compensation for injury to "feeling, dignity or self-respect," a category of compensation that is very important in human rights law.[44] Saskatchewan's statutory ceiling is the lowest in Canada.[45] Moreover, a significant portion of the "comparable case database" in Saskatchewan is made up of cases decided before the 2000 amendments, when the statutory ceiling was only $5,000. This statutory limit was increased in 2000 but left untouched in the 2011 amendments.

42 *Korsch v Manitoba (Human Rights Commission)*, 2011 MBQB 222 [*Korsch*] aff'd 2012 MBCA 108.

43 SHRC, "FAQ," above note 32.

44 Complainants may have mitigated their wage losses by immediately finding other employment, for example, or may be receiving wage replacement benefits from disability plans or other sources.

45 The only other human rights statute in Canada containing a ceiling on compensatory damages for injury to dignity is the *CHRA*, above note 35, which in section 53(2)(e) establishes a statutory maximum of $20,000.

One must question, as well, the SHRC's statement that directed mediation will benefit complainants by bringing previously uncooperative respondents to the bargaining table:

> The process encourages respondents to provide a reasonable settlement in order to avoid the expense of litigation, and provides the complainant more negotiating power knowing that an unreasonable offer from a respondent will lead to the complaint being taken forward to a hearing.

In fact, the detour into directed mediation will not give respondents any greater motivation to seek settlement than if meritorious complaints were directly referred to hearings. It has always been common for respondents to make settlement offers after that direction, frequently "on the courthouse steps."

The reality is that the risk of dismissal immediately decreases complainants' bargaining power and exerts downward pressures on what they will accept by way of settlement. In addition, the day-to-day business of case management may not always reflect the requirements of *Korsch*. There are institutional pressures on human rights commissions and on individual staff members to close complaint files as quickly as possible. HRCs may lack the resources for adequate investigation of the *Korsch* factors in all cases. There is also the issue of non-monetary remedies. For example, will settlements include systemic remedies where there is evidence of systemic discrimination, or preventive measures where they appear to be needed? Because terms of settlement are usually kept confidential, public scrutiny of the adequacy of remedies is unlikely to occur.

It may be claimed that directed mediation is a response to complainants with unrealistically high expectations, who could force HRCs to litigate complaints where settlements should be achievable. It should be possible to deal with such cases in other ways. Parties are typically given "reality checks" by mediators and by adjudicators at pre-hearing conferences, and the SHRC may now dismiss complaints because "having regard to all the circumstances of the complaint, a hearing of the complaint is not warranted." Moreover, the reach of the directed mediation section will not be limited to cases on the brink of a hearing because of intransigent, unreasonable complainants. It will have a system-wide impact on virtually all mediated complaints. The pressures on complainants to accept low settlements during directed mediation will have a "trickle-down" effect because complainants will be told at every stage that, even if their complaint is ultimately substantiated, it will be referred to directed mediation and dismissed unless the complainant's expectations are considered reasonable by the Chief Commissioner. Within this context, and given the length, difficulty, and uncertainty of investigation and litigation, complainants will be vulnerable to pressures to accept significantly less compensation than the seriousness of their allegations might lead one to expect.

Are the downward pressures on compensation fair? The trade-off of a portion of compensation for certainty of outcome may seem reasonable and is the reality in civil litigation. It may be asked, however, whether remedies in human rights cases should be subject to the same "saw-offs" as standard civil litigation. The public interest in the protection of human dignity is put at risk by this sort of scenario. Human rights complainants also face pressures that civil litigants do not: the Chief Commissioner's power of dismissal (complainants cannot, like civil litigants, gamble that they will be awarded more than has already been paid into court); the institutional pressures to close complaint files quickly; and the generally inadequate baseline of compensation in comparable cases in Saskatchewan. The overall picture gives cause for concern that complainants will effectively be required to accept low, even token amounts of compensation for serious violations of their rights to equality and human dignity.

The directed mediation provision offends the principles of fairness and accessibility. It favours respondents by pressuring complainants to accept low settlements, and enables the Chief Commissioner to make discretionary decisions that deprive complainants of access to adjudication even though their complaints have merit. The provision serves the principle of economy where it avoids a hearing by permitting dismissal of a complaint.

It may be noted that human rights statutes in a number of jurisdictions allow HRCs to terminate the complaint process at any stage if the respondent makes a reasonable offer of settlement that the complainant rejects.[46] In 2012, Manitoba joined those jurisdictions by repealing section 29(2) of its *Human Rights Code* and replacing it with the following, more general provision:

1 2 3 4 5 6 7 8 9 10 11 12 13 14

---

46 See, for example, *Alberta Human Rights Act*, RSA 2000, c A-25.5, ss 22(1)(b) and 26(3)(a)(ii); Prince Edward Island *Human Rights Act*, RSPEI 1988, c H-12, ss 22(4)(b) and 25(3)(a)(ii); Yukon *Human Rights Act*, RSY 2002, c 116, as amended by RSY 2009, c 6, s 20(1)(g).

> 24.1(4) If a complainant rejects a settlement offer made by the respondent before an adjudicator is appointed to hear the complaint, the Commission must terminate its proceedings in respect of the complaint if the Commission considers the offer to be reasonable.

Such provisions enable HRCs to dismiss complaints after little or no investigation, at points where it may be impossible to satisfy the requirements of *Korsch*. Without an adequate factual record, HRCs are unable to assess either the strengths and weaknesses of a complaint or the harm caused by the alleged discrimination.

5) No Reporting Requirements

Prior to 2011, the *Code* required the commission to publish an annual report containing detailed information about its handling of human rights complaints. Section 49 stated:

> 49(1) The commission shall, in each fiscal year, in accordance with The Tabling of Documents Act, submit to the minister a report upon the administration of this Act and in particular upon:
> (a) the number, nature and disposition of inquiries into complaints directed to it under this Act;
> (b) the number, nature and disposition of inquiries or investigations, public hearings and educational programs held under this Act;
> (c) the number, nature and disposition of formal inquiries made under the authority of this Act and the results of any appeal; and
> (d) any other information the commission may consider necessary.

The 2011 amendments repealed sections 49(1)(a), (b), and (c), replacing them with the vaguer requirement in the new section 49(1)(c.1) that the commission report upon "the commission's business for the preceding fiscal year." Consequently, the commission is no longer required to publish statistical or any other information about its processing of complaints. Unless the SHRC chooses to report this information, it will be impossible for any interested party to examine the commission's enforcement activities. This situation is fundamentally incompatible with the principles of transparency and accountability, and is especially troubling given the amendments' expansion of the Chief Commissioner's discretionary powers and their new restrictions on an individual's ability to access the human rights complaint process.

F. THE ROLE OF LITIGATION

There are many valid reasons for wanting to resolve complaints through alternatives to adjudication. Nevertheless, litigation has an important role to play in the protection and promotion of human rights.

Unfortunately, the SHRC appears to have taken an extreme stance against litigation, referring to it as "punitive" and "retributive."[47] This characterization of human rights litigation is inaccurate and unhelpful. As the Supreme Court of Canada stated in *Blencoe v British Columbia (Human Rights Commission)*: "The purpose of human rights proceedings is not to punish but to eradicate discrimination. Tribunal orders are compensatory rather than punitive."[48] The preventive, remedial, and compensatory purposes of human rights litigation are made clear in the *Code* by section 31.3, which outlines the remedies a court may order and contains many references to rectifying injury, compensating for injury, and taking steps to prevent similar contraventions in the future.

A core goal of human rights legislation is to establish standards of behaviour which respect individual dignity and equality. This is much more likely to happen through a thoughtful, open process of adjudicative decision making that engages in a public, principled discussion of issues and creates precedents that guide the development of human rights law than through settlements that are made behind closed doors and rarely publicized. As retired Supreme Court of Canada Justice Ian Binnie stated in an interview with *The Globe & Mail* on 10 April 2012:

> One of the most interesting aspects of being on the Supreme Court was to see how quickly the law was changing under our feet. Issues were being decided with new approaches and the law is forever being modified. For that modification to take place, there has to be this stream of nutrients flowing up . . . . When that stream is impaired — as it is by taking work out and giving it to alternative dispute resolution — then the work at the top suffers because the judges are

47 SHRC, "FAQ," above note 32.
48 *Blencoe v British Columbia (Human Rights Commission)*, 2000 SCC 44 at para 94.

> not exposed to the same range of problems, with the same depth and the same frequency.[49]

The virtual elimination of litigation as a legitimate option effectively brings adjudication "in house," where complaint decisions are made by government appointees without a full airing of the facts and issues. This turns an administrative body designed to conduct preliminary screening into the final adjudicator of fundamental rights and freedoms. Such an approach could be expected to attract criticism from the UN Human Rights Committee, which in its 2006 response to Canada's fifth periodic report on the *International Covenant on Civil and Political Rights* made the following recommendation:

> The State party should ensure that the relevant human rights legislation is amended at federal, provincial and territorial levels and its legal system enhanced, so that all victims of discrimination have full and effective access to a competent tribunal and to an effective remedy.[50]

Some litigation is also needed to fulfill the public education mandate of HRCs. Human resource managers, for example, are hungry for information on how to handle human rights issues. They wish to comply with legislation and to avoid complaints, not simply to keep settlements low. Moreover, the decisions in many human rights complaints — such as those involving the duty to accommodate — depend upon all the circumstances of a case. People need information about the specific facts of real cases. If the approach of HRCs is to avoid litigation at almost any cost, then the public will be deprived of authoritative information about many of the complex human rights issues being brought to HRCs on an ongoing basis. The genuine availability of enforcement is necessary to achieve both effective public education and systemic change.

Finally, as noted above, mediators look to adjudicated decisions for guidance regarding both liability and appropriate compensation. An extreme unwillingness to resort to litigation may not only block the

---

49 Jacquie McNish, "The Supreme Court's Retired, but Hardly Retiring, Ian Binnie" *The Globe and Mail* (10 April 2012), online: *The Globe and Mail* www.theglobeandmail.com/report-on-business/industry-news/the-law-page/the-supreme-courts-retired-but-hardly-retiring-ian-binnie/article4099999/.

50 Human Rights Committee, *Concluding Observations: Canada*, UN Doc CCPR/C/CAN/CO/5, 2006, Recommendation at para 11.

judicial development of human rights principles and protections, but also restrict settlements to parameters which become increasingly inadequate.

G. CONCLUSION AND RECOMMENDATIONS

The 2011 amendments to the *Code* significantly elevated the gatekeeping function of the SHRC at the expense of access to justice. They increased the Chief Commissioner's discretionary authority, increased threshold requirements for the acceptance of complaints, added new grounds for dismissing complaints, made the mediation of meritorious complaints mandatory, created downward pressures on compensation for discrimination, eliminated the statutory right to a review of a dismissal decision, and eliminated the SHRC's obligation to include details of its complaint and litigation activities in annual reports. Although some amendments may serve the interests of economy, many are inconsistent with the principles of fairness, accessibility, transparency, and accountability. Taken as a whole, the amendments have a negative impact on human rights protections in Saskatchewan.

Although gatekeeping is a necessary function of HRCs, it should not be prioritized to the point where it blocks access to human rights protections unjustifiably or trivializes redress for discrimination. Some steps can be taken to avoid such outcomes.

First, HRCs should receive stable, adequate funding which enables them to fulfill the fundamental goals of human rights legislation: the promotion, recognition, and protection of the equality, inherent dignity, and equal inalienable rights of all members of the human family. The independence of HRCs should also be enhanced by giving Chief Commissioners the status of Officers of the Legislature who are appointed by and report directly to the legislative assembly. Independence and adequate funding are two safeguards against pressures which can lead to negative outcomes such as the inappropriate rejection of complaints.

Human rights statutes could also contain provisions which reflect a principled approach to gatekeeping while avoiding some of the missteps of the 2011 amendments to the Saskatchewan *Code*. For example:

1) Human rights statutes should only be amended after meaningful public consultation. Amendments should consider the input of all

stakeholders, including complainants and respondents. At the same time, they should be consistent with the nature and objectives of human rights legislation, illustrate an understanding of the disadvantages often experienced by complainants, and ensure that the enforcement process is genuinely accessible to all those who experience discrimination.

2) The threshold requirements for acceptance of a complaint should not demand more than typical complainants can provide. It should be sufficient for a complainant to provide information indicating that there may have been a discriminatory reason for the action in question and that the alleged violation falls within the HRC's jurisdiction.
3) Human rights statutes should require HRC decision makers to provide written reasons for their decisions to reject, decline to process, or dismiss complaints and should specify the required content of certain decisions. For example, they could require a dismissal decision to summarize the facts, legal principles, and analysis upon which it is based, in plain language and in sufficiently specific terms that a party can consider its reasonableness and accuracy.
4) Human rights statutes and regulations should contain other provisions designed to make the discretionary decisions of HRCs transparent and accountable. For example, they could require HRCs to publicize the guidelines they will use when deciding whether to extend the limitation period for making a complaint.[51] HRCs could take such steps on a voluntary basis as well. In the interests of prevention and public education, HRCs should publicize as much information as possible about complaints they have settled.
5) Human rights statutes should provide complainants with a statutory right to have complaint dismissals reviewed by a body independent of the HRC.

---

51 Nilson, *Hansard*, above note 20. MLA John Nilson stated at second reading of Bill 160:

> We know that the commissioner will have the power to use discretion to extend that limitation period . . . . But it's much like what we do too often in this legislature. We set out the law and then we actually put the substance of the law in regulations or in the discretion of a minister or senior official. And so the law isn't as clear as it could be as to what exactly will happen.

6) Provisions which enable HRCs to dismiss a complaint if the complainant refuses a reasonable offer of settlement should be reconsidered, particularly with regard to early stages of the complaint process when few facts are known and the probable outcome of adjudication cannot be fairly assessed. Where such provisions are retained, human rights statutes should specify a narrow range of circumstances in which the drastic step of dismissal is permissible. Where rejection of a reasonable offer can lead to dismissal, statutes should place comparable pressures on respondents and complainants. For example, a respondent who refuses to make a reasonable offer might be made liable for the costs of litigation.
7) Human rights statutes should seek to provide levels of compensation that reflect the importance of human rights and human dignity. Statutory ceilings on damages for injuries to dignity should be eliminated.
8) Human rights statutes should require HRCs to publish periodic reports containing detailed information, including statistical information, on their complaint processing activities.

Notwithstanding the many benefits of alternative dispute resolution, HRCs and human rights legislation should also recognize the importance of litigation as a valuable and sometimes necessary strategy for enforcing human rights. Litigation assists the development of human rights law, it can provide a full range of remedies, it promotes prevention through public explanations of what does and does not constitute discrimination, and it supports the development of the "common standard of achievement" to which the *UDHR* aspires.

1 2 3 4 **5** 6 7 8 9 10 11 12 13 14

CHAPTER 6

ONTARIO AND THE DIRECT ACCESS MODEL TO HUMAN RIGHTS[1]

Michelle Flaherty[2]

A. INTRODUCTION

Human rights are part of our society's most fundamental values. Striving to achieve freedom from discrimination because of certain personal characteristics, including sex, race, sexual orientation, and disability, is part of what it means to live in a society that values human dignity and protects some of its most vulnerable members.[3] At least as important as the substantive right to be free from discrimination,[4] however, is the existence of institutions that allow for the effective enforcement of

---

1 The Human Rights Tribunal of Ontario has been the subject of a three-year review. Section 57 of the *Human Rights Code*, RSO 1990 c H.19, as amended [*Code*] specifically provides for an independent review of the Tribunal, the Ontario Human Rights Commission, and the Human Rights Legal Support Centre three years after the 2008 amendments came into effect. In 2012, Andrew Pinto released his report. This chapter was written prior to the public release of the report and, therefore, has not considered its contents. See Andrew Pinto, *Report of the Ontario Human Rights Review 2012* (Toronto: Ministry of the Attorney General, 2012), online: Ministry of the Attorney General www.attorneygeneral.jus.gov.on.ca/english/about/pubs/human_rights/Pinto_human_rights_report_2012-ENG.pdf.

2 Michelle Flaherty is a professor of law at the University of Ottawa and a part-time member of the Human Rights Tribunal of Ontario. The author wishes to thank Lucie Lamarche, Leslie Reaume, Jennifer Trépanier, and David Wright for their very helpful feedback and suggestions.

3 *Code*, above note 1. For a full list of prohibited grounds and the social areas of discrimination, see Part I of the *Code*.

4 See, for example, s 5 of the *Code*, *ibid* and s 15 of the *Canadian Charter of Rights and Freedoms*, Part I of the *Constitution Act, 1982*, being Schedule B

those rights. The measure of our society turns not only on the vigour of the language it uses in human rights laws, but also on whether individuals have real access to an enforcement process that gives meaning to their rights.[5] While Ontario has long had relatively robust human rights statutes,[6] its principal and ongoing challenge has been to create an effective mechanism for enforcing those rights.

Stakeholders had long complained that Ontario's human rights system was characterized by lengthy delays, disenfranchised and dissatisfied parties, a lack of transparency, and limited access to Human Rights Tribunal of Ontario (Tribunal) adjudication. In 2006, the Attorney General for Ontario referred to the human rights system then in place in Ontario as "broken."[7] Many parties felt that the system at the time was so ineffective that there was no point in even making a claim.[8] In June 2008, the Ontario human rights system underwent a major overhaul. Principal among the changes brought to the Ontario *Human Rights Code*[9] (*Code*) was a structural move from a commission-based human rights system to a direct-access model. The 2008 amendments to the *Code* fundamentally reshape how human rights are enforced in Ontario;

---

to the *Canada Act* 1982 (UK), 1982, c 11, both of which contain important protections against discrimination on a number of grounds.

5 This includes, of course, access to effective remedies.

6 Ontario was the first province to enact human rights legislation: *Racial Discrimination Act*, SO 1944, c 51 [*Racial Discrimination Act*, 1944]. See Mary Cornish, Fay Faraday, & Jo-Anne Pickel, *Enforcing Human Rights in Ontario* (Aurora: Canada Law Book, 2009) ch 2 [Cornish]; Judith Keene, *Human Rights in Ontario*, 2d ed (Toronto: Carswell, 1992) at 1–2 [Keene] regarding the history of human rights in the province and the breadth of the substantive rights it protects.

7 Ontario, Legislative Assembly, Official Report of Debates (*Hansard*), 38th Parl, 2d Sess, (26 April 2006) at 1410 [*Hansard*, 26 April 2006]; Ontario, Human Rights Code Review Task Force, *Achieving Equality: A Report on Human Rights Reform* (Toronto: Policy Services Branch Ministry of Citizenship, 26 June 1992) at 20 [Task Force Report].

8 See Task Force Report, *ibid* at 20. Before the 2008 amendments, the *Code* referred to human rights claims as "complaints." Since the amendments, it speaks of "applications." I use the term "application" (or "claim") to refer to claims filed under the *Code*, whether before or after the 2008 amendments. In the same vein, I use the word "Tribunal" to refer to both the Ontario Human Rights Tribunal and its predecessor, the Board of Inquiry.

9 *Code*, above note 1.

they redefine the structure of human rights institutions in the province and redistribute roles and responsibilities among them.[10]

To summarize briefly, prior to June 2008 the Ontario Human Rights Commission (Commission) was charged with the administration of the *Code*.[11] It played three key roles. First, the Commission was responsible for human rights education in the province. Second, it received, processed, investigated, and, in some cases, determined human rights complaints. The Commission was often referred to as a "gatekeeper" to adjudication because it decided whether a matter would be referred to the Tribunal for adjudication. The Commission could refuse to refer an application, which would result in the matter's dismissal.[12] It could do so with or without conducting an investigation and without any requirement that there be a hearing.[13] Third, where cases were referred to the Tribunal, the Commission played a key role in the litigation of claims and generally presented the case.[14]

---

10 In addition, the amendments expand the courts' role regarding human rights. Section 46.1 of the *Code* gives the courts jurisdiction over *Code* rights raised in a "civil proceeding" as well as the power to order monetary and non-monetary compensation for losses arising out of *Code* infringements.

11 There are historic reasons that led to the adoption of this Commission-based system, including the expectation that many human rights applicants would be self-represented and would need the assistance of a body like the Commission to navigate the human rights system. The system was also designed so that cases could be triaged and to ensure that the adjudicative process would not be weighed down by a large number of frivolous or vexatious claims. See Cornish, above note 6; Keene, above, note 6. While a detailed review of the basis for the creation of the Commission-based system in Ontario is beyond the scope of this chapter, it bears noting that some of the concerns that led to its creation persisted and were also at the root of the 2008 reforms.

12 Although this decision was subject to judicial review.

13 For a more detailed description of the role of the Commission and its powers regarding complaints, including its investigative powers and attempts to achieve settlement, see Cornish, above note 6 at 20–21.

14 See Cornish, above note 6; Keene, above note 6. A detailed discussion of the factors that led to the creation of the Commission is beyond the scope of this chapter. The Commission was created in 1962 with the enactment of the first Ontario *Human Rights Code* in 1962 and was charged with the implementation of the act: SO 1961–1962, c 93, s 27(2) [*Code*, 1962]. See Keene, above note 6 at 1. As John Dwyer explains, the Commission-based model was adopted as a "deliberate policy choice that recognized that the legal and juridical systems in place were insufficient and ill-equipped to handle certain human rights matters." A Commission system was preferred over a court-based model because court proceedings were thought to be formal, cumbersome, expensive, and adversarial. The hope was that a Commission-based model

1 2 3 4 5 6 7 8 9 10 11 12 13 14

Under the new direct-access model, parties file human rights applications directly with the Tribunal. The Commission's role has shifted from gatekeeping to focus on existing policy development and public education roles. The Tribunal, which once dealt only with matters referred to it by the Commission, is now responsible for all aspects of applications, including processing, mediation, and adjudication.[15] A new body, the Ontario Human Rights Legal Support Centre (Support Centre), was created to provide legal services to applicants. The direct access model and the institutional and structural changes it created have now been in effect for approximately four years. These years have seen important shifts, including new procedures, significant developments in the Tribunal's jurisprudence, emphasis on mediation, and dramatic increases in the number of hearings and decisions at the Tribunal level.

This chapter looks at Ontario's direct access model to human rights and, more particularly, at whether the legislative changes have improved access to fair and effective human rights adjudication.[16] I begin with a brief history of human rights systems in Ontario and discuss some of the concerns that led to reform in 2008. I then consider the Tribunal's "new" role in Ontario's direct-access model and I reflect on lessons learned throughout the four years of this system. As a current member and former vice-chair of the Tribunal, I had the great privilege of being involved in the Tribunal's work from 2008 to the present. While the Tribunal continues to strive to meet challenges, it has, I think, seen considerable success.

---

would meet the particular needs and vulnerabilities of parties in a human rights context, including flexibility and access to alternative dispute resolution. See John Dwyer, "Roles and Responsibilities in Implementing HR: Similarities and Differences in Approaches to Access to Justice" in Helena Birt, ed, *Access to a Specialized Human Rights Tribunal: an Urgent Need to Act in Quebec*? (Cowansville, QC: Yvon Blais, 2008) 277 at 292–93 [Dwyer].

15 In 1993, the United Nations General Assembly adopted the *Principles Relating to the Status of National Institutions*, annex to *National Institutions for the Promotion and Protection of Human Rights*, CHR Res 54, UNESCOR, Supp No 2, UN Doc E/1992/22, (1992); GA Res 48/134, UNGAOR, 48th Sess, (1993) Annex [Paris Principles]. These have become internationally-recognized standards applicable to human rights institutions. See ch 7.

16 The notions of "fairness" and "efficiency" as competing objectives within the human rights system are discussed in more detail, below, when I consider possible measures of the Tribunal's performance.

B. BRIEF HISTORY OF HUMAN RIGHTS IN ONTARIO

To appreciate Ontario's direct access model to human rights, it is important to consider together all three human rights institutions created by the *Code*: the Commission, the Support Centre, and the Tribunal. However, I have focused in this chapter on the Tribunal and its particular role within the direct access system.[17] While the focus of this chapter is Ontario's "new" human rights regime and the role of the Tribunal within that system, to appreciate what is new, it is necessary to have some understanding of the old. I begin by providing a brief history of human rights in Ontario and then provide some background to the 2008 reform and, in particular, the shift from a Commission-based to a direct-access approach to human rights.

Ontario has a long history of protecting and enforcing human rights and its approach has long served as a model for other human rights systems in Canada.[18] The *Code*, which was first enacted in 1962, consolidated a number of existing anti-discrimination statutes[19] and expanded the scope of protection from discrimination available through those existing statutes. It also created two key bodies to promote human rights and enforce the *Code*: the Ontario Human Rights Commission and the Board of Inquiry.[20]

Historically, the Commission's role has been pivotal. It managed every human rights claim filed between 1962 and 2008 and it made key decisions, including ones that resulted in the dismissal of the claim.[21] Under this system, only a small percentage of cases proceeded to Tribunal adjudication. For example, in the years leading up to the 2008 reform, an average of 2,500 complaints were filed with the Commission each

---

17 Each of these human rights institutions has its own *raison d'être*, history, and challenges. While I touch on some of these briefly, any reference to the Commission or the Support Centre is not meant to be a thorough review and is included only as context to my analysis of the Tribunal's role.

18 It enacted the first anti-discrimination legislation in Canada: *Racial Discrimination Act*, 1944, above note 6. In addition it created the first human rights commission in the country: *Code*, 1962, above note 14.

19 See, for example, *Racial Discrimination Act*, 1944, above note 6; *Fair Accommodation Practices Act*, SO 1954, c 28; *Female Employees Fair Remuneration Act*, SO 1951, c 265.

20 Keene, above note 6; Cornish, above note 6. See also Heather M MacNaughton, "Direct Access: the B.C. Experience" in Birt, above note 14 at 173–79.

21 Keene, above note 6; Cornish, above note 6.

year but only an average of approximately seventy-five cases per year proceeded to adjudication.

Access to adjudication was an issue principally because, even where parties wished to proceed,[22] claims could be dismissed by the Commission before ever reaching the stage of Tribunal adjudication. Because of the nature of the Commission's powers, some said they felt disempowered; others expressed concerns the Commission determined their cases without an open and transparent adjudicative process.[23] Second, the Commission's gatekeeper functions and the significant delays they occasion frustrated and deterred some rights-seekers.[24] Third, applicants and respondents alike stated that uncertainty about access to adjudication informed their settlement positions and, in some cases, made mediated settlements more difficult to achieve.[25] The Commission had carriage of those matters it did refer to adjudication, which meant that it presented each case at the Tribunal level, leading evidence and making legal argument. This aspect of the Commission's role contributed to concerns that applicants were disempowered in the process, particularly where their own and the public's interest diverge. Importantly, although it had carriage of the case, the Commission did not act for the applicant; its role was to represent the public interest. This meant, for example, that the Commission might refuse to proceed with a matter because the applicant rejected a reasonable settlement offer, one that was perceived to be in the public's interest.[26]

The 1962 *Code* also created the Board of Inquiry, the forerunner of the Ontario Human Rights Tribunal.[27] The Board of Inquiry's role was to

---

22 Some matters never reached the hearing stage because they were voluntarily resolved by the parties.

23 Cornish, above note 6 at 17–18.

24 Above note 1.

25 For example, delays and uncertainty about the availability of adjudication led some respondents to delay serious mediation discussions until after the Commission had referred the matter to adjudication. Conversely, applicants explained that they felt pressured to accept less-than-fair settlement offers early in the process rather than run the risk that the Commission would dismiss their case. See Cornish, above note 6 at 17.

26 *Losenno v Ontario (Human Rights Commission)* (2005), 78 OR (3d) 161 at para 58 (CA). It might also insist that a particular public interest remedy be included in a settlement agreement, even if this might make resolution of the individual complaint less likely.

27 Boards of Inquiry were initially appointed on an *ad hoc* basis. In 1995, the Board of Inquiry was established as a permanent, stand-alone tribunal. In 2002, its name was changed to the Human Rights Tribunal of Ontario. See

adjudicate human rights matters referred to it by the Commission. It typically held full and formal hearings: only a small number of cases were referred to adjudication and these were presented and had been fully investigated by the Commission.[28]

C. BACKGROUND TO THE 2008 *CODE* REFORM

Following Ontario's example, many jurisdictions in Canada also adopted a Commission-based human rights model. Across the country, the call for reform of this human rights model was long-standing and broad-based. It stemmed, *inter alia*, from Canada's Auditor General,[29] the United Nations Human Rights Committee,[30] applicant groups, respondent groups, the bar, and from the Commission itself.[31] In 1992, in response to widespread demand for reform, the Ontario government appointed the Ontario Human Rights Code Review Task Force (Task Force) to review the human rights regime in Ontario and to make recommendations regarding possible reform.[32] As part of its work, the

---

Ontario Ministry of the Attorney General, "A New Human Rights System for Ontario," online: Ontario Ministry of the Attorney General www.attorneygeneral.jus.gov.on.ca/english/ohrc/ohrc.asp.

28 For a more detailed description of the Commission and the Board of Inquiry's respective roles under the "old" human rights system, see Cornish, above note 6 at 21; Task Force Report, above note 7 at 17–20.

29 Office of the Auditor General, *September 1998 Report of the Auditor General of Canada*, ch 10 (Ottawa: Office of the Auditor General, 1998), online: OAG www.oag-bvg.gc.ca/internet/English/parl_oag_199809_10_e_9316.html. Although this report was specifically directed at the federal system, it shares many of the same characteristics and is plagued by many of the same difficulties as the pre-2008 model in Ontario. See Canadian Human Rights Act Review Panel, *Promoting Equality: A New Vision* (Ottawa: Minister of Justice, 2000) [*Promoting Equality*].

30 Human Rights Committee, *Concluding Observations: Canada*, UN Doc CCPR/C/CAN/CO/5 (2006) at para 11. These observations were cited by the Attorney General when he introduced the bill to amend the *Code*. See also Maxwell Yalden, "Looking Back — Looking Forward" in Birt, above note 14, 55 at 78.

31 Task Force Report, above note 7 at 14.

32 Similar reviews were conducted elsewhere in Canada. Federally, the Auditor General identified concerns with the existing system and this lead to the appointment of the Canadian Human Rights Act Review Panel [La Forest Panel], which released a report in 2000. Issues concerning delay and limited access to adjudication were at the fore of the report. Although it has not

Task Force heard submissions from a number of different human rights stakeholders and their submissions brought into stark relief many competing views of how best to fix human rights in Ontario.[33] The Task Force released its report in June 1992 and it used strong language to identify a number of "serious and systemic" issues within Ontario's existing human rights system.[34] It described stakeholder dissatisfaction as centred around three issues: long delays in the processing of complaints, the disempowerment of parties in the claim process, and limited access to adjudication.[35]

The Task Force spoke of the frustration and anger parties experienced because their human rights matters often took years to be determined.[36] The problem of delay was a persistent one. For example, the Commission's Annual Report for fiscal year 2006–2007 (the year before *Code* reform), states that it took on average 29.4 months for a complaint to be investigated and for the Commission to decide whether to dismiss the matter or refer it to adjudication.[37] That year, the Commission received over 2,300 new complaints and referred 140 matters to the Tribunal. The average age of complaints at the time they were referred to adjudication

---

been implemented, federally, the La Forest Panel also recommended a direct access model. See *Promoting Equality*, above note 29. Following the La Forest Panel's recommendations, the Commission made a number of changes to how it carries out its mandate. See Canadian Human Rights Commission, "Overview" [CHRC, "Overview"], online: CHRC www.chrc-ccdp.ca/about/icm_page1_gci-eng.aspx?print=1. The British Columbia human rights system underwent several reviews between 1993 and 2002. See, for example, William W Black, *Report Concerning Internal Procedure of the B.C. Council of Human Rights and Related Agencies* (British Columbia, 15 November 1993) [Black]; William W Black & Kathryn Thomson, *Report on Legal Representation Models under the British Columbia Human Rights Code* (British Columbia, 1998) [Black & Thomson]. See also Cornish, above note 6 at 25–30.

33 For a more detailed summary of the submissions made to the Task Force in 1992, see Michael Gottheil & Katherine Laird, "Direct Access to a Specialized Human Rights Tribunal" in Birt, above note 14, 145 at 155 [Gottheil].

34 Task Force Report, above note 7 at 10.

35 *Ibid* at 20–22.

36 *Ibid* at 20.

37 Under s 34 of the "old" *Code*, the Commission also had the power to dismiss complaints on preliminary objections, based on written submissions. In 2006–2007, it dismissed 7 percent of cases it received under section 34 after an average of over ten months. See Ontario Human Rights Commission, *Annual Report, 2006–2007* (Toronto: OHRC, 2007) at 25, online: OHRC www.ohrc.on.ca/sites/default/files/attachments/Annual_report_2006-2007.pdf.

was 33.4 months.[38] By the time the Tribunal heard a case and rendered a decision, the case had been in the system for an average of approximately five years.[39]

In terms of access to adjudication and the Commission's gatekeeper function, the Task Force heard competing objections: applicants' groups felt that the Commission dismissed too many meritorious complaints, while respondents' groups felt that it did not dismiss trivial or vexatious claims quickly enough. Both groups complained about disempowerment and a lack of transparency. Complainants wanted better and quicker access to a hearing; respondents expressed concern that the Commission addressed matters behind closed doors and that its decision-making process lacked transparency.[40] The Task Force made a number of recommendations for reform, including that Ontario move to a direct-access model. It felt that direct access would improve access to adjudication, allow for more timely hearings, and create a more open, clear, and streamlined decision-making process.[41] For almost fifteen years, little came of the Task Force's recommendations. During this time, the broad-based call for reform did not abate and, indeed, many of the problems (including delays) exacerbated significantly. Despite this, it was not until 2006 that the government of the day reignited the debate and introduced the *Human Rights Code Amendment Act, 2006*, referred to as Bill 107.[42]

In the meantime, other jurisdictions within Canada had considered and, in some cases, implemented reform. British Columbia created a direct access model to human rights, eliminating its human rights commission and providing additional funding to legal aid clinics.[43] Federally, the direct access model was considered but rejected.[44] Following recommendations, however, the federal human rights commission devoted fewer resources to litigation and focused on a limited number of hearings it felt raised broader issues. In a "new reading" of its enabling statute, the

---

38 *Ibid* at 26–27.
39 *Hansard*, 26 April 2006, above note 7 at 1610.
40 Task Force Report, above note 7 at 5 and 23–25.
41 *Ibid* at 4–5.
42 *An Act to amend the Human Rights Code*, 2d Sess, 38th Leg, Ontario, 2006 (assented to 20 December 2006), SO 2006, c 30.
43 While a detailed discussion is beyond the scope of the paper, some argue that the British Columbia model does not respect the Paris Principles, a series of internationally-recognized minimum standards for human rights institutions. See Dwyer, above note 14 at 302–20.
44 *Promoting Equality*, above note 29; La Forest Panel, above note 32.

Commission concluded that it did not have exclusive carriage over human rights complaints.[45]

When the prospect of human rights reform arose again in Ontario in 2006, the renewed discussion was again heated and politicized. Stakeholders were far from united in their views on the Task Force recommendations, and there was little support for reforms similar to those implemented federally or in British Columbia.[46] Among the challenges to developing human rights reform were stakeholders' disparate views on what changes were necessary. While some argued in favour of direct access, many groups did not support a shift to a direct-access approach and argued that, while the current system clearly needed fixing, the solution was not to divest the Commission of its key roles. Some worried that a direct access model would mean privatizing human rights to the detriment of public interest remedies. Both supporters and opponents of the reform expressed concern that the system would not be sufficiently funded.[47] Ultimately, Ontario opted for a direct-access system that maintained the Commission, although in a much-altered role. The new *Code* has created a human rights system that, in important ways, is different from either the British Columbia or the federal models. In sum, Ontario developed its own statutory approach.

---

45 See CRHC, "Overview," above note 32. This means that, in the federal human rights system, many hearings proceed without the Commission and applicants are left without the litigation support it had previously provided. While the British Columbia model includes funding for legal clinics, the federal system does not. See Black, above note 32; Black & Thomson, above note 32. This is the case notwithstanding that a key component of the La Forest Panel's recommendation was the creation of a legal clinic. See above notes 29 and 32. Coupled with the reality of limited Commission-involvement in federal Tribunal matters, the Tribunal has no ability to award costs. See *Canada (Canadian Human Rights Commission) v Canada (Attorney General)*, 2011 SCC 53. This has led to questions about whether the federal system contains systemic barriers to a meaningful complaint process.

46 See the Attorney General's comments at *Hansard*, 26 April 2006, above note 7 at 1630 and 1640. In terms of the British Columbia model, in particular, stakeholders were concerned that it left applicants without the necessary support and that many claims continued to be screened out without parties having access to tribunal adjudication. See below notes 57–62 regarding the competing interests of stakeholders.

47 See Gottheil, above note 33 at 155.

D. DIRECT ACCESS AND THE 2008 *CODE* AMENDMENTS

The 2008 amendments to the *Code* relate principally to the restructuring of human rights institutions, most notably, the redefinition of the role of the Tribunal and the Commission, and the creation of the Support Centre. They also set out a number of procedural and remedial changes and entitlements that accompany this reform, but they do not alter the substantive rights of Ontarians to protection from discrimination in specific social areas[48] based on enumerated grounds.[49] In the next sections, I briefly describe the new role of each of the three human rights institutions following the reform.[50] I then consider, in more detail, how the Tribunal fits within this framework and some of the challenges it has faced and adaptations it has made.

1) The Commission

As I have indicated, the Commission's mandate has been revised to focus on its existing role of proactively providing public education, developing policy, and promoting compliance with the *Code*.[51] While these responsibilities had always been part of the Commission's mandate, the vast majority of the Commission's resources had been directed at the processing of individual complaints.[52] With the reforms, the Commission's involvement in Tribunal hearings is much more limited than it once was

---

48 "Social areas" refers to the spheres of activity to which the *Code* applies. These include employment, contracts, accommodation, goods, services, and facilities.

49 Procedural changes include, for example, s 42(2), which stipulates that the Tribunal will not finally determine a matter within its jurisdiction without giving the parties an opportunity to make oral submissions. The amendments provide for broader remedial powers and they expand, for example, the powers of courts to address human rights issues and award damages for breaches of the *Code* and they remove caps on the quantum of damages that can be awarded by the Tribunal. See the *Code*, above note 3, ss 45.2 and 46.

50 My purpose in doing so is not to thoroughly set out the roles of these other institutions. Rather, I aim to situate the Tribunal's role within the new legal framework.

51 See *Code*, above note 3, s 29.

52 See *ibid*, Part III.

and most of its work takes place within the community, outside of the Tribunal litigation context.[53]

2) The Support Centre

The Support Centre is a publicly-funded independent agency, created under the *Code*, whose role is to provide legal services and support to applicants and prospective applicants in all stages of the human rights process.[54] The Support Centre has taken over some of the functions previously fulfilled by the Commission, although its mandate is different in some important respects and its role is much more like conventional legal representation. For example, the Support Centre is not a gatekeeper to Tribunal adjudication and an application can proceed with or without the Support Centre. It becomes involved only where an applicant seeks advice or requests representation and, even in those cases, it has no decision-making role regarding the adjudication or processing of the application. In practice, although it may have been part of the government's objective in creating the Support Centre, this has not translated into full legal representation for all or even many applicants before the Tribunal.[55] Much of the Support Centre's work has been to provide

53 Its work includes, for example, conducting education sessions and public consultations, building partnerships (for example, Project Charter with the Toronto Police Service), advocating for change in discussions with various groups, making submissions on proposed legislation, intervening in litigation in other fora (including before the Supreme Court of Canada), and designing policies and educational tools. See, for example, Ontario Human Rights Commission, *Annual Report, 2010–2011* (Toronto: OHRC, 2011) [OHRC, *Annual Report 2010–2011*], online: OHRC www.ohrc.on.ca/sites/default/files/attachments/Annual_Report_2010-2011%3A_Looking_back%2C_moving_forward.pdf. See also the Commission's written submissions in the context of the three-year review, Ontario Human Rights Commission, *Ontario Human Rights Commission Submission Regarding Section 57 Three-Year Statutory Review of the Ontario Human Rights System, 4. The OHRC's 2008–2012 priorities, initiatives and impact* [OHRC, *Three-Year Review*], online: OHRC www.ohrc.on.ca/en/ontario-human-rights-commission-submission-regarding-section-57-three-year-statutory-review-ontario/4-ohrc's-2008-2012-priorities-initiatives-and-impacts.

54 See *Code*, above note 3, ss 13 and 45.12.

55 See *Hansard*, 26 April 2006, above note 7 at 1410. In introducing Bill 107, the Attorney General, referring to the Support Centre, stated:

> We would ensure that, regardless of levels of income, abilities, disabilities or personal circumstances, all Ontarians would be entitled to

assistance and support, rather than representation.[56] Consequently, the overwhelming majority of applicants in Tribunal proceedings are self-represented. Only a fraction of them obtain legal representation for hearings or mediations from the Support Centre and most others cannot or do not otherwise obtain counsel.[57] While many applicants access some form of legal advice, from the Support Centre or otherwise,[58] stakeholders have expressed concern that this limited access to legal representation is a significant barrier to meaningful access to justice in the human rights context.[59]

3) The "New" Tribunal

Litigation before the Tribunal is very different from what it once was. Before 2008, the Tribunal had rarely received more than 150 new hearing referrals per year, all of which had already been through an extensive

---

share in receiving equal and effective protection of human rights, and all will receive that full legal representation.

56 See Ontario Human Rights Legal Support Centre, *Annual Report 2010–2011* (Toronto: HRLSC, 2011) at 9, online: HRLSC www.hrlsc.on.ca/docs/en/AnnualReport2010-11.pdf. Unlike the regime surrounding legal aid clinics, the *Code* does not establish and the Support Centre does not specifically apply any income-related criteria in determining how to allocate legal services. Instead, the Support Centre considers the merits of the claim and it gives "priority service" to disadvantaged individuals who face heightened barriers to the human rights process.

57 According to its *2010–2011 Annual Report*, the Support Centre represented only a total of 544 individuals before the Tribunal, in either mediations or hearings. See *ibid* at 10. During that same fiscal year, the Tribunal received 3,164 applications, and in response it conducted hundreds of hearings and well over a thousand mediations. Social Justice Tribunals Ontario, *2010–2011 Annual Report* (Toronto: SJTO, 2011) at 31–33 [SJTO, *2010–2011 Annual Report*], online: SJTO www.sjto.gov.on.ca/stellent/groups/public/@abcs/@www/@sjc/documents/abstract/ec160192.pdf.

58 Others sources of legal advice may include legal clinics (other than the Support Centre) and counsel consulted by the parties.

59 See *Code*, above note 3, s 43(2), which requires that parties to applications that are within the Tribunal's jurisdiction be given an opportunity to make oral submissions before their matter is finally determined. The issue arises, in part, because of the particular vulnerability of some human rights applicants. Unless some of these individuals obtain publicly-funded representation, the concern is that they will be deterred from pursuing human rights claims. Some argue that, in the human rights context, representation services should be publicly-funded because our society, generally, derives a benefit from the eradication of *Code* violations.

intake, investigation, and conciliation process with the Commission.[60] Cases were generally presented by the Commission. Since 2008, however, the Tribunal receives an average of over 3,000 new applications per year and it is responsible for all aspects of processing, mediating, and adjudicating these matters.[61] Now, most of the parties who appear before it are self-represented.[62]

In creating the Tribunal's new role, the 2008 *Code* conferred broad powers to actively adjudicate matters and control its proceedings.[63] These new powers include, for example, the ability to question witnesses, to direct the order of evidence, and to limit evidence or submissions. Further, in keeping with some of the *Code* amendments, institutional changes and innovations have taken place within the Tribunal itself, ranging from increases to the number of vice-chairs, to approaches to mediation, to processing of applications, to developing active adjudication models. Notably, the *Code* amendments respond to concerns about the accessibility of adjudication. While the Commission could refuse to deal with cases based only on written submissions, the *Code* now stipulates that the Tribunal will give parties an opportunity to make oral submissions before finally determining any matter that falls within its jurisdiction.[64] This means that, unless the parties settle their disputes or expressly

---

60 See the comparative statistics compiled by the Commission, *OHRC Comparative Indicators*, online: OHRC www.hrlsc.on.ca/docs/en/OHRCComparativeNumbers.pdf.

61 SJTO, *2010–2011 Annual Report*, above note 57 at 31–33. See also the Ontario Human Rights Tribunal, *Annual Report 2008–2009* (Toronto: HRTO, 2009) and the Ontario Human Rights Tribunal, *Annual Report 2009–2010* (Toronto: HRTO, 2010) [OHRT, *Annual Reports 2008–09 & 2009–10*], both online: HRTO www.hrto.ca/hrto/?q=en/node/26. In addition to these "new applications," the Tribunal is responsible for resolving two other types of cases that originated in the old system: (1) transitional applications, which are matters that were filed with the Tribunal between 30 June 2008 and 30 June 2009, based on complaints originally filed with the Ontario Human Rights Commission under the old system; and (2) Commission-referred complaints, which are matters that were filed under the old system and that the Commission referred to the Tribunal for hearing. This chapter and the statistics it references relate to new applications only.

62 While a detailed discussion is beyond the scope of the paper, "access to adjudication" takes on a new dimension when most parties are self-represented, including ensuring that processes, decisions, and practices can be understood and applied by non-represented litigants.

63 See *Code*, above note 3, s 49. The powers are described in more detail, below. See below, notes 67–84.

64 See *Code*, above note 3, s 42(2).

waive the right to make oral submissions, the Tribunal holds in-person or telephone conference hearings in all matters before finally determining them, unless it finds they are outside jurisdiction.

Having considered some of the major changes brought about by *Code* reform, we turn now to how the Tribunal has implemented these changes and I attempt to identify some benchmarks against which the Tribunal's performance can be considered.

E. MEASURES OF PERFORMANCE

There are many difficulties associated with measuring the work of an adjudicative body. Even if clear and appropriate benchmarks can be established, many of the possible measures are highly subjective.[65] Further, the adversarial process and the very nature of the Tribunal's work is such that the parties before it have very different interests and objectives. Applicant and respondent communities have different ideas about how the Tribunal should function. For example, applicants judge the Tribunal based on its ability and willingness to provide them with a timely and full opportunity to present their case before finally determining it. Conversely, many respondents judge the Tribunal based on whether it addresses cases efficiently (particularly where they seemingly lack merit) and without requiring respondents to expend significant resources.

The Tribunal has defined its mandate as follows: "To provide an expeditious and accessible process to assist parties to resolve applications through mediation, and to decide those applications where the parties are unable to reach a resolution through settlement."[66] Some of these notions are echoed in the terms of reference for the three-year review, which suggest a benchmark for measuring the Tribunal's performance: namely, whether it is "providing quicker and direct access for applicants, and a fair dispute resolution process for all parties, including respondents." While the first element of this benchmark (quicker and direct access to adjudication) is quantifiable, whether the Tribunal is of-

65 A qualitative review of the Tribunal's jurisprudence is both beyond the scope of this paper and subjective in nature.

66 Human Rights Tribunal of Ontario, "About HRTO," online: HRTO www.hrto.ca/hrto/?q=en/node/1.

fering a "fair dispute resolution process" is less easily defined and much more difficult to measure.

The task is complicated because notions of "fairness" and "efficiency" must be considered in tandem.[67] On the one hand, the benchmarks require that the Tribunal's processes are "fair" in the sense that they, for example, afford the parties with an opportunity to be heard, allow for appropriate measures of certainty and flexibility, give parties adequate notice and disclosure, and do not advantage one party over another. On the other hand, the Tribunal also strives for efficiency: it must deal with a large volume of cases in a timely manner, making the best use of limited adjudicative resources. While the Tribunal's ability to balance the "fairness" and "efficiency" components of its mandate is a key measure of its success, this, too, is difficult to measure. The appropriate balance between "fairness" and "efficiency" is a subjective notion and different stakeholder groups will bring different perspectives to the question. Thus, a possible indicator of success is feedback from stakeholders and, more generally, factors that indicate whether the Tribunal has gained the confidence of the communities it serves. This can be gleaned not only from direct stakeholder feedback, but also from the number of applications the Tribunal receives over time. Although there are a range of other variables that may come into play, an increase or decrease in the number of applications filed per year could be indicative of at least applicants' confidence in the human rights system.

The Tribunal's ability to provide a "fair dispute resolution process" depends also upon the legislative framework of the *Code*. As we shall see, much of the criticism of the Commission-based model was based on the legal framework and procedures it created. The legal framework has now changed, largely in response to stakeholder criticism. One of the measures of the Tribunal's success is its ability to adapt within that statutory framework and to ensure that its approach and processes strike an appropriate balance between fairness and efficiency. Thus, to appreciate the Tribunal's work, we need to consider a combination of factors, including Tribunal statistics regarding hearings, mediations, and wait times, stakeholder feedback and indicia of levels of stakeholder confidence, and whether developments in the Tribunal's processes are in keeping with its mandate to be both fair and efficient. Taken together,

---

67 Consider the Tribunal's stated mandate and the terms of reference of the three-year review, which incorporate both elements: see OHRC, *Three-Year Review*, above note 53.

these factors will help us assess the impact of the legislative changes on the Tribunal's work.

From a purely quantitative perspective, the Tribunal is clearly providing quicker access to adjudication than was available under the old system. While, under the old system, parties might wait five years to have their matter adjudicated, most cases are now being resolved more quickly. The Tribunal's stated objective is that 75 percent of complete applications will be resolved within one year. In fiscal year 2009–2010, 95 percent of matters were resolved within this time frame. In fiscal year 2010–2011, however, only 62 percent of applications were resolved within one year so that, by the close of the 2010–2011 fiscal year, the Tribunal had a year's worth (3,680) of active applications pending. Statistics recently published on the Tribunal's website show promising patterns in its management of applications. The Tribunal is now resolving more cases than it is opening, and with its ongoing work to add efficiencies to its processes, this trend is expected to continue.[68] At the end of the first quarter in 2010, the Tribunal had 3,162 active cases pending and, in that quarter alone, it closed over 150 files more than it opened.

In terms of access to adjudication, there have been some important developments. As we have seen, direct access to the Tribunal is at the root of and is mandated by *Code* reforms. Moreover, because the *Code* requires that parties have an opportunity to make oral submissions, this means that "access to adjudication" under the *Code* generally includes a hearing.

Turning now to stakeholder feedback and confidence levels, these have generally expressed satisfaction about the Tribunal's work. While stakeholder groups continue to make suggestions for improvements, groups on all sides of the issues seem to agree that the 2008 *Code* reform has improved many aspects of the human rights system in Ontario. Judging from the submissions to the Review Panel, the Tribunal's work, in particular, has been positively received.[69]

To summarize briefly, submissions provided in the context of the three-year review show that, again, there are two sides to many of the issues. For example, applicant groups want to ensure that legal services

---

68 See above note 61. For example, the Tribunal now schedules mediations over a half-day rather than a full day. It has also instituted a new rule that allows for a summary hearing process. These changes are discussed in more detail, below.

69 *Ibid.*

are available to them and they identify the Support Centre's limited resources, the cost of securing private legal services, and the difficulties in navigating the formality of the legal process without representation as the main barriers to accessing human rights in Ontario.[70] Respondent groups raise concern that similar legal services have not been made available to them. They also worry that the availability of free legal support for applicants, combined with the fact that the Tribunal does not have the jurisdiction to award costs, increase the number of human rights claims and decrease applicants' appetite for their early resolution.[71]

A further measure of success is whether, within its legislative framework, the Tribunal has developed and applied its powers and procedures in a way that appropriately balances fairness and efficiency. In this regard, the Tribunal has done significant work and its approach has evolved over time, along with its developing experience. For example, in keeping with its mission to be fair and efficient in its determination of claims, the Tribunal has taken a hands-on approach to managing applications. It frequently, of its own initiative, seeks submissions from parties on issues including jurisdiction, dismissal, and deferral. It typically requires respondents to file a full response, even if they are raising preliminary objections to the application.[72] This approach prevents

70 See, for example, the Canadian Mental Health Association, *Submission to Andrew Pinto Chair, Ontario Human Rights Review 2012* (Toronto: CMHA, 2012). See also ARCH Disability Law Centre, *Written Submissions of ARCH Disability Law Centre — Ontario Human Rights Review* (Toronto: ARCH Disability Law Centre, 2012), online: ARCH Disability Law Centre www.archdisabilitylaw.ca/?q=written-submissions-arch-disability-law-centre-ontario-human-rights-review-0.

71 See, for example, the Canadian Association of Counsel to Employers, *Submissions of the Canadian Association of Counsel to Employers on the Ontario Human Rights Review* (Toronto: CACE, 2012), online: CACE www.counseltoemployers.ca/Advocacy/CACE%20Submission%20on%20Ontario%20Human%20Rights%20Review%20March%201-12.pdf; Ontario Bar Association, *Written Submissions to the Ontario Human Rights Review 2011–2012* (Toronto: OBA, 2012), online: OBA www.oba.org/En/publicaffairs_en/PDF/OBA%20Submission-%20Ontario%20Human%20Rights%20Review%202011-2012-final.pdf (this also argues that enhanced publicly-funded legal services should be made available to applicants); Association for Reformed Political Action (Hamilton Area), *Submissions to the Ontario Human Rights Review Panel*, online: ARPA http://arpacanada.ca/attachments/article/1518/Submission%20to%20OHRC%20from%20Hamilton%20ARPA.pdf.

72 For a summary of exceptions to this general rule, see *Masood v Bruce Power*, 2008 HRTO 381.

cases from getting bogged down in procedure and allows the Tribunal to assess whether to address issues on a preliminary basis. This means that the application's adjudicative path is ultimately directed by the Tribunal, even where parties seek to raise a number of preliminary and procedural issues. In determining how a matter should proceed, the Tribunal is guided by what is both fair and efficient in the circumstances.

The Tribunal has also been innovative in its approach to mediation. It has tried to optimize alternative dispute resolution methods, and both mediation and mediation-adjudication have served as some of the Tribunal's key tools. The Tribunal sees its role as to facilitate and encourage such voluntary settlement negotiations and to hear and determine disputes where no agreement is possible.[73] Since 2008, an average of over 60 percent of cases has resolved at mediation.[74] The Tribunal does not employ designated mediators, but instead uses vice-chairs and members to facilitate mediations. Because they also conduct hearings and render decisions, vice-chairs and members have the expertise to be effective rights-based mediators, and they can speak with authority about the issues in dispute. The Tribunal has emphasized mediation training and skill development for vice-chairs and members and it has worked to refine its approach. In 2010, mediations, which had been held over a full day, shifted to half-day slots. Despite this change, settlement rates did not decrease significantly. Thus, not only is the Tribunal conducting more mediations, it is helping resolve more cases more quickly.

In July 2010, the Tribunal amended its *Rules of Procedure* to formalize a mediation-adjudication process.[75] Mediation-adjudication is a voluntary process that takes place within the context of a hearing. If the parties agree and sign an agreement to this effect, the hearing adjudicator may attempt to mediate the dispute between them at the outset or during the course of the scheduled hearing. If the mediation does not result

---

73 See "About HRTO," above note 66; OHRC, *Annual Report 2010–2011*, above note 53.

74 For example, in fiscal year 2009–2010, the HRTO held over 1,200 mediations of new applications, with a settlement rate of approximately 67 percent. In fiscal year 2010–2011, for the period in which statistics were kept, the settlement rate was just over 60 percent. See STJO, *2010–2011 Annual Report*, above note 57 at 32; OHRT, *Annual Reports 2008–09 & 2009–10*, above note 61.

75 See Ontario Human Rights Tribunal, *Rules of Procedure: Applications under the Human Rights Code*, Part IV RSO 1990, c H.19, as amended [OHRT, *Rules of Procedure*].

1 2 3 4 5 6 7 8 9 10 11 12 13 14

in a settlement agreement, the same adjudicator will then conduct the hearing.

Part of what now characterizes the Tribunal is its willingness to develop new active adjudication tools afforded in the *Code*.[76] Many Tribunal adjudicators play an active role in the hearing process, although the specific approach to each hearing may vary.[77] Parties appearing before the Tribunal, whether represented or not, should be prepared for an active adjudicator who may, among other things, determine the order of the evidence, take the lead in questioning the witnesses, and seek submissions from parties (at various stages of the proceedings) as to the reasonable prospect of success of the application.[78]

In 2010, the Tribunal's *Rules of Procedure* were amended to create a summary hearing process.[79] This is an expeditious proceeding, used where an application is within the Tribunal's jurisdiction but appears, on its face, to have no reasonable prospect of success. It also gives applicants access to adjudication and a fair opportunity to argue their case, while ensuring that matters without apparent merit are dealt with expeditiously and without either party having to expend significant resources. The legal issue in a summary hearing is whether the application should be dismissed, in whole or in part, because it has no reasonable prospect of success.[80] This can mean a number of different things, depending on the nature of the allegations. For example, a summary hearing is typical-

---

76 See *Code*, above note 3, s 43(3).

77 It may depend on a number of factors, including the nature of the issues and, for example, whether they are expected to be complex or straightforward; whether the matter is expected to turn on factual or legal issues.

78 See *Code*, above note 3, s 49. See, for example, *Newton v Toronto (City)*, 2010 HRTO 1023 at paras 14–15; *Pellerin v Conseil scolaire de district catholique Centre-Sud*, 2011 HRTO 1777 [*Pellerin*]; *Hoekstra v First Hamilton Christian Reformed Church*, 2011 HRTO 2108 at paras 7–12. The Tribunal will generally hear submissions from the parties and will often obtain their consent to non-traditional adjudicative methods, such as the adjudicator conducting the examination or cross-examination of witnesses. However, the Tribunal has concluded that it had the power to adopt such methods even where these are opposed by the parties. See *Clennon v Toronto East General Hospital*, 2009 HRTO 1242.

79 See OHRT, *Rules of Procedure*, above note 75, r 19A. The Tribunal can order that a matter proceed by summary hearing at its own initiative or in response to a request by a respondent. Typically, summary hearings are conducted by telephone.

80 The Tribunal sets out the principles that apply in a summary hearing in *Dabic v Windsor Police Service*, 2010 HRTO 1994 at paras 6–10.

ly ordered in cases where the allegations appear to have no connection to the *Code* and seem to concern general issues of fairness rather than differential treatment based on *Code* grounds.[81] Similarly, summary hearings are often ordered because the application contains only bald allegations without any suggestion that they are or could be supported by evidence reasonably available to the applicant.[82] Further, the Tribunal has begun to incorporate the summary hearing test (and the threshold of no reasonable prospect of success) into its merits-based hearings.[83] At appropriate stages in the hearing, often once the applicant has presented his or her case or has had an opportunity to question key respondent witnesses, the Tribunal may invite submissions from the parties regarding whether the application has a reasonable prospect of success. This use of the summary hearing test as part of merits hearings may make effective use of the parties' and the Tribunal's resources, ensuring that limited adjudicative time is not spent pursuing a case when it becomes apparent that it cannot succeed.[84]

Many of the practices outlined above were developed with both fairness and efficiency in mind and with a view to giving both parties timely access to justice. Efficiency, provided that it is appropriately balanced with fairness, benefits the parties: their matters are dealt with more quickly, they have access to a timely hearing, and less time and resources are devoted to litigation. Similarly, the Tribunal's approach to mediation not only helps it manage its caseload, it gives willing parties meaningful opportunities to resolve their matters, allowing them to have a hand in crafting their own agreement rather than risking an all-or-nothing outcome following a hearing.

---

81 *Ibid*. See also *Forde v Elementary Teachers' Federation of Ontario*, 2011 HRTO 1389 at paras 17–18 [*Forde*]; *Diab v Ontario Lottery and Gaming Corporation*, 2011 HRTO 2093; *Saxon v Amherstburg Police Services Board*, 2011 HRTO 77; *Basic v Felix Sabayle*, 2011 HRTO 802.

82 See *Forde*, above note 81.

83 *Pellerin*, above note 78. See also *Vandervelde v Goodlife Fitness Centres*, 2012 HRTO 1042.

84 This is a relatively recent jurisprudential development and it has yet to fully bear itself out in the caselaw. It remains to be seen to what extent the "no reasonable prospect" test will be used in merits hearings.

F. CONCLUSION

This analysis suggests that, four years into the revamping of its human rights legislation, Ontario has effectively transitioned to a direct access model for human rights. The human rights system and the institutions created through the 2008 reform to the *Code* have resulted in the more timely resolution of claims. They also ensure that parties have direct access to the Tribunal and can make oral submissions before their matter is finally determined. The human rights community continues to propose changes to enhance human rights in the province. As required by section 57 of the *Code*, a review of the reforms is underway. As of the date of writing, the report was not yet available. However, the submissions to the review panel show that, while human rights stakeholders continue to see room for improvement in the system, they do not voice the same level of deep dissatisfaction and loss of confidence that characterized the Task Force's Review in 1992. To some extent, improvements to the human rights system can be traced back to the legislative reforms themselves. As we have seen, the amendments to the *Code* attempt to balance competing interests in a way that is mindful of the procedural and substantive rights of all parties. While the human rights system under the "old" *Code* was broken, the "new" *Code* conceived of a workable framework for human rights enforcement in the province. Importantly, however, a human rights system is more than just a statute. On its own, however well-conceived, the legislation could not guarantee the success of the human rights system. Ultimately, this also requires effective human rights institutions, striving together to fulfill their mandates under the *Code*.

This chapter focused on the Tribunal's work and attempted to consider its work against a number of benchmarks. The Tribunal's statistics are promising and the feedback regarding its work is generally positive. We have seen that, to meet the challenges inherent in its new role, the Tribunal has been adaptable, resourceful, and (most importantly) mindful of striking an appropriate balance between fairness and efficiency.

CHAPTER 7

THE PARIS PRINCIPLES TWENTY YEARS AFTER[1]

Maxwell Yalden[2]

A. INTRODUCTION

In October 1991, in my capacity as Chief Commissioner of the Canadian Human Rights Commission, I attended an international conference in Paris on National Institutions for the Promotion and Protection of Human Rights. The meeting had been organized at the invitation of the French government, in cooperation with the French National Commission on Human Rights[3] and the UN Centre for Human Rights.[4] The agenda called for a review of patterns of cooperation between national and international institutions (such as the United Nations and its agencies) and an exploration of ways of increasing their effectiveness.

When the conference reached agreement on a declaration of principles and criteria for the establishment and governance of National Human Rights Institutions (NHRIs), or the "Paris Principles"[5] as they came to be known, one could hardly have anticipated how extensive

1 The author is indebted to Karen Hamilton and John Dwyer, and to Sulini Sarugaser-Hug and other officials of the Canadian Human Rights Commission, for their contributions to this article.

2 Maxwell Yalden is a former member of the United Nations Human Rights Committee.

3 La Commission nationale consultative française des droits de l'homme.

4 Later replaced by the Office of the High Commissioner for Human Rights.

5 Properly known as the *Principles Relating to the Status of National Institutions*, annex to *National Institutions for the Promotion and Protection of Human Rights*, CHR Res 54, UNESCOR, Supp No 2, UN Doc E/1992/22, (1992); GA Res 48/134, UNGAOR, 48th Sess (1993) Annex [*Paris Principles*].

their impact would be in the field of human rights. With the passage of time, the essential place of the Principles and of the NHRIs that bridge domestic systems and the international human rights regime has become evident. The Office of the High Commissioner for Human Rights itself recognized their importance as early as 1993: "It has . . . become increasingly apparent that the effective enjoyment of human rights calls for the establishment of national infrastructures for their protection and promotion."[6]

In the twenty years since that observation, reliance on national institutions has continued to grow. It has also become increasingly clear that an international framework is needed to develop a worldwide assortment of otherwise diverse institutions into a more coherent system in the defence of human rights.

B. THE BEGINNINGS

The Paris Conference was not the first time these issues had surfaced. It followed upon a number of earlier UN initiatives directed towards enhancing the role of national institutions. A 1960 resolution of the Economic and Social Council (ECOSOC), for example, recognized the unique role such institutions could play in the protection and promotion of human rights.[7] It went on to invite governments to encourage the creation and development of such bodies, and to communicate their ideas on the subject to the Secretary-General.

The first World Conference on Human Rights was held in Teheran from 22 April to 13 May 1968, to review the progress made in the twenty years since the adoption of the *Universal Declaration of Human Rights* and to formulate a programme for the future. It approved the Proclamation of Teheran,[8] which, *inter alia*, reaffirmed that:

---

6 Office of the High Commissioner for Human Rights, "Fact Sheet No. 19: National Institutions for the Promotion and Protection of Human Rights" (Geneva: OHCHR, April 1993) ["Fact Sheet No 19"], online: OHCHR www.ohchr.org/Documents/Publications/FactSheet19en.pdf.

7 United Nations Economic and Social Council, *Resolutions of National Advisory Committees on Human Rights*, E/30, UNESCOR, 30th Sess, Supp No 1, UN Doc E/3422, (1960) 14.

8 *Proclamation of Teheran, Final Act of the International Conference on Human Rights, Teheran 22 April to 13 May, 1968*, UNGAOR, 1968, UN Doc A/CONF.32/41, 3 [*Teheran Proclamation*].

> The Universal Declaration of Human Rights states a common understanding of the peoples of the world concerning the inalienable and inviolable rights of all members of the human family and constitutes an obligation for the members of the international community.[9]

Other conferences and workshops followed, and the Commission on Human Rights[10] decided in 1978 to organize a meeting on national and local institutions to draft guidelines for the structure and functioning of such bodies. Accordingly, a seminar on "National and Local Institutions for the Promotion and Protection of Human Rights" was held in Geneva from 18 to 29 September of that year, at which a series of guidelines was approved. The guidelines were subsequently endorsed by the Commission on Human Rights and the General Assembly.[11]

In 1990, the Commission on Human Rights recommended that a workshop be convened, with the participation of national and regional institutions involved in the protection and promotion of human rights. As I have noted above, the meeting was eventually held in Paris, in October 1991. Participants included representatives of national institutions, UN member states, the United Nations and its specialized agencies, and intergovernmental and non-governmental organizations (NGOs). The Paris Principles, which the meeting approved, were subsequently endorsed by the Commission on Human Rights in March 1992[12] and by the UN General Assembly in December 1993.[13] They have since become the leading statement of the role, composition, status, and functions of national human rights institutions.

From 14 to 25 June 1993, the representatives of 171 states attended the second World Conference on Human Rights in Vienna. Some thirty national institutions were also present and held a number of meetings in parallel with the sessions of the full conference. Underlining the significance of their presence, the Vienna Declaration, adopted by the World Conference, states:

> . . . the World Conference on Human Rights reaffirms the important and constructive role played by national institutions for the

9 *Ibid*, art 2.
10 Since 2006, the UN Human Rights Council.
11 "Fact Sheet No 19," above note 6 at 2.
12 *Paris Principles*, above note 5.
13 *National institutions for the promotion and protection of human rights*, GA Res 48/134, UNGAOR, 1993, UN Doc A/RES/48/134.

> promotion and protection of human rights, in particular in their advisory capacity to the competent authorities, their role in remedying human rights violations, in the dissemination of human rights information, and education in human rights.[14]

And a further assessment by the Office of the High Commissioner in 2010 asserts:

> The 1993 World Conference on Human Rights in Vienna was a watershed for NHRIs. For the first time NHRIs compliant with the Paris Principles were formally recognized as important and constructive actors in the promotion and protection of human rights, and their establishment and strengthening formally encouraged . . . .[15]

So far, so good. Nevertheless, much remained to be done. National institutions were to grow substantially in number and what is known today as the International Coordinating Committee[16] (ICC) was to be established for the purpose of seeing to the creation and strengthening of those institutions in conformity with the Paris Principles. The status of the ICC and its main functions are discussed further below.

C. A SUMMARY OF THE PRINCIPLES

The Paris Principles seek to ensure the establishment of effective national institutions. They embody minimum requirements and guidelines concerning the competence and responsibilities, composition, guarantees of independence, and methods of operation for national institutions. They are drafted in very broad language in order to cover the interests of all the parties involved, and the different systems of human rights protection that have been developed in various parts of the world. However, while they are broad enough to encompass a range of models, they

---

14 *Vienna Declaration and Programme of Action*, UNGAOR, 1993, UN Doc A/CONF.157/23 [*Vienna Declaration*].

15 Office of the High Commissioner for Human Rights, *National Human Rights Institutions, History, Principles, Roles and Responsibilities* (New York: United Nations, 2010) at 7, online: OHCHR www.ohchr.org/Documents/Publications/PTS-4Rev1-NHRI_en.pdf.

16 Properly known as the International Coordinating Committee of National Human Rights Institutions for the Promotion and Protection of Human Rights.

are also sufficiently specific to allow the ICC to make judgments about which institutions do and which do not meet the basic criteria. Given that they have remained one of the principal sources of guidance for national institutions over the years, it is important to review their major elements.

The first section of the Principles relates to the competence and responsibilities of national institutions. These provisions suggest as broad a mandate as possible to protect and promote human rights. Thus, national institutions have the responsibility to prepare and submit to government various proposals, opinions, recommendations, and reports on any matters concerning the protection and promotion of human rights. They are assigned the responsibility to provide information on the national situation, including both topical and thematic reports. They are to promote and recommend the harmonization of laws and practices in conformity with international human rights standards, such as any treaties to which the state is a party. They are also to encourage ratification of human rights instruments to which the state is not a party, to contribute to treaty body reports, and to assist in the formulation of teaching and research programs. They should be active in publicizing measures to promote human rights and efforts to combat discrimination and in increasing public awareness of what has been achieved and remains to be accomplished. And, finally, "they may be authorized to hear and consider complaints and petitions concerning individual situations."[17]

The second group of principles deals with the composition of national institutions and guarantees of independence and pluralism. In order to ensure broad participation, it is recommended that national institutions canvass NGOs, unions, social and professional organizations, specialists in philosophical and religious thought, academic experts, and parliamentary representatives for membership.[18] Governmental representatives may participate, but it is recommended that they do so only in an advisory capacity. It is also essential, as a prerequisite for ensuring independence, that national institutions have secure, adequate financial

17 *Paris Principles*, above note 5. I shall return below to this quasi-optional complaints-taking function.

18 It is notable that the drafting of these requirements was much influenced by the French model for national institutions, particularly with respect to the emphasis given to the concept of "pluralism" described above, and to educational and advocacy responsibilities, as against individual petitions or complaints functions.

resources. Finally, it is noted that they will be most effective when they are established by constitutional provisions[19] or through legislation: bodies set up by executive decision may find it difficult to avoid problems in maintaining their independence.

The list of possibilities with respect to methods of operation is very broad. National institutions shall freely consider any questions falling within their competence and hear any person and obtain any documentation necessary for assessing situations within their jurisdiction. They shall publish their opinions and recommendations. They should meet on a regular basis, establish working groups as required, and set up local or regional sections. Finally, the Principles emphasize the importance of consultation with other bodies with similar responsibilities for the promotion and protection of human rights, including NGOs.

The last group of principles has been described as optional. In particular, they would allow national institutions to be authorized to hear and consider complaints and petitions concerning individual situations. Should they be granted this power, they may be given the authority, in the first instance, to seek an amicable settlement where possible; to inform the party who filed the petition or complaint of the remedies available to him and facilitate access to them; and either to hear complaints or petitions themselves or transmit them to another competent authority. If they consider that it falls within their jurisdiction, they may also make recommendations regarding the complaint, especially by proposing amendments or reforms to any laws, regulations, or administrative practices that have contributed to the restriction of the petitioner's human rights.

As of May 2013, there were 106 national institutions that had been assessed by the ICC with respect to their compliance with the Paris Principles. Seventy institutions were accredited as being in compliance with the Principles and were given "A" designations, twenty-six were judged not fully to meet the requirements of the Principles and were designated "B," and ten institutions that did not comply had a "C" designation.

19 It is worth noting that the Supreme Court of Canada has described human rights legislation as "quasi-constitutional" in nature. See, for example, *Insurance Corp of British Columbia v Heerspink*, [1982] 2 SCR 145.

D. THE INTERNATIONAL COORDINATING COMMITTEE

At the 1993 World Conference in Vienna, an informal coordinating group comprising eight members was created with representatives from each of the world's regions.[20] In addition to representing the full group of NHRIs in dealing with other participants at the conference, the group adopted resolutions dealing with the rights of the child, women's rights, and the rights of disabled persons. It was also successful in ensuring that language emphasizing the importance of national institutions was included in the *Vienna Declaration and Programme of Action*,[21] building on resolutions that had previously been adopted at the UN Commission on Human Rights, the ECOSOC, and the General Assembly.

However, although the Vienna meeting advanced the process substantially, there was still a great deal of unfinished business. A further NHRI workshop was held in Tunis in December 1993, at which the International Coordinating Committee of National Human Rights Institutions was formally created, with the aim of bringing together the activities of the NHRI network.[22] A third meeting was convened in Manila in April 1995, at which a major subject of discussion was the desire of national institutions to be accorded their own status within the United Nations system. In the early days, national institutions were often obliged to speak at the UN from their country's seat, obviously an unsatisfactory situation for ostensibly independent agencies. Nor were such institutions to be considered NGOs; they wished to be able to speak with their own voice. Accordingly, participants in the Manila workshop adopted a recommendation calling on the then-commission on human rights to recognize the unique status of national institutions and take appropriate measures to assure their participation in their own right; and the ICC also made a sustained attempt to obtain recognition, both for itself and for national institutions. In due course this effort succeeded,

---

20 Initially, Australia, Cameroon, Canada, France, Mexico, New Zealand, Philippines, and Tunisia. It is interesting to note that New Zealand, a third member from the Asia-Pacific region, was included by general agreement in order to ensure the presence of at least one woman in the group (Margaret Mulgan, the Chief Commissioner of the New Zealand Human Rights Commission).

21 *Vienna Declaration*, above note 14.

22 It was agreed that, following the informal arrangements that had been set up in Vienna, I would continue to serve as the chairman of the committee; I retained those responsibilities until 1996.

1 2 3 4 5 6 7 8 9 10 11 12 13 14

and the ICC and NHRIs continue to participate in their own right at Human Rights Council meetings.

In 1998, rules of procedure were developed for the ICC and its membership was enlarged to sixteen members, four from each of the geographical regions. At that same meeting, the ICC resolved to create a process for accrediting institutions. In 2008, the ICC discussed governance issues, including incorporation of the ICC in order to cope with the changing environment, including the role of NHRIs in the international human rights system, and it decided to incorporate itself as a legal entity under Swiss law. It also streamlined its rules of procedure and defined its membership and the role and governance of its annual meeting and international conferences.[23]

The ICC currently comprises four regional groupings: Africa, the Americas, Asia-Pacific, and Europe, each regional grouping being represented by four delegates. Meetings are normally held in conjunction with sessions of the Human Rights Council or the biennial International Conference on National Institutions.

Simply put, the primary functions of the ICC are to encourage international coordination of joint activities and cooperation among national human rights institutions, to organize international conferences, to serve as a liaison with the United Nations and other international organizations, and to assist governments to establish institutions in conformity with the Paris Principles.[24]

One of the major contributions to this enterprise is the accreditation of candidates for NHRI status. Formally approved by the Bureau of the ICC, the Sub-Committee on Accreditation established by the ICC carries out the actual work of reviewing accreditation credentials and providing reasons for accreditation decisions. The Sub-Committee is composed of one representative of each geographical grouping, each with A-status accreditation. The chair of the Sub-Committee is selected by the members, on a rotational basis.

An applicant institution is required to provide detail on its legislative mandate, its operational methods, and its program implementation. It is also required to submit supporting documentation, including a copy of its enabling legislation and its most recent annual report or equivalent. Following a review of this documentation and information from other

---

23 Office of the High Commissioner for Human Rights, "OHCHR and NHRIs," online: OHCHR www.ohchr.org/en/countries/nhri/pages/nhrimain.aspx.

24 International Coordinating Committee, *Rules of Procedure*.

sources, the National Institutions Unit of the Office of the High Commissioner for Human Rights (OHCHR) prepares a summary highlighting any problem areas. The summary is provided to the applicant institution, which may provide additional information, documentation, or written commentary to respond to the problems noted in it. The Sub-Committee may also receive and consider submissions by NGOs and the OHCHR in support of or opposing an application. These will also be shared with the applicant institution, which may comment on them. Finally, the applicant institution is contacted directly if the Sub-Committee believes that it needs to clarify any matter relevant to the application.

The significance of the accreditation procedure lies of course in the legitimacy that it provides as to the conformity of the institution concerned with the Paris Principles. A-status accreditation also opens the door for that institution to participate in the work of the ICC, the Human Rights Council, and other UN bodies. As the Secretary-General has stated:

> NHRIs accredited by the ICC as being in compliance with the Paris Principles may participate and address the Council in an independent capacity . . . . It is important that the principle that only those national institutions deemed to be in compliance with the Paris Principles are able to address the Council be upheld.[25]

Failure to be accredited suggests that a national institution is not fully independent or effective and therefore not entirely credible.

There is provision for direct liaison between the ICC and the Office of the High Commissioner. As I have noted, the OHCHR has created a National Institutions Unit that serves, *inter alia*, as a secretariat for the ICC, and supports the work of the ICC Bureau and the Sub-Committee on Accreditation.

There is also a role for NHRIs to play in the Universal Periodic Review of States members of the United Nations Human Rights Council.

And there has in addition been a developing relationship between the ICC and OHCHR with regard to the UN treaty bodies. National institutions have also received increasing attention from the human rights treaty bodies themselves, as they can be important factors in ensuring compliance with treaty standards.

---

25 Human Rights Council, *Report of the Secretary-General on national institutions for the promotion and protection of human rights*, UN Doc A/HRC/4/91 (2007) at para 15.

As the Secretary-General reported in 2011:

> The cooperation of national human rights institutions with the United Nations and United Nations system agencies, funds and programmes is a key requirement of the Paris Principles . . . .
>
> The Office of the United Nations High Commissioner for Human Rights has continued to support the participation of national human rights institutions in treaty body sessions during the reporting period.[26]

E. LIMITS TO THE PRINCIPLES

The Paris Principles are not without limitations. Some arise not from the substance of the Principles themselves, but from the inability to implement them effectively. For instance, some governments do not fully respect the requirements of an appointment process that genuinely guarantees independence and many institutions do not have "adequate funding." Shortcomings like these are of particular concern, because they cannot be resolved through the elaboration of revised or expanded principles: they require fundamental changes at the national level if they are to be remedied.

On the other hand, there are deficiencies that are inherent in the language and scope of the Principles themselves. For example, from the point of view of Canada, including the complaints-taking function in a last quasi-optional group of principles is obviously a weakness. We would see the capacity to take complaints, to deal with them either through mediation or other alternative dispute resolution procedures or to bring them before a competent tribunal or court, as being essential to the system. The International Council on Human Rights Policy has put this point succinctly:

> Complainants expect national institutions to deal with bodies against which complaints are made. Procedures should be simple, accessible, affordable and speedy. Securing compliance with

26 General Assembly, *National Institutions for the Promotion and Protection of Human Rights: Report by the Secretary-General*, UN Doc A/66/274, (2011), online: United Nations www.un.org/ga/search/view_doc.asp?symbol=A/66/274&referer=http://www.un.org/en/ga/documents/symbol.shtml&Lang=E.

> the NHRI's recommendation is also crucial. National institutions should have power to refer their findings to courts or specialized tribunals for adjudication when their good offices fail.[27]

That is not the case, however, for countries that employ different means, such as ombudsman offices, in dealing with complaints and concentrate their commissions' activities on a broad mandate to advise and recommend changes to legislation and other state action that is in conformity with human rights principles. Nevertheless, various commentators have noted that developments in this area are moving towards more institutions having a complaints mandate as well.

Additionally, the Principles do not set out any non-derogable standards. Some national institutions, for example, are barred by statute from inquiring into abuses by the armed forces or the security services. And some apparently cannot take action on their own initiative. The Principles are not altogether clear on these and similar issues.

Furthermore, it remains a serious weakness that, in the light of worldwide experience, simply being in conformity with the Paris Principles does not guarantee the effectiveness of a national institution. In practice, on the ground, the ICC and its Sub-Committee on Accreditation have no capacity for checkups, except what they can glean from OHCHR agents, NGOs, and others, and from interviewing prospective candidates or NHRIs up for review. As one observer has put it, the Principles "focus more on factors relevant to the establishment of such bodies, rather than how they perform once created . . . ."[28] In other words, they are more suited to determining whether an agency qualifies as an "A" designated NHRI or a lesser qualification, rather than assessing how it is operating on a day-to-day basis, although the accreditation process is moving toward more coverage of activities as against founding qualifications.

There are also perhaps some ambiguities regarding the appointments process. The Principles suggest, for example, that appointments should be made by an "official act," and it has sometimes been suggested that executive appointments may be deficient in that respect. At the same time, under various systems (including the Canadian, to some degree) many appointments of this sort are made, technically speaking, by

---

27 The International Council on Human Rights Policy, *Assessing the Effectiveness of National Human Rights Institutions* (Geneva: OHCHR, 2005) at 9, online: ICHRP www.ichrp.org/files/reports/18/125_report.pdf.

28 Rachel Murray, "National Human Rights Institutions — Criteria and Factors for Assessing their Effectiveness" (2007) 25:2 Nethl QHR 189 at 190.

the executive (in Canada, the "Governor in Council") without their independence necessarily being compromised, as long as their term is set out by statute and cannot be terminated without cause.

Finally, there are two considerations of a somewhat tangential nature that are nevertheless relevant to the future of national institutions and the coordinating committee that binds them together. First, there are a total of 106 NHRIs.[29] Given that the UN comprises 193 states, one might well ask where the rest of them are vis-à-vis the national institutions community. There may be a number of reasons that explain in part their absence. For example, there are thought to be potential complications in certain federal states as to which institution should properly represent them. On this issue, the ICC may not yet be out of the woods. Still, it should not be taken to affect the common sense position of state or provincial commissions, for example, in Canada, which rightly look to the Paris Principles for guidance on matters such as their independence or proper methods of protection and promotion of human rights. It had also been felt that initially limiting the use of languages in meetings to English and French, before the provision of translation facilities, might have caused difficulties for certain NHRIs, though it should no longer present a problem since simultaneous interpretation has been made available. And of course there were and are problems of a political nature in various states. Nevertheless, it cannot be denied that it would be worthwhile to try to achieve greater universality.

Second, duplication in UN agencies and institutions remains a concern, as I have argued in my book, *Transforming Rights*,[30] with respect to the treaty bodies and other agencies working in essentially the same area. It is entirely possible in the European context, for example, for entities such as the European Union, the Council of Europe, the European Court, the Commission on Security and Cooperation in Europe, and various UN bodies to examine the same countries' performance using essentially the same sort of criteria. Elsewhere, a similar situation may sometimes prevail with respect to various American, Asian, and African human rights institutions. To my mind, this has proven a major waste of scarce resources and funds. For example, when I was a member of the UN Human Rights Committee,[31] it consistently duplicated enquiries and

---

29 As of May 2012.

30 Maxwell Yalden, *Transforming Rights* (Toronto: University of Toronto Press, 2009).

31 1996–2004.

hearings undertaken by other treaty bodies and various agencies working in the human rights field. Even granting how difficult it is to undo an agency or institution, once created and settled in to its place in the international family, it will always repay trying to reduce duplication as far as possible.

F. SUGGESTIONS FOR REFORM OF THE PRINCIPLES

It will be useful to outline a few key points that might enhance the effectiveness of the Paris Principles.

First, those in the initial section that deal with competence and responsibilities might include a provision recommending that the mandate of national institutions should permit jurisdiction to extend to other categories of rights, including, in so far as practicable, certain types of economic, social, and cultural rights.

Second, there may be value in stipulating that national institutions should not be excluded from looking at important components of society such as the armed forces or the security services and indeed some private sector institutions.

Third, hearing individual complaints should be one of the accepted functions of a national institution, as it allows for greater accessibility and avoids the expense involved in recourse to the courts.

Fourth, independence is a key consideration in establishing the public legitimacy of national institutions, as is diversity in membership. It has been suggested that neither need require a revision of the Principles, but simply further guidance from the ICC. As a result, there may be value in the ICC adopting interpretative guidelines that would provide greater clarity on the types of procedures and mechanisms that could best guarantee the independence of national institutions, including the appointment of members and staff who are representative of society at large.

Finally, public reporting is important, particularly a regular report to parliament or other legislative body. While the Principles do not stipulate that national institutions should produce an annual report, consideration should be given to adding language on the importance of developing and publishing such a document, with a view to identifying priorities, and reporting on progress and shortcomings in all relevant areas of the human rights domain.

G. THE BOTTOM LINE

Where does all this leave us, twenty years on?

From a broad point of view, progress has been considerable: both the Paris Principles and the ICC seem to have served well. In the beginning, the national institutions that turned up in Paris in 1991 were small in number. The ICC also began as a small, simple, informal group. Over the years, there have been substantial developments, both in terms of numbers of institutions and the work of the ICC. In the course of this evolution, a template has been developed for the accreditation of NHRIs that expands on the original Principles, and the ICC has devised helpful criteria for deciding whether or not an NHRI qualifies as meeting the standards of the Paris Principles.

ICC statutes and rules of procedure have also been developed. Regular meetings are held between the whole membership, the ICC, its Bureau, or its Sub-Committee on Accreditation, and NGOs and other interested parties.

NHRIs have also developed relations with the Office of the High Commissioner, with the treaty bodies, and with the Universal Periodic Review procedure of the UN Human Rights Council.

Thus, in principle, all the structures are there to ensure a working system. However, the test of the machinery is not what it looks like qua machinery, but the extent to which it works in practice.

Do ICC accreditations really identify effective NHRIs and separate the wheat from the chaff? There is virtually no investigatory mechanism to confirm the findings of the Sub-Committee on Accreditation or assess performance as against presumptive compliance. It is essentially a paper exercise, except for information provided by the OHCHR agents and interviews with prospective applicants.

In that context, one must ask, for example, whether some 70 percent of institutions qualified as "A" is not a rather high number to have met the ostensibly rigorous standards set out in the Paris Principles. One must question, to take only one example, whether the Russian Commission, functioning under what we know of the present regime, is genuinely comparable with, say, the French or Australian Commissions, all of which are designated as "A" institutions. Or for that matter, countries with NHRIs that I recall being submitted to a periodic review by the Human Rights Committee which found that even judges' independence was questionable.

The relationship between NHRIs and other important members of the UN human rights family requires further reinforcement and development. It is questionable, for example, to what extent they have so far been taken seriously by the treaty bodies. Further, although they have been involved in the UN Human Rights Council's Universal Periodic Review procedure, it is worth noting that some observers have called their participation "limited," "with few seeking to pursue their priorities and policies through direct participation in Geneva."[32]

I have also alluded to the matter of universality. There is certainly no lack of desire to establish a national institution of one sort or another. As the former High Commissioner for Human Rights, Mary Robinson, has noted, "while there is not yet an independent national institution in each State there is one in every corner of the globe — from Mongolia to New Zealand, Denmark to South Africa, Argentina to Canada."[33] However, a conglomeration of human rights bodies that does not include, for example, Brazil, China, and the United States, not to mention dozens of smaller players, can only be placed in question as to its coverage of worldwide human rights problems. Of course, it has to be recognized that the ICC and individual NHRIs are not in the business of "recruiting" new members. They do, however, have an interest in encouraging their establishment, and the importance of covering the rights of all the human family should not be neglected.

H. CONCLUSION

None of these shortcomings, or others that may be identified elsewhere, should be taken to mean that the system is without value. There are many human rights organizations, within and outside the UN, that suffer from weaknesses in their powers of investigation and ability to confirm competence to deal with human rights abuses. Even so, they provide a valuable contribution to a more solid structure of human rights institutions.

---

32 See Thomas Pegram & Mary Massay, contributions to the e-Discussion on *UN Engagement with the Universal Periodic Review*, May 2012 [contents archived with the author].

33 Mary Robinson, United Nations High Commissioner for Human Rights, "To the International Co-ordinating Committee of National Institutions for the Protection and Promotion of Human Rights" (Delivered in Geneva, 17 April 2002), online: NHRI www.nhri.net/pdf/ICC.170402.pdf.

Moreover, as I have noted at the outset, the Secretary-General of the United Nations has made it plain that strong human rights institutions at the country level are a *sine qua non* of any effective defence and re-inforcement of human rights. It is equally clear that this entails national institutions that adhere to minimum standards. However, as I have also argued, it is less obvious what changes to the Paris Principles and the ICC might be necessary to ensure that those standards are in place.

My own experience at the UN, principally but not exclusively with the treaty bodies and the Human Rights Commission, has made it clear that substantial ameliorations with respect to this sort of institution are much easier to talk about than to accomplish in practice. During my eight years on the Human Rights Committee, for example, "reform" of the treaty bodies was one of the favourite topics of discussion; however, ingrained habits die hard, and the difficulty of amassing support from a wide body of disparate countries can prove more than a little challenging. Moreover, practical problems such as the prohibitive cost of an effective inspection capacity, and the likely reaction of some states that it would represent an unacceptable intrusion into their internal affairs, are all hard to overcome.

I daresay the same may be said of NHRIs and the ICC. Moreover, the problem would be particularly resistant in the case of foundational documents like the Paris Principles themselves. In the circumstances, we are likely to be obliged to live with what we have; to encourage continuing incremental improvements to the ICC; and, where possible, to refine the Principles over time. This may be disheartening for some, but it is my belief that, realistically, it is the best we are likely to achieve. And furthermore that it will on the whole surpass the expectations of those who were involved in the drafting of the Principles some twenty years ago.

PART 3

Discrimination and Political Struggle: Three Case Studies

CHAPTER 8

SEXUAL HARASSMENT: A FEMINIST PHRASE THAT TRANSFORMED THE WORKPLACE[1]

Constance Backhouse[2]

A. INTRODUCTION

I stood at the speaker's podium and tentatively surveyed my audience. The room was packed. The members of the audience seemed both tense and uncertain. It was 20 March 1981, and a crowd had assembled in Ottawa's city hall to listen to the city's first workshop on the controversial and novel topic: "sexual harassment of working women." I was the featured guest speaker, invited because I was a co-author of the first book published in Canada on the subject. Maude Barlow, who ran the office of equal opportunity for Ottawa's socially progressive mayor Marian Dewar, had been the one who approached me to ask if I would speak to

---

1 Constance Backhouse, "Sexual Harassment: A Feminist Phrase That Transformed the Workplace" (2012) 24:2 CJWL 275. Reprinted with permission from University of Toronto Press www.utpjournals.com. Article © 2012 by the *Canadian Journal of Women and the Law*. Copyright in the content of the article remains with *CJWL*.

2 Constance Backhouse, CM, O Ont, FRSC, is a professor of law at the University of Ottawa.

The author would like to thank Beth Atcheson for suggesting that she document the history of the efforts taken to eliminate sexual harassment over the past decades. Without her urging, this narrative might never have been written. The author also wants to thank the women — Beth Atcheson, Beth Symes, Diana Majury, and Lorraine Greaves — who have worked with her in the Feminist History Society to chronicle the history of the feminist movement in Canada and Québec through the publication of a series of books. See Feminist History Society, online: Feminist History Society www.FeministHistories.ca.

the group. I had not met Maude before, but her warm welcome reassured me greatly that morning. She was wonderful — astute, charismatic, and inspiring. Over breakfast, she had fully coached me on the gender politics of the event. Sexual harassment was a huge problem within the city's workforce. Some of the women who would be seated in the audience had suffered personally from unwanted sexual overtures. Among the men would be some of the city's most tenacious and flagrant perpetrators, who had been told that their attendance at the workshop was mandatory. They would be sitting in the front rows, arms crossed in defiance, ready for a fight. The feminists at city hall wanted to transform the culture. They hoped someone like me, perceived as a radical outside agitator, might be able to set the stage.

I remember joking with Maude, telling her that they needed a "miracle worker." It was a tall order. And it was at that precise moment that I realized that these brave women in Ottawa truly believed that a speech about sexual harassment could dismantle a piece of the sexist world around them. I caught my breath as I recognized how much power we understood to be wrapped up in this new idea of "sexual harassment." I looked around the room again, took a deep breath, and launched into a speech I had given several hundred times across Canada and the United States in the past two years. And as I did, in the back of my mind, I could not help but reflect on what had brought me to this place and this moment.

My life had been deeply enmeshed in the feminist campaign to eradicate sexual harassment since the spring of 1978, when Leah Cohen and I had begun full-time work on a book. The story of how that book came to be published a year later as *The Secret Oppression: Sexual Harassment of Working Women*, may offer one way of trying to understand how the idea of sexual harassment came to hold such potency.[3] My reflections are those of a single feminist, working within a much wider and powerful movement. Many feminists played pivotal roles in advancing the campaign against sexual harassment, and others would tell this story differently, and probably better. I offer these memories simply as the recounting of one path, one set of observations, along a trajectory that was much broader than any one woman's comprehension.

3 Constance Backhouse & Leah Cohen, *The Secret Oppression: Sexual Harassment of Working Women* (Toronto: Macmillan, 1978) [Backhouse & Cohen].

B. THE ORIGINS OF THE SECRET OPPRESSION

My version of this story would have been greatly enhanced by Leah Cohen's assistance, but her premature death from cancer on 10 May 2007, has left me to construct this recollection without her. The day I first met Leah, fortunately, remains perfectly etched in my memory. We met at a business conference in a downtown Toronto hotel in the spring of 1976. She was a manager at a multinational corporation, and I was a newly graduated lawyer working for the government. We began to chat quite by accident, both of us dismayed and angry over the stream of sexist jokes that the all-male conference speakers seemed to feel was an obligatory start to each presentation.

Looking back on it, I would describe myself as a "feminist late bloomer." I had been raised in a family where women were encouraged to think beyond traditional gender barriers, and I had chosen the male-dominated profession of law. Yet I had avoided identification with feminism, naïvely believing that equality was within personal reach. After I entered the full-time workforce, I began to recognize sexism more clearly, but I had never thought much about the women's movement or my potential role within it.

Leah was far ahead of me. As we conversed that morning, she spoke with self-confidence and pride about feminism and its ideals. I marvelled at how much she knew about the women's movement, its dreams and accomplishments. Our conversation ranged widely, as we moved quickly beyond introductions to in-depth discussions about our jobs, the challenges facing women at work, and the evidence of deeply embedded sexism in society. I was fascinated by Leah's inclusive depiction of feminism. She welcomed me to the women's movement with warmth and optimism. She was so positive about the potential of feminism to transform women's lives. Her delightful sense of humour was infectious. Before the end of the conference, she suggested I come for brunch the next Sunday at her High Park apartment. I was hooked.[4]

In the months that followed, we became inseparable. We devoured the wonderful books that were pouring out of newly established feminist publishing houses. We recruited other women to join us in a variety of local activist projects. The 1970s was a decade of enormous energy

---

4 A fuller account of how I came to meet Leah Cohen is published as "Seven Hundred Men in Suits" in Marguerite Andersen, ed, *Feminist Journeys/Voies féministes* (Ottawa: Feminist History Society, 2010) 49.

for the Canadian women's movement. Rape crisis centres and battered women's shelters were opening their doors across the country. Take Back the Night marches and anti-pornography demonstrations brought a public pulse to feminist demands to end violence against women. Workplaces vibrated with calls for equal pay and the newly crafted goal of equal pay for work of equal value, as well as affirmative action plans to launch women into positions previously barred by sexism. The question was not whether to join the growing women's movement but, rather, where to put our time and energy.

We both harboured a secret desire to write, and feminist writing beckoned as an obvious niche. Leah, who had already acquired a compelling journalistic style, generously taught me to shift my essay-writing style to more accessible prose. Using Leah's business contacts, we managed to place two articles in the *Toronto Board of Trade Journal*. Both focused on gender in a changing workplace: one on shifting rules of etiquette and the other on the difficulties faced by female graduates of a master's degree in business administration.[5] We were casting about for new topics, wanting to capture the explosion of energy that women were bringing to the workforce.

Both Leah and I had in the past experienced incidents of sexual harassment that had had significant consequences in our lives. We commiserated endlessly, exploring what had happened and what it signified. Although both of us understood our situations as sex discrimination, like most women then and now, we weighed the risks associated with public disclosure and future career repercussions and decided against formal complaint.[6] We began to talk with female friends and colleagues and learned to our surprise that most of them had similar stories to tell. In fact, although none seemed to have a name to identify the problem, it took very little probing before every single woman described at least one experience of unwelcome male sexual aggression at work. Aha, we thought, here was the topic for a blockbuster magazine article!

---

5 Constance Backhouse, "Emily Post Revisited: Etiquette between Male and Female Co-Workers" *Toronto Board of Trade Journal* (Fall 1977); Constance Backhouse, "Women MBA's: The New Elite?" *Toronto Board of Trade Journal* (Spring 1978). Both were co-authored with Leah Cohen, under pseudonyms.

6 Neither of us broke our silence in public for the many years in which we advocated against sexual harassment. Even with the passage of time, as I write this article more than thirty years later, I still do not feel confident that I could write about it fairly and fully.

I cannot remember when we first adopted the phrase "sexual harassment." However, the term was coined in April 1975 in Ithaca, New York, when feminists struggling to name this pervasive problem held a meeting, dismissed phrases such as "sexual abuse," "sexual coercion," "sexual intimidation," and "sexual exploitation on the job" and issued a press release calling for an end to "sexual harassment." The last term prompted "almost instant agreement" within the group because it encompassed both "subtle and unsubtle persistent behaviours."[7] The group's activism culminated in a public "speak out" where 275 women gathered to protest sexual harassment.[8]

I do not recall reading any of the sporadic press coverage that began to chronicle the handful of women who courageously came forward to demand change in the months that followed.[9] Yet I do recall vividly how *Ms.* magazine's cover article in November 1977 turned "sexual harassment" into a household word. The American-based premier feminist magazine of the day dedicated an entire issue to sexual harassment, with personal testimonials from secretaries, advertising agents, waitresses, congressional aides, factory workers, and students. *Ms.* also profiled two new organizations — the Working Women United Institute (WWUI) in

---

7 Eight women attended the meeting at the Human Affairs Program at Cornell University to support Carmita Wood, a forty-four-year-old woman who had been forced to resign as an administrative assistant to a Cornell professor because of his sexual advances. The earliest written use of the term appears to have been in a letter of 28 March 1975, from one of the women at that meeting, Karen Sauvigné to Mauri Heins. See Carrie N Baker, *The Women's Movement against Sexual Harassment* (Cambridge: Cambridge University Press, 2008) at 27–31, 35, and 207 [Baker].

8 The group held a "speak-out" on 2 April 1975, to foster public consciousness about the problem and set up the Working Women United Institute (WWUI) to serve as an institutional agent for change. Their press release on 3 April 1975, was the first public use of the phrase "sexual harassment." See Baker, *ibid* at 27–31, 35, and 207.

9 The first national media to use the phrase was a syndicated article by Enid Nemy, "Women Begin to Speak-Out against Sexual Harassment at Work" *The New York Times* (19 August 1975) 38. Baker, above note 7 at 35–38 and Lin Farley, *Sexual Shakedown: The Sexual Harassment of Women on the Job* (New York: McGraw Hill, 1978) at 18–21 [Farley], document other early coverage. The first efforts to quantify the incidence of sexual harassment occurred in 1975 at the office of the Human Affairs Program at Cornell University, in 1976 at *Redbook* magazine, at the Ad Hoc Group on Equal Rights at the United Nations Secretariat, and in 1977 at the University of Texas in San Antonio. See Farley, *ibid* at 20–21; Backhouse & Cohen, above note 3 at 39–41.

New York City and the Alliance Against Sexual Coercion (AASC) in Boston — that were mounting spirited campaigns to eradicate it.[10] As we devoured *Ms.* magazine that November, both Leah and I realized that the time for magazine stories had passed us by.

We decided to think bigger: a book. It was a scary prospect since neither one of us had any experience with book publishing. The economic implications of taking extensive time off from the paid labour force to complete the research and writing were equally sobering. However, we were buoyed by the strength of the feminist movement, the sheer number of women who were willing to disclose their experiences with sexual harassment, and our sense that this was one way we could turn our personal misfortunes into positive change. There was an infectious excitement in the women's movement that made almost everything seem possible.

Through the fall of 1977 and winter of 1978, we spent untold hours talking to more sexually harassed women. At first, we used the grapevine approach — we asked everyone we talked to if they knew anyone else we should talk to. This method "snowballed" into a rich continuum of sexual harassment interviewees. An advertisement in a Toronto newspaper resulted in another rich vein of names. With very few exceptions, the women we met had never sought redress and were loathe to take their complaints public. Yet all believed the time had come to demand change, and they were more than willing to describe the full details of their experiences, provided they could maintain their privacy. We promised all of them that the case studies we profiled in the book would be anonymous. Leah was firmly of the view that the movement to end sexual harassment should not demand "sacrificial lambs" and that no individual women should be harmed further as we took this cause into the public realm.

By March, we were approaching publishers with a title and full synopsis. It took quite a few tries before we found a publisher willing to take a risk on us, but we finally signed a contract with editors Ann Hill and Virgil Duff at Macmillan of Canada in Toronto in the summer of 1978.[11]

---

10 Karen Lindsey, "Sexual Harassment on the Job and How to Stop It" *Ms.* (November 1977) 47; Karen Lindsey, "A National Resource" *Ms.* (November 1977) 49; Rochelle Lefkowitz, "Help for the Sexually Harassed: A Grass-Roots Model" *Ms.* (November 1977) 49; Mimi Kelber, "Sexual Harassment . . . The UN's Dirty Little Secret" *Ms.* (November 1977) 51.

11 Ann Hill was one of the MBA graduates we had interviewed for the earlier *Toronto Board of Trade Journal* article, and her positive sponsorship was

In retrospect, it seems remarkable that we were also able to negotiate an advance that would allow us to travel to New York City and Boston to interview the activists at WWUI and AASC. Two neophyte book authors, we were now launched on a writing project that would dominate our every waking moment for the next year.

C. CREATING THE SECRET OPPRESSION

The 13 March entry in my appointment book for 1978 says, in bold block-printed letters, "BEGINNING BOOK." It was a testament to the excitement I felt as we jumped with both feet full time into the book project, months before we had secured a publishing contract. Each morning, I rode the Queen streetcar, from the little apartment I rented in the Beaches neighbourhood on the eastern edge of Toronto, to Sunnyside in the far west end, where Leah drove down to pick me up in her shiny white Fiat. Her car was her signature: she adored Emma Peel from *The Avengers* television show. Her obituary, thirty years later, would capture it well, reminiscing how Leah relished the image of herself as "a spy or secret agent, relentlessly pursuing social injustice," decked out in "style."[12] She also owned a Selectric IBM typewriter, the most high-tech machine then on the market and the pinnacle of a writer's dream, which made our task immeasurably easier. The house Leah was renting in High Park, decorated with her extraordinary personal flair, became our official writing premises.

Our work was a combination of research, drafting, and editing. We sorted through the notes from the women's interviews, selecting the best ones to illustrate wider themes, and then tried to chronicle the narratives while altering enough details to prevent identification. We winnowed our sample down to seven case studies. One was a clerical worker at a small advertising agency harassed by her company's vice-president.

---

pivotal. Virgil Duff, who would go on to become a successful executive editor at the University of Toronto Press, was equally helpful. Beth Symes, a young feminist lawyer, friend, and fellow activist, generously acted *pro bono* as our counsel in the negotiation of terms. Although we also explored possible publication with Women's Press in Toronto, the only feminist press in the country, the discussions did not culminate in a contract.

12 Naomi Lightman, "Lives Lived: Leah Cohen" *The Globe and Mail* (14 September 2007) L8.

Her boss demanded that she sleep with him and then followed up with coercive physical overtures when she refused. Another was a waitress who offered a litany of examples of crude remarks, leering, grabbing, and pinching. She was harassed from all sides: from her customers, from the restaurant manager, from the bartender, and from the cook. A female electrician reported hollering and whistling from co-workers on the all-male construction site, a dildo left in her lunch bucket, obscene phone calls, threatening letters, and repeated physical assaults. She understood these tactics to be nothing less than a concerted effort to keep women out of the trades. A graduate student described how her psychology professor sent her poems, dropped by her apartment uninvited on the pretext of delivering notes, and kissed her without consent in his office. A young female lawyer described how the senior partner, a corporation lawyer at her law firm, suggested they have an affair. She ruefully added that she had quit her job right afterwards, desperate to avoid further unwelcome overtures and terrified over the senior lawyer's level of power inside the profession. An exotic dancer explained how she was raped by a nightclub owner when she sought work at his establishment. An investigation officer at a human rights commission described how her director insisted on talking about sex interminably and demanded sex from her while in a drunken stupor at an out-of-town staff conference.

The diversity of stories was astonishing. Women working in professional positions, white-collar office work, pink-collar female jobs, and blue-collar trades all reported sexual harassment. The problem affected women of all ages, appearances, races, religions and ethnicities, diverse marital and family status, and income levels. The omnipresence of sexual harassment was appalling, but there was a flipside to the pervasiveness. It was a time when the growing women's movement was forging connections between women from all walks of life. Sexual harassment was an issue with an unprecedented capacity to bring different women together in solidarity and identity of purpose.

Although each experience was unique, there were identifiable patterns. Some sexual harassment was exclusively verbal. Women reported employers whose overtures began with subtle hints or crude suggestive comments. These often escalated to relentless proposals for intimacy, including overt requests for dates and sexual favours. Other sexual harassment manifested itself physically. Women reported pinching, grabbing, hugging, patting, leering, brushing against, and touching. Some sexual harassers' blatant demands for sex escalated to outright sexual assault and rape.

In many cases, sexual harassment was accompanied by threats of dismissal or job-related sanctions for non-compliance. Other harassers were more subtle. There were no direct threats, but women who rejected the sexual overtures or complained about sexism found their workplaces dramatically changed for the worse: they received the worst work assignments, their previously unblemished work performance suddenly inspired a rash of complaints, raises and promotions vanished into thin air, and interpersonal relations turned frosty overnight. Still other harassers carried out no obvious reprisals, but the inherent power imbalance alone was enough to cause women great anxiety. Working relationships were significantly altered after the overture, women felt there was no future in their jobs, they could no longer count on the good will of their supervisor, and they felt forced to look for new positions. Nor was sexual harassment restricted to employers and supervisors. Co-workers and customers were equally capable of poisoning the work environment with verbal and physical sexual overtures, innuendo, and sexist "humour."

Sexual harassers crossed all age, class, race, and religious boundaries. The unnerving thing was that there was no indication that the harassers were psychologically disturbed, perverted, or even immature. They were simply ordinary men acting out their desires for sex in a setting where their gender and labour-market power combined to allow them to treat women like "perks" of the job. They benefited not only from sexual interactions that they did not individually merit but also from the multiple ways that these behaviours reinforced women's inferior gender and employment status. The coerced sexual activity ran roughshod over women's right to choose whether, where, when, and with whom to have sex. The economic toll was enormous: lost jobs, poisoned working environments, and a pervasive erosion of women's equality.

As the stories unfolded, the devastation wrought by sexual harassment became tragically clear. Gender-role socialization made it difficult for women to rebuff unwelcome male sexual attention. Complicated further by the inherent power imbalance that infected so many workplace relationships, the situation became a landmine. Most women tried to ignore the unwanted overtures long past the danger point and then attempted to hide the situation from family, friends, and co-workers. Raised to believe that it was women who were responsible for controlling

1 2 3 4 5 6 7 **8** 9 10 11 12 13 14

sexual matters, they internalized their failure in a deep sense of guilt. Sexual harassment victims reacted with anxiety, dismay, anger, embarrassment, shame, and humiliation. Many experienced psychological depression and despair, culminating in a host of stress-related physical ailments such as stomach aches, headaches, nausea, involuntary muscular spasms, insomnia, and hypertension. Most also insisted that they were terrified to complain about sexual harassment, fearing that they would be ridiculed, ignored, blamed, or labelled a troublemaker.

Hoping to place these stories into a wider context, Leah and I toiled away in libraries, poring over books and articles on women's history, searching for elusive accounts of sexual harassment from the past. We tracked down legislation and law reports, seeking words to explain the legal options in ways that readers could understand. We debated between ourselves interminably over the causes of sexual harassment and what solutions might bring it to an end. The most fascinating research took place in people's offices and homes, public meeting rooms, and restaurants, where we interviewed managers and business executives, human resources specialists, union officials, feminists, historians, lawyers, and educators. The gender divide was palpable. The woman we spoke to nodded affirmatively when questioned about intrusive male sexual licence at work. They might not have yet fastened the label "sexual harassment" to it, but they were well aware of the problem and its endemic nature. Most seemed largely resigned to trying to cope with it by counselling female victims to transfer or quit and to find new jobs.

The men seemed unable to get a grasp of the concept. They admitted to observing sexual interaction at work but utterly failed to distinguish between consensual and coercive sexuality. They described unwelcome sexual invitations attached to threats for non-compliance as harmless flirtation. They scoffed at women's fear of rebuffing employers' advances, insisting that a "simple no" would deter any man. They insisted that the so-called victims must have invited the advances. They raised misogynist stereotypes of women who made false allegations. The unfair use of job-related power to extract sexual activity was entirely invisible to them. Some of the most intriguing interviews we conducted were with men who had been identified to us as sexual harassers. Although we did not confront them with these allegations, we did ask them about sexual harassment generally. Their responses were astonishing. Asked about sexual harassment, they spoke of women who exploited their sexuality for gain in the workplace. Asked if it were possible to imagine an unwelcome and coercive sexual overture, one retorted: "Pinch again, honey."[13]

If there was anything that crossed over male and female interviews, it was that no one seemed to have any inkling that sexual harassment was about to burst out from under cover. The terminology was new to many. The idea that women might collectively rebel against sexual harassment seemed to be beyond credulity. And even those who expressed deep frustration about sexual harassment, including feminists and leaders of women's unions, seemed largely resigned to passivity. It was not until we flew to New York City and Boston in June 1978, to meet with the women who were spearheading the struggle against sexual harassment there, that we met up with feminists who were ahead of the curve.

It was electrifying to be in the company of brilliant and committed women who were working full time on the eradication of sexual harassment. The late 1970s was an era when there was a great deal of sharing of ideas and inspiration between American and Canadian feminists. Even the Women's Section, Studio D of the National Film Board of Canada, put out a film titled *Some American Feminists*. Although we might have made a different decision in another era, Leah and I did not even consider writing our book from an exclusively Canadian perspective. We wanted our readers to be aware of the vanguard work south of the border.

The non-profit organization WWUI had originated in Ithaca in May 1975, to support Carmita Wood, an African-American sexually harassed by a white physics professor and forced to resign her job as an administrative assistant at Cornell University. WWUI had sponsored the first

---

13 Catharine MacKinnon's book, published six months after ours, would characterize the motivation and behaviour of sexual harassers brilliantly:

> Sexual assault as experienced during sexual harassment seems less an ordinary act of sexual desire directed toward the wrong person than an expression of dominance laced with impersonal contempt, the habit of getting what one wants, and the perception (usually accurate) that the situation can be safely exploited in this way — all expressed sexually. It is dominance eroticized. The sense that emerges from incidents of sexual harassment is less that men mean to arouse or gratify the women's sexual desires, or often even their own, and more that they want to know that they can go this far any time they wish and get away with it. The fact that they can do this seems itself to be sexually arousing.

Catharine A MacKinnon, *Sexual Harassment of Working Women* (New Haven, CT: Yale University Press, 1979) at 162 [MacKinnon].

"speak out" that year. By 1977, the organization moved to the basement of a Presbyterian church on Park Avenue in New York City, where a few paid staff and volunteers divided their time between research, the collection and dissemination of legal information, and public education.[14] Leah and I marvelled at the foresight of the New York City organization, which was applying for research grants and building a national network of lawyers knowledgeable about sexual harassment.

Even more impressive was AASC, which was a larger volunteer feminist collective based in Boston. Freada Klein, a founding member, had already amassed a reputation as one of the country's most influential experts on sexual harassment. Her roots lay as an activist in the anti-rape movement, and her failure to convince overburdened rape crisis centres to take on sexual harassment had been the impetus to establish the new organization. AASC opened its doors in June 1976 to provide a sexual harassment hotline that was soon inundated with calls from across the country. The collective provided crisis intervention counselling and extra-legal "direct action" to support victims. Its members also published groundbreaking informational brochures, did public speaking, offered training and consulting to employers and unions, and helped women's groups in other cities set up similar services. Fees generated from the sale of literature, speaking, and workshops helped pay the cost of office rental. Most of the members of the AASC collective had "day jobs" that paid their bills, but they viewed their true work as feminist activism.[15]

It is difficult to articulate, decades later, what it was like to sit down with the AASC members in their storefront office and have them share everything they had learned about the dynamics of sexual harassment. AASC was publishing handbooks that offered the most impressive theoretical analysis of sexual harassment available anywhere at the time, in which they advanced sophisticated arguments about the connections between sexual harassment, sexism, racism, and class discrimination.[16]

---

14 For a detailed description of WWUI's creation, activities, and demise in 1987, see Baker, above note 7 at 27–40, 102, 103, 152–54, and 190–98.

15 For details on the work of the Alliance against Sexual Coercion (AASC) and its closure in 1984 due to lack of funds, see Baker, above note 7 at 41–46, 85–87, and 152–54.

16 Baker, above note 7, describes some of the early AASC publications at 41–46, 86, & 87, including a seventy-six-page training manual for organizations providing services to sexual harassment victims, entitled *Fighting Sexual Harassment: An Advocacy Handbook* (New York: Alyson and AASC, 1979) [*Fighting Sexual Harassment*], articles in the feminist periodical *Aegis* on

Leah and I were amazed at their openness and generosity of spirit, the depth of their analysis, their eagerness to hear what we were finding in Canada, and their willingness to coordinate ideas and strategies. We were heartened that the patterns we had identified from our own research were similar to those diagnosed by the women at AASC. Our conversations buoyed our confidence in our own research. Indeed, we came away sufficiently reassured about our initial findings that we felt much freer to write definitively. It solidified and clarified our thinking and shaped the thoughts that eventually saw light in *The Secret Oppression*. My links with AASC would continue to grow in the years to come. Directly upon the completion of our book, I would leave to do a master's degree at Harvard Law School and joined AASC, where I was able to work one day a week for a year on their exciting sexual harassment initiatives.[17]

However, first, Leah and I flew back to Toronto to finish writing the book. Inspired and validated by the comradeship of our American contacts, the joint book writing endeavour evolved into a delightful blend of pleasure and work. Leah used to worry that I did not feed myself properly and would often insist upon cooking a full breakfast of scrambled eggs, bacon, and tea before we began the day. It was my first initiation into the wing of the women's movement that insisted that delicious food must accompany every feminist meeting. We did almost all of the research as a twosome and soon developed an unusual interviewing technique that allowed us to work as a team in asking questions, which vastly improved the directions that the conversations took. Although we began with each of us drafting on our own, the task of editing jointly caused our voices to

---

myths and facts about sexual harassment, on the pervasiveness of sexual harassment, and on strategies to combat sexual harassment (1979), a study on why men harass (1979), an annotated bibliography on sexual harassment and a handbook on how to establish grievance procedures for sexual harassment on college campuses (1980), a report on sexual harassment in Massachusetts schools (1981), a handbook on the law of sexual harassment (1981), and articles in *Radical America* and *Aegis* on strategies to combat sexual harassment (1981).

17 From September 1978 to May 1979, I became involved in staffing the crisis line, helping to draft the handbook entitled *Fighting Sexual Harassment*, above note 16, offering training workshops to employer organizations in the New England area, and participating in the first "direct action" picketing of a sexual harasser in Boston. The connection with AASC members also offered me an extraordinary entree into the feminist movement in Boston. I attended feminist social gatherings, film screenings, workshops on violence against women, battering, prostitution, rape, and child sexual abuse, marches, and meetings with other feminist organizations.

1 2 3 4 5 6 7 8 9 10 11 12 13 14

blend into one uniform style. Before the end, our thoughts, terminology, and grammar structure had merged seamlessly, and we were finishing each other's sentences. Our distinct personalities also combined well in the joint project. I kept Leah on deadline (mostly), and she tempered my workaholic instincts by insisting that we take the odd afternoon off for the frivolity of a movie and that we end the workday at a respectable hour with sherry, crackers, and cheese. It was a glorious six months, and we celebrated with a sense of spirited elation in August 1978, when we sent the completed manuscript off to the publisher.

D. THE EXPLOSION INTO PUBLIC VENUES

The Secret Oppression burst into print and public consciousness on 7 April 1979. Although ours was the first Canadian book to emerge, six months earlier in October 1978 in New York, Lin Farley, one of the founders of WWUI, had published *Sexual Shake-Down: The Sexual Harassment of Women on the Job*, the first book on the subject.[18] Catharine MacKinnon, then a New Haven lawyer and Yale University professor, released *Sexual Harassment of Working Women* five months after our book.[19] It was a tribute to how connected all of the early activists were that the group of us exchanged books among ourselves within days of each one rolling off the presses.

In addition to a spectacular "book party" that Leah hosted at her home, attended by well over a hundred well-wishers on 7 April 1979, our book basked in a media frenzy. This attention had begun well before the book even came out. A speech on sexual harassment that Leah gave to a dinner meeting of the Association of Women Executives in April 1978 had garnered a stream of radio, television, and newspaper articles through 1978 and into 1979. On the heels of the book's release, the coverage escalated. Press articles sprouted across the country, as virtually every newspaper and national magazine wrote features on sexual harassment and our book. Local and national radio reporters conducted innumerable interviews, and we filled the airwaves of endless dialogue shows and open-line phone-ins. The hosts of television public affairs programs, round tables, and talk shows invited us into their studios.

---

18 Farley, above note 9.

19 MacKinnon, above note 13, was published on 10 September 1979.

Most of the coverage was surprisingly supportive, although we did get the occasional attack-dog piece, such as a *Maclean's* magazine column by Barbara Amiel spluttering that our book was a feminist rant. *Canadian Lawyer* gave front-cover attention to the spin-off piece Leah and I wrote on the sexual harassment of women lawyers. The magazine selected the cover art all on its own — a photograph of a naked woman in a bathtub filled with bubbles, waited on by a fully-gowned male lawyer in courtroom garb, who was pouring her champagne while she smiled broadly — graced with the caption "Are women lawyers sexually harassed?" The magazine staff had also taken the liberty of changing our title from the innocuous "Women Lawyers: Part of the Secret Oppression" to "Take That, You Male Chauvinist Sexist Pig!" The strange thing was that they then printed our full article, filled with narratives about egregious sexual harassment from male lawyers, judges, and clients, without further comment.[20] The cover and title offered us yet another illustration of masculinist incomprehension, spicing up our speeches to gales of laughter for years to come. Perhaps the most bizarre request came from the CTV staff at the flagship investigative journalism program *W5*, who were hoping to film a "real-life" incident of sexual harassment as it was taking place.

Women's groups in Montréal found funding to fly me from Boston, and Leah from Toronto, in January 1979, a precursor of what would become a pipeline of speaking invitations across Canada, and occasionally in the United States, over the next several years. We spoke to multinational employers, government ministries, human resources associations, unions, boards of education, industrial relations associations, psychologists' associations, lawyers' groups, law clerks, women's Canadian Clubs, home economists, librarians, nurses, teachers, sororities, secretaries' associations, Young Women's Christian Associations, women's credit unions, rape crisis centres, regional feminist organizations, university women's clubs, business and professional women's clubs, Zonta clubs, student organizations, universities, community colleges, high schools, and academic and professional conferences. I tried to juggle my new full-time teaching position in the Faculty of Law at the University of Western Ontario with speaking engagements that were happening on average three times per week. Leah, who was working in Toronto on a new book on discrimination against older women, was

20 Constance Backhouse & Leah Cohen, "Take That, You Male Chauvinist Sexist Pig!" (February 1980) Can Law 16.

also fully booked. The upside was the growing confidence with which we began to approach public speaking. Leah had always been a natural in front of a crowd, but I started out tongue-tied, awkward, and painfully self-conscious. With the luxury of being able to deliver the same speech several hundred times, even I improved.

At the time, we were running on empty just trying to meet the seemingly endless demands. We had no time, energy, or capacity to analyze what was happening or why. In retrospect, it seems clear that we were in the eye of a storm of change. Our book had become a focal point for an intensifying public debate about male sexual privilege in the workplace. In less than two months of its Canadian release, 1,100 copies had sold. In December 1980, Prentice-Hall brought out a revised edition in the United States.[21] *The Secret Oppression* served as an entry way for media pundits, opinion leaders, and the larger public to contest traditional practices and to imagine a more level playing field for women and men. Much of this would have happened without *The Secret Oppression*. But it is worth probing what this book, published in the spring of 1979, tapped into in terms of the winds of change.

E. THE WIDER CONTEXT: FACTORS FORCING A CULTURAL SHIFT

The question of why things exploded when they did is also premised on why things had been so bottled up for decades. Sexualized economic exploitation had a history that spanned centuries, but its victims considered the practice so shameful that it had remained a problem without a name. It was conducted in private and trivialized as unique to specific personalities and simply a "personal" matter. It was screened from criticism, hidden from the political, social, and legal arenas. It was also dismissed as "universal," or "natural," even "biological," a characterization that rendered it too embedded and invariable to permit any possibility of change. As Catharine MacKinnon would later quip, it was illogically

21 Constance Backhouse & Leah Cohen, *Sexual Harassment on the Job: How to Avoid the Working Woman's Nightmare* (Englewood Cliffs, NJ: Prentice Hall, 1980).

viewed as both "too small, too unique, too infinitely varied" *and* "too big, too immutable, too invariant" to tackle.[22]

What changed? First off, the problem obtained a "handle," a proper name, in 1975. The naming that took place in Ithaca that spring, and the public baptism that the new name received at the ensuing "speak out," was pivotal. Language runs to the core of life's meaning and exercises enormous influence upon our beliefs and behaviour. Brilliant feminist scholars such as Mary Daly, Dale Spender, and Nicole Brossard were demonstrating how deeply our linguistic heritage had been skewed by male-dominant terminology.[23] Their efforts to reclaim female language and women's voices positively bristled with revolutionary potential. The birthing of the "sexual harassment" terminology was a remarkable illustration of the awesome power of words.

Second, timing was everything. That these events occurred in 1975 and that they mushroomed with lightning speed into a powerful wider movement was no accident. Sexual harassment claimed ascendancy on the coattails of second-wave feminism, which was about to hit its stride. Many would pinpoint the decades of the 1960s, 1970s, and 1980s as the strongest years of the second wave. The year that sexual harassment catapulted onto the public stage — 1975 — was right at the mid-point of the heyday.

At the height of its power, the women's movement was breaking through centuries of silence on issues such as abortion, rape, child sexual abuse, battering, pornography, and prostitution. Rape crisis centres were documenting the pervasiveness of sexual violence and insisting that the root causes were not biological male urges sourced in testosterone but, rather, layers of uncontested patriarchal privilege. Working women's groups were protesting ghettoization in the workplace and demanding pay rates commensurate with their skills as well as a toppling of unfair hurdles placed before women on the job. Sexual harassment had a foot in two camps. It was rooted in the movement to eradicate sexism in the labour market, and it was also defined as violence against women, on a crossroads between two of the most active wings of the feminist movement.

---

22 MacKinnon, above note 13 at 83.

23 Mary Daly, *Gyn/Ecology: The Metaethics of Radical Feminism* (Boston: Beacon Press, 1978); Dale Spender, *Man Made Language* (London: Routledge and Kegan Paul, 1980); Nicole Brossard, *The Aerial Letter*, translated by Marlene Wildeman (Toronto: Women's Press, 1988).

Second-wave feminists took as their mantra the principle that "the personal is political." Through consciousness-raising groups and in activist organizations, they broke their silence about experiences of sexual harassment and discovered with a mixture of relief and growing anger that the problem was anything but "unique." Strengthened by sisterhood, women were feeling bolder about asserting their right to sexual autonomy, identity, and equality. They were less fearful of setting boundaries and demanding rights. They scoffed at the idea that gender inequalities were immutable. They saw with clarity that Catharine MacKinnon was right — sexual harassment was neither too small, nor too big, to challenge. And they raised their voices everywhere they turned. Feminists began to demand public speakers and consultations on sexual harassment within their community organizations, their educational institutions, and their places of employment.

A third factor was the sexual revolution that began in the 1960s, which occurred contemporaneously with the surge of second-wave feminism. Transformational shifts in the culture of sexuality have always served as a double-edged sword for women. Undeniably, women's opportunities for sexual self-realization expanded. Yet the 1960s sexual revolution also made male sexual licence in the workplace more flagrant, more brazen. And more avenues opened for public discussions of sexuality. All three factors impacted on sexual harassment. Harassers felt free to be more overt, which made the problem appear worse. Women who suffered from sexual harassment felt greater licence to speak up about it. And their speech received public dissemination.

The fourth factor, favourable media depiction of sexual harassment, was in part an offshoot of the third. The media perceived itself as being freer to explore issues of "sex," and publishers also concluded that "sex sells." This recognition made coverage of sexual harassment a foregone conclusion. However, the balanced and generally fair media coverage of sexual harassment was quite unanticipated. When we first took our message to the press, we worried that our ideas would be lambasted and ridiculed by reporters whom we imagined to be stereotypical chain-smoking, Scotch-swilling cynics. But even in the newsrooms, change was afoot. The "straight up" coverage given to the feminist analysis of sexual harassment came primarily from a cadre of young women reporters, who were infiltrating all-male newsrooms and simultaneously asserting their own rights to be taken seriously on the job.

Lastly, the demands for an end to sexual harassment grew with the burgeoning numbers of women working for pay. After the Second World War, increasing numbers of women began to pursue lifelong careers in the paid job market. Some of the newcomers were middle-class and professional women, whose economic privilege gave them substantial voice. They added their growing power to the swelling protests against sexual harassment, earmarking it as a barrier that must be toppled if they were to realize their investments in long-term employment.

F. WHAT CHANGED?

Our objective, the total eradication of sexual harassment from the workplace, remains but a dream. This can feel disheartening, and occasionally we lapse into bleakness and disparagement. However, our shared sadness over the failure to achieve revolutionary victory can eclipse the very real changes that have occurred. Others who have been centrally involved in the struggle against sexual harassment in more recent decades will have a fuller appreciation of the victories and losses and will ultimately write definitive accounts.[24] What follows are my personal reflections on what I believe might loosely be characterized as cultural, intellectual, legal, and workplace-based changes.

Culturally, sexual harassment emerged from the shrouds of silence, kicking and screaming, into a public venue where it became defined as wrongful behaviour. The Hollywood hit movie, *Nine to Five*, released in 1980 and starring Jane Fonda, Dolly Parton, and Lily Tomlin, depicted female office workers turning tables on their harasser boss with triumphal glee. That same year, the well-known actor Ed Asner narrated an award-winning documentary film identifying sexual harassment as an "abuse of power."[25] Sexual harassment was no longer cool or winked at around the water cooler. It was newly perceived as risky, as a practice that could bring denunciation and negative consequences down upon its perpetrators.

While we failed to transform the misogynist labels that stuck to women who complained of sexual harassment, we raised the spectre

---

24 See, for example, Baker, above note 7, and the current research of Sandy Welsh, professor of sociology, University of Toronto.

25 Baker, above note 7 at 89 and 105.

that there might be a complaint. Would-be harassers were forced to take the prospect of notoriety and public embarrassment into the equation. Of course, many harassers failed to see that their actions were offensive or coercive, and they were left in some bewilderment as to what all the fuss was about. However, even they began to recognize that sexualized behaviour at work could potentially prove detrimental. The media frenzy that surrounded Anita Hill's sexual harassment allegations against Clarence Thomas in his 1991 US Supreme Court confirmation hearings took the discussion to new heights. Clarence Thomas may have achieved appointment to the court, but no one who witnessed the hearings would ever imagine again that behaviour such as his was free of risk.[26]

Intellectually, the scope of sexual harassment expanded enormously. The brand new concept birthed in 1975 grew by leaps and bounds as women began to articulate their diverse experiences. The first cases had been mainly examples of unwelcome overtures for sex — sometimes described as "put out or get out" or "quid pro quo" sexual harassment. The second group involved women who were harmed by a more generally sexualized workplace — sometimes described as "gender harassment" or "poisoned environment." There was no outright request for sex but, rather, a pattern of demeaning sexual comments, jokes, abusive anonymous phone calls, pornographic visual material, and bizarre practices that stereotyped and demeaned women as sex objects. Women who were moving into all-male workplaces often reported this type of harassment, which seemed designed to run them out of the job. Furthermore, the venues expanded to include harassment in education, housing, on the street, and on the Internet.

Sexual harassment also bumped up against the concept of "intersectionality." Workplace harassment was not limited solely to sex but was also based on race, ethnicity, nationality, religion, sexual identity, class, disability, and other forms of discrimination. As women began to report diverse forms of harassment, we learned more about these complicating factors. For example, Black and Aboriginal women reported that race lay at the root of much of the harassment they experienced and that racist stereotypes shaped the forms of the harassment itself. They explained that it was impossible to untangle the racism from the sexism. Lesbians reported that homophobia was central to the harassment that

26 See Toni Morrison, ed, *Race-ing Justice, En-gender-ing Power: Essays on Anita Hill, Clarence Thomas, and the Construction of Social Reality* (New York: Pantheon, 1992).

was directed at them. Women with disabilities reported that stereotypes about mental and physical disabilities were interlaced with coercive sexual overtures.

The feminist movement was being challenged more broadly to take account of issues such as racism, homophobia, and disability, and this critique helped pave the way towards recognizing that issues of gender could not be resolved in isolation. Calls to end sexual harassment grew to include demands to eradicate racial harassment, disability harassment, religious harassment, sexual identity harassment, age harassment, and ultimately "personal" harassment, which was understood as bullying or ostracizing that was perpetrated upon any employee — female or male — in the workplace. Some have critiqued this most recent focus on "personal harassment" or "workplace bullying" as potentially problematic, arguing that the newly neutralized concept risks stripping out the real dynamics of gender discrimination. Nevertheless, the many new directions have heralded important corrections to our initial preoccupation with gender alone.[27]

The legal landscape was also transformed. When *The Secret Oppression* was published, there were no laws that specifically addressed sexual harassment. Within a year, the first Canadian human rights tribunal to rule on the subject held that sexual harassment was prohibited under the Ontario *Human Rights Code* as a form of "sex discrimination."[28] Shortly thereafter, many Canadian jurisdictions amended their human rights statutes to prohibit sexual harassment explicitly.[29]

---

27 Some of the earliest activists against sexual harassment had acknowledged intersectionality from the outset. See Baker, above note 7, describing at 96–100 the work of Freada Klein and others.

28 *Bell v Ladas* (1980), 1 CHRR D/155 (ON Board of Inquiry). Despite this progressive interpretation, Chair Owen Shime concluded that the two women waitresses had not proved their allegations of sexual harassment against their manager and dismissed their claim. This was to become a pattern, where adjudicators dismissed women's claims based on assessments of credibility that borrowed heavily from the deeply flawed criminal law of evidence and sexual assault. Constance Backhouse, "*Bell v The Flaming Steer Steak House Tavern*: Canada's First Sexual Harassment Decision," Case Comment (1981) 19 UWO L Rev 141. Ontario *Human Rights Code*, RSO 1990, c H.19.

29 The federal *Canadian Human Rights Act*, RSC 1985, c H-6, and the majority of the provincial human rights statutes now prohibit harassment — in many jurisdictions, ranging well beyond sexual harassment to include harassment on grounds additional to sex. Arjun P Aggarwal, *Sexual Harassment: A Guide for Understanding and Prevention*, 2d ed (Toronto: Butterworths,

Bonnie Robichaud's 1980 complaint against the federal Department of National Defence was the first to reach the Supreme Court of Canada. The first woman hired as a "lead hand cleaner" in North Bay, Robichaud found herself the victim of physically coercive sexual assaults by her male supervisor. She emerged victorious in 1987, after a gruelling litigation journey that provoked serious work reprisals, suspension without pay, and a $30,000 lawsuit for defamation. Although she never recouped more than minimal compensation, Robichaud did obtain a public apology and a new posting to a secure governmental job in Ottawa. Most importantly, she obtained a ruling from the Supreme Court of Canada that employers were liable for the sexual harassment in their workplaces.[30]

Quick on her heels, two Winnipeg waitresses, Diana Janzen and Tracey Govereau, also won in 1989, when the Supreme Court of Canada laid down a wide-ranging definition of sexual harassment in the hearing of their complaint against the restaurant cook.[31] The Women's Legal Education and Action Fund (LEAF), which was founded in April 1985, would spearhead many of the legal initiatives, providing brilliant and innovative analysis that transformed courtroom debates.

2006); Arjun Aggarwal & Madhu M Gupta, *Sexual Harassment in the Workplace*, 3d ed (Toronto: Butterworths, 2000) [Aggarwal & Gupta]; Lori McDowell, *Understanding Workplace Harassment* (Scarborough, ON: Thomson Carswell, 1997) at 137–42.

30 *Robichaud v Canada*, [1987] 2 SCR 84. The ruling overturned the initial sexist tribunal decision of RD Abbott, *Robichaud v Canada* (1983), 4 CHRR D/1272. See also Centre for Research and Education on Violence against Women and Children, "The Centre Recognizes 'Every Day Heros'" (Spring 2008) vol 1 *Building Partnerships* [newsletter] 5; Arjun P Aggarwal, "*Robichaud v R*: Confirmation of Employers' Liability for Human Rights Violations by Employees," Case Comment (1987–88) 33 McGill LJ 194.

31 *Janzen v Platy Enterprises Ltd*, [1989] 1 SCR 1252, held that "sexual harassment in the workplace may be broadly defined as unwelcome conduct of a sexual nature that detrimentally affects the work environment or leads to adverse job-related consequences for the victims of the harassment." The ruling reversed the earlier ruling below, a sexist decision by the Manitoba Court of Appeal (1986), 33 DLR (4th) 32. See Mariann Burka, "Sexual Harassment: Manitoba's Step Backward," Case Comment on *Govereau and Janzen v Platy Enterprises Ltd* (1987) 16 Man LJ 245; Alan LW D'Silva, "*Janzen v Platy*," Case Comment (1989) 14 Queen's LJ 291; Kathleen Gallivan, "Sexual Harassment after *Janzen v. Platy*: The Transformative Possibilities" (1991) 49 UT Fac L Rev 27; Ivan F Ivankovich, "Sexual Harassment in the Workplace — Two Steps Backward: *Janzen and Govereau v Platy Enterprises Ltd*." (1987–88) 26 Alta L Rev 359.

The legal victories were not without problems. Legal remedies were costly, venomously adversarial, subject to devastating delays, and almost invariably sparked retributive defamation suits.[32] Primarily white, male adjudicators frequently belittled the evidence, disbelieved the complainants, laced their decisions with sexist assumptions, and failed to award proper compensation. The harassers who were found liable were disproportionately racialized or otherwise vulnerable. The law required individualized complaints for a systemic problem, and the individual women paid dearly — their lives and livelihood often destroyed along the way. However, despite all of the perils, the whole legal infrastructure had shifted. At the level of legal principle, at least, sexual harassment was marked out for sanction in a way that seemed to tower above the more muted improvements in the laws relating to rape, battering, and employment equity.

Workplace structures also gave way. Taking stock of their new legal liability, employers began to educate their staff, and large numbers of institutions implemented sexual harassment policies. Although these too may have been more rhetorical than real, the new policies offered some harassed workers the option of internal investigations and remedies. Consultants who offered training, investigation, and mediation services sprung up to populate a new field in human resources. Unions also changed with the times. Although they often chose to protect union members who were harassers over members who were harassed, they also bargained enforceable "sexual harassment clauses" into their collective agreements.[33] There was a flowering of academic, labour relations,

---

32 Even when no harassers were named, defamation proceedings were launched. A group of Carleton University journalism students held a press conference to denounce sexual harassment within the faculty in March 1980. Three male professors brought suit for $100,000 because they felt they had been unfairly implicated.

33 Susan Attenborough, "Sexual Harassment: An Issue for Unions" in Linda Briskin & Lynda Yanz, eds, *Union Sisters: Women in the Labour Movement* (Toronto: Women's Educational Press, 1983) 136; Susan Attenborough, *Sexual Harassment at Work* (Ottawa: National Union of Provincial Government Employees, 1981); Judy Haiven, "Zero Tolerance: Can It Work in a Unionized Environment?" (2006) 58 Labour/Le Travail 169; Pradeep Kumar & Lynn Acri, "Unions' Collective Bargaining Agenda on Women's Issues: The Ontario Experience" (1992) 47 Industrial Relations 623; Lori L Park, "Fair Representation and Conflict of Interest: Sexual Harassment Complaints between Co-Workers" (1997) 6 Dal J Leg Stud 121; K Wayne Taylor, "Penalty Standards for Sexual Harassment Offences in Unionized Workplaces" (1998) 53 Industrial Relations 1.

business management, and feminist writing on sexual harassment.[34] In short, workplaces too changed in discernible and palpable ways.

G. OTTAWA CITY HALL, NOVEMBER 1981

When we started, we hoped to change the world. We did not come close to creating a society in which sexual harassment would be unthinkable. Women from a vast array of diverse occupations — policing, firefighting, the military, and the law, to mention but a few — continue to suffer untold egregious forms of sexual harassment. However, as I reflect back to that morning in Ottawa's city hall, when I stood at the podium, anxiously hoping to measure up to at least some of the expectations of the feminists who had asked me to speak on sexual harassment, the memory of the sense of electricity is almost palpable. I remember all too well the hostile facial expressions and body language of the men in the front rows. And yet I also remember that looking out over that packed room, I was heartened by the positive, expectant expressions on the faces of others.

I spoke uninterrupted for about thirty minutes, as I related the stories of women who had suffered from sexual harassment and described the shocking epidemic of coercive male sexual aggression in the workplace. I spoke about the patterns of gender dynamics, the behaviours that flowed from male dominance and female subordination. I talked about the deep chasm that separated men and women in our culture and the damage that ensued from this disjunction. I tried to unmask the injustice of patriarchal attitudes and to exhort women to join the collective struggle to resist. I challenged all of the people in that room to turn the tide to eradicate sexual harassment at work. I do not know whether I changed anyone's mind that morning. One can never know what innumerable factors bear upon something as complex as human beliefs and behaviour. However, I do know that I overheard people after the workshop talking heatedly in the aisles. At least one man commented with some astonishment that a gender war had been unleashed. At least one woman added: "About time."

---

34 See the bibliography at the end of this chapter.

BIBLIOGRAPHY

Arjun Aggarwal & Madhu M Gupta, Sexual Harassment in the Workplace, 3d ed (Toronto: Butterworths, 2000)

Arjun P Aggarwal & Madhu M Gupta, "Same-Sex Sexual Harassment: Is It Sex Discrimination? A Review of Canadian and American Law" (1999) 27 Man LJ 333

Janine Benedet, "Same-Sex Sexual Harassment in Employment" (2000–01) 26 Queen's LJ 101

Josée Bouchard, "La personne raisonnable en matière de harcèlement sexuel: Une appréciation féministe" (1995) 8 CJWL 89

Josée Bouchard, "Les mesures de redressement pour les victimes de harcèlement sexuel: Le *Code des droits de la personne* de l'Ontario" (1993–94) 19 Queen's LJ 551

Josée Bouchard, "L'indemnisation des victimes de harcèlement sexuel au Québec" (1995) 36 C de D 125

Joan Brockman, "The Use of Self-Regulation to Curb Discrimination and Sexual Harassment in the Legal Profession" (1997) 35 Osgoode Hall LJ 209

Deborah Ann Campbell, *The Evolution of Sexual Harassment Case Law in Canada* (Kingston, ON: Industrial Relations Centre, 1992)

J-Maurice Cantin, "Le harcèlement sexuel: une préoccupation majeure dans le monde des relation de travail" (1986) 17 RGD 271

Madeleine Caron, "Aux frontières du droit civil et du droit statutaire: Un cas de harcèlement sexuel: *Foisy c Bell Canada*" (1985) 19 RJT 79

Shirish P Chotalia, "Are Academic Freedom and Free Speech Defences to Poisoned Educational Environment? — What Can *Ross* Tell Us about Sexual Harassment?" (1994) 33 Alta L Rev 573

Shirish P Chotalia, "Sexual Harassment Laws in Canada: It's All a Question of Power" (1994–95) 3 Journal of Individual Employment Rights 155

Mary Cornish & Suzanne Lopez, "Changing the Workplace Culture through Effective Harassment Remedies" (1994–95) 3 CLELJ 95

Gillian Demeyere, "Common Law Actions for Sexual Harassment: The Jurisdiction Question Revisited" (2002–03) 28 Queen's LJ 637

Janet Dine & Bob Watt, "Sexual Harassment: Moving Away from Discrimination" (1995) 58 Mod L Rev 343

Pierre Douville, "Harcèlement sexuel: Les sanctions" in Denis Nadeau & Benoît Pelletier, eds, *Relation d'emploi et droits de la personne: Évolution et tensions!* (Cowansville, QC: Yvon Blais, 1994) 105

Maurice Drapeau, *Le harcèlement sexuel au travail: le régime juridique de protection* (Cowansville, QC: Yvon Blais, 1991)

Maurice Drapeau, "Le harcèlement sexuel," in Barreau du Québec, *Développements récents en droit du travail* (Cowansville, QC: Yvon Blais, 1992) 27

Maurice Drapeau, "Les conséquences de l'arrêt *Béliveau Saint-Jacques* sur les droits de recours des victimes de harcèlement discriminatoire ayant causé une lésion professionnelle?" in Barreau du Québec, *Développements récents en responsabilité civile* (Cowansville, QC: Yvon Blais, 1997) 1

Fay Faraday, "Dealing with Sexual Harassment in the Workplace: The Promise and Limitations of Human Rights Discourse" (1994) 32 Osgoode Hall LJ 33

Monique Gauvin, "Le harcèlement sexuel et sexiste comme pratique d'appropriation des femmes: La situation dans les universités canadiennes" (1991) Égalité 189

Nora A Gillespie, "Sexual Harassment Policies in the University Context" (1994–95) 3 CLELJ 225

Sandy Goundry, "Sexual Harassment in the Employment Context: The Legal Management of Working Women's Experience" (1985) 43 UT Fac L Rev 1

Linda Geller-Schwartz, *Comprendre pour agir: Stratégies d'élimination du harcèlement sexuel en milieu de travail* (Ottawa: Ministre des Approvisionnements et Services Canada, 1994)

MA Hickling, "Employer's Liability for Sexual Harassment" (1987) 17 Man LJ 124

Patricia Hughes, "The Evolving Conceptual Framework of Sexual Harassment" (1994–95) 3 CLELJ 1

Holly Johnson, "Work-Related Sexual Harassment" (1994) 6:4 Perspectives on Labour and Income 1

Marlene Kadar, "Sexual Harassment: Where We Stand Research and Policy" (1983) 3 Windsor YB Access Just 358

Lynn Kaye, "Where Women Refuse to be Victims" (1985) 10 Status of Women 4

John Kilcoyne, "The 'Politics of Policies': Responding to Sexual Harassment on Campus" (1994–95) 3 CLELJ 33

Lucie Lamarche, "Définition de harcèlement sexuel prohibé sur les lieux de travail en droit canadien" (1986–88) 2 CJWL 113

Louise Langevin, "Le harcèment sexuel au travail: L'impact de la decision *Béliveau Saint-Jacques*" (1997) 9 CJWL 17

Louise Langevin, "Responsabilité extracontractuelle et harcèlement sexuel: Le modèle évaluation peut-il être neutre?" (1995) 36 C de D 99

Katherine Lippel & Diane Demers, *Access to Justice for Sexual Harassment Victims: The Impact of Béliveau St-Jacques on Female Workers' Right to Damages* (Ottawa: Status of Women Canada, 1998)

Katherine Lippel & Diane Demers, "La harcèlement sexuel au travail: La rencontre du droit de la santé au travail et des droits de la personne" (2000) 12 CJWL 32

Kathleen E Mahoney, "Problems in the Law of Sexual Harassment" in E Diane Pask, Kathleen E Mahoney, & Catherine A Brown, eds, *Women, the Law and the Economy* (Toronto: Butterworths, 1985) 41

Kirsti McLean, "The Disclosure of Clinical Records in the Context of Sexual Harassment" (1996) 6 ELLR 89

Maeve McMahon, *Women on Guard: Discrimination and Harassment in Corrections* (Toronto: University of Toronto Press, 1999)

Caroline Meilleur & Mylène Sabourin, "Le harcèlement sexuel en milieu de travail" in Denis Nadeau & Benoît Pelletier, eds, *Relation d'emploi et droits de la personne: Évolution et tensions!* (Cowansville, QC: Yvon Blais, 1994) 121

Nina Moritsugu, "Sex Discrimination in the Workplace May Be Hazardous to Your Health: A Call for Workers' Compensation Benefits for Victims of Sexual Harassment" (1994) 10 J L & Soc Pol'y 217

Barbara Orser, *Sexual Harassment Is Still a Management Issue* (Ottawa: Conference Board of Canada, 2001)

Rachel L Osborne, "Sexual Harassment in Universities: A Critical View of the Institutional Response" (1992) 12 Canadian Woman Studies 72

Chantal Richard, "Surviving Student to Student Sexual Harassment: Legal Remedies and Prevention Programmes" (1996) 19 Dal LJ 169

Dominique Savoie & Viateur Larouche, "Le harcèlement sexuel au travail: Définition et mesure du phénomène" (1988) 43 RI 509

Karen Schucher, "Achieving a Workplace Free of Sexual Harassment: The Employer's Obligations" (1994–95) 3 CLELJ 171

Aysan Sev'Er, "Sexual Harassment: Where We Were, Where We Are and Prospects for the New Millennium: Introduction to the Special Issue" (1999) 36 Canadian Review of Sociology and Anthropology 469

Colleen Sheppard, "Systemic Inequality and Workplace Culture: Challenging the Institutionalization of Sexual Harassment" (1994–95) 3 CLELJ 249

Kathleen Storrie, "Work Environment, Sexual Harassment and Women's Health" in B Singh Bolaria & Rosemary Bolaria, eds, *Women, Medicine and Health* (Halifax: Fernwood, 1994) 301

Kathleen Storrie, Pearl Dykstra, & Kelleen Wiseman, "Bibliography on Sexual Harassment" (1981–82) 10 Resources for Feminist Research 25

Russel J Summers & Karin Myklebust, "The Influence of a History of Romance on Judgments and Responses to a Complaint of Sexual Harassment" (1992) 27 Sex Roles 345

Sylvain Toupin, "Le harcèlement sexuel en milieu de travail" (1988) 43 RI 531
Marvin A Zuker & Wilfred J Wilkinson, "Sexual Harassment: *A v E*," Case Comment (1993) 4 Educ & LJ 309.

CHAPTER 9

FROM SEXUAL TO PSYCHOLOGICAL HARASSMENT: ONE STEP FORWARD, TWENTY-FIVE YEARS BACK FOR WOMEN'S EQUALITY AT WORK?

Rachel Cox[1]

A. INTRODUCTION

In 2004, adoption of legislation guaranteeing a work environment free from psychological harassment in Québec appeared to be a victory for all employees, but particularly so for women. Psychological harassment itself is a gendered phenomenon. In Québec, as is the situation elsewhere, women are more often than men the targets of psychological harassment, and men are more often than women the ones doing the harassing.[2] It would appear that gender even trumps hierarchical rela-

---

1 Rachel Cox is a professor of law at the Faculty of Political Science and Law of the Université du Québec à Montréal (UQÀM) and a member of the Québec Bar.

2 Katherine Lippel, "Le harcèlement psychologique au travail : portrait des recours juridiques au Québec et des décisions rendues par la Commission des lésions professionnelles" (2005) 7:3 Perspectives interdisciplinaires sur le travail et la santé (PISTES), online: PISTES www.pistes.uqam.ca/v7n3/pdf/v7n3a13.pdf; Carole Dupéré, "Pour en connaître d'avantage sur les personnes ayant porté plainte pour harcèlement psychologique à la Commission des normes du travail" (2009) 5 Regards sur le travail 40; Ruth Simpson & Claire Cohen, "Dangerous Work; The Gendered Nature of Bullying in the Context of Higher Education" (2004) 11:2 Gender, Work and Organisation 163. For racialized women, see Susy Fox & Lamont E Stallworth, "Race and Ethnicity as Factors in Workplace Bullying" (Paper delivered at the symposium Work, Stress, and Health March 2008 Conference, Washington, DC) [Fox & Stallworth, "Race and Ethnicity"]. Careful analysis is necessary to determine to what extent the sexual segregation of the labour market and the nature of typical women's work are related to these findings.

tionships at work, as hierarchical power in the workplace insulates men, but not women, from harassment by their hierarchical subordinates.[3]

Power and specifically unequal power relationships are central to the notion of psychological harassment,[4] just as they are to sexual harassment[5] and racial harassment.[6] Research on incivility and harassment in the workplace reveals a latent, systemically discriminatory element even in cases in which the incivility or harassment initially appears to be of a purely individual nature.[7] At the same time, blatant sex and race discrimination has become less socially acceptable.[8] This suggests that in the current legal framework, psychological harassment legislation could be a crucial addition to human rights legislation in order to protect women workers from more insidious manifestations of power imbalances between men and women. Recourse in cases of psycho-

---

3 Katherine Lippel et al., "Chapitre 5: Violence au travail : harcèlement psychologique, harcèlement sexuel et violence physique" in Institut national de santé publique du Québec, Institut de la statistique du Québec et Institut de recherche Robert-Sauvé en santé et sécurité du travail, *Enquête québécoise sur des conditions de travail d'emploi et de santé et de sécurité du travail (EQCOTESST)* (Montréal: IRSST, 2011) at 335 [EQCOTESST], online: Institut national de santé publique du Québec www.inspq.qc.ca/pdf/publications/1336_EnqQuebCondTravailEmpSantSecTravail.pdf.

4 Denise Salin, "Workplace Bullying among Business Professionals: Prevalence, Gender Differences and the Role of Organizational Politics" (2005) 7:3 Perspectives interdisciplinaires sur le travail et la santé (PISTES), online: PISTES www.pistes.uqam.ca/v7n3/pdf/v7n3a2en.pdf.

5 Catharine MacKinnon, *The Sexual Harassment of Working Women: A Case of Sex Discrimination* (New Haven, CT: Yale University Press, 1979) [MacKinnon, *Sexual Harassment*].

6 *Québec (Commission des droits de la personne et des droits de la jeunesse) c Québec (Procureur général)*, 2008 QCTDP 8 at paras 123ff [*Pavilus*].

7 For example, higher prevalence rates of harassment for African-American teachers dropped off when school principals were also African-Americans. Perpetrators tend to select racial and ethnic minorities as the targets of their (apparently) purely psychological harassment. See Fox & Stallworth, "Race and Ethnicity," above note 2. See also Susy Fox & Lamont E Stallworth, "Racial/ethnic Bullying: Exploring the Links between Bullying and Racism in the U.S. Workplace" (2005) 66 Journal of Vocational Behavior 438.

8 Sandy Lim & Lilia M Cortina, "Interpersonal Mistreatment in the Workplace: The Interface and Impact of General Incivility and Sexual Harassment" (2005) 90 Journal of Applied Psychology 483; Lilia M Cortina, "Unseen Injustice: Incivility as Modern Discrimination in Organizations" (2008) 33 Academy of Management Review 55; Ruth Simpson & Claire Cohen, "Dangerous Work; The Gendered Nature of Bullying in the Context of Higher Education" (2004) 11:2 Gender, Work and Organisation 163.

logical harassment is thus potentially one more tool in women's struggle for equality in the workplace.

In Québec, provisions on psychological harassment are housed in the *Act respecting Labour Standards*.[9] Psychological harassment is defined as:

> . . . any vexatious behaviour in the form of repeated and hostile or unwanted conduct, verbal comments, actions or gestures, that affects an employee's dignity or psychological or physical integrity and that results in a harmful work environment for the employee.
>
> A single serious incidence of such behaviour that has a lasting harmful effect on an employee may also constitute psychological harassment.[10]

The definition of psychological harassment is largely inspired by the definition of sexual harassment laid out by the Supreme Court of Canada in the landmark *Janzen v Platy Enterprises Ltd* case[11] and elaborated on by the Québec Court of Appeal in *Habachi c Québec (Commission des droits de la personne)*.[12] It is common ground that the definition of psychological harassment encompasses all forms of discriminatory harassment including sexual and racial harassment.[13]

The non-unionized employee who believes that she or he is being harassed at work can lay a complaint with the Labour Standards Commission as soon as her or his dignity is affected. The Commission conducts an investigation into the complaint and works with the parties in an attempt to settle the complaint.[14] If the Commission considers the complaint to be well-founded and attempts at mediation are unsuccessful, the Commission's litigation department assumes carriage of the complaint (at no charge to the worker) before the Labour Relations Board.[15] The Labour Relations Board then holds a hearing and renders a decision on the complaint.[16]

---

9 RSQ 1979, c N-1.1 [*Labour Standards Act*].

10 *Ibid*, s 81.18.

11 *Janzen v Platy Enterprises Ltd.*, [1989] 1 SCR 1252 [*Janzen*].

12 *Habachi c Québec (Commission des droits de la personne)*, 1999 CanLII 13338 (QC CA).

13 *JurisClasseur Rapports individuels et collectifs du travail*, fasc 23 by Katherine Lippel, Rachel Cox, & Isabelle Aubé, No 321 [JurisClasseur].

14 *Labour Standards Act*, above note 9, ss 123.8, 123.10, and 123.12.

15 *Ibid*, ss 123.12–123.13.

16 *Ibid*, ss 123.14–123.16.

Unionized workers[17] also benefit from the provisions on psychological harassment. The definitions and remedies set out in the *Labour Standards Act* are deemed to be a part of all collective agreements.[18] Recourse against psychological harassment is then via a grievance under the collective agreement.

In the eight years before the coming into effect of Québec's legislation on psychological harassment in June 2004, the Québec Human Rights Tribunal rendered twenty-five decisions on sexual and racial harassment at work. The vast majority of these decisions involve non-unionized workers (see Annex 1).[19] In the eight years since,[20] the Tribunal's caselaw on harassment at work has fallen off dramatically. Since June 2004, the Tribunal has rendered only two decisions on harassment at work — both involving third party harassers — that took place after the psychological harassment legislation came into effect.[21] In the first case, in a one-time incident, a public transit inspector (a man) was harassed by a member of the public because he was Black. In the other, a warehouse foreman (a man) was harassed by an independent computer consultant who had discovered that he was gay (see Annex 2).

---

17 Forty percent of the Québec workforce is unionized. See Statistics Canada, *Labour Force Historical Review 2007* (Ottawa: StatCan, 2008).

18 *Labour Standards Act*, above note 9, s 81.20. Colleen Sheppard questions the "fairness of requiring some employees to pursue a more private enforcement system (i.e. grievance arbitration) rather than a public system (i.e. the human rights or unjust dismissal tribunal)." See Colleen Sheppard, *Rights, Respect and Dignity: Interface of Labour Standards and Human Rights Legislation* (Research Report, prepared for the Federal Labour Standards Task Force, November 2005), online: Human Resources and Skill Development Canada www.rhdcc.gc.ca/fra/travail/normes_travail/ntf/recherche/recherche14/page00.shtml. However, this question goes beyond the scope of this chapter.

19 Methods involved searching the SOQUIJ Azimut in the "Tribunaux judiciaires" database for decisions citing section 10.1 of the *Charter of Human Rights and Freedoms*, RSQ 1975, c C-12 [*Charter*] (interdiction to harass on the basis of a prohibited ground of discrimination).

20 Research is up to date as of 31 May 2012.

21 Three further decisions are based on facts that took place well before 2004. See *Pavilus*, above note 6; *Québec (Commission des droits de la personne et des droits de la jeunesse) c D.L.*, 2007 QCTDP 23; *Québec (Commission des droits de la personne et des droits de la jeunesse) c Épicerie boucherie St-Antonin*, 2005 CanLII 18112 (QC TDP). Presumably these cases involve complaints laid before June 2004 (the decisions do not usually mention the date on which the initial complaint was laid at the Human Rights Commission).

The ineluctable conclusion is that since the coming into effect of the psychological harassment law in June 2004, in non-unionized workplaces, psychological harassment complaints have for all intents and purposes replaced human rights complaints of harassment at work. Similarly, while there are numerous grievance arbitration awards on psychological harassment,[22] there is also a dearth of Québec Human Rights Tribunal decisions on discriminatory harassment at work in unionized workplaces, though perhaps for somewhat different reasons than in non-unionized workplaces.[23] This chapter makes a preliminary inquiry as to what this change of forum means for women's equality rights. More specifically, what does it mean when sexual or racial harassment or other kinds of discriminatory harassment[24] at work is framed as psychological harassment?

---

22 Rachel Cox, "Psychological Harassment Legislation in Québec: The First Five Years" (2010) 32 International Comparative Labor Law and Policy Journal 55 [Cox, "Psychological Harassment Legislation"].

23 In 2003, the Supreme Court of Canada decided that, regardless of the actual provisions of the collective agreement, recourse in case of discriminatory acts in unionized work environments lies with grievance arbitration. See *Parry Sound (District), Social Services Administration Board v OPSEU, Local* 324, 2003 SCC 42 [*Parry Sound*]. The Supreme Court recognized that even if human rights tribunals have greater expertise on human rights issues than grievance arbitrators, "any concerns in respect of this matter are outweighed by the significant benefits associated with the availability of an accessible and informal forum for the prompt resolution of allegations of human rights violations in the workplace" (*ibid* at para 53). Rendered just before Québec adopted its psychological harassment law, the *Parry Sound* decision might have single-handedly prevented unionized workers from laying human rights complaints regarding harassment at work. However, even before 2003, the vast majority of Québec Human Rights Tribunal decisions concern non-unionized workers (twenty-three out of twenty-five, see Annex 1). The small number of grievances for discriminatory harassment could also be explained in part because of unions' ability to deal with many situations of discriminatory harassment without having to go to arbitration. See Rachel Cox, "Harcèlement psychologique : Perspectives syndicales sur un phénomène social" (Presentation delivered at the Centrale syndicale du Québec, Health and Safety Delegates' Network, Ste-Foy, Québec, 16 May 2012), [unpublished, archived with the author].

24 Following the pattern set by the caselaw, which in turn reflects who has rights that can be sanctioned and who can and does litigate, this chapter focuses on sexual and racial harassment. We are nonetheless keenly aware that working women experience harassment on many different and intersecting grounds prohibited by the *Charter*. See, for example, Jennifer L Berdahl & Celia Moore, "Workplace Harassment: Double Jeopardy for Minority Women" (2006) 91 Journal of Applied Psychology 426. In the same

In order to answer these questions, this chapter looks both at Québec's Human Rights Tribunal caselaw on discriminatory harassment at work as well as at the decisions of Québec's Labour Relations Board and grievance arbitrators on psychological harassment. Careful analysis of the caselaw on *psychological* harassment complaints by non-unionized workers reveals that even though the harassment is not necessarily named as "sexual"[25] or "racial"[26] or "based on religious belief,"[27] several decisions clearly involve harassment based on discriminatory grounds (see Annex 3). Furthermore, framing sexual or racial harassment as psychological harassment appears to have had particular consequences on the success or failure of the complaint.

To give one example, the ninety-day time period for filing a complaint of psychological harassment has led to refusal of complaints of sexual harassment framed as psychological harassment. Had the same facts been argued as sexual or racial harassment under the *Charter of Human Rights and Freedoms*[28] (*Charter*), the complainant would have had two years after the last relevant fact before her rights were extinguished (see Section B, below).

Too, many jurists initially saw the inclusion of sexual harassment in the definition of psychological harassment as representing a less onerous burden of proof for complainants, given that under psychological

---

vein, the decisions on racial harassment looked at for this chapter involve only complainants who are men. While the analogy is not perfect, we discuss these cases as the nearest available proxy for caselaw on harassment of racialized working women.

25 *Desjardins c Maison du Spaghetti (A et Compagnie A)*, 2007 QCCRT 28; *GS c HF*, 2007 QCCRT 295, aff'd 2007 QCCRT 530; *Roy c Maisons Laprise*, 2008 QCCRT 86 [*Maisons Laprise*]; *SH c Compagnie A*, 2007 QCCRT 348 [*SH*]; *CC c Gestion A Bossé Inc*, 2008 QCCRT 399, aff'd 2010 QCCS 1159 [*Gestion A Bossé*]; *Lizotte c Alimentation Coop La Pocatière*, 2008 QCCRT 240, aff'd 2008 QCCRT 521; *Rodriguez Vergara c 9169-1022 Québec inc*, 2009 QCCRT 224 [*Rodriguez Vergara*]; *Dupuis c Commission scolaire de la Riveraine*, 2009 QCCRT 3, aff'd 2010 QCCS 481 [*Dupuis*]; *Rioux c Commission touristique du Port-Joli inc*, 2011 QCCRT 473 [*Rioux*].

26 *Dian c Pêcheries Norref Québec inc*, 2007 QCCRT 551 [*Norref*]; *Cebert c Groupe d'imprimerie Saint-Joseph inc*, 2009 QCCRT 373, aff'd 2010 QCCS 7114 [*Cebert*]; *Monongo c Coffres-forts CB 2000 inc*, 2010 QCCRT 290, aff'd 2012 QCCS 4085.

27 *Cheikh-Bandar et Pfizer Canada inc*, 2008 QCCRT 124, aff'd 2008 QCCS 4811 [*Cheikh-Bandar*]. See Annex 3. Methods involved updating a database constructed in the context of the author's doctoral research project. See Cox , "Psychological Harassment Legislation," above note 22.

28 *Charter*, above note 19.

harassment legislation, it is not necessary to prove a link between the harassment and a prohibited ground of discrimination. A number of authors have pointed out that the line between sexual and psychological harassment can be a fine — and shifting — one.[29] However, a careful reading of several decisions reveals that if a complaint of sexual or racial harassment is heard as a psychological harassment complaint, in certain respects, the burden of proof on the harassed worker may be heavier than before. There are additional elements to prove such as injury to dignity and, in the case of a single serious incidence of harassment, a lasting harmful effect on the target. Complaints of sexual or racial harassment that would appear to be well-founded under the *Charter* have been rejected under the psychological harassment law (see Section C, below).

Whereas human rights law holds employers vicariously responsible for damages suffered by targets of harassment, employers' obligations under psychological harassment law are of "reasonable means" rather than performance obligations. A psychological harassment complaint can be rejected even if harassment has been proven, as long as the employer demonstrates due diligence in putting a stop to it (see Section D, below). And a psychological harassment complaint can only be laid against the employer, thus sheltering the harasser from any personal responsibility for his — or more rarely, her — acts (see Section E, below).

Taking a more global perspective, sexual harassment, in particular, has historically been seen as a question of women's equality, central to women's struggle for substantive equality both in economic and sexual terms. Sexual and racial harassment remain significant obstacles

---

29 Marie-France Hirigoyen, *Malaise dans le travail, harcèlement moral : Démêler le vrai du faux* (Paris: Éditions La Découverte & Syros, 2001) at 30 and 81; Ada Garcia, Bernard Hacourt, & Viriginie Bara, "Harcèlement moral et sexuel. Stratégies d'adaptation et conséquences sur la santé des travailleurs et des travailleuses" (2005) 7:3 Perspectives interdisciplinaires sur le travail et la santé (PISTES), online: PISTES www.pistes.uqam.ca/v7n3/pdf/v7n3a6.pdf. The *Québec (Human Rights Commission) v O'Hashi*, 1996 CanLII 12 (QC TDP) case, involving harassment of a nurse by a doctor, also illustrates that, in some cases, proving the link between the harassment and a prohibited ground of discrimination can be difficult. See also *Québec (Commission des droits de la personne et des droits de la jeunesse) c Buffet Trio*, 1999 CanLII 55 (QC TDP); *Lapointe c Sécur*, 1997 CanLII 68 (QC TDP) as examples of cases where managerial abuse is proven but where the complainant failed to prove a connection with a protected ground.

for women's equal access to the labour market.[30] Several studies confirm that women who refuse to meet gender expectations and hold jobs traditionally held by men are at a high risk of being harassed.[31] However, when sexual harassment is framed as a question of psychological harassment, the debate is diverted from the question of women's *equality* in a labour market marked by persistent systemic discrimination against women, to one of the individual's *dignity* in a given supposedly gender-neutral workplace. Psychological harassment lends itself to an individual analysis of a situation of harassment and thus tends to obscure its more systemic effects[32] . . . who is harassed where, by whom, and why, with what result (see Section F, below).

Finally, these considerations that came into play with the adoption of the provisions on psychological harassment are one more layer in a broader process of making physical and psychological violence against women at work invisible as such. This process is exemplified by the Supreme Court of Canada's 1996 ruling in *Béliveau St Jacques c Fédération des employées et employés de services publics inc*[33] that if a woman's health is compromised because of harassment at work, she is considered to have suffered an employment injury for which her exclusive recourse is a claim for workers' compensation benefits. The Supreme Court decided that the

---

30 Sandy Lim & Lilia M Cortina, "Interpersonal Mistreatment in the Workplace: The Interface and Impact of General Incivility and Sexual Harassment" (2005) 90:3 Journal of Applied Psychology 483; Alain Marchand, Pierre Durand, & Andrée Demers, "Work and Mental Health: The Experience of the Quebec Workforce between 1987 and 1998" (2005) 25:2 Work 135; Colleen Sheppard, "Systemic Inequality and Workplace Culture: Challenging the Institutionalization of Sexual Harassment" (1995) 3 CLELJ 249; Deborah Lee, "Gendered Workplace Bullying in the Restructured UK Civil Service" (2002) 31:1–2 Personnel Review 205 [Lee].

31 See, for example, Lee, *ibid*; Sharon K Parker & Mark A Griffin, "What Is So Bad about a Little Name-Calling? Negative Consequences of Gender Harassment for Overperformance Demands and Distress" (2002) 7:3 Journal of Occupational Health Psychology 195; Julie Konik & Lilia M Cortina, "Policing Gender at Work: Intersections of Harassment Based on Sex and Sexuality" (2008) 21 Social Justice Research 313 [Konik & Cortina]. The same is true for men in jobs traditionally held by women: Denise Salin, "Workplace Bullying among Business Professionals: Prevalence, Gender Differences and the Role of Organizational Politics" (2005) 7:3 Perspectives interdisciplinaires sur le travail et la santé (PISTES), online: PISTES www.pistes.uqam.ca/v7n3/pdf/v7n3a2en.pdf.

32 Cox, "Psychological Harassment Legislation," above note 22.

33 *Béliveau St Jacques c Fédération des employées et employés de services publics inc*, [1996] 2 SCR 345 [*Béliveau St Jacques*].

provisions of the *Act respecting industrial accidents and occupational diseases*[34] granting employers civil immunity in cases of employment injury prevail over the provisions of the *Charter* providing remedy in case of violation of fundamental rights.[35] Then in 1998, in *Québec (Commission des droits de la personne et des droits de la jeunesse) c Genest*, the Québec Court of Appeal went on to confirm that regardless of whether sexually harassed workers have actually filed a claim at the Workers' Compensation Board, if their health has been compromised, it is no longer possible for them to claim any damages at all in a human rights complaint.[36] Several authors have explored the far-reaching legal and political implications of these decisions.[37] This chapter touches just briefly on the specific implications of these decisions for a sexually or racially harassed woman's right to return to work and also, more generally, on the consequences for harassed women of access to remedy and redress only through multiple and sometimes, this chapter will argue, unsuitable avenues of recourse (see Section G, below).

B. EXTINGUISHING FUNDAMENTAL RIGHTS: SHORTER DELAYS TO FILE COMPLAINTS

One of the first consequences of framing sexual or racial harassment as psychological harassment lies with the shorter time period in which targets of sexual harassment may file a complaint. At first glance, the shorter timeline may appear to be a rather technical question. A closer

---

34 RSQ 1985, c A-3.001.

35 *Béliveau St Jacques*, above note 33.

36 *Québec (Commission des droits de la personne et des droits de la jeunesse) c Genest*, 1997 CanLII 66 (QC TDP) [*Genest*], leave to appeal to SCC refused, 28436 (20 September 2001). This is so whether it be a claim against their employer or the co-worker who harassed them.

37 See, for example, Katherine Lippel & Diane Demers, "Le harcèlement sexuel au travail: la rencontre du droit de la santé au travail et du droit de la personne" (2000) 12:1 CJWL/RFD 32 [Lippel & Demers]; Finn Makela, "'Tell Me Where It Hurts': Workplace Sexual Harassment Compensation and the Regulation of Hysterical Victims" (2006) 51 RD McGill 27; Maurice Drapeau, "Les conséquences de l'arrêt Béliveau St-Jacques sur les droits de recours des victimes de harcèlement discriminatoire ayant causé une lésion professionnelle" in Barreau du Québec, ed, *Développements récents en responsabilité civile (1997)* (Cowansville, QC: Yvon Blais, 1997) 1.

1 2 3 4 5 6 7 8 9 10 11 12 13 14

look at the caselaw reveals how closely it can be tied to extinguishing the rights for women who are sexually harassed at work.

For non-unionized employees, a complaint of psychological harassment must be filed "within 90 days of the last incidence of the offending behaviour."[38] For unionized employees, given that a collective agreement may grant a "more advantageous" condition of employment than required by labour standards,[39] harassment grievances have generally been understood to be subject to the general delay set out in collective agreements for filing a grievance, as long as this delay is longer than ninety days.[40]

In contrast, the *Charter* provides that the Human Rights Commission "may refuse or cease to act in favour of the victim" if "the complaint is based on acts or omissions the last of which occurred more than two years before the filing of the complaint."[41] These provisions on limitations of actions are in keeping with the purpose of the *Charter*, to promote, not continuity for business and stability in the balance of power as in the case of labour relations,[42] but rather, social change and a shift in the balance of power through implementation of equality rights for historically disadvantaged groups.

Dupuis c Commission scolaire de la Riveraine[43] provides an illustration of the consequences of framing sexual harassment as psychological harassment in terms of timeliness of complaints. In May 2006, a school principal (a woman) lodged a complaint of psychological harassment against a colleague who was also a school principal (a man) as well as the Director of the School Board (a man and their mutual superior). The basis for the complaint against the other school principal included gestures and comments constituting sexual harassment, such as a series of

38 *Labour Standards Act*, above note 9, s 123.7.

39 *Ibid*, s 94.

40 JurisClasseur, above note 13 at para 281. Nonetheless, even in public sector collective agreements, timelines are considerably shorter than the two years allowed by the *Charter*. The same comment applies for any labour grievance based on equality rights which are now considered to fall under the exclusive jurisdiction of a labour arbitrator. See *Parry Sound*, above note 23.

41 *Charter*, above note 19, s 77.

42 Diane L Demers, "Les tribunaux des droits de la personne : quel rôle et quelle place 'leur' réserve-t-on?" in Le Tribunal des droits de la personne & le Barreau du Québec, eds, *La Charte des droits et libertés de la personne: pour qui et jusqu'où?* (Cowansville, QC: Yvon Blais, 2005) 175.

43 *Dupuis*, above note 25.

inappropriate comments on the complainant's hair, clothes, and lips as well as demeaning nicknames ("babine" and "poupoune").

In 2008, the Labour Relations Board rejected the psychological harassment complaint against the other school principal on the basis that none of the gestures constituting sexual harassment had occurred in the ninety-day period preceding the complaint.[44] Indeed, according to the complainant, when she took matters into her own hands and formally requested that her colleague cease his embarrassing and humiliating comments, he then began to completely ignore her (in private) or interrupt and mock her (in public). The Labour Relations Board decision states that had she wished to complain about her colleague's behaviour, she should have done so within ninety days of the last sexual comment. As for his refusal to acknowledge her after she put him on notice to cease his inappropriate comments, the board found this to be, in the circumstances, an understandable reaction and not a further incidence of harassment.

To use the language of prescription, the short ninety-day "lapse of time" released her co-worker and their mutual employer from any responsibility for the months during which she endured the sexual harassment; her right to a work environment free from (psychological) harassment was extinguished because she had not "used" it promptly enough.[45] Had she framed her complaint as one of sexual harassment under the *Charter* and filed a complaint at the Human Rights Commission, only a "lapse of time" of two years would have been sufficient to release her colleague and employer from their responsibility for the comments and gestures constituting sexual harassment.

Alleged gestures of psychological harassment on behalf of the school board director coincided with the complainant's request that he intervene to stop the harassment by the other school principal. However, the Labour Relations Board found that the school board director's behaviour was a legitimate exercise of management rights in a context of relationships at work marked by a "niggling" and "unreasonable" attitude on the part of the complainant, namely in her attitude towards dealing with the other school principal who was sexually harassing her (one

---

44 *Dupuis c Commission scolaire de la Riveraine*, 2008 QCCRT 408, aff'd 2009 QCCRT 3, aff'd 2010 QCCS 481.

45 According to the *Civil Code*: "Prescription is a means . . . of being released by the lapse of time and according to the conditions fixed by law" (art 2875 CCQ). Extinctive prescription is defined as " . . . a means of extinguishing a right which has not been used . . . ." (art 2921 CCQ).

is tempted to ask, was the harasser not just as niggling and unreasonable?).

The complainant developed a psychological disability associated with her situation at work. The veritable legal saga that ensued illustrates the multiple avenues of recourse that a target of harassment must undertake to attempt to obtain remedy and redress. In 2006, as well as her psychological harassment complaint, she also filed a claim at the Québec workers' compensation board (CSST), which was eventually accepted during an administrative review process. In 2009, the appeals tribunal (Commission des lésions professionnelles) overturned the CSST's decision on review and refused her claim. Following the 2008 Labour Relations Board's decision, the appeals tribunal justified its decision on the basis that the facts on which the complaint of psychological harassment was based constituted a legitimate exercise of management rights. As for the alleged incidents of sexual harassment, the tribunal found "surprising" that the claimant's testimony was not corroborated. It nonetheless found the claimant to be credible and qualified several incidents as "completely inappropriate" and "simply unacceptable." However, the tribunal refused to recognize any relationship between these "isolated incidents" and the claimant's uncontested psychological disability (adjustment disorder with anxiety and depressed mood), pointing out that to do so would be inconsistent with the evidence that the claimant had not spoken about the sexual harassment until many months later, nor had she used an internal complaint process at the school board.[46] The tribunal's position was, to borrow from Catharine MacKinnon: "Not that the acts did not occur, but rather that it was unreasonable to experience them as harmful."[47]

In April 2012 (six years later), the Québec Court of Appeal overturned a 2010 Superior Court decision that the appeals tribunal decision was unreasonable and, in the end, the claimant received no compensation of any kind.[48] Her saga — six years of litigation on two different legal fronts — is not entirely exceptional. Since the psychological harassment law came into effect, on numerous occasions, women and men who develop a disability in relation to harassment at work have been dragged into litigation over jurisdictional and procedural issues, espe-

---

46 *Commission scolaire de la Riveraine et Dupuis*, 2009 QCCLP 3111 at paras 25 and 30–32, aff'd 2010 QCCS 6516.

47 MacKinnon, *Sexual Harassment*, above note 5 at 108.

48 *Commission scolaire de la Riveraine c Dupuis*, 2012 QCCA 626.

cially involving the interface between their employment injury claim and their recourse against the harassment *per se*.[49] Notable is the fact that, in this case, although the harassed woman received no compensation or validation of her experience of any kind, incidents of sexual harassment were proven both before the Labour Relations Board and the employment injury appeals tribunal.

C. ADDING TO THE BURDEN OF PROOF FOR COMPLAINANTS OF SEXUAL AND RACIAL HARASSMENT[50]

If a complaint of sexual or racial harassment is heard as a psychological harassment complaint, in certain respects, the burden of proof on the harassed worker may be heavier than before. There are additional elements to prove such as injury to dignity and, in the case of a single serious incidence of harassment, a lasting harmful effect on the target. Complaints of sexual or racial harassment that would appear to be well-founded under the *Charter* have been rejected under the psychological harassment law.

For example, in *Dian c Pêcheries Norref Québec inc*,[51] although vexatious behaviour was proven, the Labour Relations Board Commissioner found that the complainant's dignity had nonetheless remained intact and rejected the complaint. The complainant, a Black man working for a fishery company, had been the target of blatantly racist comments made by the assistant foreman. The assistant foreman attempted to fire the complainant who was then sent back to work by other management representatives. The complainant had worked previously for the company but had left to pursue his studies, yet comments were made insinuating that he was not literate. Some of the comments tended to be barely veiled threats. For example, one day, in the hostile context previously described, the foreman bragged, "I had my way with my Black guy, he worked here but I threw him out." The assistant foreman replied, looking directly at

---

49 Cox, "Psychological Harassment Legislation," above note 22; Anne-Marie Laflamme & Jennifer Nadeau, "Le harcèlement psychologique au travail: une atteinte à la santé ou à la dignité de la personne?" in *Conférence des juristes de l'État 2011* (Cowansville, QC: Yvon Blais, 2011) 437.

50 This section draws in part from Cox, "Psychological Harassment Legislation," above note 22 at 72–75.

51 *Norref*, above note 26.

the complainant, "I'm gonna have my way with my Black guy too." After an altercation in a corridor of the fisheries plant, the complainant complained to the police. Following an investigation by the police, the assistant foreman was charged with bodily assault of the complainant. The Labour Relations Board nonetheless rejected the complaint:

> The comments about blacks and immigrants are not admissible in a democratic society and this is even more the case in the workplace. The comments could be considered as humiliating or abusive, hostile or unwanted. It is clear that there was repetition of these comments. Can we then, however, conclude that they affected the dignity or the psychological or physical integrity of the complainant? The evidence is silent in this respect, unless we espouse an intellectual fiction that anyone who can be called "black" and an "immigrant" would feel that his or her dignity had been affected in similar circumstances.[52] [author's translation]

The Commissioner cites the fact that the complainant (with remarkable composure, one is tempted to add) systematically attempted to refute the racist comments and unwarranted criticism of his job performance by the assistant foreman to support his conclusion that, rather than a situation of psychological harassment, the facts were suggestive of an interpersonal conflict between the two men. This conclusion is surprising, given that the decision clearly describes how the complainant asked the assistant foreman why he was trying to humiliate him in front of the other employees. Even more poignant is the description of how, after being assaulted by his harasser, the complainant left the workplace in tears and never returned.[53]

In this case, it is clear that all of the elements necessary for a complaint of harassment on the basis of race and ethnic or national origin to succeed under the *Charter* are present. Yet under the *Labour Standards Act*, dignity is not considered to be affected, and the psychological harassment complaint is rejected.

In contrast, in 2010, the Human Rights Tribunal rendered a decision on a one-time incident of racial harassment in which a Black public transit inspector was the target of hostile and aggressive behaviour on the part of a tow truck driver parked illegally in a reserved bus lane. The tow truck driver yelled "I'm gonna make sure you lose your job, goddam

52 *Ibid* at para 51.
53 *Ibid* at paras 16 and 28.

nigger!" at the complainant, but was considerably politer to his non-racialized companion inspector.[54]

After having recalled that racial discrimination in all its forms is prohibited by international law and that Canada has legal obligations to fight racism to which Québec has also adhered, the Human Rights Tribunal describes the harmful effects of racism. It refers first to a decision on racial prejudice amongst jurors where the Supreme Court stated that: "Racial prejudice and its effects are as invasive and elusive as they are corrosive."[55] In the same decision, the Supreme Court also warned against underestimating "the insidious nature of racial prejudice and the stereotyping that underlies it" and pointed out that

> . . . racial prejudice . . . is a form of discrimination. It involves making distinctions on the basis of class or category without regard to individual merit. It rests on preconceptions and unchallenged assumptions that unconsciously shape the daily behaviour of individuals . . . .[56]

The Tribunal goes on to discuss the effects that language with racist overtones can have on racialized people:

> The effect that this kind of racist insult can have is never well understood by those that have never experienced it themselves. The person is robbed of his or her dignity and his or her self-esteem is violated, perhaps irreparably.[57] [author's translation]

The Tribunal then awarded $7,500 in moral damages and $500 in punitive damages to the complainant.

On one hand, in the *Norref* case where racial harassment was framed as psychological harassment, the Labour Relations Board refuted the existence of any "intellectual fiction" that when an employer representative constantly makes racist comments and slurs to a racialized

---

54 *Québec (Commission des droits de la personne et des droits de la jeunesse) c Remorquage Sud-Ouest (9148-7314 Québec inc.)*, 2010 QCTDP 12 [*Remorquage Sud-Ouest*]. For another example of a Québec Human Rights Tribunal decision on racial harassment and discrimination, see *Pavilus*, above note 6. Although the decision was rendered in 2008, the complainant's employment was terminated in 2001.

55 *R v Williams*, [1998] 1 SCR 1128 at para 22.

56 *Ibid* at para 21.

57 *Hinds v Canada (Employment and Immigration Commission)*, 1988 CanLII 109 (CHRT) Lederman J, cited in *Remorquage Sud-Ouest*, above note 54 at para 63.

employee, this affects the employee's dignity. On the other hand, for the Human Rights Tribunal, this supposedly non-existent "intellectual fiction" is seen to be an integral part of human rights law.[58] The contrast is striking.

Similarly, in *Lizotte c Alimentation Coop La Pocatière*,[59] the Labour Relations Board shows little sensitivity to or knowledge of the consequences and typical reactions and strategies women adopt when faced with sexual harassment at work. Although the Labour Relations Board Commissioner found a single serious incidence of vexatious behaviour in the form of a sexual assault, she found no "lasting harmful effect" on the complainant and rejected the complaint. The Commissioner found that the complainant, a woman who worked in a supermarket, had been the victim of vexatious behaviour by her supervisor. Specifically, in a context where her supervisor had been taking disciplinary action against her for alleged poor job performance, during a conference that she attended at the employer's request, her supervisor and another male employee, having consumed alcohol throughout the evening, came to the hotel room that she shared with a female colleague during the night. The director lay down in her bed and touched her breast. The next morning, he asked her not to talk about the incident. The following evening, he lewdly suggested to his male colleague that the latter pursue his conversation with the complainant in the intimacy of her hotel room.

Having rejected other allegations that her supervisor humiliated her and was excessively controlling of her activities at work, the Labour Relations Board Commissioner decided to consider the hotel room incident and lewd suggestion of the next day as a single serious incidence of vexatious behaviour. As previously discussed, a single serious incidence of vexatious behaviour can constitute psychological harassment on the condition that it "has a lasting harmful effect on an employee" (if harassment takes the form of *repeated* vexatious behaviour, the complainant need only prove a "harmful work environment"). The Labour Relations Board rejected the psychological harassment complaint, as the Commissioner found no evidence of a *lasting* harmful effect on the complainant. The Commissioner specifically cited the fact that a friend described the complainant at breakfast the next day as not seeming particularly bothered when she recounted the event in question.

---

58 See, namely, *Remorquage Sud-Ouest*, above note 54.

59 *Lizotte c Alimentation Coop La Pocatière*, 2008 QCCRT 240, aff'd 2008 QCCRT 521.

The Labour Relations Board review panel upheld the decision. The panel rejected the argument that any form of sexual assault on a woman by her supervisor necessarily creates a lasting harmful effect and affirmed that no such "presumption" is provided for by the provisions on psychological harassment.

Again, in contrast, for a complaint under the *Charter* to succeed, there is no requirement that a complainant prove the "lasting harmful effect" of sexual harassment or even a "harmful work environment." The Human Rights Tribunal caselaw is clear on this point:

> A violation of the right to not be subjected to harassment within the meaning of section 10.1 of the *Charter* constitutes, amongst other things, . . . a violation of every person's right to the safeguard of his or her dignity, as set out by section 4 [of the *Charter*], and does not require the existence of definitive consequences in order to find a violation.[60] [author's translation]

And according to the Supreme Court of Canada, sexual harassment in and of itself is considered as an affront to a woman's dignity:

> When sexual harassment occurs in the workplace, it is an abuse of both economic and sexual power. Sexual harassment is a demeaning practice, one that constitutes a profound affront to the dignity of the employees forced to endure it. By requiring an employee to contend with unwelcome sexual actions or explicit sexual demands, sexual harassment in the workplace attacks the dignity and self-respect of the victim both as an employee and as a human being.[61]

---

60 *Québec (Commission des droits de la personne et des droits de la jeunesse) c Caisse populaire Desjardins d'Amqui*, 2003 CanLII 48209 at para 67 (QC TDP), leave to appeal to QC CA refused, (23 January 2004), Québec 200-09-004700-040 [*Caisse populaire*].

61 *Janzen*, above note 11 at 1284. This point of view is consistent with the Québec Human Rights Tribunal's analysis of sexual harassment. For example, see *Québec (Commission des droits de la personne et des droits de la jeunesse) c Lavoie*, 1997 CanLII 51 (QC TDP); *Québec (Commission des droits de la personne et des droits de la jeunesse) c Syed*, 1998 CanLII 56 (QC TDP) in which the Human Rights Tribunal cites the *Inter-American Convention on the Prevention, Punishment and Eradication of Violence against Women*, 9 June 1994, 33:6 ILM 1534 (entered into force 5 March 1995) (violence against women including sexual harassment is described as a "manifestation of the historically unequal power relations between women and men") to support the idea that in and of itself, sexual harassment is an affront to women's dignity. See *Québec (Commission des droits de la personne et des droits de la jeunesse) c Sfiridis*, 2002

Indeed, dignity is the core value and a defining element of equality rights.[62] How, then, could racial harassment — by the Commissioner's own admission, repeated inadmissible "humiliating" comments about Blacks and immigrants made by a white foreman to a Black employee (the *Norref* case) — *not* affect the employee's dignity? How, then, could sexual assault by her supervisor *not* create a lasting harmful effect on a working woman?

Under psychological harassment legislation, on a practical level, the burden of proof on the complainant has thus been made heavier, which was surely not the intention when the psychological harassment legislation was adopted. Common forms of sexual and racial harassment as well as the harmful effects of sexism and racism that this harassment perpetuates seem to be invisible to several Labour Relations Board Commissioners who hear complaints of psychological harassment.

The complexity of women's experience of harassment is also poorly understood. As Kathrin Zippel points out:

> Sexual harassment is not like other forms of bullying, mobbing, or moral harassment because it is a gendered problem and involves complicated issues of sexuality, power, dominance, and abuse. Hence, it is crucial to recognize the sexual nature of the problem

---

CanLII 41910 (QC TDP) at paras 143ff [*Sfiridis*], on human dignity as a value underpinning all human rights, namely in the Preamble of the *Universal Declaration of Human Rights*, GA Res 217(III), UNGAOR, 3d Sess, Supp No 13, UN Doc A/810, (1948) 71, as well as in the *Charter of Fundamental Rights of the European Union*, 7 December 2000, OJ, C364/1. See *Caisse populaire*, above note 60 at paras 51ff, on the *Convention on the Elimination of All Forms of Discrimination against Women* (CEDAW), 18 December 1979, 1249 UNTS 13 (entered into force 3 September 1981) and the provisions of the Committee on the Elimination of Discrimination Against Women, *General Recommendation No 19*, UN Doc A/47/38, (1992) on violence against women and specifically sexual harassment as a form of this violence. See also *Québec (Commission des droits de la personne et des droits de la jeunesse) c Cadorette*, 1998 CanLII 49 at para 28 (QC TDP) on sexual harassment as a manifestation of power that makes a person a sexual object in her workplace ("une manifestation de pouvoir faisant d'une personne un objet sexuel dans son milieu de travail").

62 *Law v Canada (Ministry of Employment and Immigration)*, [1999] 1 SCR 497. In *R v Kapp*, 2008 SCC 41 at para 21, the Supreme Court of Canada notes that "several difficulties have arisen from the attempt in *Law* to employ human dignity as a legal test" and stepped back from the *Law* test for identifying discrimination. The Court nonetheless reaffirms that, "the protection of all of the rights guaranteed by the *Charter* has as its lodestar the promotion of human dignity."

> and to educate those involved in implementing laws about the complexities of victims' experiences, including the embarrassment, shame, and other emotional issues that intrusions and violations of dignity can lead to . . . .[63]

A few Commissioners at the Labour Relations Board demonstrate greater sensitivity to human rights issues,[64] and some decisions regarding harassment that is clearly of a sexual or racist nature simply accept complaints without qualifying the harassment as sexual or racist or making any reference to equality rights.[65] One early decision even considers that sexual harassment automatically constitutes a violation of human dignity, a position that would seem much more in keeping with human rights law.[66] However as a tribunal, the Labour Relations Board simply does not compare to the Human Rights Tribunal in terms of "experience and expertise in, sensitivity to and interest for matters of human rights and freedoms."[67]

D. DUE DILIGENCE: THE RESURRECTION OF AN OLD DEFENCE FOR EMPLOYERS FACING COMPLAINTS OF HARASSMENT

Provisions in the *Labour Standards Act* include an explicit obligation for employers to "take reasonable action to prevent psychological harassment

---

63 Kathrin S Zippel, "Gender Equality Politics in the Changing European Union: The European Union Anti-Discrimination Directive and Sexual Harassment" (2006) Center for European Studies Working paper, no. 134 [Zippel] at 9, online: Archive of European Integration http://aei.pitt.edu/9027.

64 See the decision of administrative judge France Giroux in *SH*, above note 25 and also that of administrative judge Roger Barrette in *GS c HF (Motel A)*, 2007 QCCRT 295, aff'd 2007 QCCRT 530. See also the decision of administrative judge Susan Heap on consideration of the violation of *Charter* rights as a factor when evaluating damages in *Baillie* c *Technologies Digital Shape inc*, 2008 QCCRT 549, aff'd 2009 QCCS 3090.

65 See, for example, *Maisons Laprise*, above note 25 (sexual harassment); *Gestion A Bossé*, above note 25 (sexual harassment); *Rioux*, above note 25 (sexual harassment). See also *Cebert*, above note 26 (racial harassment); *Cheikh-Bandar*, above note 27 (harassment on the basis of religious belief and ethnic origin).

66 *SH*, above note 25.

67 The Québec Human Rights Tribunal judges and assessors are chosen on this basis: see *Charter*, above note 19, s 101.

and, whenever they become aware of such behaviour, to put a stop to it." The corollary of this obligation, however, is that even if psychological harassment is proven, a complaint will be rejected if an employer can prove that when he became aware of the harassment, he took reasonable action to put a stop to it.[68] Indeed, this due diligence defence has led to rejection of a complaint on several occasions.[69]

To illustrate, in one case, a cleaning woman was greeted at the door of a hotel room by a naked man who grabbed her by the arm and declared that he wanted to have sex with her. Informed of the incident, the woman's supervisors (she worked for a cleaning company that had contracted to clean the hotel) went to the man's room, but he was no longer there. The hotel supervisor eventually contacted the man who opted not to have his room cleaned for the rest of his stay. Unsatisfied by the employer's reaction and believing that her hours of work had been reduced after the incident (though the evidence did not support this last allegation), she filed a complaint of psychological harassment. The Labour Relations Board rejected her complaint, denying any compensation to the cleaner (who was, understandably, shaken and upset by the incident). The board concluded that the employer had taken all reasonable means to put a stop to the harassment.[70]

In another case, a public service worker (a woman) complained of harassment by a colleague (a man) who had taken a dislike to her in the context of a conflict related to union politics. He regularly insulted her, going out of his way, often several times a day, to go to her desk to do so, cursing her, calling her names, and making disparaging comments and hostile gestures in front of colleagues and clients alike. An employer witness described the man as "brusque, unpredictable and on occasion impolite with clients, colleagues and supervisors." Eventually the complainant informed her supervisor of the man's visits to her desk. The supervisor then met with him regularly, inviting the harasser to "develop his rational brain in order to control his reptilian brain" and laying out behaviour "expectations."

---

68 JurisClasseur, above note 13.

69 *Syndicat de la fonction publique du Québec et Québec (Ministère des transports)*, 2012 CanLII 58630 (QC SAT); *Rodriguez Vergara*, above note 25; *Gougeon c Cheminées Sécurité International ltée*, 2010 QCCRT 120; *Syndicat de la fonction publique du Québec* et *Québec (Ministère de l'Emploi et de la Solidarité sociale)*, 2009 CanLII 39275 (QC SAT), aff'd 2010 QCCS 548 [*SFPQ*].

70 *Rodriguez Vergara*, above note 25.

Despite these actions by the supervisor, however, one day, the harasser intentionally rammed himself into the complainant's shoulder and side — a move described as resembling a hockey-style bodycheck — when she was in the middle of talking with two team leaders. She then decided to file a complaint of psychological harassment as well as a complaint with the police. Even after her complaints, the harasser still felt licensed to give her the finger at work and otherwise behave disobligingly with respect to her from time to time, in spite of further "behaviour expectations" now consigned in a "contract" with the supervisor.

After an internal investigation under the ministry's psychological harassment complaint procedure, the complainant was invited to a mediation session with the harasser, which she refused. The committee proposed moving her office to another location right beside her supervisor (with whom she had had frequent and somewhat tense dealings in her role as a union officer), which she also refused, eventually moving to another location when office space became free. Both she and the harasser were offered help through the Employee Assistance Program. The harasser was invited to, and did, offer her a letter of apology.

The arbitrator concluded that the employer had fulfilled all of his obligations to prevent and stop the harassment and rejected the grievance. He rejected the complainant's argument that more severe disciplinary measures should have been taken against the harasser, stating that if the harasser was as dangerous as the complainant and other witnesses suggested, it was wiser to follow the supervisor's "slow but safe" method of working with him.[71]

In short, adoption of the psychological harassment provisions created a "due diligence" defence for employers that is not available to employers under the *Charter*. Both in *Robichaud v Canada (Treasury Board)* and in *Janzen*, the Supreme Court of Canada clearly stated that in the context

---

71 See *SFPQ*, above note 69 at para 255 :

> J'invite la plaignante à évaluer les risques qu'elle aurait courus pour sa propre sécurité si l'employeur avait imposé, comme elle le voulait, une mesure disciplinaire très sévère au mis en cause. Aurait-il accepté la mesure sans réagir contre la plaignante? Il l'agonissait déjà d'injures lorsqu'elle signalait ses frasques. Allait-il adopter une attitude mesurée si le cadre lui imposait une suspension ou un congédiement? Si le mis en cause est aussi dangereux qu'elle le dit, appuyée dans cette assertion par plusieurs témoins, ne valait-il pas mieux adopter la méthode plus lente mais plus sécuritaire choisie par leur supérieur commun?

1 2 3 4 5 6 7 8 9 10 11 12 13 14

of human rights legislation, employer responsibility is determined by rules designed to ensure fulfillment of the remedial objectives of the legislation, namely, to provide a healthy work environment to all, and to suppress the discriminatory acts that get in the way of that goal by "redressing socially undesirable conditions quite apart from the reasons for their existence."[72]

Indeed, in the seminal harassment case of *Robichaud*, the employer argued that his responsibility was not engaged because under the legislation in effect at the time of the harassment, he had only a "reasonable-means" obligation to stop the harassment. Supreme Court Justice La Forest responded that, in keeping with the remedial purpose of the Act, amendments to the *Canadian Human Rights Act*[73] had abolished the reasonable means or due diligence defence. Employers still had a vested interest in reacting promptly and effectively to complaints of harassment to reduce the extent of damages and the scope of remedies ordered, but could no longer exonerate themselves from responsibility for damages caused:

> I should perhaps add that while the conduct of an employer is theoretically irrelevant to the imposition of liability in a case like this, it may nonetheless have important practical implications for the employer. Its conduct may preclude or render redundant many of the contemplated remedies. For example, an employer who responds quickly and effectively to a complaint by instituting a scheme to remedy and prevent recurrence will not be liable to the same extent, if at all, as an employer who fails to adopt such steps. These matters, however, go to remedial consequences, not liability.[74]

Likewise, doctrine and jurisprudence confirm that under the *Charter*, an employer cannot be exonerated from responsibility for damages caused by discriminatory harassment at work.[75]

---

72 *Robichaud v Canada (Treasury Board)*, [1987] 2 SCR 84 at para 10 [*Robichaud*].

73 RSC, 1985, c H-6.

74 *Robichaud*, above note 72 at 19.

75 See Christian Brunelle, "La protection quasi-constitutionnelle contre le harcèlement" in Barreau du Québec, ed, *Développements récents en droit du travail 2000* (Cowansville, QC: Yvon Blais, 2000) 185; Louise Langevin, "Le harcèlement sexuel au travail: l'impact de la décision *Béliveau St-Jacques*" (1997) 9 CJWL/RFD 17 at 39. For an illustration of the Québec Human Rights Tribunal caselaw on the irreversible nature of the presumption of employer responsibility under Québec civil law, see *Caisse populaire*, above note 60 at para 96.

Here again, framing sexual harassment as psychological harassment leads to a lower standard of employer responsibility to compensate employees who are not able to enjoy a healthy workplace in spite of some, obviously not totally successful, efforts by an employer in this direction. The premise of the psychological harassment law is that these unfortunate employees for whom the employer's reasonable efforts to prevent harassment failed are a random group, and the harassment is an unfortunate blip on the screen of an otherwise healthy, gender-equal work environment. When it comes to discriminatory harassment such as sexual or racial harassment, however, the group of targets is not a random group but one clearly comprised of individuals selected from a disadvantaged group (women, racialized or not; racialized men, and so on), often historically excluded from the workplace, and in the case of targets of sexual harassment, often economically vulnerable.[76] The harassment is part and parcel of a larger picture of discrimination. Leaving these victims uncompensated for harm caused by harassment is not just an individual injustice; it inevitably leaves intact part of the structure of systemic discrimination against women (or against racialized women and men, and so on) in the workforce.

E. THE PERSONAL RESPONSIBILITY OF PERPETRATORS OF SEXUAL AND RACIAL HARASSMENT SET ASIDE

When harassment is framed as psychological harassment rather than discriminatory harassment, the individual responsibility of perpetrators of harassment disappears. In twenty-four cases out of twenty-five (see Annex 1), the human rights complaints name both the perpetrator and the employer as defendants,[77] whereas by definition, psychological

76 MA Hickling, "Employer's Liability for Sexual Harassment" (1988) 17 Man LJ 124 at 127, as quoted by the Supreme Court in *Janzen*, above note 11 at 1285. See also the results of EQCOTESST, above note 3 on the relationship between precarious work status and sexual harassment and Elsa Underhill & Michael Quinlan, "How Precarious Employment Affects Health and Safety at Work: The Case of Temporary Agency Workers" (2011) 66:3 RI 397.

77 In only one case, *Québec (Commission des droits de la personne et des droits de la jeunesse) c Birkett*, 2000 CanLII 81 (QC TDP) [*Birkett*], was the complaint laid only against the perpetrator. In this case, upon learning of the harassment, the employer immediately fired the perpetrator and rehired the complainant, who was still employed by the company at the time of the

harassment complaints are laid only against the employer. In several cases, this precludes any possibility of obtaining punitive damages from the perpetrator, a common conclusion in Human Rights Tribunal decisions on harassment.[78] Too, if the perpetrator and the employer are jointly and severally condemned to pay the material and moral damages, if the employer goes bankrupt, the complainant has a greater chance of actually obtaining the damages awarded.[79]

F. THE CONNECTIONS BETWEEN HARASSMENT IN THE WORKPLACE AND EQUALITY IN THE WORKPLACE OBSCURED

In 1979, in the United States, Catharine MacKinnon published her seminal book entitled *Sexual Harassment of Working Women: A Case of Sex Discrimination*, arguing that sexual harassment institutionalized the sexualized subordination of women to men in the workplace.[80] Meanwhile, in the rest of Canada as well as Québec, employers had begun arguing that human rights legislation prohibiting sex discrimination did not prohibit sexual harassment. In the 1980s, many human rights laws, including the *Charter* in 1982, were amended to make it clear that

---

hearing. In a few other cases, there is only one party named as a defendant but they are cases where the sole proprietor of a business was also the perpetrator of the harassment. See, for example, *Sfiridis*, above note 61.

78 See *Québec (Commission des droits de la personne et des droits de la jeunesse) c Tremblay*, 2003 CanLII 68799 (QC TDP) (perpetrator ordered to pay $2,000 punitive damages); *Québec (Commission des droits de la personne et des droits de la jeunesse) c Produits forestiers Domtar inc*, 2000 CanLII 72 (QC TDP), leave to appeal to QC CA refused, 200-09-003168-009 (28 June 2000) (perpetrator ordered to pay $1,000 punitive damages).

79 See, for example, *Québec (Commission des droits de la personne et des droits de la jeunesse) c Café Java Haus Inc*, 2000 CanLII 27 (QC TDP). In *Québec (Commission des droits de la personne et des droits de la jeunesse) c Provigo Distribution inc, division Maxi*, 2002 CanLII 36232 (QC TDP), leave to appeal refused 2002 CanLII 31291 (QC CA), though the Tribunal found that the complainant was bound by a transaction signed with the employer, the case was still heard and the perpetrator was ordered to pay damages.

80 MacKinnon, *Sexual Harassment*, above note 5. For commentary on the evolution of this idea, see Kathryn Abrams, "A New Jurisprudence of Sexual Harassment" (1998) 83 Cornell L Rev 1169.

sexual harassment was a form of sex discrimination.[81] In 1989, in *Janzen*, the Supreme Court settled the debate, ruling that sexual harassment was indeed a form of sex discrimination:

> All female employees were potentially subject to sexual harassment by the respondent . . . . That his discriminatory behaviour was pinpointed against two of the female employees would have been small comfort to other women contemplating entering such a workplace. Any female considering employment at the Pharos restaurant was a potential victim . . . and as such was disadvantaged because of her sex. A potential female employee would recognize that if she were a male employee she would not have to run the same risks of sexual harassment . . . . Because they were women, the appellants were subject to a disadvantage to which no man at the restaurant would have been subject. As the LEAF factum puts it, " . . . sexual harassment is a form of sex discrimination because it denies women equality of opportunity in employment because of their sex." It is one of the purposes of anti-discrimination legislation to remove such denials of equality of opportunity.[82]

The Québec Human Rights Tribunal has also elaborated on the links between sexual harassment and discrimination against women at work:

> . . . section 10 of the *Charter* sets out a general interdiction against discrimination on prohibited grounds; section 10.1 sets out an autonomous right to protection against harassment which aims at "reinforcing the suppression of unacceptable behaviour that has been tolerated for too long in our society, principally, need we add, directed against women and homosexuals . . . . "
>
> However, sexual harassment at work, to take one example, also constitutes a form of sex discrimination because it involves practises and attitudes that also have the effect of compromising the working conditions of certain persons precisely because of their sex.[83] [author's translation; references omitted]

---

81 See generally Colleen Sheppard, "Systemic Inequality and Workplace Culture: Challenging the Institutionalization of Sexual Harassment" (1995) 3 CLELJ 249; Constance Backhouse & Leah Cohen, *Secret Oppression: Sexual Harassment of Working Women* (Toronto: Macmillan of Canada, 1978).

82 *Janzen*, above note 11.

83 *Caisse populaire*, above note 60 at paras 65–66.

In the 1980s, Catharine MacKinnon enthusiastically described the new sexual harassment law in the United States. Though evolution of the law was somewhat different in Québec and Canada, the interface between law and society is similar:

> The existence of a law against sexual harassment has affected both the context of meaning within which social life is lived and the concrete delivery of rights through the legal system. The sexually harassed have been given a name for their suffering and an analysis that connects it with gender. They have been given a forum, legitimacy to speak, authority to make claims, and an avenue for possible relief. Before, what happened to them was all right. Now, it is not.
>
> This matters. Sexual abuse mutes victims socially through the violation itself. . . . When the state also forecloses a validated space for denouncing and rectifying the victimization, it seals this secrecy and reinforces this silence. The harm of this process, a process that utterly precludes speech, then becomes all of a piece. If there is no right place to go to say, this hurt me, then a woman is simply the one who can be treated this way, and no harm, as they say, is done.[84]

MacKinnon nonetheless also referred to sexual harassment as an example of "legally prohibited but socially permitted" behaviour. One of the reasons for the persistent ineffectiveness of the law on sexual harassment is the stigma attached to filing a complaint and the reprisals that often occur against a woman who does complain of sexual harassment.[85] Targets of sexual harassment frequently do not lay complaints, preferring to simply leave their jobs.[86] If they do file a complaint, for non-unionized workers, often it is when they have already left their job.[87]

---

84 Catharine MacKinnon, *Feminism Unmodified: Discourses on Life and Law* (Cambridge, MA: Harvard University Press, 1987) at 103–4 [MacKinnon, *Feminism Unmodified*].

85 *Ibid* at 111.

86 Colleen Sheppard, "Harcèlement en milieu de travail: vers une approche systémique" in Jean-Louis Baudouin & Patrice Deslauriers, eds, *Droit à l'égalité et discrimination: Aspects nouveaux* (Cowansville, QC: Yvon Blais, 2002) 139 at 145.

87 In the twenty-five decisions on sexual and racial harassment rendered by the Human Rights Tribunal before 2004, only one complainant was still employed at the time she filed a complaint. She had been fired by her harasser and supervisor but then immediately reinstated by her employer when he learned of the harasser's behaviour: *Birkett*, above note 77. See also Cox, "Psychological Harassment Legislation," above note 22 at 125.

In *Québec (Commission des droits de la personne et des droits de la personne) c Québec (Procureur général)*[88] (*Lippé*), the Québec Human Rights Tribunal heard a complaint by a correctional services officer that illustrates the taboo of denouncing sexual harassment. During her first year on the job, Ms Lippé had managed to survive "without making waves" (her words) in this job traditionally held by men. However, when complaints of sexual harassment were filed by two unidentified colleagues, a rumour circulated that she was one of the complainants. Things changed drastically. Her already challenging work environment became poisoned by overt sexual and sexist harassment (including threats of sexual assault): "I'm gonna hurt you so bad that you're not gonna want to have anything to do with men afterwards" [author's translation] as well as various subtle and less subtle forms of professional sabotage.

In its decision granting the complaint and reinstating Ms Lippé in her job with back pay, the Human Rights Tribunal recalled that sexual harassment is aimed at keeping women, individually as well as collectively, in a position of inferiority.[89] The Tribunal recognized the range of behaviours that constitute sexual harassment and, in combination, work to keep women in a position of inferiority in the workplace:

> Sexual harassment of the hostile environment type is therefore a more subtle and more insidious manifestation than harassment with sexual connotations. This type of situation usually does not involve elements that could imply seduction. On the contrary, words, gestures or acts converge to demonstrate that the person does not belong in the workplace — which is generally predominantly but not exclusively occupied by males — simply because one of the grounds set forth in section 10 of the *Charter* is present, i.e. because she is a woman. Hence, this type of sexual harassment can be considered gender-based, as gender rather than sexuality is the object of the harassment.
>
> Gender-based harassment is likely to take various forms, ranging from the use of coarse language, dirty jokes, unpleasant remarks, snubs, hazing, verbal abuse, and insults, to threats, assault or other forms of aggression. It also includes caricatures, graffiti, and damage to the victim's property or to the premises or objects

---

88 *Québec (Commission des droits de la personne et des droits de la personne) c Québec (Procureur général)*, 1998 CanLII 30 (QC TDP) [*Lippé*].

89 *Ibid* at para 148.

> at her disposal, with particular emphasis on obviously female characteristics. Essentially, this type of harassment seeks to isolate the women involved, reminding them that the environment is not meant for them, that they are weak and that they are integrating themselves into the environment at their own risk. The environment has its own codes and rules, which tend to reinforce the prejudices and stereotypes under which abuse of power occurs. [90] [references omitted]

The Tribunal noted that when a woman says she is being sexually harassed or files a complaint, reprisals without an overtly sexual connotation are commonplace:

> Furthermore, often coupled with incidents with a sexual or sexist connotation are more or less serious acts and behaviour in the nature of reprisals against the victim, i.e. attitudes, behaviour or practices that reflect the animosity toward her, for example, sabotaging her work, causing unmerited sanctions to be imposed on her, imposing conditions or additional burdens, in short, creating around her a hostile and abusive work environment in which she is treated differently from people of the opposite sex. [91] [references omitted]

To go back to MacKinnon, in a world where harassment cannot be denounced, the harm caused by the silencing of targets of harassment is of a piece with the harm caused by the harassment itself.

In stark contrast to the Human Rights Tribunal's decision in the *Lippé* case, is the decision in *EG c Compagnie A*.[92] In this case, a woman diagnosed with an adaptive disorder with anxiety applied for workers' compensation benefits. After her previous job in a garment factory was abolished, she had used her seniority rights to transfer to a position in another factory in a male-dominated job (300 men, 15 women at the time of the events). One day, during a machine stoppage, she enquired after a colleague's mother who had breast cancer. Another colleague — a man — arrived and stated, "If she'd gotten breast cancer, maybe it was because her breasts hadn't been grabbed enough." As she left the conversation, the same man slapped her on the buttocks. He had previously bragged

90 *Ibid* at paras 167–68.
91 *Ibid* at para 169.
92 *EG c Compagnie A*, 2005 CanLII 74145 (QC CLP), aff'd (2006), 2006 CanLII 64753 (QC CLP) [*EG c Compagnie A*].

to her about doing something similar to another woman colleague, and presumably was flaunting her warning that he shouldn't try to do the same thing to her. He had also mentioned to her that he "preferred seeing her working on all fours" rather than upright.

The situation then went from bad to worse for the worker. She contacted her union representative to file a complaint. With reference to the problems anticipated with respect to the arrival of women in the previously all-male factory floor workforce, the union representative's response was to say to her: "That's it! Here we go!" She then complained to her employer, who refused to consider her as credible until the other man present corroborated her story. In the meantime, her colleagues turned against her. Some of the other women called her a goody-goody ("sainte nitouche"). Almost two weeks later, the employer's inquiry led him to suspend her aggressor for a week, but by then her work environment had become so poisoned that she had been put on disability by an emergency room doctor.

Her claim for workers' compensation benefits was refused by the Appeals Tribunal (Commission des lésions professionnelles). The Appeals Tribunal declared that while the remarks about breast cancer were stupid and foolish, they did not constitute either psychological harassment or sexual harassment, emphasizing that the remarks were of little import as they did not concern her directly.[93] Moving on to consider the slap on the buttocks, while again the Appeals Tribunal stated that this was "completely inappropriate," in and of itself, it could not be considered as psychological or sexual harassment. The fact that this blue-collar woman swore copiously at the man after he slapped her and told him in no uncertain terms not to do it again, was cited as evidence that she was angry but not hurt, and also that her testimony that she was afraid of him after the incident was not convincing.[94] The tribunal's position was, again, to borrow from MacKinnon: "Not that the acts did not occur, but rather that it was unreasonable to experience them as harmful."[95]

---

93 We note that this type of remark is clearly recognized by the social science literature as sexual harassment in the form of gender harassment, specifically "disparaging conduct not intended to elicit sexual cooperation; rather, . . . verbal, physical, and symbolic behaviors that convey hostile and offensive attitudes about women." See Konik & Cortina, above note 31 at 314.

94 *EG c Compagnie A*, above note 92 at paras 61–63.

95 MacKinnon, *Feminism Unmodified*, above note 84 at 108.

The Appeals Tribunal found that the most probable cause of the woman's disability was — and here I do not disagree — the treatment of her complaint after the incident, and her ensuing isolation and ostracization in the workplace. However, the Appeals Tribunal then found this to be in the realm of labour relations. Her disability was therefore considered a non-compensable injury, and her claim was rejected.[96]

In this case (*EG c Compagnie A*), the woman also filed a grievance for psychological harassment under the collective agreement. However, by the time the grievance hearing date was set, the Appeals Tribunal had already rendered its decision on the woman's claim for workers' compensation. The arbitrator refused outright to admit any evidence of incidents of sexual or psychological harassment that had already been filed before the Appeals Tribunal, accepting the employer's position that the Appeals Tribunal decision was *res judicata* and constituted final judgment on these questions.[97] The situation is Kafkaesque.

The Appeals Tribunal decision exemplifies how a de-contextualized, incident by incident, approach to sexual harassment leads to minimizing and ultimately denying the harm of sexual harassment. A narrow vision of sexual harassment that excludes the silencing process when a woman attempts to denounce harassment is an important part of this denial. So does the fact that being a witness to offensive and sexist comments about one woman might affect another woman worker. The Appeals Tribunal's insistence that the woman couldn't have been hurt because she swore at the perpetrator again reflects a lack of understanding of the complexities of sexual harassment, where victimization and resilience can be intertwined.[98] The Appeals Tribunal's analysis of sexual harass-

96 *EG c Compagnie A*, above note 92 at para 66.

97 *Conseil du Québec — Unite Here c Compagnie A(EG)*, 2006 CanLII 40685 (QC SAT). There are currently two schools of thought, both for grievance arbitrators and for the Labour Relations Board, on whether this is good law. See JurisClasseur, above note 13 at paras 304ff. See also Anne-Marie Laflamme, "Le harcèlement psychologique au travail : une atteinte à la dignité ou à la santé de la personne?" in Barreau du Québec, ed, *Développements récents en santé et sécurité au travail (2012)* (Cowansville, QC: Éditions Yvon Blais, 2012) 437 [Laflamme].

98 We note that our methodology does not allow us to generalize about lack of understanding of sexual harassment on the part of the Appeals Tribunal (Commission des lésions professionnelles). Not all administrative judges of the Commission lack understanding of the complexities of sexual harassment. For a case involving the sexual harassment of a waitress and single working mother whose claim was accepted, see *MC et Compagnie A*, 2011 QCCLP 2615, Administrative Judge Richard Hudon [*Hudon decision*].

ment contrasts sharply with that of the Human Rights Tribunal in the *Lippé* case.[99] The arbitrator's interpretation of the psychological harassment legislation then allows the Appeals Tribunal's narrow analysis to decide the harassment grievance.

In the 2008 *CC c Gestion A Bossé Inc*[100] (*Gestion A Bossé*) decision rendered by the Labour Relations Board, we read that a woman was hired as a barmaid at a small-town restaurant-bar that represents one of the only local employers. The owner sexually harassed her without mercy in front of clients and staff, saying things like: "What do I have to do to be allowed to grab your tits?"[author's translation]. After his sexual advances met with resistance on her part, he became extremely abusive, ultimately threatening to kill her. (He was later convicted of uttering death threats and sentenced to twelve months in prison.) He then fired her. The worker testified that she was traumatized by the experience and unable to work for several months.

Of note is the fact that the words "sexual harassment" do not once appear in the decision on compensation for the complainant who was eventually awarded $25,000 in moral and punitive damages as well as back pay and an indemnity for loss of employment. In justifying awarding punitive damages, the administrative judge simply mentions that:

> In 2008, it is high time that everyone understands that the time when the master was the owner of those that serve him and could abuse them as he wished is long gone.[101] [author's translation]

The fact that the master is a man, the abuse is sexual, and the target is a woman is not mentioned. As Catharine MacKinnon points out,

> . . . there is a gender definition of traditionally female jobs that includes sexualisation of the woman worker as part of the job. Until it is changed, this makes sexual harassment systemically inevitable for the masses of women who must take the only jobs society opens to them.[102]

Just as — if not more — important as the legacy of the master-servant relationship in Québec civil law is the legacy of sexual subordination of women to men. It seems trite to point out that sexual harassment

99 *Lippé*, above note 88.
100 *Gestion A Bossé*, above note 25.
101 *Ibid* at para 113.
102 MacKinnon, *Feminism Unmodified*, above note 84 at 19.

of women at work involves not only the subordination of any worker to his or her employer but also the objectification of women. Yet the Labour Relations Board decision does not recognize that the sexual harassment affected not only the economic well-being and dignity of the target but also her right to gender equality.[103]

Arbitration awards on psychological harassment rarely concern factual situations of sexual harassment. This may be because in unionized environments, complaints involving sexual harassment are often settled promptly rather than litigated.[104] In one case, an arbitrator did mention in passing that sexist comments constituted a form of vexatious conduct that could amount to sexual harassment but then went on to reject the grievance.[105] In another case, a worker was forced to perform oral sex on her boss, the owner of a grocery store, and then assaulted the following day by another employer representative who forcibly kissed her and touched her thigh as part of a bet with the owner/assailant. Her psychological harassment grievance was upheld when the arbitrator found the woman's testimony to be more credible than that of her assailant.[106]

In the end, in the last case, this single mother settled out of court and presumably received damages. But as in the *Gestion A Bossé* case, something is missing in terms of recognition of the harm caused to the goal of gender equality when economically vulnerable women are sexually harassed or sexually assaulted at work by their boss.[107]

---

103 See Zippel, above note 63 at 2, who writes that sexual harassment " . . . cuts across several important fault lines of gender inequality, because the problem is about the abuse of power in the workplace and hence affects economic well-being as well as rights to sexual self-determination."

104 The traces of sexual harassment are found more often in the awards on disciplinary measures imposed on harassers by employers.

105 *Centre de Santé et de Services Sociaux du Sud-Ouest — Verdun (Résidence Yvon-Brunet)*, [2008] RJDT 346 (QC SAT). This decision has received little publicity, as none of the key words assigned to it by the data bank SOQUIJ (Azimut) have to do with sexual harassment or sexist comments.

106 *9008-4062 Québec inc (Frutta'si) c Travailleurs et travailleuses unis de l'alimentation et du commerce, local 500*, 2010 CanLII 75192 (QC SAT). The arbitrator reserved jurisdiction over remedy and the parties settled out of court.

107 We note that in France, sexual assault is not included in the 2012 definition of sexual harassment and remains a distinct infraction. See Loïc Lerouge, "Harcèlement: nouvelles dispositions issues de la loi du 6 août 2012" 10 Droit social (Actualités) 1 [Lerouge].

G. GENDER EQUALITY AND THE UNFORTUNATE CONSEQUENCES OF TREATING DISABILITY RELATED TO HARASSMENT AS EMPLOYMENT INJURY

I have argued that framing sexual and racial harassment as psychological harassment makes violence against women at work invisible. However, the considerations that come into play with the adoption of the psychological harassment law are just one more layer in a broader process of making violence against women at work invisible by subsuming it in policies and practices that obscure its links with gender and racial inequality.

Specifically, recourse against sexual and racial harassment as well as psychological harassment must be understood in the particular legal context where disability related to harassment at work is treated as an employment injury for which exclusive recourse lies with a claim for workers' compensation benefits.[108] A complaint or grievance of harassment involves a legal process aimed at establishing responsibility for certain events and, as the case may be, awarding damages to the victim.

In contrast, a claim for workers' compensation benefits is by definition made within a no-fault scheme. Amongst other things, this precludes the possibility for a woman who is harassed to sue her employer or a co-worker who harassed her.[109] What's more, a workers' compensation claim involves a medico-legal process centred on the disability of the claimant: diagnosis by a doctor, medical treatment (including psychotherapy but also medication such as anti-depressants), duration of the period of disability, functional limitations resulting from the "accident," as well as scrutiny of the work-related character of the illness as opposed to illness of "personal" origin.

Given that a workers' compensation claim is the only recourse open to harassed women to recover lost salary and healthcare expenses, in order for women to be compensated, the pathology of harassment is searched for and must be found within the harassed women's bodies and minds. While the harasser remains at work, the harassed woman must

---

108 See notes 30 & 31. This topic goes beyond the scope of this chapter but merits critical inquiry in and of itself.

109 See *An Act respecting industrial accidents and occupational diseases*, RSQ 1985, c A-3.001, ss 438 and 441ff. See, however, the recent caselaw in *Hardy c Financière Banque Nationale inc*, 2009 QCCS 5789; *Gagnon c Desjardins Sécurité financière, compagnie d'assurance-vie*, 2011 QCCS 4149.

undergo psychiatric evaluation by her own doctor or psychiatrist, and more often than not, by a psychiatrist hired by the employer.[110] This further draws the legal debate to her mental health, the inadequacies of her personal and family life, her personality flaws, and weaknesses . . . rather than those of the harasser. The existence of these psychiatric expert reports may then find their way into the evidence in Labour Relations Board and arbitration hearings on psychological harassment, discrediting the target of harassment.[111] Women whose past has been fraught with violence may find it more difficult to obtain compensation than women for whom harassment at work is the first form of violence that they have encountered.[112]

Furthermore, any claim involving chronic stress at work such as that caused by sexual harassment is likely to initially be denied (90 percent refusal rate) by the CSST,[113] obliging the claimant to take her case to the Appeals Tribunal. In 2010, the CSST reported a total of only thirteen successful sexual harassment claims.[114]

The fact that if a woman's health is compromised because of harassment at work, she is considered to have suffered an employment injury also has specific implications for the right to return to work.[115] If the harassed woman's treating physician declares her fit to return to work albeit with a "functional limitation" that she not have contact with her harasser, a successful claimant may see her employment legally terminated. After all, in Québec law, employers have no duty to accommodate

---

110 In one case, while the identity of the sexually harassed claimant was published, the harasser's identity was protected as a third party to the claim. See *Gervais et Établissements de détentions* (2006), [2005] CLP 1467 (QC CLP) [*Gervais*].

111 Rachel Cox, "Harcèlement psychologique au travail : entre psychologisation et victimisation, Une étude de la jurisprudence arbitrale québécoise" 81 Dr et Soc 343 [Cox, "Harcèlement psychologique"].

112 Katherine Lippel & Nancy Malo, "Le harcèlement sexuel au travail : s'agit-il d'un accident du travail comme les autres?" (Presentation delivered at the 6e Conférence mondiale sur la prévention et le contrôle des traumatismes, Montréal, 14 May 2002), [unpublished, archived with the author, abstract online: INSPQ www.inspq.qc.ca/pdf/publications/129_trauma2002.pdf].

113 Commission de la santé et de la sécurité du travail du Québec, *Statistiques sur les lésions attribuables au stress en milieu de travail* (Québec: CSST, 2012) at 36.

114 *Ibid* at 14. The same document reports forty-five successful claims related to psychological harassment. There are no statistics available on racial harassment or any other kind of discriminatory harassment.

115 See above notes 30 & 31.

work accident victims under the *Charter*,[116] nor are they obliged to create a new position in order to allow a work-accident victim to return to work.[117] Depending on the size and nature of the workplace, the employer may be successful[118] or not[119] in arguing that there is no appropriate job available

---

116 *Société des établissements de plein air du Québec* c *SCFP*, 2009 QCCA 329, leave to appeal to SCC refused, 33135 (10 September 2009).

117 Anne-Marie Laflamme, "Le droit de retour au travail et l'obligation d'accommodement: le régime de réparation des lésions professionnelles peut-il résister à l'envahisseur?" (2007) 48 C de D 215 at 233.

118 *Blouin et AFG Industries ltée*, 2007 QCCLP 2577. Here, the claimant was a mechanic (a man) who had been harassed by his co-workers when he refused to follow a union decision to refuse to do overtime as a pressure tactic. His grievance for compensation for having lost his job because of the psychological harassment — a remedy specifically provided for in section 123.15 of the *Labour Standards Act*, above note 9 — was refused. The arbitrator was of the opinion that the benefits received from the workers' compensation board had covered all aspects of any damages due to him by the employer: see *AFG Industries et Syndicat national (TCA)*, [2008] RJDT 531 (QC SAT). In a similar story, Ms Dionne, a forewoman working for the City of Montréal, was harassed by a blue-collar worker under her supervision. She successfully claimed for Workers' Compensation benefits but then saw her employment terminated when the city argued that there was no position available to her where, as her doctor had specified, she would not be in contact with any blue-collar workers. Despite use of every available avenue of recourse, she was unsuccessful in her efforts to ask the Workers' Compensation Board to overturn (see *Dionne c Montréal (City of)*, 2006 CanLII 65950 (QC CLP), aff'd 2007 QCCLP 641, aff'd 2008 QCCS 2158, leave to appeal refused, 2008 QCCA 1270 [*Dionne*]) or reconsider (see *Dionne c Montréal (City of)*, 2009 QCCLP 8549) its decision that there was no appropriate position available for her at the City of Montréal. She is currently litigating over her right to return to work under the collective agreement: see *Montréal et Syndicat des fonctionnaires municipaux de Montréal* (2011), AZ-50807353 (Azimut) (QC SAT) for a favourable but preliminary decision on the arbitrator's jurisdiction to hear her grievance.

119 *Gervais*, above note 110. In this case, a Correctional Services Agent (a woman) was sexually harassed by a co-worker. Her doctor declared that she was permanently unable to work with the man in question. Her employer argued that Ms Gervais could not return to work in a position that respected the limitations prescribed by her doctor, as given his rights under the collective agreement, there was nothing to stop the perpetrator of the harassment from applying for a transfer to the region where Ms Gervais wished to be relocated. The Appeals Tribunal allowed Ms Gervais to return to work, stating that a narrow interpretation of the functional limitations set out by the doctor was necessary in order to respect the right of work accident victims to return to work. See France Cormier, "La victime de harcèlement et le processus de réadaptation professionnelle" in Barreau du Québec, ed, *Développements récents en droit de la santé et de la sécurité au travail (2007)* (Cowansville, QC: Yvon Blais, 2007) 113.

where the harassed worker is certain not to encounter the perpetrator. In any case, this issue often generates further, costly (in economic and human terms) litigation for the harassed woman.[120]

Finally, the interface between the workers' compensation scheme and the labour standards framework for recourse against harassment is not yet clearly defined. A legal framework in which a harassed and ill woman must claim at the CSST for salary and healthcare expenses including psychotherapy, and at the same time, file a grievance or a complaint to obtain an order for the employer to (a) take steps to stop the harassment, (b) correct the worker's disciplinary record, or (c) pay a sum of money to compensate for loss of employment, has been highly conducive to litigation over procedural issues.[121] In this chapter, the multiple decisions rendered by different jurisdictions on individual cases of harassment illustrate the complexity of the legal framework for recourse against psychological and sexual harassment.

In short, the consequences of framing sexual harassment as psychological harassment are felt in a context where, to the extent that the harassment caused disability, the implications of sexual and racial harassment have already been detached in part from questions of gender and racial equality.

H. CONCLUSION

Although this chapter lays out some unsettling consequences of framing sexual and racial harassment as psychological harassment, I nonetheless take issue with the idea that a choice has to — or should — be made between an avenue of recourse in cases of sexual or racial harassment (with the goal of ensuring gender and racial equality) and an avenue of recourse in cases of psychological harassment (with the goal of ensuring dignity at work).[122]

---

120 The *Dionne* affair is a case in point, above note 118.

121 Cox, "Psychological Harassment Legislation," above note 22 at 85–87; Laflamme, above note 97.

122 On potential conflict between the pursuit of goals of anti-discrimination and goals of dignity at work, see Gabrielle S Friedman & James Q Whitman, "The European Transformation of Harassment Law: Discrimination versus Dignity" (2003) Yale Law School, Public Law & Legal Theory Research Paper Series, Research Paper No. 37, online: SSRN http://ssrn.

First, as discussed earlier, not all gendered aspects of psychological harassment are subsumed in sexual harassment.[123] Psychological harassment often plays a role in policing gender or racial or some other type of social conformity.[124] Second, as the saying goes, no one is free until we are all free. Psychological harassment is about abuse of power. Women are in need of protection from psychological harassment at work. It is simply not possible to imagine a work environment with a culture of gender and racial equality yet where managerial abuse is permitted and individuals chosen at random can be persecuted by their colleagues with impunity. Third, any abuse of power such as harassment at work is experienced by women in the larger context of their sexual and economic inequality. The consequences of being psychologically harassed at work are necessarily gendered — one has only to think of a single mother or a woman living with conjugal violence contemplating the prospect of losing her job to illustrate this point.

Both recently in framing sexual and racial harassment as psychological harassment and before that in framing disability related to harassment as an employment injury, the trend is towards directing issues of violence against women at work into broader avenues of recourse where they are not dealt with as such. These forms of violence against women thus become invisible, as does, arguably, the goal of gender and racial equality. In order to slow or halt this trend, I would argue for better dovetailing and letting complainants choose freely between the available avenues of recourse. Women (and men) should have the possibility of framing sexual and racial harassment as a human rights issue rather than having to claim for salary and healthcare expenses through the workers' compensation regime.[125] And in any case, the burden of

---

com/abstract=383900. On recognition of the "interconnected yet distinct" [author's translation] nature of sexual and psychological harassment in French law, see Lerouge, above note 107.

123 Jordi Escartin, Denise Salin, & Alvaro Rodriguez-Caballeira, "Conceptualizations of Workplace Bullying: Gendered rather than Gender-Neutral" (2011) 10:4 Journal of Personnel Psychology 157.

124 See, for example, Stig B Mathiesen, Brita Bjorkelo, & Ronald J Burke, "Workplace Bullying as the Dark Side of Whistleblowing" in S Einarsen et al, eds, *Workplace Bullying: Development in Theory, Research and Practice* (London: Taylor & Francis, 2011) at 301.

125 For an argument in favour of leaving open the possibility of framing sexual harassment as a human rights complaint rather than as an employment injury, see Lippel & Demers, above note 37. In the same vein, women and men alike should also be allowed to frame psychological harassment as such

1 2 3 4 5 6 7 8 9 10 11 12 13 14

proving psychological harassment should not be heavier than that of proving harassment on grounds prohibited by the *Charter*. Discriminatory harassment should automatically be considered as a violation of human dignity.[126]

Furthermore, on closer scrutiny, it is a mix of policy and practice that combine to make the links between violence against women at work and gender inequality invisible. The role of practice comes into play when, as discussed in this chapter, decision makers with little or no expertise on or sensitivity to human rights issues apply a legislative framework that ignores the existence of gender and racial inequality and the importance of human rights. Yet in spite of a "gender-blind" legal framework, a small handful of decisions explicitly take into account the complex nature of and specific harm caused by sexual harassment.[127] I would thus also argue that judicial education of administrative judges and grievance arbitrators on the connections between harassment and systemic sex and race discrimination, as well as women's experience of harassment and especially sexual harassment could play an important role in mitigating the negative effects of framing sexual harassment as psychological harassment or employment injury.

Finally, the substantial contribution of the Québec Human Rights Tribunal to women's equality rights at work up until 2004 makes the absence of complaints of harassment under the *Charter* a troubling prospect. Some of the most egregious examples of sexual harassment and sexual assault at work reported in the caselaw occurred in non-unionized workplaces.[128] Theoretically, non-unionized employees have a choice of pursuing a human rights complaint or complaining through

---

rather than having to claim for salary and healthcare expenses through workers' compensation.

126 For example, I have previously suggested that judicial notice could be taken of this question: Cox, "Psychological Harassment Legislation," above note 22 at 75–76.

127 See *Hudon decision*, above note 98 which takes into account the particular vulnerability of a low-income, sexually active, single mother to sexual harassment by her employer. See also Labour Relations Board Administrative Judges Susan Heap, France Giroux, and Roger Barrette's decisions, above note 64. Aside from the decisions of the Québec Human Rights Tribunal (which is a judicial tribunal), I found no decisions illustrating the expertise and sensitivity of administrative judges to concerns of racial equality in a legal framework that is as "race-blind" as it is "gender-blind."

128 See, for example, *Gestion A Bossé*, above note 25 or *Rioux*, above note 25 (Administrative Judge Line Lanseigne).

the labour standards process. However, after the psychological harassment law came into effect, it would seem that the Québec Human Rights Commission started advising people inquiring about how to file a complaint of harassment at work under the *Charter* to also file a complaint of psychological harassment at the Labour Standards Commission.[129] This might explain why, since the coming into effect of the psychological harassment legislation in June 2004, the Québec Human Rights Tribunal is no longer seized of cases of sexual or racial harassment at work.[130] Further research is necessary to understand why the Québec Human Rights Commission is no longer bringing any complaints of sexual or racial harassment to the Québec Human Rights Tribunal. We might then be able to identify how to ensure that the Québec Human Rights Tribunal's vital contribution to defining women's equality rights at work could resume, notwithstanding the existence of distinct recourse against psychological harassment.

129 This means that the Human Rights Commission can either close the file or suspend processing of the human rights complaint until the Labour Standards Commission had ruled on or settled the complaint of psychological harassment. See Carole Henry, *Harcèlement psychologique au travail, Cinq ans plus tard, où en sommes-nous?* (Montréal: Au Bas de l'échelle, 2009) at 31.

130 Unless the harassment is by individuals who are third parties to the employment relationship. See Section A, above in this chapter.

ANNEX 1

Québec Human Rights Tribunal (QC TDP) decisions on sexual and racial harassment at work *before* the coming into effect of the legislation on psychological harassment (1 June 1996–31 May 2004)

* = Unionized employee

1) **Québec (Commission des droits de la personne et des droits de la jeunesse) c Caisse populaire Desjardins d'Amqui* (2003), [2004] RJQ 355, leave to appeal to QC CA refused (23 January 2004), Québec 200-09-004700-040.
2) *Québec (Commission des droits de la personne et des droits de la jeunesse) c Groupe Agrinet*, 2003 CanLII 43256 (QC TDP).
3) *Québec (Commission des droits de la personne et des droits de la jeunesse) c Tremblay*, 2003 CanLII 68799 (QC TDP).
4) *Québec (Commission des droits de la personne et des droits de la jeunesse) c Pigeon*, 2002 CanLII 21498 (QC TDP).
5) *Québec (Commission des droits de la personne et des droits de la jeunesse) c Provigo Distribution inc, division Maxi inc*, 2002 CanLII 36232, leave to appeal to QC CA refused, [2003] RJQ 22.
6) *Québec (Commission des droits de la personne et des droits de la jeunesse) c Éditions commerciales Jaguar inc*, 2002 CanLII 23919 (QC TDP).
7) *Québec (Commission des droits de la personne et des droits de la jeunesse) c Produits de sécurité north ltée*, 2002 CanLII 6147 (QC TDP).
8) *Québec (Commission des droits de la personne et des droits de la jeunesse) c Sfiridis*, 2002 CanLII 41910 (QC TDP).
9) *Québec (Commission des droits de la personne et des droits de la jeunesse) c Mansoura*, 2000 CanLII 29 (QC TDP).
10) *Québec (Commission des droits de la personne et des droits de la jeunesse) c Café Java Haus inc*, 2000 CanLII 27 (QC TDP).
11) *Québec (Commission des droits de la personne et des droits de la jeunesse) c Produits forestiers Domtar inc*, 2000 CanLII 72 (QC TDP), leave to appeal to QC CA refused (28 June 2000), Québec 200-09-003168-009.
12) *Québec (Commission des droits de la personne et des droits de la jeunesse) c Birkett*, 2000 CanLII 81 (QC TDP).
13) *Québec (Commission des droits de la personne et des droits de la jeunesse) c Buffet Trio inc*, 1999 CanLII 55 (QC TDP).
14) **Québec (Commission des droits de la personne et des droits de la jeunesse) c* Québec *(Procureur général)*, [1998] RJQ 3397 (QC TDP).
15) *Québec (Commission des droits de la personne et des droits de la jeunesse) c Syed*, 1998 CanLII 56 (QC TDP).

16) *Québec (Commission des droits de la personne et des droits de la jeunesse) c Virage Santé mentale inc*, [1998] RJQ 2199 (QC TDP).
17) *Québec (Commission des droits de la personne et des droits de la jeunesse) c Gestion René Landry inc (Restaurant Harvey's)*, 1998 CanLII 51 (QC TDP), leave to appeal to QC CA refused (8 July 1998), Montréal 500-09-006742-985.
18) *Québec (Commission des droits de la personne et des droits de la jeunesse) c Cadorette*, 1998 CanLII 49 (QC TDP).
19) *Québec (Commission des droits de la personne et des droits de la jeunesse) c Coiffures Woncor inc*, 1998 CanLII 44 (QC TDP).
20) *Québec (Commission des droits de la personne et des droits de la jeunesse) c Lavoie*, 1997 CanLII 51 (QC TDP).
21) *Québec (Commission des droits de la personne et des droits de la jeunesse) c Zervakis*, 1997 CanLII 3 (QC TDP).
22) *Lapointe c Sécur inc*, 1997 CanLII 68 (QC TDP).
23) *Québec (Commission des droits de la personne et des droits de la jeunesse) c 2641-0431 Québec inc (André Gosselin Bois de foyer, Transport André Gosselin)*, [1997] RJQ 1481 (QC TDP).
24) *Québec (Commission des droits de la personne et des droits de la jeunesse) c Genest*, [1997] RJQ 1488 (QC TDP), leave to appeal to QC CA granted, 2001 CanLII 11888, leave to appeal to SCC refused, 28436 (20 September 2001).
25) *Québec (Human Rights Commission) v O'Hashi*, 1996 CanLII 12 (QC TDP).

ANNEX 2

Quebec Human Rights Tribunal (QC TDP) decisions on sexual and racial harassment at work *after* the coming into effect of the legislation on psychological harassment (1 June 2004 – 31 May 2012)

1) *Québec (Commission des droits de la personne et des droits de la jeunesse) c Villemaire*, 2010 QCTDP 8.
2) *Québec (Commission des droits de la personne et des droits de la jeunesse) c Remorquage Sud-Ouest (9148-7314 Québec inc)*, 2010 QCTDP 12.
   During this period, the QC TDP also rendered three decisions based on facts that took place well before 2004.
3) *Québec (Commission des droits de la personne et des droits de la jeunesse) c Québec (AG)*, 2008 QCTDP 8 [*Pavilus*].
4) *Québec (Commission des droits de la personne et des droits de la jeunesse) c DL*, 2007 QCTDP 23.

1 2 3 4 5 6 7 8 9 10 11 12 13 14

5) *Québec (Commission des droits de la personne et des droits de la jeunesse) c Épicerie boucherie St-Antonin*, 2005 CanLII 18112 (QC TDP).

ANNEX 3

Examples of decisions on psychological harassment complaints laid by non-unionized workers that involve harassment based on discriminatory grounds

1) *Desjardins c Maison du Spaghetti (A et Compagnie A)*, 2007 QCCRT 28.
2) *GS c HF (Motel A)*, 2007 QCCRT 295, aff'd 2007 QCCRT 530.
3) *Roy c Maison Laprise*, 2008 QCCRT 86.
4) *SH c Compagnie A*, 2007 QCCRT 348.
5) *CC c Gestion A Bossé Inc*, 2008 QCCRT 399, aff'd 2010 QCCS 1159.
6) *Lizotte c Alimentation Coop La Pocatière*, 2008 QCCRT 240, aff'd 2008 QCCRT 521.
7) *Craig c Poliseno Marine International inc*, 2009 QCCRT 11.
8) *Rodriguez Vergara c 9169-1022 Québec inc*, 2009 QCCRT 224.
9) *Baillie c Technologies Digital Shape inc*, 2008 QCCRT 549, aff'd 2009 QCCS 3090.
10) *Dupuis c Commission scolaire de la Riveraine*, 2009 QCCRT 3, aff'd 2010 QCCS 481.
11) *Rioux c Commission touristique du Port-Joli inc*, 2011 QCCRT 473.
12) *Dian c Pêcheries Norref Québec inc*, 2007 QCCRT 551.
13) *Cebert c Groupe d'imprimerie Saint-Joseph inc*, 2009 QCCRT 373, aff'd 2010 QCCS 7114.
14) *Hassam c Le Groupe Comagest inc*, 2009 QCCRT 267.
15) *Monongo c Coffres-forts CB 2000 inc*, 2010 QCCRT 290, aff'd 2012 QCCS 4085.
16) *Cheikh-Bandar c Pfizer Canada Inc*, 2008 QCCRT 124, aff'd 2008 QCCS 4811.
17) *St-Hilaire-Gravel c 9165-8526 Québec inc (Boston Pizza)*, 2008 QCCRT 0364.

CHAPTER 10

THE HATE SPEECH DIVERSION

Richard Moon[1]

A. INTRODUCTION

I am surprised sometimes by the fervour with which some individuals oppose all forms of hate speech regulation. In a few cases, the opposition to hate speech restriction is simply a more palatable way of defending hate speech — the message it carries. Hate mongers have found it strategically useful to present themselves as defenders of free speech. The shift from advocate of hate to defender of free speech fits well with the hate monger's self-understanding as a victim of state oppression and a defender of Western values against multiculturalism. More often, though, the opposition to hate speech regulation has a principled basis. There are many committed civil libertarians who regard hate speech as odious but are nevertheless prepared to defend the right of others to engage in it. Their opposition to the restriction of hate speech rests on a commitment to individual liberty and a concern about the reach of state power. While I think the "civil libertarian" position is mistaken, it is not without merit. What is perplexing though is the extraordinary energy that these advocates of free speech put into the fight against hate speech regulation. They seem convinced that the integrity of the free speech edifice depends on holding the line here. Yet they seem indifferent to the more significant ways in which freedom of expression is being eroded in Western democracies. Whether by design or not, the obsessive opposition to

1 Richard Moon is a professor of law at the University of Windsor. This chapter draws on Richard Moon, "The Attack on Human Rights Commissions and the Decline of Public Discourse" (2010) 73 Sask L Rev 93 [Moon].

hate speech regulation diverts our attention away from more fundamental free speech issues concerning the character and structure of public discourse, and more particularly the domination of public discourse by commercial messages and the advertising form. But, of course, these are not issues that can be addressed by the courts, except in indirect ways, and that may partly explain the lack of attention they receive.[2]

In recent years the critics of hate speech regulation in Canada have focused on human rights code restrictions. Some critics are opposed not to hate speech regulation *per se* but only to this form of restriction. Their concern is that the human rights process is poorly suited to the regulation of hate speech. I count myself among this group. Other critics are opposed to any form of hate speech restriction and human rights code regulation is simply the battleground on which they have chosen to conduct their fight. But there is another dimension to the attack on human rights code regulation of hate speech. Much of the recent criticism of such regulation seems designed to undermine the entire human rights system. Critics such as Ezra Levant and Mark Steyn have focused on hate speech regulation as the most vulnerable part of that system. In their criticism of this regulation, they spend more time talking about the "corruption" and "incompetence" of human rights institutions than about the value of free speech. The logic of their (unfounded) claims of "corruption" is that these institutions have no legitimate role and should be abolished. Their claims are rooted in a more general libertarian view that state power is inherently oppressive and corrupt.

Let me add a caution here. I want to be careful about attributing a clear political outlook to Levant, Steyn, and other critics. It often seems that they are interested less in advancing a political agenda than in promoting themselves.[3] I say this not just because of their indifference to

2 For a discussion, see Richard Moon, *The Constitutional Protection of Freedom of Expression* (Toronto: University of Toronto Press, 2000).

3 Levant and Steyn were each the subject of a human rights complaint. A complaint was made to the Alberta Human Rights Commission against Levant, and the *Western Standard*, following his publication of the "Danish Cartoons." Complaints against Steyn and *Maclean's* magazine were made to the Ontario Human Rights Commission (Ontario Commission), the BC Human Rights Tribunal (BC Tribunal), and the Canadian Human Rights Commission (CHRC), following publication by *Maclean's* of an excerpt from Steyn's book *America Alone* (Washington, DC: Regnery Publishing, 2006). The complaint against Steyn was dismissed by the CHRC and did not go to adjudication. The BC Tribunal dismissed the complaint following a hearing. The province of British Columbia abolished its human rights com-

factual accuracy (which is discussed below) but because of their lack of interest in the consequences of their speech. In a piece in *Maclean's* (which was the subject of a human rights complaint), Steyn argued that Muslims will soon become the majority community in many European countries (through higher birth rates and immigration), that their goal is to impose Sharia law, and that many Muslims are prepared to use violence to achieve that goal. Steyn offered what he called "the obligatory 'of courses'": "Of course not all Muslims are terrorists"; "Of course not all Muslims support terrorism." But in the context of his piece, this caveat was about as comforting as the statement that: "Of course not every Jew is a crook" or "Of course not all gay men are pedophiles." It was presented as an exception to the assumed norm. Steyn seemed surprised when he discovered that his writing had been used by Anders Breivik, the Norwegian mass murderer, to justify his horrendous actions. But why should Steyn have been surprised? Any reader who believed Steyn's false claims — that Muslims are seeking to take over Europe and are prepared to use violence to do so — would have to conclude that radical action was called for. It is the risk that some readers or listeners might take seriously this kind of false claim that justifies the restriction of hate speech.[4]

In this chapter, I will say something about the current state of hate speech regulation in Canada, before looking more closely at the attack on human rights laws and institutions, and the resonance these attacks have had in the mainstream media.

---

mission in 2003 and so human rights code complaints are made directly to the BC Tribunal. The BC *Human Rights Code*, RSBC 1996, c 210 [BC *Code*] provides that a respondent may ask the Tribunal to dismiss the complaint in advance of a hearing on the grounds that the complaint is unlikely to succeed. Steyn, though, chose not to bring such a motion, presumably because he wanted to fully embrace the process and its publicity. The Ontario Commission does not have a provision similar to section 13 of the *Canadian Human Rights Act*, RSC 1985, c H-6 [*CHRA*] and the Ontario Commission held that it did not have jurisdiction to receive the complaint.

4 See Mark Steyn, "Gagging Us Softly" *National Review* (29 August 2011), online: SteynOnline www.steynonline.com/4409/gagging-us-softly. Steyn tries to distance himself from Breivik's actions in two ways: first by pointing out that Breivik murdered non-Muslim Norwegians (who he viewed as "race-traitors"); second, by noting that Breivik cited other writers, including Locke and Voltaire.

1 2 3 4 5 6 7 8 9 10 11 12 13 14

B. HATE SPEECH REGULATION IN CANADA

Hate speech in Canada is currently restricted by both federal and provincial laws. The *Criminal Code* of Canada prohibits the advocacy or promotion of genocide, the incitement of hatred against an identifiable group, when this incitement is likely to lead to a breach of the peace, and the wilful promotion of hatred against an identifiable group.[5] An individual may be charged under either the incitement or wilful promotion provisions only with the consent of the provincial Attorney General. To be convicted under either of these provisions, the accused must be shown to have committed the relevant act and to have done so either intentionally or with awareness of the nature of her/his actions. If found by the court to have committed the offence, he/she may be sentenced to a fine or a term of imprisonment. The *Criminal Code* also includes a section that enables a court to order the seizure or erasure of material that is judged to be "hate propaganda."[6]

Hate speech is also restricted under section 13 of the *Canadian Human Rights Act* (*CHRA*), although this provision will soon be repealed.[7] The section 13 ban on hate speech applies to telephonic or Internet communication that is likely to expose the members of an identifiable group to hatred or contempt. The purpose of section 13 is to prevent or rectify discriminatory practices or to compensate the victims of discrimination for the harm they have suffered. An individual may be found to have breached section 13 even though she/he did not intend to expose others to hatred or realize that his/her communication might have this effect. The focus is on the effect of the act and not the intention with which it is performed. The ordinary remedy against an individual, who is found to have breached the section, is an order that she/he cease her/his discriminatory practices.

The *CHRA* prohibits several different forms of discrimination, including discrimination in employment and in the provision of goods and services. But while the ban on these other forms of discrimination has been interpreted broadly by the courts and the Canadian Human Rights Tribunal (CHRT), the scope of the section 13 ban has been more narrowly

---

5 *Criminal Code*, RSC 1985, c C-46, ss 318 & 319(1)–(2) [*Criminal Code*].

6 *Ibid*, ss 320–320.1.

7 *CHRA*, above note 3. Bill C-304, *An Act to amend the Canadian Human Rights Act (protecting freedom)*, 1st Sess, 41st Parl, 2011 (Royal Assent 26 June 2013). The bill will repeal s 13 and will take effect one year after receiving Royal Assent.

defined. In *Canada (Human Rights Commission) v Taylor*[8] (*Taylor*) a majority of the Supreme Court of Canada, in a judgment written by Chief Justice Dickson, held that section 13 of the *CHRA* prohibits only a very narrow category of extreme expression that can be shown to contribute to the spread of hatred in the community. According to Dickson CJ, section 13 applies to expression that encourages "unusually strong and deep-felt emotions of detestation, calumny and vilification." He thought that "as long as the Human Rights Tribunal continues to be well aware of the purpose of section 13(1) and pays heed to the ardent and extreme nature of the feeling described in the phrase 'hatred or contempt,' there is little danger that subjective opinion as to offensiveness will supplant the proper meaning of the section."[9]

The process established under the *CHRA* is complaint-driven. An individual who has reasonable grounds for believing that a person is engaging or has engaged in a discriminatory practice can file a complaint with the Canadian Human Rights Commission (CHRC).[10] If the CHRC receives a complaint that falls within the general scope of the *CHRA* and is not trivial, frivolous, vexatious, or made in bad faith, it is obliged to investigate the complaint to determine whether it should be referred to the CHRT for adjudication. The CHRT is a separate and independent body from the CHRC. If a complaint is referred by the CHRC to the CHRT for adjudication, the CHRC may appear at the hearing "to represent the public interest." The complainant has carriage of the action before the CHRT.

It appears that section 13 of the *CHRA* will soon be repealed. However, similar provisions remain part of the human rights codes of British Columbia, Alberta, Saskatchewan, and the Northwest Territories — but are applicable to signs and publications rather than to the Internet.[11] (There is no equivalent provision in the other provincial and territorial

---

8 *Canada (Human Rights Commission) v Taylor*, [1990] 3 SCR 892 [*Taylor*].

9 *Ibid*. In *Warman v Kouba*, 2006 CHRT 50 at para 82, the CHRT identified certain "hallmarks of hate," factors the Tribunal considered relevant in deciding whether the expression meets the *Taylor* test for breach of section 13. All the complaints referred to the Tribunal for adjudication involved postings on white supremacist or neo-Nazi websites that were extreme in content and tone.

10 The CHRC may also initiate a complaint, but in the case of section 13 it has done so on only one occasion.

11 *Alberta Human Rights Act*, RSA 2000, c A-25.5; BC *Code*, above note 3; *Northwest Territories Human Rights Act*, SNWT 2002, c 18; *Saskatchewan Human Rights Code*, SS 1979, c S-24.1, s 14.

codes.) In the recent decision of *Saskatchewan (Human Rights Commission) v Whatcott*, the Supreme Court of Canada held that the hate speech ban in the *Saskatchewan Human Rights Code* did not breach the *Canadian Charter of Rights and Freedoms*[12] (*Charter*). Section 14(1)(b) of the Saskatchewan *Code* prohibits signs and other representations that expose or tend to expose to hatred an individual or groups of individuals based on their membership in a group. The section also prohibits speech that ridicules, belittles, or affronts the dignity of group members; however, the Court found that this element of the ban was not compatible with the *Charter* and so severed it from the section.[13] There is some variation in the investigative and adjudicative processes established under the different provincial codes. In British Columbia, all complaints go directly to the BC Human Rights Tribunal, which must hear the complaint, unless it is shown to be trivial. In Alberta, a complaint is first considered by the human rights commission, which determines if it should be adjudicated by an appointed tribunal. In Saskatchewan, complaints are investigated by the provincial human rights commission; however, if the commission decides that the complaint has substance, it will refer the complaint to the Court of Queen's Bench for adjudication.

---

12 *Saskatchewan (Human Rights Commission) v Whatcott*, 2003 SCC 11 [*Whatcott*]. According to the Court, the section bans only a narrow category of extreme expression — expression that vilifies the members of a group. The difficulty with this claim is that the harm, which human rights codes are designed to prevent, is described by the Court in very broad terms — as harm to "the societal standing of vulnerable groups" or discrimination against the members of such groups. But is it only extreme speech that contributes to these harms? A wide range of speech acts including derogatory remarks, stereotypical representations, and ridicule, may injure the group's social standing or encourage discrimination against the group's members. The challenge for the Court in *Whatcott*, as it was in *Taylor*, is to resolve the tension between the broad understanding of discrimination adopted in human rights laws (and reflected in their processes) and the recognition that a commitment to freedom of expression requires that a ban on hate speech be very narrowly drawn — and focus on only extreme speech. *Canadian Charter of Rights and Freedoms*, Part I of the *Constitution Act, 1982*, being Schedule B to the *Canada Act* 1982 (UK), 1982, c 11.

13 The courts in Saskatchewan had already, in practice, read these words out of the section. See, for example, *Owens v Saskatchewan (Human Rights Commission)*, 2006 SKCA 41 at para 52.

C. THE REPEAL OF SECTION 13 OF THE *CHRA*

In the fall of 2008, I prepared a report for the CHRC in which I recommended the repeal of section 13 of the *CHRA* so that the restriction of Internet hate speech would occur exclusively under the *Criminal Code*.[14] In my report, I made three arguments: (1) the state should ban extreme expression; (2) the state should not ban more "mainstream" instances of prejudiced expression; (3) the human rights code process is not well suited to the regulation of extreme expression.

1) The Restriction of Extreme Expression

The first claim is that the failure to ban the extreme or radical edge of prejudiced speech carries too many risks, particularly when it circulates within the racist subculture that subsists on the Internet. Despite our commitment to freedom of expression and our faith in public reason, we know that in some times and places, reason does not always operate. Hate speech on the Internet is often directed at the members of a relatively insular racist subculture. When directed at such an audience, extreme speech may reinforce and extend bigoted views without being exposed to public criticism. Individuals, already weighed down by prejudice or susceptible to manipulation or already part of an extremist subculture, will see in these claims a plausible account of their social and economic difficulties and a justification for radical action. Because the Internet audience is highly fragmented, it is easy for a particular website to operate at the margins and avoid critical public scrutiny. While most Internet websites are public in the sense that they are generally accessible, the audience for a particular site is often self-selecting and small. Smaller hate sites (or those that are less easily accessed such as chat rooms) that link like-minded individuals are able to encourage a sense of intimacy and identity and to operate below the radar. Thus these sites can be an effective means for individuals and groups, who hold hateful views, to encourage others to adopt more extreme views or to take violent action.

The focus of restriction should be on the extreme or radical edge of prejudiced speech — that which threatens, justifies, or advocates

---

14 Richard Moon, *Report to the Canadian Human Rights Commission Concerning Section 13 of the* Canadian Human Rights Act *and the Regulation of Hate Speech on the Internet* (October 2008), online: CHRC www.chrc-ccdp.ca/pdf/moon_report_en.pdf [Moon, *Report*].

1 2 3 4 5 6 7 8 9 10 11 12 13 14

violence either explicitly or implicitly. Speech can be understood as supporting violence, when its message is so extreme (when it represents the target groups as dangerous or threatening or inhuman) that a receptive audience member would conclude that violent action against the group was justified. Extreme speech carries too many risks, particularly when it is directed at the members of a racist subculture or occurs in a context in which there is little opportunity for response. The encouragement of extreme action may be a concern because, in the words of the Cohen Committee, "in times of stress such 'hate' could mushroom into a real and monstrous threat to our way of life"[15] or more likely because it may lead to "isolated" acts of violence against members of an identifiable group, acts such as "gay-bashing." Hate crimes are committed most often not by organized groups but by individuals who have immersed themselves in the extremist subculture that operates principally on the Internet. Internet content is notoriously difficult to regulate because material can be posted anonymously and redirected quickly and because it can be generated anywhere in the world. Indeed, it is sometimes argued that there should not be a law prohibiting hate on the Internet, for the simple reason that it will be ineffective. But even if we are unable to prevent some, perhaps even most, instances of hate speech, we ought to prevent those that we can. Every instance of hate speech — every threat or encouragement of violence — is harmful and ought to be prohibited.

2) Less Extreme Speech

The second claim I made in the report is that less extreme forms of discriminatory expression cannot simply be censored out of public discourse. Expression that stereotypes or defames the members of an identifiable group is insulting to the group's members and may negatively impact their position and treatment in the community. It may also serve as the foundation for more extreme "hate speech." Nevertheless, because discriminatory views or assumptions are so widely held and circulate generally in society, they cannot be eradicated through censorship. Any attempt to exclude speech that stereotypes or defames the

---

15 Canada, Parliament House of Commons Special Committee on Hate Propaganda in Canada, *Report to the Minister of Justice of the Special Committee on Hate Propaganda in Canada* (Ottawa: Roger Duhamel, 1966) at 24 [Cohen Report].

members of an identifiable group from public discourse would require extraordinary intervention by the state and would dramatically compromise the public commitment to freedom of expression. Because these less extreme forms of discriminatory expression are so commonplace, it is impossible to establish clear and effective rules for their identification and exclusion. Because they are so pervasive, it is vital that they be addressed or confronted rather than censored. They are often spread or reinforced without a clear intent by the speaker or conscious acceptance by the audience. The only effective response, then, is to expose the prejudiced character of commonplace assumptions and bring it to clearer, and hopefully more critical, consciousness.

Because hate speech laws focus on extreme speech, they leave untouched expression that employs stereotypes, or makes misleading claims, about the members of an identifiable group. The familiar refrain of those who oppose the censorship of hate speech or group defamation is that the answer to bad speech should be "more speech" — group defamation should be answered, not censored. But if we are serious about the "more speech" answer, then we must think about the real opportunities that individuals and groups have to participate in public discourse and respond to speech that is unfair and discriminatory. Groups within the community should have a meaningful opportunity to respond to expression that may not be so extreme as to violate criminal or human rights laws but may nevertheless affect their position within the larger community. A "laissez-faire" approach to discriminatory speech fails the groups that are victimized and implicates the larger society in that victimization, because communicative power is inequitably distributed.

3) The Human Rights Process

The third claim is that a narrowly drawn ban on hate speech that focuses on extreme expression does not fit easily into a human rights law that takes an expansive view of discrimination, emphasizes the effect of the action on the victim rather than the intention or misconduct of the actor, and employs a process that is designed to engage the parties and facilitate a non-adjudicative resolution of the "dispute" between them.

The language of section 13 is potentially quite broad in its scope. The section prohibits the repeated communication on the phone system or the Internet of any matter "that is likely to expose a person or persons to hatred or contempt by reason of the fact that person or those persons are identifiable on the basis of a prohibited ground of discrimination." However, as noted earlier, the courts and the tribunal have interpreted the provision narrowly.

Even though the scope of the prohibition has been narrowly defined by the CHRT and the courts, there are at least two significant problems with the process. (It is worth noting that the small number of section 13 cases that have been sent by the CHRC to the CHRT, and in which the CHRT has found a breach of the section, all, or almost all, have involved expression that is so extreme that it could be seen as advocating or justifying violence against the members of an identifiable group.) The first problem is that free speech interests are affected every time an investigation occurs, particularly since the investigation engages the parties and takes eight to ten months to conclude. This is a problem because the CHRC is required to investigate a complaint unless it is trivial, vexatious, frivolous, or made in bad faith. The CHRC therefore is bound to investigate some complaints that are unlikely to proceed to adjudication. There is a risk that human rights commissions will be reluctant to exclude a complaint prior to investigation on the grounds that it is trivial, because such a finding may be seen as downplaying the genuine feelings of hurt experienced by minority group members and will preclude the possibility of a facilitated resolution of the "dispute." Because section 13 is located in a law that seeks to advance the goal of social equality through education and conciliation, the CHRC is perhaps inclined to err on the side of inclusion when deciding whether a complaint should be rejected prior to investigation.

The absence of an intention requirement in section 13 also opens the door to a broader or more discretionary application of section 13. In the *Taylor* case, the Supreme Court of Canada did not consider the absence of an intention requirement (that the respondent intended to spread hatred or knew that his/her speech was likely to do so) to be fatal to the provision's constitutionality, because the purpose of human rights legislation is to "compensate and protect" the victim rather than "stigmatize or punish" the person who discriminated. Yet, despite the familiar claim that human rights codes are about harmful effects rather than wrongful intentions, the CHRC and the CHRT do not attempt to measure the effects of hate speech. It is in fact difficult to prove the impact of expression on the attitudes and actions of audience members, who may understand and react to the communication in many different ways. A wide range of discriminatory representations may contribute to hateful attitudes and discriminatory actions in the community. Indeed, less extreme, more commonplace, instances of discriminatory speech may provide the groundwork necessary for the spread of hateful attitudes and so might be caught by section 13 on an ordinary reading of its terms. In determining whether the communication at issue breaches section 13, the CHRT looks not at the actual impact, but instead at the extreme content and hateful tone of the communication. The language of intention appears frequently in the section 13 decisions of the CHRT.

The second problem is the burden that the process puts on private complainants. Hate speech is most often directed at a receptive, or at least interested, audience and is only known to a complainant because she/he has looked for it or stumbled across it. Hate speech generally targets a group rather than an individual. An individual who makes a section 13 complaint does so on behalf of the group or society in general. She/he may not even be a member of the group targeted by the speech but has simply taken the initiative to bring a complaint. It is not accidental, then, that particular individuals have played a leading role in the initiation of complaints. Without the initiative of these individuals, section 13 might have no operation at all. The complainant carries responsibility for the complaint throughout the process, at both the investigation and adjudication stages. (While the CHRC has the legislative authority to initiate complaints under section 13, it rarely acts on this. The CHRC is not required to appear at the CHRT adjudication, but can do so as representative of the public interest.) In addition to the burden of time and money borne by complainants, they are sometimes subjected to threats of violence. It is unreasonable to expect complainants to bear such a burden. Moreover, searching neo-Nazi websites for hate speech, and engaging with individuals on those sites to determine their identity, involves ethical challenges that should not be dealt with by private citizens. Hate speech harms the group and the community. It is a public wrong. The state, not private citizens, should be responsible for the enforcement of the law.

The restriction of hate speech that threatens, advocates, or justifies violence (explicitly or implicitly) is appropriately dealt with under the criminal law. Hate speech is a serious matter that should be investigated by the police and prosecuted in the courts and should carry a significant penalty. There are, of course, some potential drawbacks to an exclusive reliance on the *Criminal Code* hate speech provisions. These include the requirement that the Attorney General of the particular province consent to prosecution, and the lack of experience on the part of some police forces in pursuing hate speech cases.

The arguments for the repeal of section 13 that I made in my report would seem to apply no less to the restrictions on hate speech in provincial human rights codes. Section 13 will soon be repealed by Parliament, although not for the reasons I put forward in my report. Instead the push to repeal section 13 seems to be based on allegations made in right wing blogs that the CHRC is incompetent and corrupt.

D. THE ATTACK ON SECTION 13 AND THE CHRC

As I was writing the report, I became aware of what can only be described as a disinformation campaign against human rights commissions. I am sure it comes as no surprise to anyone that there are Internet blogs that post things about the CHRC that are false and malicious. The problem is that the claims made in these blogs seep into mainstream discourse — they have been taken up by members of Parliament, adopted in editorials and columns in leading newspapers, and repeated on radio and television current affairs programming. They have created in the larger public, or at least a significant element of the public, a "feeling" that there is a fundamental problem with human rights commissions, and in particular the CHRC, that needs to be addressed.

There is a serious debate to be had about the regulation of hate speech by human rights commissions (HRCs). But the debate is difficult and complex and there are many reasonable positions one can take on the issue. I disagree with those who argue that the CHRC should be involved in the regulation of Internet hate speech, but I do not doubt their good faith in taking this position. The most vociferous and indeed the most media-amplified critics of the CHRC are not interested in this debate.

It is easier, and it seems more effective, to invent injustices and engage in personal attacks. This approach has several related strategic advantages: (1) the case against the HRC regulation becomes clear-cut. All complexity is washed away. There are no longer competing interests that need to be addressed; (2) the attack on hate speech regulation, when based on the corruption and incompetence of the commission, undermines the entire HRC process and not just the regulation of hate speech (particularly when the impression is given that hate speech regulation is a large part of what HRCs cover); (3) the attack on HRCs can be made without having to defend unpopular ideological positions. The regulation of hate speech can be attacked without having to rely explicitly on a libertarian free speech position — the claim that speech should never be subject to limits. And a broader challenge to anti-discrimination law can be made without having to defend the view that the market is a just and efficient mechanism for the distribution of goods that should not be subject to any form of regulation; and (4) it appears that this style of attack (personal and extreme) gets attention and is an effective means of self-promotion.

Why this style of attack is effective I will consider later. First I want to look at three claims made by the critics and recycled in the mainstream media: (1) that the CHRC has a 100 percent conviction rate for section 13 cases; (2) that the CHRC has engaged in corrupt behaviour; and (3) that HRCs, in general, make unreasonable, even bizarre, decisions.

The techniques used by the critics are sadly familiar. They include (1) identifying one or two commission or tribunal decisions which seem unreasonable in their outcome, and presenting them as if they are representative of the larger body of decisions; (2) when describing a particular case, highlighting certain facts or findings and omitting mention of others to give a misleading picture of the case; (3) relying on dubious sources and reporting their claims as if true and uncontested; (4) using terms in a way that is intended to mislead the audience, such as making a claim that with some strain on the language may be "true" but which on an ordinary reading (the reading encouraged by the speaker) is false; (5) making blatantly false factual claims; and finally (6) engaging in personal attacks against those with opposing views, in order to undermine their credibility.

1) The CHRC Has a 100 Percent Conviction Rate

Ezra Levant, Mark Steyn, and others frequently assert that the CHRC has a 100 percent conviction rate in section 13 cases. Here is how Levant put it in a *National Post* op-ed:

> The CHRC already has a 100% conviction rate for censorship prosecutions — no one in 32 years has ever beat the rap. That's not hard to believe when you learn that truth, fair comment and honest belief

> are not legal defences in human rights hearings — the commissions operate more like kangaroo courts than real courts that way.[16]

Levant, in his book *Shakedown*, asserted that "no one had ever beaten a hate speech accusation . . . at the Canadian Human Rights Commission."[17] The claim was also made in a *National Post* editorial: "The CHRC, too, has a frighteningly undemocratic 100% conviction rate on hate speech cases."[18]

This claim is a little like Bill Clinton's statement: "I did not have sexual relations with that woman . . . ." It is intended to be misread. It is possible to interpret the 100 percent conviction rate claim as true, but in its "true" meaning it is entirely uninteresting and in no way a criticism of the CHRC. The ordinary reading of the claim is that the CHRC finds that section 13 is violated in every complaint it receives (every "accusation") — that the issue is fully decided by the CHRC, that it both investigates and adjudicates complaints, and that once a complaint is made — once a respondent is drawn into the process — the outcome, "conviction," is inevitable. This was the claim made in a *Windsor Star* editorial: " . . . the problem is that the CHRC is essentially the investigator, prosecutor and judge of complaints of racism and hate speech."[19]

Section 13 complaints represent a very small part of the CHRC's workload. Between January 2001 and September 2008, the CHRC received seventy-three section 13 complaints, which represented about 2 percent of the total number of complaints received by the CHRC. In the fall of 2008, when I was writing my report, fifty-eight of the seventy-three complaints received by the CHRC had been resolved: thirty-two (about half) were dismissed after investigation by the CHRC and did not go to adjudication; ten were resolved through mediation at the CHRT prior to adjudication; only sixteen were adjudicated. The CHRT found a breach of section 13 in 100 percent of the sixteen cases that it adjudicated — less than one-third of the complaints that were received and investigated by the CHRC.[20]

---

16 Ezra Levant, "Appetite for Censorship" *National Post* (16 June 2009) A16.

17 Ezra Levant, *Shakedown: How Our Government is Undermining Democracy in the Name of Human Rights* (Toronto: McClelland & Stewart, 2009) at 146 [Levant, *Shakedown*].

18 "Muzzling the Human Rights Debate," Editorial, *National Post* (18 June 2009) A20.

19 "The Code and Rights; Two Tiers We Don't Need," Editorial, *Windsor Star* (18 July 2009) A6.

20 Moon, *Report*, above note 14.

It is true that all section 13 complaints adjudicated by the CHRT were upheld — at least in the period prior to my report. The CHRT then had a 100 percent conviction rate. ("Conviction" is not the right term since the standard remedy given by the CHRT is a cease and desist order, but this is a relatively minor distortion.) It is also true that the CHRC was represented, and argued that section 13 had been breached, in all but one of the CHRT adjudications. The CHRC then had a 100 percent "conviction" rate as an advocate before the CHRT, but since so few section 13 complaints were sent to the CHRT that is not so remarkable. The CHRC dismissed approximately half of the investigated complaints because in its view the speech was not sufficiently extreme to breach section 13. Ironically, the 100 percent "conviction" rate by the CHRT could be used to support the very different claim that the CHRC is filtering out too many section 13 complaints, preventing some complaints that might succeed at adjudication from even being considered by the CHRT.

The implication of the 100 percent claim is that the process is "fixed" — that if you are accused you will be "convicted" by biased and corrupt bureaucrats. As noted earlier, there are real problems with the process that the CHRC is by law required to follow. These problems, however, are obscured by the misleading 100 percent conviction rate claim.

2) Human Rights Commissions and Tribunals Make Bad Decisions

In his book *Shakedown*,[21] Levant described a handful of human rights code cases, dealing with issues other than hate speech, in which a provincial tribunal made a decision that seemed patently unreasonable. According to Levant, the "craziest" of all the human rights decisions is the judgment of the BC Human Rights Tribunal in *Datt v McDonald's*.[22] On the CBC's *The Current*, Levant said this about the case: "A woman didn't want to wash her hands and she sued McDonald's in human rights tribunal and won. She allegedly has this human right not to have to wash her hands at McDonald's."[23] On smaller radio programs his claims became even stronger:

---

21 Levant, *Shakedown*, above note 17.

22 *Datt v McDonald's Restaurants (No. 3)*, 2007 BCHRT 324 [*Datt*].

23 Interview of Ezra Levant by Anna Maria Tremonti (28 April 2009) on *The Current*, CBC Radio, Toronto, online: CBC Radio www.cbc.ca/thecurrent/episode/2009/04/28/april-28-2009/.

> One day she said, "I don't like to wash my hands so much." . . . Nothing was wrong, she just didn't want to wash her hands . . . . There was no name for this mystery illness . . . [It was decided by the HRT that] she had the human right not to wash her hands . . . . McDonald's was ordered never to enforce its hand-washing policy on people with this hand-washing problem again . . . . That's just gross.[24]

In a blog entry on the case Levant informed us that "the British Columbia Human Rights Tribunal ruled that one of the employees there [at McDonald's] has a human right not to wash her hands when working in their kitchen"; the Tribunal "invent[ed] a human right for a worker to go to the bathroom and then handle meat without washing her hands in between."[25] The case also received passing comment in *The Globe and Mail* from columnist Rex Murphy, who referred to the trivial "rights" recognized by HRCs "like the right not to wash one's hands while working in a fast-food restaurant."[26] The impression one got from Levant's account of the case was of a tribunal that was entirely out of touch with reality and indifferent to important health and safety concerns.

Of course anyone who combs through the thousands of human rights cases that have been decided over the years is bound to discover decisions that seem wrong or unfair. This would be the case with any decision maker, including the courts. With that said, however, let me tell you what Levant leaves out of his account of this case. Ms Datt had worked for Macdonald's for twenty-three years until she developed severe dermatitis as a consequence of her frequent handwashing. There seemed to be no dispute that frequent handwashing had caused her to suffer severe dermatitis. The BCHRT, following *O'Malley v Simpson-Sears Ltd*,[27] and other decisions of the Supreme Court of Canada, noted that once it had been established that Ms Datt suffered from a disability, the burden shifted to McDonald's to establish that "her disability was not capable of being accommodated in the workplace without incurring undue

---

24 Interview of Ezra Levant by Nick Vandergragt (25 April 2009) on *Nick at Night*, 580 CFRA News Talk Radio, Ottawa.

25 Ezra Levant, "The Human Right for McDonald's Employees not to Wash their Hands" (15 April 2008), online: Ezra Levant http://ezralevant.com/2008/04/the-human-right-for-mcdonalds.html.

26 Rex Murphy, "Real Rights and Rights Commissions" *The Globe and Mail* (15 November 2008) [Murphy], online: The Globe and Mail www.theglobeandmail.com/news/national/real-rights-and-rights-commissions/article716895/.

27 *O'Malley v Simpsons-Sears*, [1985] 2 SCR 536.

hardship." The BCHRT's decision did not question the importance of hygiene in food preparation. The BCHRT member said:

> I accept that the goal of preventing the contamination of food is why McDonald's established its hand-washing policy. This goal cannot be understated and it accords with common sense in the handling and preparation of food. However, there were duties that Ms Datt could have performed that did not require her to handle food.[28]

The problem, said the BCHRT, was that McDonald's did not seem to have considered in any serious way whether there were other tasks that Ms Datt might perform that would not involve the handling of food and require handwashing with the same frequency. The BCHRT concluded:

> I am at a loss to understand why McDonald's did not take more steps to try to accommodate Ms Datt, a 23-year committed employee. Ms Datt was not entitled to a "perfect" solution, but she was entitled to a fulsome consideration of her restrictions and how those restrictions intersected with the hand-washing policies and the jobs that were available. Without having done so, neither Ms Datt nor McDonald's was in a position to know what the outcome of a return to work, with accommodations, might have been. It may be that, at the end of the day, Ms Datt could not have been accommodated at McDonald's because she simply could not meet its hand-washing policies doing any job or combination of jobs, but based on the evidence before me, I find that McDonald's failed to take all the necessary steps to make this final determination.[29]

You can disagree with the decision — although that may only be possible if you believe that employers have no duty to accommodate employees with disabilities — but the result is not shocking in the way Levant suggests. If that is among the most egregious injustices that he is able to mine from the thousands of human rights decisions, then human rights bodies must be doing far better than I might have guessed. In this and other cases discussed in *Shakedown*, Levant gives an entirely distorted account of what occurred.[30]

---

28 *Datt*, above note 22 at para 239.

29 *Ibid* at paras 249 & 250.

30 For a discussion of some of the other cases cited by Levant, see Moon, above note 1.

3) The CHRC and Its Staff Are Corrupt

The term "corruption" is used very loosely by Levant and other critics. They often use it interchangeably with incompetence to refer to what they see as the CHRC's unjustified interference with free speech or its failure to respect due process. They give the impression that the CHRC has complete discretion in deciding what complaints it will investigate and how it will conduct the investigation. Indeed, Levant often seems to suggest that the complaints originate with the CHRC; for example, when he asserts that "her [Chief Commissioner Jennifer Lynch's] persecutions of Christian clergy, mainstream conservatives, and others who merely have a different political opinion from hers is not only politically scandalous and morally odious, but it's unconstitutional." Conservative MP Brad Trost expresses on his website his belief that Canada's HRCs "have morphed into kangaroo courts that selectively oppress Canadians who hold small 'c' conservative religious or political views." But the CHRC process is complaint-driven, and, as noted above, the CHRC is bound to investigate complaints from individuals or groups that are not trivial or made in bad faith.

The critics sometimes bolster this general claim of corruption with more specific claims of corrupt behaviour. One of the more prominent of these claims is that CHRC staff members have joined neo-Nazi groups and made numerous anti-Semitic or racist postings.[31] Levant claims that "trial transcripts reveal that the staff of the CHRC's anti-hate squad, in their bid to entrap alleged hate-mongers, actually have become one of Canada's largest sources of hate speech";[32] " . . . Canada's largest 'hate group' as measured by the number of anti-Semitic, anti-gay, anti-black, and pro-Nazi comments published on the Internet . . . [is] none other than the taxpayers' own Canadian Human Rights Commission";[33] "Their goal is to goad Canadian citizens into replying with their own hateful comments — which the human rights investigators can then prosecute as human rights abuses."[34] Conservative MP Russ Heibert in an op-ed

31 Another significant claim was that the CHRC tapped into the private computer of a woman in Ottawa in order to access a neo-Nazi site. For a discussion of this baseless claim, see Moon, above note 1.

32 Levant, *Shakedown*, above note 17 at 31.

33 Ezra Levant, "Neo-Nazi Organization Infiltrates Ottawa Remembrance Day Ceremony" (10 November 2008), online: Ezra Levant www.ezralevant.com/2008/11/neonazi-activists-infiltrate-o.html.

34 Levant, *Shakedown*, above note 17 at 31.

in the *National Post* made a similar claim: "Recent hearings such as the Marc Lemire case, have revealed that current CHRC investigator Dean Steacy and former CHRC investigator Richard Warman regularly posted neo-Nazi diatribes under assumed names on white supremacist websites."[35]

When the CHRC investigates a complaint about Internet postings, it has to confirm that such postings have actually been made and it has to confirm or determine the identity of the person responsible for the postings. In order to do this the commission investigators sometimes go onto racist websites. In some cases, the complaint relates to postings in a chat room, or other location, that is accessible only to those who "join," although anyone who wishes to may join. However, there is no evidence to support the assertion that CHRC investigator Dean Steacy has made racist postings on the Stormfront site or any other site. Indeed in Marc Lemire's submissions to the CHRT in *Warman v Lemire* it was conceded that "there is no evidence he [Steacy] posted any racist material . . . . "[36] (Levant in his blog claims that the postings were racist in content — but if you follow the links he provides you will find nothing of the sort, only requests for pamphlets and information about events.)

Even though Levant's accusations refer to the CHRC, the actual focus of his claims about racist postings is Richard Warman, who has been the complainant in virtually all of the successful section 13 complaints. Warman was at one time an employee of the CHRC (from 2002 to 2004), but he did not investigate section 13 complaints for the CHRC. Levant claims that Warman "worked at the CHRC as an anti-hate investigator."[37] But that is just not true. Warman did, however, initiate complaints, as a private citizen, while he was employed by the CHRC, although most of his complaints were filed after he left the CHRC. Levant, however, attributes to the CHRC all of Warman's actions and postings, even those made after he left the employ of the CHRC. I do not want to embark on the distasteful task of parsing the online exchanges that occurred on neo-Nazi websites. I will say simply that some of the statements attributed to Warman are reformulated by Levant and taken out of context. Nothing said

---

35 Russ Heibert, "Jennifer Lynch's 'Misinformed' Human Rights Commission," Op-Ed, *National Post* (29 July 2009).

36 *Warman v Lemire*, 2009 CHRD 26. Submissions of Lemire at 400. The sentence continues " . . . but he did attempt to engage Lemire in conversation about a complaint Lemire had laid under section 13."

37 Levant, *Shakedown*, above note 17 at 32.

in response to Warman's postings has been the subject of a section 13 complaint and so the claim of entrapment has no basis. The important point, though, is that none of these postings, however they are described, comes from the CHRC or its section 13 investigators.

Again Levant's false or misleading claims about CHRC corruption fail to address the real problems with the section 13 process.

E. THE STATE OF PUBLIC DISCOURSE

Many of the claims made by Levant, Steyn, and other critics of the CHRC are false or misleading. But how have these critics been able to make these false or deceptive claims go so far? Levant's claims are not just posted on his blog. They are in his book, which is published by a major Canadian publisher.[38] They are repeated by him, almost always without challenge, in radio and television interviews. They are parroted by politicians and in newspaper editorials and columns. And, although this is more difficult to gauge, they appear to have been taken up by Canadians.

The propaganda campaign against the HRCs fits within the dominant model of contemporary political discourse, which is often referred to as "spin." Spin, described most generously, involves putting a positive gloss on an event or statement, or describing the actions of one's opponent in a negative light. More realistically described by Brooks Jackson and Kathleen Hall Jamieson, in their book, *unSpun*:

> Spin is a polite word for deception. Spinners mislead by means that range from subtle omissions to outright lies. Spin paints a false picture of reality by bending facts, mischaracterizing the words of others, ignoring or denying crucial evidence, or just "spinning a yarn" — by making things up.[39]

Political "spin" inverts the relationship between fact and opinion, with the former often following the latter. To the political spinner, facts are just supports or props for a position. "Facts" may be selected, massaged, and even invented to advance a larger "truth" or simply the self-interest of the speaker.

---

38 *Ibid.*

39 Brooks Jackson & Kathleen Hall Jamieson, *unSpun: Finding Facts in a World of Disinformation* (New York: Random House, 2007) at vii.

"Spin" is political speech in the model of commercial advertising. Commercial advertising has come to dominate public discourse not just in the sense that so much of that discourse is composed of ads, but also in the way in which these ads have become the general model for public expression — for how political and other public actors convey their views and seek to persuade others. Political speech, in the commercial model, seeks an emotional or visceral response, eschews complexity and nuance, and devalues factual accuracy. The dominance of public discourse by the advertising model has made it increasingly difficult for us to envision political speech that seeks to persuade citizens of the wisdom of a particular policy rather than simply to shape or manipulate the concerns and feelings of political consumers.

Why have mainstream media outlets been willing to provide a platform for these false and misleading claims? There are several reasons for the media's failing. The most obvious is that media reporters and interviewers have limited time and resources, making it difficult for them to fact-check — to confirm or correct the claims made. And, of course, the more these claims are repeated in the media, the less it seems necessary to check their accuracy. But there are other more significant factors that seem to support non-critical reporting of these and other baseless claims.

The first is the desire by most mainstream media outlets, in their role as reporter of news, to appear neutral or balanced in their reporting, particularly on matters of public controversy. In seeking to avoid the appearance of bias, newspapers and broadcasters, at least in their news coverage, often present different positions without commenting on their merits. The problem is that the positions reported may not have any factual grounding or may be based on factual claims that are contested. If the media simply report the factual assertions of one side without ensuring that they are accurate, or if they report competing factual claims with no comment on the accuracy of the claims, then the audience will at worst be misled and at best be denied enough information to make a reasoned judgment. Levant appeared on several CBC national radio programs. Each program allowed him to repeat his false claims with little or no challenge and so gave them validation. When Levant made his 100 percent conviction rate claim in an interview, and was not challenged by the interviewer, the audience might reasonably have assumed that his claim was true.

When the media treat factual claims the same way they treat opinions, and simply channel them to the audience, how is the audience to

1 2 3 4 5 6 7 8 9 10 11 12 13 14

know whether the claims made are true? The audience has no other meaningful access to the facts. Even when the audience hears competing versions of the facts, how are they to decide between them, if the media do not arbitrate or even comment on these factual "disputes"? Because there is often no common factual ground, it is left to the members of the audience simply to choose their position, based on "gut instinct" or ideological predisposition. Not surprisingly, individuals tend to adopt the factual claims that fit with the views they currently hold and to discount or reject those that do not. If I am already wary of "big government" or resentful of "political correctness," I will be more receptive to the claims of Levant and Steyn. On the other hand, I am more likely to discount their claims, if I believe that government has a role in protecting minority groups from discrimination. In either case, I adopt a position not as a judgment but as a preference.

The second factor, contributing to the media's non-critical reporting of the false claims about the CHRC, is the increasing prominence of columnists, who engage in advocacy rather than analysis, and are concerned less with factual accuracy and more with simply provoking a reaction in their readers. Most mainstream print publications, although seeking to be impartial in their news reporting, publish opinion columns. Most of these columns offer a careful, factually grounded, analysis of current affairs, drawing on the knowledge and experience of the columnist. However, in recent years there has been a proliferation of columns, modelled on television commentary, that are designed to be provocative — to attract readers who strongly agree or disagree with the positions taken by the columnist. The authors of these advocacy columns are prepared to address a remarkably wide range of issues about which they have little or no background knowledge. Their object is advocacy rather than accuracy, and so they make simple and dramatic claims, often with little factual support. Mark Steyn's column in *Maclean's* magazine is an obvious example. He seems to have no hesitation reshaping the "facts" to fit the conclusion he wishes to reach. Rex Murphy, in the columns he wrote for *The Globe and Mail* dealing with HRCs, took his information straight from Levant's blog, without any attempt to confirm its accuracy.[40]

A third factor contributing to the problem of factual distortion is the tendency of the television (and increasingly radio and newspapers) to avoid complex analysis and to sensationalize issues. Television, as

---

40 Murphy, above note 26.

a visual medium, does better with spectacle, and with claims that are simple, direct, and dramatic.[41] Television current affairs programming often focuses on extreme positions.[42] Accusations of corruption, deceit, or patent injustice play much better on television than do more nuanced arguments or moderate or conciliatory positions. Issues are generally presented as if they have only two sides, each of which is simple, straightforward, and diametrically opposed to the other. Even when both sides of an issue are represented, they do not engage with each other, at least not in any way that might contribute to audience understanding or to the discovery of common ground. The audience is rarely given enough information, and often lacks the background knowledge necessary, to evaluate the claims made. Because the competing positions are so far apart and rest on completely different versions of the facts, the audience cannot learn from each but must choose one over the other.

F. CONCLUSION

The dominance of the advertising model of expression, or "spin," makes it difficult for us to envision another form of public discourse — one characterized by sincerity and honesty, rather than simply their images, and intended to persuade citizens with arguments and facts, rather than simply impact consumers at a visceral or emotional level. The factual assertions made by the critics of HRCs appeal to those who are already suspicious of government power. This group is ready to accept these false or misleading claims, apparently without skepticism, or at least with indifference to their accuracy, because they represent a larger "truth." Once you accept that everyone spins then it seems the facts are no longer at issue only the preferred ideology.

In the end, the debate about human rights commissions, like so much public debate, involves no real engagement between competing positions, and no real opportunity for the audience to judge whether or not the current law is good policy. The complexity of the issue is avoided or suppressed. The merits of the case, either for or against hate speech regulation by HRCs, are lost in a sea of exaggerations and fabrications.

41 Neil Postman, *Amusing Ourselves to Death: Public Discourse in the Age of Show Business* (New York: Penguin Books, 1986).

42 Levant now has his own current affairs program on Sun TV.

It is left to the audience, if it is paying attention, to make a choice, not based on reasoned judgment, but on their existing views, on their ideological predispositions, either suspicion of government regulation or belief in the importance of human rights protection. While the critics of the CHRC have been successful in spreading their views, all they can hope for is a marginal win in a polarized debate. This is the most spin can accomplish. It will not advance democratic engagement or meaningful discussion of public policy, and it cannot bring about consensus or compromise or even respectful disagreement based on an awareness of the costs and benefits of the different responses. Spin encourages the fragmentation of the civic audience into insular ideological communities that are unable to engage with each other.[43] The costs of spin are even more fundamental than this though. Spin degrades public discourse, so that we no longer expect to be told the truth and are no longer able to evaluate positions based on the accuracy of their claims or assumptions.

43 Kathleen Hall Jamieson & Joseph N Cappella, *Echo Chamber: Rush Limbaugh and the Conservative Media Establishment* (New York: Oxford University Press, 2008).

PART 4

Human Rights Commissions and Policy-Making:
Naming – Engaging – Implementing

CHAPTER 11

ONTARIO HUMAN RIGHTS COMMISSION PROMOTION ACTIVITIES: THE EXPERIENCE OF RESPONDING TO RACIAL PROFILING BY POLICE

Shaheen Azmi[1]

A. INTRODUCTION

The Ontario Human Rights Commission (OHRC) has been directly involved in responding to racial profiling by police employing multiple approaches since 2002. This article will review the key elements of this experience and highlight its promotion elements in particular. This experience is a prime example of human rights activity by a Canadian human rights commission that strategically combines protective and promotion mandates to respond to a complex and entrenched form of discrimination that has been resistant to change for many years. It will be argued that the strategic and sustained employment of promotion activities by commissions is vital to adequately respond to entrenched forms of discrimination in Canadian society.

B. EMPLOYING THE PROMOTION MANDATE TO RESPOND TO POLICE RACIAL PROFILING

In accordance with international human rights law, human rights legislation in Canada has generally provided commissions with both human

1 Shaheen Azmi is the director of Policy, Outreach, and Education of the Ontario Human Rights Commission. The author is an employee of the Ontario Human Rights Commission, but the contents of this article are his own and do not represent the views of the OHRC.

rights protection and promotion mandates.[2] The protection mandate has involved commissions with handling of individual complaints from community members. Such activities routinely involve registration, mediation, investigation, and litigation of human rights complaints. The promotion mandate involves education, public awareness, training, research, policy development, and systemic change activities. The tendency for Canadian human rights commissions has been for the protection mandate to preoccupy resources and for promotion activity to be deemed as secondary. In part this is related to the natural tendency to focus on the legal aspects of the mandate that draw most public attention and media scrutiny but some of this is clearly related to hard choices forced on commissions dealing with limited and increasingly tight budgets.[3]

Human rights promotion is understood to be a vital component to the effective operation of a human rights system. The United Nations Office of the High Commissioner for Human Rights indicates:

> Whether human rights violations are intentional or unintentional, structural or specific, a lack of knowledge can result in actions that breach human rights principles. Sometimes traditional ways of thinking and behaving result in human rights abuse. In either case, human rights education and the inculcation of human rights values can promote change in behaviour without the need for punitive sanctions. Successful human rights promotion can therefore help prevent human rights violations from occurring in the first place.[4]

The OHRC is unique in Canada for being the only commission whose current mandate is focused primarily on a promotion mandate. As a

---

2 The Paris Principles relating to the status and functioning of national institutions for human rights adopted in 1992 by the United Nations Human Rights Commission and by the UN General Assembly in 1993 clearly indicate the importance of both protection and promotion mandates for national human rights institutions. See *Principles Relating to the Status of National Institutions*, annex to *National Institutions for the Promotion and Protection of Human Rights*, CHR Res 54, UNESCOR, Supp No 2, UN Doc E/1992/22, (1992); GA Res 48/134, UNGAOR, 48th Sess, (1993) Annex, article 3 [Paris Principles].

3 R Brian Howe & David Johnson, *Restraining Equality: Human Rights Commissions in Canada* (Toronto: University of Toronto Press, 2000) at 120–27.

4 United Nations Office for the High Commissioner for Human Rights, *National Human Rights Institutions: History, Principles, Roles and Responsibilities* (New York: United Nations, 2010) at 57–58.

result of legislative changes in 2007, the task of handling complaints was transferred from the OHRC to the Human Rights Tribunal of Ontario (HRTO).[5] However, even before this change took place, the OHRC was a leader in human rights promotion activity among human rights commissions in Canada. An official Policy and Education Branch was established in 1996 and began to coordinate policy, education, and communication activity to advance human rights in an increasingly sophisticated manner. In this year it began to release official human rights policies to provide authoritative interpretation of the Ontario *Human Rights Code*[6] (*Code*) in areas of key human rights concerns. The first such policy released in 1996 was the *Policy on Creed and the Accommodation of Religious Observances*.[7]

The usage of promotion functions by the OHRC has nowhere been as active as in its work on racial discrimination with a particular focus on racial profiling beginning in 2002. Racial profiling by police primarily involving perceptions of racially biased police stops has long been a concern of some racialized communities across North America. Scholarly research and government inquiry began to prominently identify these concerns in Ontario beginning in the 1980s.[8] Particular concern has been raised for decades by Black community members about the highly disproportionate rate of police stops affecting young Black men in particular, which they believed was related to racial profiling.[9] Many

---

5 See Ontario *Human Rights Code*, RSO 1990, c H.19, s 34(1) [*Code*]. For details, see also Mary Cornish, Fay Faraday, & Jo-Anne Pickel, *Enforcing Human Rights in Ontario* (Aurora, ON: Canada Law Book, 2009).

6 See *Code*, above note 5.

7 Steven Lavendar, *The 2013 Annotated Ontario Human Rights Code* (Toronto: Carswell, 2013) at 1069–83.

8 See, for example, Scot Wortley, "Justice for All? Race and Perceptions of Bias in the Ontario Criminal Justice System — a Toronto Survey" (1996) 38:4 Can J Crim 439; Carl E James, "'Up to No Good': Black on the Streets and Encountering Police" in Vic Satzewich, ed, *Racism and Social Inequality in Canada: Concepts, Controversies & Strategies of Resistance* (Toronto: Thompson Educational Publishing, 1998); Clare Lewis, Ontario Ministry of the Solicitor General, *The Report of the Race Relations and Policing Task Force* (Toronto: The Task Force, April 1989); *Report of the Commission on Systemic Racism in the Ontario Criminal Justice System* by David Cole & Margaret Gittens (Toronto: Commission on Systemic Racism in the Ontario Criminal Justice System, December 1995) [Cole & Gittens Report].

9 Erica Lawson et al, *Anti-Black Racism in Canada: A Report on the Canadian Government's Compliance with the International Convention on the Elimination of All Forms of Racial Discrimination* (Toronto: African Canadian Legal Clinic, 2002). See also, African Canadian Legal Clinic, *The Hidden Side of*

of these studies confirmed that racial profiling was not only a concern but a well-founded one that required concerted action. For example, the Report of the Commission on Systemic Racism in the Ontario Criminal Justice System stated:

> First we look at a police practice that has probably done more harm than any other to exacerbate tensions and fuel mistrust — exercise of the discretion to stop people in cars and on foot. Findings from the Commission's public survey about the number and the nature of stops lend considerable weight to community concerns that this discretion is exercised in a racially discriminatory manner.[10]

In response to concerns of racial profiling the Commission proceeded to propose:

> . . . that systemic strategies to promote constructive relationships between the police and the community should be built into the planning, implementation, and governance of community policing systems.[11]

The OHRC was slow to react to calls for action and formulate a role for itself in response to racial profiling. This was partially related to the fact that the OHRC routinely did not investigate police-related human rights complaints until 2002. Prior to this, the OHRC screened out complaints against police taking the position that these could be adequately addressed under the complaint provisions of the *Police Services Act*.[12] The OHRC changed this position in response to growing public concern that these complaint provisions were poorly structured to address police complaints in general and particularly to provide adequate assessment

---

Paradise: Violations of the Economic and Social Rights of African Canadians (Toronto: African Legal Clinic, 2006), online: OHCHR www2.ohchr.org/english/bodies/cescr/docs/info-ngos/ACLC.pdf.

10 Cole & Gittens Report, above note 8 at 337.

11 *Ibid.*

12 Under the provisions of section 34(a) of the then *Code*, above note 5, the OHRC in its discretion could decline to deal with a case where "the complaint is one that could or should be more appropriately dealt with under an Act other than the Code." The *Police Services Act*, RSO 1990, c P.15 system of the time placed local police services as responsible for complaints intake, investigation, and adjudication, with an independent tribunal, the Ontario Civilian Commission on Police Services reviewing how police handled complaints.

of human rights matters.[13] Primarily, there were concerns raised that the *Police Services Act* complaints process was intimidating to potential complainants and biased because these complaints at the time were required to be filed with police chiefs prior to proceeding to any later stage review. Following this change the number of human rights complaints filed against police with the OHRC quickly accelerated.

By 2007, the last full year in which the OHRC was still taking in complaints, the OHRC had 151 active complaints against twenty-one different police services with another nineteen complaints being before the HRTO for adjudication. Complaints against police services accounted for 4 percent of all active human rights complaints. Of these complaints, 110 (73 percent) of police human rights complaints related to police service delivery and about 62 percent of these were filed on the grounds of race, colour, ethnic origin, place of origin, or ancestry. The single largest theme of these race-related complaints was that of racial profiling.[14] The handling of these police complaints led to increased engagement between the OHRC and police services across Ontario with one consistent focus being on concerns of racial profiling.

Also, in 2002 a series of articles by *The Toronto Star* on race and policing in Toronto provided fresh evidence of the reality of racial profiling by the Toronto Police Service. Based on research conducted using data obtained through freedom of information legislation and gathered by the police over a six year period, the *Star* concluded that:

> Blacks arrested by Toronto police are treated more harshly than whites . . . . Black people, charged with simple drug possession, are taken to police stations more often than whites facing the same charge. Once at the station, accused blacks are held overnight, for a bail hearing, at twice the rate of whites. The Toronto crime data also shows a disproportionate number of black motorists are ticketed for violations that only surface following a traffic stop. This difference, say civil libertarians, community leaders and criminologists, suggests police use racial profiling in deciding whom to pull over.[15]

13 Scadding Court Community Centre, *Brief History of Police Complaints in Ontario* (2008), online: Bill 103 – Summit www.scaddingcourt.org/home2/Bill103-summit/briefhistory.html.

14 Ontario Human Rights Commission, *Human Rights and Policing: Creating and Sustaining Organizational Change* (Toronto: OHRC, 2011) at 13.

15 Jim Rankin et al, "Singled Out; Star Analysis of Police Crime Data Shows Justice Is Different for Blacks and Whites" *The Toronto Star* (19 October 2002) A01.

For its part the Toronto Police Service took the position that such concerns were simply wrong. In responding to the findings Chief Julian Fantino emphasized: "We're not perfect people but you're barking up the wrong tree. There's no racism . . . we don't do profiling."[16]

The research data and the articles galvanized community calls for a more active OHRC response to racial profiling. Under leadership of then Chief Commissioner Keith Norton, efforts within the OHRC to address racial profiling as a human rights issue for Commission action began. What has unfolded ever since has been a concerted and sustained effort to address racial discrimination with a particular focus on racial profiling by police. The OHRC's responses to racial profiling have included a new focus on racial profiling complaint handling and litigation,[17] a formal inquiry and report into racial profiling, the development of a policy document on racism and racial discrimination, police training partnerships with the Ontario Police College, organizational change partnerships with police service organizations, and the development and promotion of a guide to human rights organizational change for police. Each of these key initiatives will be reviewed in the following.

C. REGULAR TOOLS: INQUIRY, POLICY, AND LITIGATION

Human rights inquiry and research, policy development, and particularly litigation have been the staple of human rights commission work throughout Canada for decades. Not surprisingly, the initial tools used by the OHRC to respond to racial profiling by police relied on these.

1) Racial Profiling Inquiry and Report

On 9 December 2002, in direct response to the controversy raised by *The Toronto Star* articles, the OHRC announced that it would conduct an inquiry into the effects of racial profiling. Racial profiling was defined broadly as

> . . . any action undertaken for reasons of safety, security or public protection that relies on stereotypes about race, colour, ethnicity,

---

16 *Ibid.*

17 See *Phipps v Toronto Police Services Board*, 2009 HRTO 1604; *Maynard v Toronto Police Services Board*, 2012 HRTO 1220.

> ancestry, religion, or place of origin rather than on reasonable suspicion, to single out an individual for greater scrutiny or different treatment.[18]

The purpose of the inquiry was to "raise public awareness about racial profiling, to mobilize public action, to put an end to it and to bridge the divide between those who deny the existence of racial profiling on the one hand, and the communities who have long held that they are targets of racial profiling on the other."[19]

The inquiry was based on the premise that the reality of racial profiling was already well established, but that its impact on the lives of individuals, groups, and society as a whole was insufficiently exposed, particularly as a human rights concern.

The inquiry gathered submissions from individuals detailing their experiences relating to racial profiling. Advertisements concerning the inquiry were placed in forty-three Ontario daily newspapers, seventeen weekly French newspapers, and thirty ethnic and Aboriginal newspapers. As well, information was sent to approximately 1,000 individuals and organizations. Submissions were received by telephone (from 18 to 28 February 2003), by mail, and through an online questionnaire on the OHRC's website. The response received far exceeded expectations. Over 800 people contacted the OHRC with approximately half of those contacts being about racial profiling. Most of the remaining submissions concerned racial discrimination but did not fit within the Commission's definition of racial profiling.[20]

The inquiry report argued that racial profiling does not work from the perspective of effective policing. It summarized feedback in terms of eight different social costs to racial profiling. Included in these were:

- loss of self-esteem and confidence of young people,
- general erosion of trust in major public institutions,
- alienation of racialized individuals and communities,
- disempowerment of racialized communities,
- alternation of patterns of behaviour of individuals to avoid racial profiling scrutiny,

1 2 3 4 5 6 7 8 9 10 11 12 13 14

18 Ontario Human Rights Commission, *Paying the Price: The Human Cost of Racial Profiling: Inquiry Report* (Toronto: OHRC, 2003) at 6 [*Inquiry Report*].

19 *Ibid* at 67.

20 *Ibid* at 1.

- emotional and psychological trauma affecting those racially profiled and their families,
- physical injury for some involved in conflict relating to racial profiling incidents, and
- economic loss to individuals and society.[21]

The inquiry report also contained a special section focused on the racial profiling and its impact in Aboriginal communities.

The inquiry provided nineteen recommendations for action by organizations and institutions having some responsibility to address racial profiling including police, educational institutions, private security companies, airport and airline security, Canada customs, government, and malls and stores.

The racial profiling inquiry report[22] (Inquiry Report) was launched on 9 December 2003. It gathered considerable media and public attention. The launch of the Inquiry Report was covered live by CBC Newsworld and drew attention from many print media.[23] Predictably, many in racialized groups were supportive. However, many voices from the government, media, and police were highly critical of the Inquiry Report. Premier Ernie Eves; the Minister of Public Security and Safety, Bob Runciman; Tom Kaye, head of the Ontario Association of Chiefs of Police; Toronto Police Chief Julian Fantino; and Toronto Police Association president Craig Bromwell all spoke to the unfairness of the inquiry process and continued to deny the reality of racial profiling.[24]

Despite the negative response by most police leaders, the Inquiry Report did find a few who were supportive. For example, in January 2004, York Region Police Service organized two presentations for hundreds of its senior police service staff on the Inquiry Report. These presentations were led by Chief Commissioner Keith Norton and OHRC staff. Although most present were skeptical about racial profiling and critical of the OHRC approach to the inquiry, York Region Police Chief Armand

---

21 *Ibid* at 17–66.

22 *Ibid.*

23 See, for example, Erin Conway-Smith, "Racial Profiling Report Urges Provincial Monitor" *The Globe and Mail* (10 December 2003) A12.

24 Frances Henry & Carol Tator, *Racial Profiling in Toronto: Discourses of Domination, Mediation, and Opposition* (Toronto: Canadian Race Relations Foundation, 2005) at 65–67, online: CRR www.crr.ca/divers-files/en/pub/rep/ePubRepRacProTor2.pdf.

La Barge spoke of the need for police to take seriously the Inquiry Report results and address racial profiling concerns.[25]

Although the immediate response from most police leaders was negative, the OHRC Inquiry Report contributed to opening the door to a discussion that was almost previously unknown in policing circles in Ontario. In the Inquiry Report, the OHRC committed to hold anyone engaging in racial profiling accountable in accordance with the Ontario *Code*. Towards this end it committed to training its own staff on racial profiling issues and to raise public awareness of the negative effects of racial profiling. The OHRC also committed itself to develop a new public policy on racial discrimination. Further OHRC activity on racial profiling was to continue to have an impact to further this discussion and acceptance of racial profiling as a concern among police.

2) Policy on Racism and Racial Discrimination

Following upon its commitment in the racial profiling Inquiry Report the OHRC began intensive development of a policy addressing racism and racial discrimination in late 2003. Section 30 of the *Code* authorizes the OHRC to prepare, approve, and publish human rights policies and to provide guidance on interpreting the *Code*'s provisions. The power to develop policies is part of the OHRC's broader responsibility under section 29 to promote, protect, and advance respect for human rights in Ontario, to protect the public interest, and to eliminate discriminatory practices.[26]

Although OHRC policies and guidelines are not binding on the Tribunal or on courts, they are often given great deference and applied to the facts of human rights cases before courts or tribunals, and are quoted in the decisions of these bodies.[27] In addition, the OHRC's policies contain practical guidance relevant to the everyday lives of Ontarians. They aim to influence social behaviour to prevent human rights violations before they occur and to promote social change. They set standards for how individuals, employers, housing providers, service providers, and policy makers should act to ensure compliance with the *Code*. OHRC policies are widely used as a source of guidance by those responsible for applying

25 Personal notes taken on occasion of Chief Commissioner Keith Norton's presentation to the senior police staff of York Region Police Service in January 2006.

26 See *Code*, above note 5.

27 See, for example, *Williams v Melucci*, 2013 HRTO 547 at para 10.

the *Code*, such as lawyers, unions, human resource managers, and others. They are perceived as useful and instructive because they respond to day-to-day human rights issues.

Even without the emergence of racial profiling as an issue, the need for a policy related to the ground of "race" had become apparent to many within the OHRC and among key interested racialized community stakeholders. Annually, since the implementation of the *Code* in 1962, complaints citing the ground of "race" and related grounds (colour, ethnic origin, ancestry, citizenship, place of origin, and creed) regularly have been one of the top two sources for human rights complaints (the other top source being the ground of "disability"). Annually, 30 to 40 percent of complaints filed have cited the ground of "race" or related grounds.[28] With the release of the OHRC's *Policy and Guidelines on Disability and the Duty to Accommodate*[29] in November 2000 the need to develop a policy on the ground of race was identified as the next key priority. The increased focus on racial profiling further cemented the need for this policy.

The development process for the racism and racial discrimination policy included extensive research into caselaw and social scientific literature and several consultation events including focus groups, surveys, and a major policy dialogue conference convened in Toronto in October 2004. This conference brought together OHRC staff, stakeholders, and academics to review various policy themes and options.[30]

The *Policy and Guidelines on Racism and Racial Discrimination*[31] (Policy) was approved by the OHRC on 9 June 2005. It represented the first human rights policy on racism and racial discrimination from a statutory human rights commission in Canada. The Policy included a review of international human rights obligations relating to racism, a brief history of racism in Canada as it affected several key racialized groups, clarification of basic concepts and terms, definitions, and examples of types of racial discrimination including systemic racial discrimination and how

---

28 Ontario Human Rights Commission, *Policy and Guidelines on Racism and Racial Discrimination* (9 June 2005) at 4 [*Policy*], online: OHRC www.ohrc.on.ca/sites/default/files/attachments/Policy_and_guidelines_on_racism_and_racial_discrimination.pdf.

29 Ontario Human Rights Commission, *Policy and Guidelines on Disability and the Duty to Accommodate* (23 November 2000), online: OHRC www.ohrc.on.ca/sites/default/files/attachments/Policy_and_guidelines_on_disability_and_the_duty_to_accommodate.pdf.

30 *Policy*, above note 28 at 5.

31 *Ibid*.

to diagnose it, and best practices for monitoring and addressing racial discrimination in organizations.

The Policy identified racial profiling as a type of racial discrimination and provided the definition used earlier in the Inquiry Report into racial profiling. It detailed methods to determine where racial profiling has taken place, included clarification that race need only be a single factor in racial profiling situations, and elaborated the right of reasonable protest for those who believe that they have been racially profiled.[32] The Policy also identified an onus to collect race-based data where there is reason to believe that racial discrimination may be present. It argued that detecting some forms of racial discrimination including systemic racial discrimination and racial profiling may only be confirmed through collecting race-based data. The emphasis on data collection was in significant part related to calls from racialized community groups for police to collect stop data based on race in order to address racial profiling.[33] To support the Policy's call for race-based data collection and provide concrete guidance on how to do this, the OHRC later developed and released in 2009 its guidebook *Count Me In: Collecting Human Rights-Based Data*.[34]

The Policy proved to be a valuable tool to create better understanding of the nature of racial discrimination in general and racial profiling as a form of racial discrimination in particular. For police organizations it added to growing pressure to acknowledge and address racial profiling. Complaints of racial profiling were already starting to enter into the human rights system. The Policy served to give greater impetus to this emerging trend and provided guidance on how to better interpret these complaints. The Policy's call for race-based data collection provided sig-

---

32 *Ibid* at 19–20.

33 For example, the African Canadian Community Coalition on Racial Profiling had been advocating for race-based data collection relating to police stop practices since its foundation in 2002. In 2003, the Coalition commissioned research on best practices and responses to racial profiling by police in Canada, the United States, and the United Kingdom. This research was released in March 2004 and strongly advocated the collection of police stop data based on race. See Charles Smith, *Crisis, Conflict and Accountability: The Impact and Implications of Police Racial Profiling* (Toronto: African Canadian Community Coalition on Racial Profiling, 2004), online: CRR www.crr.ca/divers-files/en/pub/varRep/crisis_conflict_accountability.pdf.

34 Ontario Human Rights Commission, *Count Me In: Collecting Human Rights-Based Data* (Toronto: OHRC, 2009), online: OHRC www.ohrc.on.ca/sites/default/files/attachments/Count_me_in!_Collecting_human_rights_based_data.pdf.

nificant support to those in the community demanding race-based police stop data collection.

The Policy was widely promoted and had significant uptake. Ever since its release, the Policy has remained one of the most widely used and requested policies of the OHRC.

3) OHRC Litigation on Racial Profiling

The resolution of human rights complaints through the inclusion of public interest remedies, either as a result of settlement or tribunal order, has been an important feature of the Ontario human rights system since its inception. Public interest remedies often shape up as requirements to advance human rights in an organization through human rights-related awareness raising, education, training, and/or policy and program enhancement or development. There is a complementary relationship between human rights protection through complaint mechanisms and systemic human rights promotion in general. Public interest remedies obtained from respondent organizations through the enforcement system can impact other organizations in a single or related sector to engage in similar human rights advancements.

The OHRC's efforts to address racial profiling by police benefited significantly from public interest remedies obtained through the litigation of human rights complaints. Even though the OHRC ceased to directly handle complaints after the system's transition in 2007, delays involved in handling and litigation meant that it continued to be directly involved in litigation of racial profiling cases as late as 2012. The decision in 2002 to begin taking in complaints against police led to a fast growing number of racial profiling allegations being filed as complaints with the OHRC. Early efforts to address these complaints with police met with significant resistance. Police organizations were unwilling to acknowledge racial profiling as a valid issue and were generally unwilling to settle such complaints. Also, at the time, legal decisions affirming the existence of racial profiling in policing activity were just emerging.[35]

The first breakthrough in human rights complaint-related litigation against police in Ontario came from a decision of the HRTO in the case of

35 See, for example, *Halifax Regional Police Service v Johnson (No 1)* (2003), 48 CHRR D/307 (NS Board of Inquiry); *R v Brown* (2003), 64 OR (3d) 161 (ON CA); *R v Khan* (2004), 244 DLR (4th) 443 (ON Sup Ct).

Nassiah v Peel Regional Police Services[36] (*Nassiah*) released on 11 May 2007. The complaint was filed by Ms Jacqueline Nassiah related to events that took place on 18 February 2003, the very same day that the OHRC began receiving submissions related to its inquiry into racial profiling. After investigating the matter, the OHRC found evidence indicative of racial profiling. Attempts to conciliate and settle the case were unsuccessful. In the decision the Tribunal found that a Peel police officer subjected Ms Nassiah, a Black woman, to a more intensive, suspicious, and prolonged investigation because of her race.

The public interest remedies ordered by the HRTO required Peel Police to:

- prepare a new directive prohibiting racial profiling;
- develop training that would include social science literature on racial profiling and the current caselaw;
- hire an external consultant with expertise in racial profiling to assist in developing the directive and training;
- provide the new directive and training materials to the OHRC for its review to confirm compliance with the Tribunal's orders; and
- publish a one-page summary of this decision in its monthly police bulletin, outlining the HRTO's findings and orders.

These remedies required of the Peel Police had a wider impact on policing organizations in Ontario. The Peel training approved by the OHRC soon became the foundations of similar new recruit training at the Ontario Police College. The College had previously not provided any racial profiling training and took advantage of the development of the Peel training to implement its own training for all new police recruits in Ontario. The Peel directive and training materials also were later included in the resource book, *Anti-Racial Profiling Best Practices: A Self Audit to Minimize Corporate Risk*, developed and distributed in 2009 by the Ontario Association of Chiefs of Police Diversity Committee.[37] Also, several later OHRC settlements obtained in human rights complaints filed

36 *Nassiah v Peel (Regional Municipality Services Board)*, 2007 OHRT 14 [*Nassiah*].

37 Ontario Association of Chiefs of Police Diversity Committee, *Anti-Racial Profiling Best Practices: A Self Audit to Minimize Corporate Risk* (Toronto: OACP, 2009), online: OACP www.opconline.ca/conf/PastConf/Aboriginal%20&%20Diversity%20Police%20Forum/GuidelineBookWeb%20-%20Anti-Racial%20Profiling%20Best%20Practices.pdf.

against police included similar kinds of training and policy measures as obtained in the *Nassiah* case.

Another significant public interest remedy obtained by the OHRC was the agreement to collect race-related police stop data by the Ottawa Police Service in May 2012. This was obtained as a settlement of the human rights complaint alleging racial profiling in a police stop filed by Chad Aitkens in 2005.

Previously, the only police service in Canada to have collected race-related police stop data was the Kingston Police Service, which had conducted a one-year study collecting such data in 2003–04.[38] The Kingston Police Service study provided evidence of racial differences in police stop practices suggestive of racial profiling. Many in the policing community were very critical of the Kingston data collection project and of Kingston Police Chief William Closs for undertaking it. By 2008 Chief William Closs wrote with evident bitterness:

> Police services across Canada, with the tacit approval of their political leaders, have deliberately chosen to refrain from examining themselves in a meaningful, methodical, or measurable manner to determine whether they were in fact engaging in bias-free policing. Nor has any Canadian police jurisdiction made an effort to launch a data collection project consistent with the objectives of the Kingston Police. No Canadian police leader has publicly supported the efficacy of this approach to fostering trust within the community.[39]

In this context, the agreement of the Ottawa Police Service to collect race-related police stop data was a significant advance in the ongoing effort to address racial profiling by police in Ontario. As the OHRC Chief Commissioner noted about this agreement:

> This is another exciting step forward in our work with Ontario's police services and is truly ground-breaking . . . . Data collection allows organizations to measure what they do and then manage appropriately. People in every community need to feel confident in their police services. And collecting data can help police operate

38 William J Closs & Paul F McKenna, "Profiling a Problem in Canadian Police Leadership: the Kingston Police Data Collection Project" (2008) 49:2 Canadian Public Administration 143.

39 *Ibid* at 146.

with transparency so that they can maintain trust in the communities they serve.[40]

D. DIRECT ENGAGEMENT WITH POLICE ORGANIZATIONS: EDUCATION, TRAINING, CAPACITY BUILDING, AND ORGANIZATIONAL CHANGE

By 2007 the activities reviewed above had led to increased engagement between the OHRC and several police organizations across Ontario. For the most part these engagements had been conducted in the context of an adversarial relationship that was particularly inflamed by the litigation of human rights complaints. However, by that year a number of factors came together to allow the OHRC to become involved in more direct ways to support human rights advancement in police organizations. These factors were directly involved in the establishment of key partnerships with the Toronto Police Service and the Ontario Police College aimed at human rights advancement. These two projects in turn led to a number of follow up OHRC activities including a partnership with the Windsor Police Service and the development of a manual on human rights organizational change for police.

1) Partnership with the Toronto Police Service 2007–10

Changes to the human rights system were initiated in Bill 107, *An Act to amend the Human Rights Code*[41] of 2006. This Act would lead to the ending of the OHRC's role in the complaint handling system in June 2008. The OHRC would thereafter focus primarily on systemic human rights work. By 2007, efforts to transition to this primary role were well under way. Part of this transition was built on the recognition that having the complaint handling role transferred elsewhere in the human rights system opened up opportunities for the OHRC to become directly involved with institutions and organizations that previously were antagonistic due to the OHRC's previous role in the human rights complaints handling

40 Ontario Human Rights Commission, News Release, "Ottawa Police Agree to Collect Race-Based Data" (4 May 2012), online: OHRC www.ohrc.on.ca/en/news_centre.

41 2d Sess, 38th Leg, Ontario, 2006 (assented to 20 December 2006), SO 2006, c 30.

1 2 3 4 5 6 7 8 9 10 11 12 13 14

system. This new recognition was most evident in a new relationship that was emerging with police organizations and in particular with the Toronto Police Service.

The Toronto Police Service (TPS) is the largest municipal police service in Canada, with almost 6,000 sworn officers and more than 2,000 civilian staff. The relationship between the TPS and the OHRC was significantly strained with the OHRC's Inquiry Report on racial profiling and with many human rights complaints filed against the TPS at the OHRC. However, in early 2005 a new leadership was emerging at the TPS beginning with the appointment of Alok Mukharjee as chair of the Toronto Police Services Board (TPSB). Mukharjee had a long history of academic and professional work in human rights, race relations, and diversity management. Shortly, after his appointment as chair, the TPSB began its search for a new chief and made hiring of an individual committed to diversity issues a priority in this search. Bill Blair was selected partially on this basis and became the new chief in April 2005. Under the new leadership, issues of diversity emerged as a major focus. In 2006, the TPS created a Diversity Management Unit, the first of its kind for police in Canada. The new unit's mandate was to coordinate human rights issues and activities across the service and address barriers and gaps in order to create a more inclusive workplace. The TPS also embarked on major initiatives including conducting a comprehensive employment systems review related to enhancement of equity and development of revised recruitment processes.

By 2007, the OHRC, the TPSB, and the TPS were involved in many different negotiations to resolve human rights complaints involving potential public interest remedies. In these negotiations, the TPSB and TPS argued that they had already begun to move on a number of fronts to address human rights concerns on a systemic basis. The OHRC recognized this shift in direction but believed this to be nascent and insufficient. What emerged were discussions on a new more collaborative way to engage each other in promoting human rights and anti-discrimination within the TPS. Negotiations ultimately culminated in the signing of an agreement termed the *Human Rights Project Charter* (Project Charter) at a TPSB meeting in May 2007.[42] TPSB member Hamlin Grange speaking at

42 See Ontario Human Rights Commission, *Framework of Relationship between the Ontario Human Rights Commission (OHRC), the Toronto Police Services Board (TPSB) and the Toronto Police Service (TPS): Human Rights Project*

the meeting termed the Project Charter "a historic partnership that had great potential to change the culture of the police service."[43]

The Project Charter established a three-year partnership (Partnership Project) between the three organizations that would aim at "the identification and elimination of any discrimination that may exist in the employment and service practices of the Toronto Police Service that may be contrary to the Ontario *Human Rights Code*."[44] It indicated that each partner was a voluntary participant and that decisions were to be made on the basis of consensus. It established a "sponsors committee" made up of the heads of each of the partner organizations to provide direct oversight and guidance throughout the life of the project. Four specific strategically selected areas of focus for change were identified: (1) recruitment, selection, promotion, and retention; (2) police accountability; (3) public education; and (4) training. Multi-stakeholder committees involving all three partners would identify human rights concerns related to each focal area and identify possible solutions and initiatives. These initiatives aimed at establishing fundamental organizational change that would develop the long-term capacity to prevent and effectively handle human rights issues when and where they would arise.

The three-year partnership helped to identify a number of new tools and techniques to enhance human rights capacity within police organizations. The initiatives that emerged from the partnership included:

- the development of new TPSB level human rights and accommodation policies;
- new human rights and racial profiling training;
- the establishment of new forms and training dealing with complaints to ensure clearer focus on human rights implications;
- the revision of the performance management system to include a new focus on diversity and human rights behaviour;
- the inclusion of a human rights advancement role for community consultative committees;
- the development of a new disability-focused consultative committee;
- the review and revision of many TPS procedures to address human rights concerns;

Charter (Toronto: OHRC, 2007), online: OHRC www.ohrc.on.ca/en/human-rights-project-charter-tps-tpsb.

43 Personal notes taken by the author during the meeting of the Toronto Police Services Board in May 2007.

44 *Ibid*.

- an inclusive design review of the TPS to assess its employment and service practices from the viewpoint of religion and creed;
- an external evaluation project assessing the impact of the project to be conducted by Ryerson University's Diversity Institute; and
- the development of a Human Rights Advisory Committee including representation from all three sponsoring organizations to monitor the implementation of the project for three years after the life of the formal project.[45]

The importance of the TPS Partnership Project cannot be understated. The project helped to develop a number of significant new tools to address human rights concerns in policing. It helped to establish a model for organizational change that other police services and organizations could emulate. Also, it helped to foster much needed goodwill between the OHRC and the TPS as well as with police organizations in general.

A direct product of this goodwill and new model was the replication of this type of partnership with the Windsor Police Service. Shortly after the conclusion of the Toronto Police Partnership Project in 2010, the Windsor Police Service approached the OHRC to consider a partnership. The OHRC seized on this opportunity as work with the Windsor Police Service represented an opportunity to fine-tune the human rights organizational change model developed in Toronto with a medium-sized police service that was more typical of other services in Ontario. A three-year agreement to do so was finalized in February 2011.[46] This partnership continues as of the writing of this article.

The TPS Partnership Project also helped to further advance the OHRC's ongoing efforts to specifically address racial profiling by police. It developed an e-learning training module on racial profiling aimed at front line officers, which was subsequently made available to police services across the country through the Police Knowledge Network. During the project the issue of race-related police stop data collection emerged as a point of contention between the OHRC and its project partners. The

---

45 See Toronto Police Services Board, *Human Rights Project Charter: Final Report* (Toronto: TPSB, 2010), online: TPSB www.tpsb.ca/FS/Docs/Publications.

46 See Ontario Human Rights Commission, *Human Rights Project Charter: Framework for the Relationship between the Windsor Police Services Board (Board), the Windsor Police Service (Service), the Ontario Human Rights Commission (OHRC), the Ontario Police College (OPC)* (Toronto: OHRC, 2011), online: OHRC www.ohrc.on.ca/en/human-rights-project-charter-windsor.

partners studied the prospect of this together extensively.[47] While the TPS and TPSB did not agree to conduct this kind of data collection, the TPSB agreed to remove a prohibition on tabulating and analyzing police service data in relationship to race and other *Code* grounds, which it did at its November 2010 board meeting.[48] The TPS also affirmed a commitment to explore the collection and analysis of race-related data in other areas of its activity. Towards this aim, the TPS contacted a United States-based team of academics who research race issues with police to explore options. Academics from this team were brought to Toronto and invited to look at current data collection and suggest options.

2) Partnership with Ontario Police College

In 2007, concurrently with the Toronto Police Partnership Project, the OHRC established a partnership with the Ontario Police College (OPC) to support human rights and racial profiling training for police.

A Race Relations and Adult Education (RRAE) unit had been established at the OPC in 1992 and race relations training had been part of new recruit training ever since. This training did not incorporate any focus on racial profiling and this deficiency was becoming increasingly apparent as significant public attention on police racial profiling emerged beginning in 2002. By early 2007, the RRAE unit had approached the OHRC to identify ways to collaborate on enhancing human rights and racial profiling training for police.[49] An agreement was soon reached for the two organizations to begin such collaboration. By 2008 the OPC had revamped its new recruit training to include clearer attention to human rights and racial profiling. Also, the partnership led to specially developed joint training for interested police organizations across the province. Willing police services were identified for full day training in human rights and racial profiling. From 2007 until 2012 special training was provided for several police services across Ontario, including Pembroke, London, Thunder Bay, Owen Sound, Hamilton, and Windsor police

47 Jim Rankin, "Police Ponder How Best to Collect Race Data" *The Toronto Star* (15 February 2010) A12.

48 Douglas Quan, "Police Routinely Suppress Racial Data in Canada, Study Says" *National Post* (1 February 2012), online: National Post http://news.nationalpost.com/2012/02/01/police-routinely-suppress-racial-data-in-canada-study-says/.

49 Interview of Saleha Khan, Instructor, Ontario Police College (2 November 2012) (archived with the author).

1 2 3 4 5 6 7 8 9 10 11 12 13 14

services. Specialized training in human rights investigation was also organized for police professional standards staff at the OPC in May 2009. A two-day forum entitled the *Advanced Human Rights Leadership and Professional Practice Conference* was organized in October 2009 for police leaders to promote best practices related to human rights. The growing cooperation with the OPC also led to its involvement as a sponsoring partner in the Windsor Police service human rights project.

The partnership with the OPC was instrumental in the OHRC's efforts to address racial profiling in policing. It helped to foster new training on racial profiling and human rights not only for new recruits but also for existing staff in police organizations across Ontario that has now been implemented on multiple occasions. Perhaps even more significantly, the partnership helped to develop linkages and relationships between the OHRC and police leaders and staff across the province. These linkages and relationships allowed for the gradual normalization of issues of human rights and racial profiling among what had long been a skeptical and hostile audience. Previously, police in Ontario simply did not see *Code* matters as an essential and regular feature of policing activity. The recognition of this was newly being fostered through the many interactions the OHRC was having with police across the province.

3) Human Rights Organizational Change for Police Manual

Following the three-year partnership with the TPS in 2010, the OHRC put together a manual entitled *Human Rights and Police: Creating and Sustaining Organizational Change*.[50] The manual was based on extensive research into organizational change practices and relied heavily on the experience of the Toronto Police partnership to document the human rights organizational change model piloted in Toronto. It reviews key terms and concepts, the history and shape of human rights complaints against police in Ontario, organizational change best practices, and identifies various specific initiatives that have been developed to address human rights concerns.

The manual was supported by testimonials from key police organization leaders, including leaders of the Ontario Association of Chiefs of Police, the Ontario Association of Police Services Boards, the Ontario Police College, the TPS, and the Ontario Provincial Police. It was promoted

50 Ontario Human Rights Commission, *Human Rights and Policing: Creating and Sustaining Organizational Change* (Toronto: OHRC, 2011).

at several major police events and training on its contents was provided in several locations across Ontario. The support and recognition shown to the manual demonstrated the significant improvement in the relationship between the OHRC and police in Ontario.

The manual has been heavily promoted in the police community and has drawn attention from police organizations across Ontario and from elsewhere in Canada. Several police services have now received training on the manual from the OHRC and have expressed interest in further collaborations with the OHRC.

E. CONCLUSION

Despite more than ten years of ongoing work by the OHRC to address human rights concerns in policing with a special focus on racial profiling, it still cannot be said that this form of racial discrimination has ended. Some racialized groups, particularly in the Black community, continue to raise alarm about the impact racial profiling by police has on members of their communities. Research on practices of the TPS conducted by *The Toronto Star* and reported on in 2010 and 2012 continues to show significantly disproportionate police stops faced by young Black men in particular.[51]

While the prevalence of racial profiling by police remains a major concern, police leaders and organizations have moved significantly to acknowledge this concern and take some measures to address it. In 2002, almost all police leaders in Ontario denied racial profiling by police was a reality or a concern, by 2012 most have come to acknowledge it, and many have now been involved in initiatives to address it. In a 16 June 2010 resolution entitled "racial profiling," the Ontario Association of

---

51 See Jim Rankin, "Race Matters: Blacks Documented by Police at High Rate" *The Toronto Star* (6 February 2010), online: Toronto Star www.thestar.com/news/crime/raceandcrime/2010/02/06/race_matters_blacks_documented_by_police_at_high_rate.html; Jim Rankin & Patty Winsa, "Known to Police: Toronto Police Stop and Document Black and Brown People Far More than Whites" *The Toronto Star* (9 March 2012), online: Toronto Star www.thestar.com/news/insight/2012/03/09/known_to_police_toronto_police_stop_and_document_black_and_brown_people_far_more_than_whites.html.

Chiefs of Police acknowledged the reality of racial bias in society and in policing and called on

> . . . police services throughout Ontario to continue implementing on-going positive measures to prevent bias in policing and to promote harmonious relationships with all the diverse communities they serve. The measures referred to above include: policy, human resources and training processes, systems of supervision and accountability as well as proactive community engagement.[52]

While there is undoubtedly plenty more that can and needs to be done to address racial profiling by police, the transformation of police attitudes is notable. The OHRC's activities have undoubtedly played a significant role in this transformation. This article demonstrates that the consistent usage of both protection and especially promotion mandates has been instrumental in fostering this change in attitudes and has helped to create training, monitoring, capacity building, and organizational change tools and approaches to support police in addressing the problem directly.

The OHRC's development of direct engagement with respondent organizations and sectors in the context of its work with police is not without its detractors. There are those in the human rights community and among racialized community groups who see this type of work as compromising the ability of the OHRC to act as a forceful advocate for human rights change. The shift in emphasis from one relying primarily on litigation and public interest remedies to create change to an approach that actively includes cooperative approaches is criticized as opening up the door to being co-opted by respondent organizations and sectors. The 2012 Pinto review of the Ontario human rights system recommends an increased involvement of the OHRC in public interest litigation and seems to suggest that the OHRC should consider sacrificing a bit of buy-in from stakeholders partially related to such concerns.[53] While, such concerns undoubtedly have some legitimacy, the OHRC's experience responding to police racial profiling suggests that it

---

52 Ontario Association of Chiefs of Police, *Resolution 2010-04: Racial Profiling* (16 June 2010), online: OACP www.oacp.on.ca/content/resolutions/view_resolution.html?id=125.

53 Andrew Pinto, *Report of the Ontario Human Rights Review 2012* (Toronto: OAG, 2012), online: OAG www.attorneygeneral.jus.gov.on.ca/english/about/pubs/human_rights/Pinto_human_rights_report_2012-ENG.pdf.

is important not to allow such concerns to undermine the effective utilization of all tools available to promote human rights.

Racial profiling is typical of many complex and entrenched forms of discrimination which are resistant to easy solutions. Litigation alone has generally failed to address these types of discrimination, as have the usage of educational and policy tools alone. Such forms of discrimination can only be adequately responded to by employing the full range of protection and promotion mandates afforded human rights commissions and need to be strategic, coordinated, and extended to have any hope of having any impact at all. The OHRC's work on racial profiling by police can serve as a valuable demonstration and example of this kind of work for other human rights commissions and actors to learn from.

Ontario's unique human rights system has significantly enabled the OHRC's promotion mandate thus rendering this kind of work more of a possibility for it. However, the basic approaches are replicable by other human rights commissions in Canada as well. Greater promotion activity of this type by other human rights commissions would be a valuable addition to the struggle for human rights in Canada in general but particularly in response to pernicious human rights issues like racial profiling.

CHAPTER 12

THE QUÉBEC HUMAN RIGHTS COMMISSION AND THE CONSTRUCTION OF THE CONCEPT OF SOCIAL PROFILING[1]

Paul Eid[2]

A. INTRODUCTION

The Commission des droits de la personne et des droits de la jeunesse (Commission) is mandated, among other things, to ensure that Québec's laws, bylaws, standards, and institutional practices, both public and private, comply with the *Charter of human rights and freedoms*[3] (*Charter*), a quasi-constitutional law. Since its early days in the late 1970s, the Commission has had a research team comprised of approximately half legal experts and half social scientists. This parity is informed by the notion that any attempt to properly investigate human rights issues needs to rest on an understanding of the social, cultural, political, and economic factors that contribute to either foster or hamper one's ability to effectively exercise one's rights protected by the *Charter*. To this end, a cross-fertilization of the sociological and legal lenses provides an in-depth understanding of how the legal framework interacts with social relations (of power) in preventing vulnerable groups from effectively

1 Except for the introduction and the conclusion, this chapter is an adaptation of Commission des droits de la personne et des droits de la jeunesse, *La judiciarisation des personnes itinérantes à Montréal: un profilage social* (Québec: CDPDJ, 2009) at 45–111 [CDPDJ], co-authored by Paul Eid & Me Christine Campbell.

2 Paul Eid is a professor in the Department of Sociology at the Université du Québec à Montréal (UQÀM), and a member of the Chaire de recherche en immigration, ethnicité et citoyenneté (CRIEC).

3 RSQ 1975, c C-12 [*Charter*].

converting their formal equality *Charter* rights into substantive equality rights.

Such a perspective is consistent with the systemic approach to discrimination, which has been given increasing judicial credence since the 1980s. Indeed, the Supreme Court, as well as lower level courts across the country, have contributed to the building and enriching of our understanding of this notion over the past decades. As will be made clear below, the way the Commission conceptualized the notion of social profiling and analyzed its various manifestations in its landmark 2009 report[4] is fully in keeping with this systemic approach to discrimination.

The first part of this paper presents the contextual background and the conceptual framework underlying the notion of social profiling. First, I sketch out the context and provide the data that prompted the Commission to investigate the issue of biased policing against homeless people (Section B(1)). Then, I explain the meaning attached to the notion of social profiling, and the reason why this concept is appropriate to capture the kind of discriminatory law enforcement practices that the homeless experience on a regular basis in their contacts with the police (Section B(2)). Thirdly, I will go over certain cues that were identified by the Commission as social profiling benchmarks (Section B(3)), and point out which kind of human rights violations can result from social profiling under the *Charter* (Section B(4)).

The second part of the paper demonstrates how social profiling in Montréal can be best understood as a form of systemic discrimination induced, among other things, by law enforcement authorities' official policies, standards, and decision-making procedures. I will first shed light on the way homeless people were portrayed in the Service de police de la Ville de Montréal (SPVM)'s institutional standards and policies shaping what became to be known as the "fight against 'incivilities'" (Section C(1)). Then in Section C(2), I explain how the stigmatization of homeless people in these official documents has fuelled, over the past five years or so, systemic social profiling in law enforcement practices. Lastly, drawing on the Commission's report, I will critically engage with the rationales put forth by the SPVM in its institutional standards and policies to justify its portrayal of the homeless as a high-risk population deserving

4 CDPDJ, above note 1.

special police oversight (Section C(3)). It will be shown how both sociologically and legally, these rationales do not have any ground to stand on.

B. CONTEXTUAL AND CONCEPTUAL BACKGROUND

1) The Context

As early as 2003, the Réseau d'aide aux personnes seules et itinérantes de Montréal (RAPSIM), a Montréal-based umbrella non-governmental organization (NGO) defending homeless rights, had voiced to the Commission its growing concern with the increasing tendency of Montréal's police forces to over-judicialize the homeless, mainly under municipal bylaws, causing this population to be over-incarcerated for unpaid tickets. In 2005, a tripartite working group made up of the Commission, the RAPSIM, and various City of Montréal representatives (including police officials) was formed in order to find alternative solutions to the over-judicialization of the homeless in Montréal. After a few years, it became clear that the parties would not agree on which avenues to explore in order to identify the main contributing factors to this phenomenon. Most notably, Montréal's police and city representatives were highly reluctant to examine the possible role played by discrimination in the process. Therefore, the Commission took it upon itself to determine to what extent municipal regulations and law enforcement practices leading to the prosecution of the homeless in Montréal were in line with the *Charter*, specifically with section 10 that protects equality rights.

When the Commission started to investigate this topic in 2008, it was already known, from previous research and data, that the homeless were disproportionately targeted by Montréal's police forces as part of their efforts to enforce municipal bylaws. Thus, it was known from data collected as part of research conducted by Céline Bellot and colleagues that, between 1994 and 2005, the number of tickets issued to the homeless under municipal bylaws increased by 327 percent (from 575 to 2,455 tickets a year), whereas tickets issued to this population under the subway bylaws during this same period increased by almost 700 percent (from 494 to 3,942 tickets a year).[5] During the 2006–10 period, the number

5 Céline Bellot et al, *Judiciarisation et criminalisation des populations itinérantes à Montréal*, Rapport de recherche préparé pour le Secrétariat National

of tickets served to homeless people under Montréal's statutory bylaws remained relatively stable, fluctuating between 2,230 and 3,000.[6] However, the number of tickets issued to this population under the subway bylaws jumped from 2,493 in 2006 to 4,055 in 2010, which represents a 63 percent increase.[7] This pattern can be largely accounted for by the fact that, starting in 2007, the SPVM created a special Subway unit that was instructed to enforce the Société des transports de Montréal's (STM) bylaws in place of STM security agents, which were previously in charge of doing so.

Even more preoccupying from the Commission's perspective was the fact that, when crossing the SPVM's data with that of Bellot,[8] it turned out that 31.6 percent of the Montréalers who received a ticket under Montréal's bylaws in 2004 were homeless people, whereas the figure for 2005 was 20.3 percent. According to more recent data,[9] between 2007 and 2010, close to 25 percent of Montréalers who were issued a ticket for violating a municipal bylaw were homeless people. In 2010, 23.5 percent of all statutory bylaw tickets were served to homeless persons.[10] Given that the homeless are estimated to make up around 1 percent of Montréal's population, these figures suggest that they are dramatically overrepresented among citizens who, in Montréal, are issued tickets for breaking a bylaw.

In light of Bellot and Sylvestre's compilation, it appears that, for the 2006–10 period, the majority of the top ten most common provisions under which homeless people were prosecuted in Montréal are "victimless" offences, in the sense that they generally did not jeopardize security or infringe property (private or public). These ten most commonly enforced provisions were (in order):

1) found lying or loitering drunk in a public place;

---

des Sans-abri (October 2005) [Bellot et al], online : RAPSIM www.rapsim.org/docs/rapport_Bellot_05_VF.pdf.

6 Céline Bellot & Marie-Ève Sylvestre, *La judiciarisation des personnes en situation d'itinérance à Montréal. 15 années de recherche: faits et enjeux. Extraits du rapport final* (février 2012) at 12 [Bellot & Sylvestre], online: Politiques sociales www.politiquessociales.net/IMG/pdf/Extraits15ansjudiciarisation2012.pdf. Full report online: Homeless Hub www.homelesshub.ca/ResourceFiles/judiciarisationquebec_nov7_web_1.pdf.

7 *Ibid.*

8 Bellot et al, above note 5.

9 Bellot & Sylvestre, above note 6 at 28.

10 *Ibid.*

2) consuming alcohol in public places;
3) impeding or obstructing pedestrian and vehicular traffic by standing still or loitering in public places (a provision often used against homeless individuals whose presence is deemed undesirable);
4) being in a public park after closing hours (a provision often used against homeless persons found sleeping in parks at night);
5) spreading a liquid on public property;
6) using street furniture for a purpose other than the one for which it is intended (a provision often used against homeless persons lying on a public bench);
7) refusal to cease to engage in a violation;
8) knife possession;
9) making noise resulting from cries, clamours, singing, altercations, cursing or uproar; and
10) urinating or defecating in public spaces.[11]

Most of these offences relate to behaviours in which homeless people are more likely to engage in public for lack of having their own dwelling (sleeping on a bench, in a park, urinating, loitering) and/or because they are struggling with an alcohol dependency. In any case, most of them are minor offences but, starting in 2003, they became subject to much stricter enforcement as the SPVM started to identify fighting against "incivilities" and "public disorders" as one of its top organizational priorities in its annual strategic orientations and guidelines.

The Commission worked from the hypothesis that the homeless were victims of a systemic form of discrimination, that is, a discrimination that cannot be reduced to a few isolated cases involving police officers with malicious intents. Rather, it seemed to us that the gross overrepresentation of homeless persons within the judicial system was probably accounted for by more systemic factors. The Commission identified two main contributing factors: (1) social profiling fostered by the SPVM's institutional standards and policies, and (2) lawmaking resulting in discrimination against the homeless, including one municipal ordinance[12] imposing night closure on two of the last downtown parks where homeless persons could still stay overnight; a municipal

---

11 *Ibid* at 16.

12 Ville de Montréal, arrondissement de Ville-Marie, revised bylaw RRVM c P-3, o 8.1, *Ordonnance modifiant l'ordonnance sur les heures de fermeture des parcs (8)* (1 August 2006).

bylaw[13] prohibiting dogs from entering two downtown parks known to be attended by homeless dog owners; and a provincial law[14] providing for imprisonment when outstanding fines remain unpaid.

In what follows, I will only focus on the first of these factors, that is, social profiling in law enforcement practices due to biased policing. Let us start by clarifying what is meant by social profiling.

2) What Is Social Profiling?

Social condition is a prohibited ground of discrimination under section 10 of the *Charter*.[15] The Québec Court of Appeal clearly established that this ground was applicable to deprived or vulnerable persons whose social condition amounts to an imposed burden weighing them down in life.[16] Therefore, the Commission had no difficulty concluding that homelessness, whether actual or presumed, ought to be considered as a potential ground for discrimination based on one's "social condition." It follows that, like racial profiling, social profiling is a form of discrimination prohibited by section 10 of the *Charter*. Now let me restate the definition of racial profiling that was adopted by the Commission back in 2005:

> Racial profiling is any action taken by one or more people in authority with respect to a person or group of persons, for reasons of safety, security or public order, that is based on actual or presumed membership in a group defined by race, colour, ethnic or national origin or religion, without factual grounds or reasonable suspicion, that

---

13 Ville de Montréal, arrondissement de Ville-Marie, bylaw RRVM c C-10, *Règlement sur le contrôle des chiens et autres animaux*, (amended in 2007), s 14.

14 *Code of Penal Procedure*, RSQ 1987, c C-25.1, ss 237, 346, & 347 [CPP].

15 *Charter*, above note 3, s 10:

> Every person has a right to full and equal recognition and exercise of his human rights and freedoms, without distinction, exclusion or preference based on race, colour, sex, pregnancy, sexual orientation, civil status, age except as provided by law, religion, political convictions, language, ethnic or national origin, social condition, a handicap or the use of any means to palliate a handicap. Discrimination exists where such a distinction, exclusion or preference has the effect of nullifying or impairing such right.

16 *Ordre des comptables généraux licenciés du Québec c Québec (Procureur général)*, [2004] RJQ 1164 at para 69 (QC CA).

> results in the person or group being exposed to differential treatment or scrutiny.
>
> Racial profiling includes any action by a person in a situation of authority who applies a measure in a disproportionate way to certain segments of the population on the basis, in particular, of their racial, ethnic, national or religious background, whether actual or presumed.[17]

To what extent could this definition, which was originally meant to conceptualize racially biased law enforcement practices, be fruitfully applied to the over-judicialization of homeless people? First, it became clear that the first paragraph of the above definition was perhaps not fitting well with the specific form of profiling that the homeless are likely to experience in their daily interactions with the police. Indeed, the differential treatment they receive from the police does not generally consist in being disproportionately stopped *without factual grounds or reasonable suspicion*. Originally, this part of the definition was meant to capture the well documented fact that Black pedestrians or car drivers were typically stopped more often and searched only because their skin colour made them suspicious in the eyes of the police. By contrast, from gathered information, it appeared that most of the time, the police officer issuing a ticket to a homeless person did so after having observed an actual bylaw violation, such as jaywalking, loitering, spitting, making a loud noise, consuming alcohol, or being drunk in a public place. In other words, in most cases homeless people are not stopped by police officers based on groundless suspicions, but rather on factual observations.

However, the second paragraph of the above-quoted definition better captures the sort of biased policing that homeless people are likely to experience. Specifically, it seems that certain law-infringing behaviours are more likely to be fined when they are perpetrated by a homeless person or at least by someone perceived as such by the police. This would mean that homeless people are dramatically over-judicialized not so much because they are more likely to break the law than other citizens, but because police officers are more likely to scrutinize them, notice their offences, and eventually fine them as a result. I will expound on

17 Commission des droits de la personne et des droits de la jeunesse, Racial Profiling: Context and Definition by Michèle Turenne (June 2005) at 18, online: The Star http://media.thestar.topscms.com/acrobat/7b/a1/011b013400bbc65bb67e656cf3d.pdf.

this latter point in the second part of this chapter, but, first, let me elaborate on the benchmarks against which social profiling can be measured.

3) Social Profiling Benchmarks

In the following, I will briefly go over four indicators that one has to look for when assessing whether a police intervention has been tainted with social profiling. It should be noted that these benchmarks are partly derived and/or inspired from a 2006 document in which the Commission identified, based on the prevailing caselaw, the type of evidence that is required in court in order to substantiate allegations of racial profiling.[18]

a) The Triggering Factor behind the Intervention

As in the case of racial profiling, the catalyst of social profiling is not actual group membership, but rather the assumption made by law enforcers that a given individual belongs to a profiled group. In other words, it does not matter whether the profiled individual fits this or that definition of homelessness — not to mention the fact that there is no consensus among social scientists over what qualifies as homelessness. What is legally and sociologically relevant here is whether the said individual has been categorized as a homeless person by the law enforcer based on a series of cues which, alone or combined, act as social signifiers of poverty and/or marginality. For example, dishevelled hair, clothes or appearance, bad hygiene, body odours, erratic behaviours and attitudes, are all socially constructed signs of poverty and marginality that can prompt a police officer to enforce municipal bylaws in a biased manner.

b) Double Standards in Law Enforcement Practices

Perhaps an important sign that one has to look for when trying to track down social profiling occurs at the initial stage of the judicialization process, that is when the police officer makes the decision to issue a ticket after having witnessed a law-breaking behaviour, or what he or she considers as such. Specifically, it can be suspected that social profiling has tainted a police officer's intervention whenever a homeless person is given a ticket for minor offences that are usually never or sel-

18 Commission des droits de la personne et des droits de la jeunesse, *Proving Racial Profiling: Perspectives for Civil Cases* by Michèle Turenne (March 2006) [Turenne, *Proving Racial Profiling*], online: CDPDJ www.cdpdj.qc.ca/publications/Documents/proving_racial_profiling.pdf.

dom penalized when committed by other citizens. Examples of such behaviours include being drunk in the public domain, loitering, making loud noises, littering by throwing cigarette butts or other junk on the ground, lying on a bench, spreading a liquid on public property, ignoring traffic lights when crossing the intersection, jaywalking, etc. Of course, the fact that homeless people are disproportionately fined for these offences does not constitute sufficient evidence in itself to substantiate allegations of social profiling, although this could raise serious suspicion. Indeed, one could make the case that this overrepresentation is simply due to the fact that homeless people are more likely to engage in many of these law-breaking behaviours because they do not have access to a private dwelling to do so. However, the social profiling benchmarks are very likely to be met when one has reasons to believe that, all things being equal, the likelihood of being issued a ticket for a given behaviour is greater for someone who is categorized as a homeless person as opposed to someone who is not. Thus, citizens who do not generally display visible signs of poverty or marginality do not catch the police's attention when they engage in most of the above-mentioned behaviours (such as loitering, spitting, throwing a cigarette butt, lying on a bench, drunkenness, jaywalking, etc.). In such cases, it is reasonable to assume that the over-judicialization of homeless people for these offences owes more to a biased police decision (conscious or not) to drive them out of public places than to a neutral and impartial enforcement of the law, irrespective of one's socio-economic status.

c) Improper Behaviours on the Part of a Police Officer

In its 2006 document *Proving Racial Profiling: Perspectives for Civil Cases*, the Commission considered that "inflexible, suspicious or harassing behaviour, or discriminatory comments by the person in a situation of authority, as well as questions that are inappropriate or groundless in the circumstances . . . are all elements that can be used to show or corroborate the discriminatory nature of an intervention."[19] When applied to social profiling, such a benchmark could be met when a homeless person is being served several tickets on a short period of time by the same police officer, a situation often reported by researchers and human rights advocates, as well as by the SPVM itself. Depending on each case at hand, this type of situation can sometimes qualify as discriminatory

---

19 *Ibid* at 13.

harassment (prohibited by section 10 of the *Charter*[20]) since it is rather uncommon for police officers to exhibit such excessive zeal when they catch other citizens infringing a municipal bylaw. The SPVM confirmed the existence of this practice but argued that in most cases it is justified when the person continues to engage in the law-breaking behaviour even after the first ticket was issued. Although in some cases multiple fining may be necessary to put a stop to an actual public nuisance or security breach, in many cases one can seriously question the legitimacy of such practices against an extremely vulnerable population for whom the accumulation of unpaid tickets can lead to incarceration and, consequently, to further social disfranchisement. Serving multiple tickets to the same person over a short period of time is particularly questionable since most conducts for which homeless people are fined constitute minor offences. Finally, another form of behaviour that can be a sign of social profiling is when an officer makes an inappropriate, derogatory, or offensive comment referring to one's social condition. For example, one key informant in Céline Bellot's research with homeless persons mentions that he has been told by a police officer: "Weren't you abused when you were young?" Another informant recounts how police officers constantly remind him about his record of previous convictions when they encounter him on the street or during a new intervention against him.[21]

d) Unusual Decisions by Police Officers

According to the Commission, discriminatory profiling can also be suspected based on "unusual decisions by officers in a situation of authority that contrasts with normal practice, such as overstepping their rights or powers, the application of excessive force or a request for backup without valid grounds can be used to show differential treatment."[22] In the case of social profiling, such unusual decisions can be exemplified in cases where a bylaw provision is worded in a very general and imprecise manner, but is interpreted by the police officer in a sense that allows him or her to impose a legal sanction for conduct in which homeless people commonly engage. For example, it is not uncommon for police officers in Montréal to fine homeless people found lying on a public bench for an alleged breach of a municipal bylaw provision stipulating that "no person

20 *Charter*, above note 3, s 10.1: "No one may harass a person on the basis of any ground mentioned in section 10" (which prohibits discrimination).

21 Bellot et al, above note 5 at 93.

22 Turenne, *Proving Racial Profiling*, above note 18 at 15.

may use street furniture for a purpose other than the one for which it is intended, damage it or alter it in any way."[23] The Commission was provided with an audio recording of a Montréal Municipal Court decision[24] in which the defendant, a homeless person, was being prosecuted on that exact ground. The prosecutor was asking the judge to pronounce a guilty verdict even though the defendant did not show up to his trial. However, after having reviewed the statement of offence, the judge signified that he was uncomfortable with the way the police officer had interpreted this provision in the case at hand. The judge thus asked the police officer: "I understand from your written statement that the SPVM applies this provision to cases such as this one now? You were instructed to act this way I suppose?" The judge ended up bringing the amount of the fine down but still pronounced the defendant guilty. This example illustrates well the broad discretionary power given to police officers to determine which conduct is an offence under municipal regulations. In this case, it can be suspected that social profiling played a key part in the officer's decision since it is quite unusual for citizens who do not display signs of poverty or marginality to be fined for lying down on a public bench.

Another example of unusual decisions has to do with the way the statement of offence is delivered to the defendant. Thus, the Clinique Droits Devant[25] reported cases where homeless people who slept at the doorstep of a shelter because they were too drunk to be admitted, woke up the next morning with a ticket in their pocket for lying or loitering drunk in a public place. Such a method surely constitutes an unusual police practice, and possibly a procedural irregularity.[26] In other cases, police officers write a statement of offence to the individual without even asking him for any piece of identification. For example, in Bellot's study, a homeless person mentioned that police officers regularly prepare his

---

23 See, for example, City of Montréal, bylaw No 99-102, *By-law Concerning Cleanliness and Protection of Public Property and Street Furniture* (17 May 1999), s 20.

24 (2 February 2009), Montréal 212-157-02-09 (QC CM).

25 The Clinique Droits Devant is a Montréal-based NGO providing marginalized persons with legal assistance.

26 CPP, above note 14, s 157: "Service of a statement of offence may be made at the time of the commission of an offence. A duplicate of the statement shall in such a case be delivered to the defendant by the prosecutor or the person authorized to issue a statement on his behalf." One can reasonably question whether a ticket slipped in the defendant's pocket while he or she was drunk and unconscious has been properly "delivered" within the meaning of the law.

statement of offence from their car patrol without asking him to identify himself.[27] This same participant also reported that he sometimes received tickets via other persons living in the same makeshift camp without having seen the police officer who wrote the statement. In the same study, another participant mentioned he was given a ticket for jaywalking by a police officer without having been previously asked to provide identification documents. For these informants, these unusual practices can be accounted for by the fact that they are already known to local police. Therefore officers do not even bother anymore to ask them to identify themselves (name and address) before serving them a ticket. Although not illegal, this type of police conduct is certainly out of the ordinary. Moreover, in the absence of a human contact previous to the delivery of the ticket, it becomes impossible for the defendant to give his or her side of the story or to point out mitigating or contextual factors that would lead the police officer to be more lenient or tolerant.

Conversely, according to the Clinique Droits Devant, it is not uncommon for police officers to ask homeless people to identify themselves without any reasonable ground to do so. Of course, whether conscious or not, this type of conduct is illegal since a police officer may only require someone to give his name and address if there are reasonable grounds to believe that this person has committed an offence or is about to commit one.

4) The Infringed Rights

Social profiling infringes upon the *Charter* rights of the homeless and other socially marginalized populations. First, social profiling violates the right of every person to full and equal recognition, without discrimination, of his or her right to the safeguard of his dignity (sections 10 and 4 of the *Charter*). The Supreme Court of Canada circumscribed the contours of the notion of dignity in *Law v Canada*:

> Human dignity is harmed by unfair treatment premised upon personal traits or circumstances which do not relate to individual needs, capacities, or merits. It is enhanced by laws which are sensitive to the needs, capacities, and merits of different individuals, taking into account the context underlying their differences. Human dignity is harmed when individuals and groups are marginalized,

27 Bellot et al, above note 5 at 92.

> ignored, or devalued, and is enhanced when laws recognize the full place of all individuals and groups within Canadian society.[28]

Whenever laws, statutory bylaws, or institutional policies and standards are nurturing group-based discrimination while reinforcing preexisting stereotypes and prejudices, it can be said that the dignity of the group members will be harmed.[29] As will be demonstrated in the second part of this paper, the Commission considered that the SPVM's organizational standards and policies were doing just that since, by prompting police officers to specifically target homeless people, they were fuelling century-old social biases according to which these populations pose a threat and constitute a public nuisance to society, and therefore ought to be expelled from public places. In other words, social profiling reinforces the notion that homeless people are *persona non grata* in the public domain, thus "perpetuating or promoting the view that the individual is less capable, or less worthy of recognition or value as a human being or as a member of Canadian society."[30] This in turn will jeopardize homeless persons' ability to exercise their right to the safeguard of their dignity without discrimination based on their social condition.

Biased law enforcement practices against homeless people are at risk of violating other *Charter* protected rights and freedoms. However, these violations will vary depending on the nature of the offence. For example, if a homeless person is fined for loitering as a result of social profiling, this will jeopardize his right to exercise, without discrimination, his freedom of movement (section 1), and his right to access public places (section 15). If a group of two or more street youths are served tickets for loitering as a result of social profiling, their freedom of peaceful assembly and freedom of association (section 3) might be infringed. If a police officer asks a homeless person to provide pieces of identification for an offence that, all things being equal, would have been overlooked or unnoticed had the person not been in a state of (perceived) homelessness, then he or she might be infringing upon this person's right to a private life without discrimination (section 5). When a homeless person is served a ticket for sleeping on a public bench because of his social condition, he is then prevented from enjoying full equality in exercising his right to personal security and freedom (section 1). These are only meant

28 *Law v Canada (Minister of Employment and Immigration)*, [1999] 1 RCS 497 at para 53 [*Law*].

29 *Québec (Procureur général) c Lambert*, [2002] RJQ 599 (CA).

30 *Law*, above note 28 at para 51.

as examples of discriminatory human rights infringements that can result from biased police misconduct against the homeless.

C. THE SPVM'S FIGHT AGAINST INCIVILITIES, OR WHEN SOCIAL PROFILING BECOMES SYSTEMIC

In this second part of the chapter, I will lay out the Commission's reasoning and analysis that led to the conclusion that social profiling in Montréal does not boil down to a few isolated cases, but consists of a systemic form of discrimination. The concept of systemic discrimination was established by the Supreme Court in the 1980s,[31] and was subsequently appropriated and enriched by human rights tribunals.[32] In an important 2008 decision, Québec's Human Rights Tribunal (Tribunal) defined the notion as follows:

> Evidence of systemic discrimination thus rests essentially on a set of facts, such as institutional policies, decision-making procedures, behaviours and attitudes that, in an often apparently unconscious and innocuous way, have and maintain, when combined, disproportionately exclusionary effects on members of groups contemplated by the prohibition of discrimination. As useful as it is when available and relevant, statistical evidence is not, in fact, indispensable in demonstrating discrimination.[33]

In the case at hand, statistical evidence showed that the homeless were and still are grossly overrepresented among Montréalers who are fined for violating municipal bylaws (see Section B(1)). Although useful to establish systemic discrimination, as the Tribunal stated, such evidence alone is not sufficient. This led the Commission to critically review the SPVM's written documents informing what became to be known as "the fight against incivilities." The purpose here was to verify whether

---

31 See *CN v Canada (CHRC)*, [1987] 1 SCR 1114.

32 See *National Capital Alliance on Race Relations v Canada (Department of Health & Welfare)* (1997), 28 CHRR 179 (CHRT); *Radek v Henderson Development (Canada) Ltd (No 3)*, 2005 BCHRT 302 [*Radek*]; *Québec (Commission des droits de la personne et des droits de la jeunesse) v Gaz métropolitain inc*, 2008 TDPQ 24 [*Gaz métropolitain*, 2008], aff'd 2011 QCCA 1201 [*Gaz métropolitain*, 2011].

33 *Gaz métropolitain*, 2008, above note 32 at para 67.

the SPVM "institutional policies, standards and decision-making procedures" were framed in a neutral and non-discriminatory manner or if, on the contrary, they were likely to lead police officers to specifically target homeless people when enforcing bylaw regulations, in which case there would be strong evidence supporting the systemic discrimination hypothesis.

1) The Portrayal of the Homeless in the SPVM's Standards and Policies

In 2003, the SPVM published an important guiding policy entitled *Rapport d'optimisation de la police de quartier*[34] (*Rapport d'optimisation*), which was meant to assess to what extent the SPVM had successfully met the objectives it set for itself in 1997 when it had officially decided to adopt a community-based approach to policing. This model involved more police officers on the streets as well as an extensive use of foot patrols with a view to be more attentive and responsive to citizens' needs and expectations in terms of crime prevention. Six years later, in its 2003 *Rapport d'optimisation*, the SPVM presented the results of surveys, consultations, and focus groups that it either conducted or commissioned in order to better identify what Montréalers most prioritize in matters of security and crime prevention. Drawing on these surveys and consultations, the SPVM concluded that minor public disorders and incivilities were identified by Montréalers as one of their main concerns and, as such, needed to be promoted to the rank of top crime prevention priority. But what is exactly an "incivility" in the SPVM's view? As conceded by the SPVM itself, such a term is a vague and hard to define notion, not least because it does not correspond to any known legal category. Nonetheless, according to the SPVM, the term incivility encompasses "criminal behaviours as much as disturbing behaviours."[35] In the same document, the SPVM then underlined those behaviours that were most problematic in the eyes of citizens and elected representatives: "*Incivilities such as noise, vandalism, homelessness are always major concerns voiced by elected officials and emerging from surveys.* Also, over half of Montréalers consider that there are

1 2 3 4 5 6 7 8 9 10 11 12 13 14

34 Service de police de la Ville de Montréal, *Rapport d'optimisation de la police de quartier* (10 October 2003), online: SPVM www.spvm.qc.ca/upload/documentations/Rapport_optimisation_2003_10_10.pdf.

35 *Ibid* at 9.

problems of vandalism, graffiti, and dirtiness in their neighbourhood."[36] [author's emphasis and translation]

Based on the latter excerpt, it can be said that according to the SPVM homelessness seems to be a form of incivility in itself. In any case, since the SPVM was aware that the meaning of incivility needed to be clarified for patrollers, it added twenty-six new entries to its existing list of twelve call codes ("codes d'appel"[37]). Each new entry corresponded to one of the top key concerns and priorities voiced by citizens and officials, at least in the SPVM's reading. Most of these new call codes refer to behaviours that are already illegal, such as vandalism, selling or consuming drugs, graffiti, making loud noises after 11 p.m., fighting, brawling, etc. However, other codes do not refer to behaviours as such, but to certain categories of people, such as homeless people, beggars, prostitutes, and squeegee kids, who are tagged as potentially "disturbing" populations by virtue of their mere presence in the urban landscape. These new codes came into effect in 2004 but, according to the SPVM, they have gradually fallen into disuse because, in practice, police officers failed to use them on a regular basis. Nonetheless, the SPVM confirmed that these codes were still in effect at the time the Commission's report was being written.

From 2004 on, the SPVM, acting upon the recommendations set forth in its 2003 *Rapport d'optimisation*, identified the "fight against incivilities" as one of its top organizational priorities in all of its annual action plans from 2004 to 2010.[38] Moreover, in its annual action plans of 2007, 2008, 2009, and 2010, the SPVM always justified the importance of fighting incivilities and disorders in the public domain by arguing that, by doing so, it is merely fulfilling Montréalers' expectations while trying to appease their sense of insecurity. Furthermore, the SPVM systematically identified marginalized groups as the main perpetrators of public disorders of the type that tend to make citizens feel insecure. Thus, the

---

36 *Ibid.*

37 These codes are used by call dispatchers to categorize incoming 911 calls based on the type of intervention that is required, as well as by police officers in order to identify the nature of their intervention once completed.

38 Service de police de la Ville de Montréal, *Plan d'action du SPVM — 2004* (10 December 2003); *Plan d'action du SPVM — 2005* (23 December 2004); *Plan d'action du SPVM — 2006* (23 January 2006); *Plan d'action du SPVM — 2007* (7 December 2006); *Plan d'action 2008 du SPVM* (6 December 2007); *Plan d'action 2009 du SPVM* (8 January 2009); *Plan d'action 2010 du SPVM* (19 January 2010), online: SPVM www.spvm.qc.ca/upload/documentations/Plan_actions_2010.pdf.

following passage could be systematically found in all of the SPVM annual plans from 2007 to 2010 inclusively:

> Montréal is a safe city and its residents are well aware of it. . . . Thus 92 percent of them consider that their neighbourhood is either very or reasonably safe. However, incivilities and problems related to marginality and public disorders worry Montréalers. Some persons are experiencing complex social problems which lead them to violate someone else's private space or to occupy the public domain. This category of people includes homeless persons, street youth, street prostitutes, drug consumers and taggers. All of them are often blamed because their occupation of the public domain is deemed disturbing and inappropriate. This gives rise to many difficult situations, among which are violations of laws and bylaws.[39] [author's translation]

Thus, in these documents, the presence of homeless people and other marginalized groups in public places is construed as a major source of concern for Montréalers, and citizens are presumed to blame these groups for their disturbing and inappropriate way of occupying the public domain (the same way noise, vandalism graffiti, or dirtiness are socially condemned). It must be said, however, that from 2009 onwards, the action plans started to emphasize, along with repression, the need for the SPVM to build partnerships with NGOs and institutions dedicated to providing homeless people with psychosocial help and services. Nonetheless, in a 2009 document entitled *Homelessness in the Context of Urban Space Managing: The Vision and Orientations of the SPVM*, it is said that because homeless persons live in serious poverty, they will often engage in more or less legal activities to survive (prostitution, theft, consuming or selling drugs, squeegeeing, begging).[40] Homeless persons are thus presumed, as a group, to be more likely to engage in illegal activities, although no data is provided to substantiate such a claim.

The Commission also took into account the findings of Marie-Ève Sylvestre's studies.[41] Following a recommendation from the 2003 *Rapport*

39 Service de police de la Ville de Montréal, *Plan d'action 2010 du SPVM*, *ibid* at 4.

40 SPVM, *L'itinérance dans un contexte de gestion des espaces urbains: la vision et les orientations du SPVM, Service du développement stratégique* (SPVM: Montréal, September 2009) at 4.

41 Marie-Ève Sylvestre, *La pénalisation et la judiciarisation des personnes itinérantes au Québec: des pratiques coûteuses, inefficaces et contre-productives dans la prévention de l'itinérance et la réinsertion des personnes itinérantes*

1 2 3 4 5 6 7 8 9 10 11 12 13 14

d'optimisation, the SPVM requested that each of its neighbourhood police stations identify three to five incivilities to be prioritized as part of the fight against incivilities. Sylvestre was given access to the lists of priority goals set by each one of Montréal's police stations in order to keep incivilities and public disorders in check. Sylvestre found that all the police stations servicing a neighbourhood with a significant homeless population set for themselves the following priorities in their fight against incivilities: "disturbing presence of homeless people and beggars," "street prostitution," "disturbing presence of squeegees," "drug dealing," "uncivil behaviour such as loitering, spitting, urinating in public," etc.

However, it must be said that in its 2011 annual action plan,[42] the SPVM was careful not to refer to homeless persons and other marginalized populations as being specifically predisposed to engaging in acts of incivility. Furthermore, in January 2012, the SPVM released a three-year strategic plan laying out its policy orientations with respect to racial and social profiling.[43] In it, the SPVM not only acknowledges for the first time the existence of social profiling in Montréal, but even stresses that both social and racial profiling need to be treated as systemic problems calling for systemic solutions that focus on prevention, staff training, and internal monitoring. It remains to be seen, however, whether these initiatives will effectively translate into practice.

2) The Stigmatization of Homeless People in the SPVM's Standards and Policies: A Source of Systemic Discrimination

By considering that "the disturbing presence" of homeless people ought to become a law enforcement priority, the SPVM's institutional standards and policies both echo and reproduce the stereotypes and prejudices which have historically legitimized the exclusion of vagrants from

---

(Mémoire présenté à la Commission parlementaire sur l'itinérance, 2008) [Sylvestre, 2008], online: University of Ottawa www.droitcivil.uottawa.ca; Marie-Ève Sylvestre, "Policing the Homeless in Montreal: Is This Really What the Population Wants?" (2010) 20 Policing & Society 432 [Sylvestre, 2010].

42 Service de police de la Ville de Montréal, *Une organisation agile et forte de sa mission première: Plan d'action 2011 du SPVM* (9 March 2011), online: SPVM www.spvm.qc.ca/upload/documentations/Plan_daction_2011_du_SPVM.pdf.

43 Service de police de la Ville de Montréal, *Des valeurs partagées, un intérêt mutuel. Plan stratégique en matière de profilage racial et social (2012–2014)* (January 2012), online: SPVM www.spvm.qc.ca/upload/documentations/Plan_strategique_LOREZ.pdf.

the public domain. Their organizational standards and policies rest upon the notion that the mere presence of the homeless in public places is in itself more likely to be regarded by citizens as a nuisance or a "social disorder." Such rhetoric is a reminder of a time, not so long ago, when homelessness was legally considered as a crime. Nowadays, homelessness and panhandling are not illegal anymore, but homeless people and panhandlers are still strongly stigmatized. Consequently, they belong to a category of undesirable people in the mind of large segments of the population. Thus, the SPVM's standards and policies are very much at risk of encouraging patrollers to specifically target those groups whose presence in the public domain is presumed to be "disturbing" or "bothering" for society.

The SPVM also repeatedly portrayed the homeless in its official policies as being a source of "public disorder," or more specifically a source of "social disorder" to use a term coined by the SPVM (as opposed to "physical disorders" such as graffiti and vandalism). But as criminology and sociology taught us, notions of order and disorder are far from being neutral and need to be deconstructed. The meaning attached to these notions is derived from a complex symbolic system hierarchizing behaviours depending on their degree of conformity with dominant normative models. Since the nineteenth century, the modern state has relied on its institutional apparatus in order to discipline and normalize socially deviant behaviours, whether by therapeutic (such as psychiatric institutions), educational (such as rehabilitative institutions), or repressive (such as tribunals and prisons) means.[44] Whether this is done through informal social norms or through the state's institutions, the reproduction of the dominant social order is always contingent upon some form of sanction exerted on "deviant" behaviours. Furthermore, individuals who are labelled as "deviant" are not evenly distributed across the population. In the public domain, those groups displaying visible signs of poverty or experiencing social marginalization are much more likely than others to be socially condemned, and thus to be held responsible for causing "public disorders."[45] Similar to New York Mayor Rudolph Giuliani's Quality of

---

44 Michel Foucault, *Surveiller et punir. Naissance de la prison* (Paris: Gallimard, 1975); Jean-Marie Fecteau, *La liberté du pauvre: sur la régulation du crime et de la pauvreté au XIXe siècle québécois* (Montréal: VLB, 2004) [Fecteau].

45 Conseil national du bien-être social, *La justice et les pauvres* (Ottawa: Public Works and Government Services Canada, 2000); Loïc Wacquant, "The Penalization of Poverty and the Rise of Neo-liberalism" (2001) 9 Eur J on Crim

Life Initiative in the 1990s, the SPVM's fight against minor public disorders resulted in specifically targeting certain groups from the "urban margins" who are already socially stigmatized, such as homeless people, squeegee kids, and prostitutes. According to the Commission, this rhetoric was bound to echo as much as to reinforce preconceived notions about which groups fall into the "troublemaker" category.

By so doing, the SPVM gave further legitimacy to the notion that these groups need to be closely monitored by the police, and eventually excluded from public places. In other words, by associating public disorders with certain groups, the SPVM makes it easier for citizens to turn a blind eye to the (discriminatory) double standards applied by law enforcement officers when dealing with them. Of course, the social image of the disorderly and disturbing citizen only makes sense by comparison with that of the "good citizen" in need of protection from the threat and/or nuisance associated with the former. This dichotomy between bad and good citizens, between those who cause and those who suffer from public disorders, clearly contributes to give credence to the notion that the former are not full-fledged citizens. Thus, the SPVM repeatedly emphasizes how it needs to be in tune with what citizens really expect from their police services when it comes to fighting public disorders and incivilities. However, one cannot fail to notice that whenever the SPVM refers to "citizens' expectations," it does not seem to have in mind the expectations of marginalized groups such as the homeless, prostitutes, street youth, and squeegee kids, who are thus symbolically expelled from the realm of citizenship. How could it be otherwise since the latter groups have been stamped from the outset as the perpetrators of public disorders, as opposed to the other law-abiding citizens who presumably suffer harm from them?

Based on this briefly summarized analysis, the Commission concluded that it was no coincidence that the homeless in Montréal were so disproportionately represented among citizens who are served tickets by the SPVM and subway security agents. Surely, their lifestyle and the fact that many of them live on the streets make them more at risk of violating certain municipal bylaws, but there seems to be more to it. More specifically, it became clear that this gross overrepresentation had largely to do with the fact that the homeless are strongly stigmatized in the SPVM's organizational standards and policies, which makes them more likely

Pol'y & Research 401; Bernard Harcourt, *L'illusion de l'ordre. Incivilités et violences urbaines : tolérance zéro?* (Paris: Descartes & Cie, 2006) [Harcourt].

than any other group to be targeted by police officers as part of their mission to eradicate public disorders.

Such an inference is given jurisprudential support in light of a 2005 decision by the British Columbia Human Rights Tribunal.[46] In this ruling, the tribunal found that a shopping mall's "site post orders" designed to provide security agents with cues to help them identify customers' suspicious behaviours and characteristics would lead security agents to discriminate against Aboriginal and disabled people. Similarly, Québec's Court of Appeal[47] upheld a Human Rights Tribunal decision[48] in which Gaz métropolitain, a large corporation, was found guilty of systemic discrimination against women in their recruitment process designed to fill non-traditional jobs. As previously mentioned, according to the trial judge in this matter, the central element to proving systemic discrimination is not so much statistical evidence, but rather the exclusionary effect that can be rationally inferred from certain gender biases permeating institutional policies and decision-making procedures.[49]

Based on this caselaw, the Commission became convinced that the disproportionate judicialization of homeless people in Montréal was mainly attributable to the SPVM's institutional standards, policies, and procedures. Such policies and procedures fuelled a systemic form of discrimination against the homeless since, by construing them as a socially problematic population, they were turned into "designated" targets susceptible to closer police surveillance, as well as to stricter law enforcement practices. It thus became clear to the Commission that the SPVM's "fight against incivilities" was directly modelled after the Quality of Life Initiative designed by New York Mayor Rudolph Giuliani in the late 1990s. Such a model is informed by the "broken window" theory, according to which minor public disorders must be systematically prosecuted or else, the theory goes, a climate of insecurity will rapidly come to prevail in the neighbourhood, which in turn is presumably conducive to more serious criminality.[50] Giuliani's plan consisted precisely in a zero-tolerance approach to petty crime and public disorders, which resulted in the New York City Police Department (NYPD) targeting and over-

---

46 *Radek*, above note 32.

47 *Gaz métropolitain*, 2011, above note 32.

48 *Gaz métropolitain*, 2008, above note 32.

49 *Ibid* at para 67.

50 This theory was initially elaborated in James Q Wilson & George L Kelling, "Broken Window. The Police and Neighborhood Safety" *Atlantic Monthly* (March 1982) at 29.

judicializing Manhattan's homeless population as well as other marginalized groups making up the urban landscape (such as prostitutes, street youth, squeegee kids, etc).[51] In a similar fashion, in all of the SPVM documents analyzed by the Commission, homeless persons, as well as other marginalized groups such as prostitutes, squeegee kids, and street youth, were systematically portrayed as a potential threat to law and order, and as a major source of insecurity for their fellow citizens.

By doing so, the SPVM's standards and policies resulted in reinforcing the discriminatory biases which, for centuries, have legitimized the banning of vagrants and beggars from the public domain, often by incarcerating them.[52] Nowadays, images of homeless persons and beggars still carry the stigma of the past, which rests upon the notion that their way of life, whether real or imagined, constitutes both a deviant and devious lifestyle. Historically, beggars and vagrants have always bothered their fellow citizens and have always been socially perceived as undesirable, mostly because they epitomize, in popular imagery, the most extreme form of social disenfranchisement. The fact that they have neither a place called home or paid work clashes significantly with the standards against which a successful or "normal" civic integration is usually measured.

3) Is Social Profiling Reasonably Necessary to Meet the SPVM's Objectives?

Once it has been proven that a norm or practice leads to *prima facie* discrimination against a protected group, the onus then shifts to the defendant or incriminated party to demonstrate that such discrimination is reasonably necessary. In *British Columbia (Superintendent of Motor Vehicles) v British Columbia (Council of Human Rights)*,[53] the Supreme Court

---

51 Loïc Wacquant, "La mondialisation de la 'tolérance zéro'" (1999) 22 Agone 127; Tanya Erzen, "Turnstile Jumpers and Broken Windows. Policing Disorder in New York City" in Andrea McArdle & Tanya Erzen, eds, *Zero Tolerance. Quality of Life and the New Police Brutality in New York City* (New York: New York University Press, 2001) 19 [Erzen]; Harcourt, above note 45.

52 It should be noted that between 1994 and 2004, 72 percent of homeless persons judicialized under Montréal's municipal bylaws ended up being incarcerated for unpaid tickets. See Bellot et al, above note 5 at 101. However, it appears that since 2005, tribunals have ceased to order incarceration for unpaid tickets.

53 *British Columbia (Superintendent of Motor Vehicles) v British Columbia (Council of Human Rights)*, [1999] 3 SCR 868.

laid out a test designed to determine whether discrimination in service provision cases could be justified:

> (1) it [the organization] adopted the standard for a purpose or goal that is rationally connected to the function being performed;
>
> (2) . . . ;
>
> (3) the standard is reasonably necessary to accomplish its purpose or goal, in the sense that the defendant cannot accommodate persons with the characteristics of the claimant without incurring undue hardship.[54]

In the case at hand, the construction of homelessness as a security problem, as well as the social profiling to which it leads, tend to be justified by the SPVM by the need to (1) restore a sense of security among the population, and (2) address the complaints generated by the "bothering presence" of homeless people. These two rationales are in fact interrelated since homelessness tends to be considered as a nuisance in part because it generates a sense of insecurity within the population. The Commission argued that these rationales could hardly be considered as reasonable justifications for the identification of homeless people as a group warranting special police surveillance and attention as part of the SPVM's fight against incivilities.

a) The Sense of Insecurity Argument

The argument according to which homeless people undermine people's sense of security is not new. Derived from the "broken window" theory, this argument is commonly put forth by police services and elected representatives to justify judicial repression against homeless and other disfranchised populations in large cities. This reasoning is in line with a risk-reduction approach to crime legitimizing the exercise of greater police control and surveillance of groups considered more likely to put public safety at risk. From this perspective, closer police oversight must be exerted against marginalized groups because they carry within them the seeds of social deviance, delinquency, and even more serious criminality.

If this risk-reduction approach to crime can be "socially reassuring" to many, it can also exacerbate the exclusion of already stigmatized

---

54 *Ibid* at para 20.

1 2 3 4 5 6 7 8 9 10 11 12 13 14

groups.[55] The problem with this approach is that the targeted groups, that is, those warranting extra police scrutiny, are not identified based on *ex post facto* observations, but on an assessment of the risk they pose to public safety. However, as sociology and criminology teach us, the notion of "risk" is a social construction, and is thus very much tainted by preconceived notions about which groups or behaviours ought to be considered as a possible threat to the community.[56]

The identification of high-risk populations rests either on statistical previsions produced by experts (such as computing the odds that members of a given group commit a given offence based on past observations) or on surveys tapping into the general public's assessment of which groups are perceived as a potential nuisance or security threat. This latter source of information — the general public's perceptions — was pivotal in the SPVM's decision to portray the homeless as a problematic group in terms of public safety. Indeed, the SPVM did not target the homeless based on actual evidence that they represent a security threat, but solely because they are socially perceived as such. In other words, the SPVM's justification moves away from the notion that police forces must punish conduct that *objectively* jeopardizes public safety to a more malleable one according to which they must punish conduct that is *subjectively* considered as security-threatening by the general public.

From this perspective, a police officer's decision to enforce regulations against homeless people depends more on whether there is a social demand for their exclusion than on neutral and universal (applicable to all citizens) criteria for determining which behaviours objectively jeopardize public safety. By doing so, police interventions tend to sanction the social stigma attached to poverty, a stigma which has historically justified the use of criminal law and incarceration to expel from the public domain the most impoverished groups of society. Thus, throughout the nineteenth century, the poor were considered as "dangerous classes" that were morally corrupted and that needed to be re-educated. The most impoverished and socially disfranchised among them, such as vagrants

---

55 Manuelle Rozier & Valérie Vanasse, "Les mesures de réduction des méfaits : entre cadre pénal et pratiques d'intervention" in Danielle Laberge, ed, *L'errance urbaine* (Montréal: Éditions MultiMondes, 2000) 415 at 423–24; Harcourt, above note 45 at 98–124; Annamaria Colombo & Annie Larouche, "Comment sortir de la rue lorsqu'on n'est 'bienvenu nulle part' ?" (2007) 20:1 Nouvelles pratiques socials 108.

56 Jean Danet, "La frénésie pénale" in Laurent Muchielli, ed, *La frénésie sécuritaire : retour à l'ordre et nouveau contrôle social* (Paris: La Découverte, 2008) 19.

and beggars, were even displaced and, at times, incarcerated in order to free the public domain from their undesired presence.[57] Their extreme poverty, as well as their lifestyle diametrically opposed to dominant social norms, made them appear in popular imagery, not only as deviant elements, but even as potential criminals to be feared. The SPVM's argument that the presence of homeless persons in the city affects people's "sense of security" echoes these same prejudiced representations that have historically legitimized the preventive exclusion of vagrants and beggars from the public domain.

In any case, the notion — derived from the "broken window" theory — that minor public disorders are reliable predictive factors of more serious crimes has never been scientifically substantiated. In other words, there is no evidence suggesting that minor public disorders are warning signs that the offender is about to drift into the sort of crime that threatens private or public safety. For example, there is no statistically proven correlation between levels of public disorders and crime rates in any given neighbourhood.[58] It is nonetheless based on that premise that the SPVM partly justifies its discriminatory targeting of homeless people in its standards and policies relating to the fight against incivilities. Although it is conceivable that the behaviours of a minority of homeless persons make certain passers-by feel insecure, the claim that a majority of them begets a generalized sense of insecurity among the population can be seriously cast into doubt. In fact, as will be shown below, the mere notion that their presence in the public domain is an important source of concern for Montréalers is questionable.

b) Citizens' Expectations and Complaints

In all of the official documents reviewed by the Commission, the SPVM relies on Montréalers' alleged expectations to turn homelessness and public disorder caused by marginalized groups (prostitutes, beggars, street youth, squeegee kids) into a top priority for immediate action. On the one hand, this argument does not seem to be substantiated by the very data used by the SPVM to come to this conclusion. Thus, researcher Marie-Ève Sylvestre reviewed the survey data from which this SPVM's

57 Fecteau, above note 44.

58 Harcourt, above note 45 at 57–75; Ralph B Taylor, "Incivilities Reduction Policing, Zero Tolerance, and the Retreat from Coproduction: Weak Foundations and Strong Pressures" in David Weisburd & Anthony A Braga, eds, *Police Innovation : Contrasting Perspectives* (Cambridge: Cambridge University Press, 2005) 98 at 99–102.

conclusion was drawn. These include the proceedings of the plenary meeting resulting from the workshop on urban security held as part of the 2002 Montréal Summit, the transcripts of the question and answer periods following Montréal's borough council meetings, data drawn from surveys commissioned by the SPVM to external polling firms, as well as in-house surveys conducted by the SPVM itself. After analyzing these survey data and consultations transcripts, Sylvestre observed that, as far as public disorders and incivilities are concerned, Montréalers seem to be much more preoccupied by behaviours that disrupt or are detrimental to their physical environment (such as dirtiness, graffiti, vandalism, traffic, noise) than by socially marginalized groups such as homeless people.[59] For example, according to the SPVM Incivility Committee, of the 59 citizens who publicly voiced their frustration over public disorder issues during the 261 borough council meetings held between February and November 2002, none mentioned homelessness, prostitution, squeegee kids, or street youth as a source of concern.[60] The SPVM thus largely overemphasized the importance of homelessness in Montréalers' reading of which law and order issues should be prioritized by the police. If anything, noticed Sylvestre, citizens are in fact much more likely to foster social intervention than repression whenever they proffer an opinion on how local authorities should manage homelessness.

Does that mean that the contention that homeless persons are perceived as a public nuisance calling for more police interventions is a figment of the SPVM's imagination? Certainly not. However, some citizens carry more weight than others when it comes to convincing local police forces and city representatives that their concerns and interests overlap with those of the whole community. In fact, those actors holding greater social status and political influence are more likely to be successful in winning political leaders' approval over which behaviours should be considered as dangerous or harmful, or over which groups deserve to be considered as socially "deviant."[61] In Montréal, for example, condominium and business owners in the downtown area, real estate invest-

59 Sylvestre, 2008, above note 41 at 22–24.

60 *Ibid* at 24.

61 Danielle Laberge & Pierre Landreville, "De l'événement à l'infraction. Du sans-abri au délinquant. Réflexions sur le processus de catégorisation dans le champ pénal" in D Laberge, ed, *L'errance urbaine* (Montréal: Éditions MultiMondes, 2000) 121 at 128; Erzen, above note 51 at 33; Sylvestre, 2010, above note 41.

ors, and key stakeholders in the tourism industry, all have the required social capital, as well as enough financial and organizational resources, to have the SPVM and city officials endorse and advance a law and order agenda tailored to their interests.

Indeed, because luxury condominiums have been mushrooming in downtown Montréal over the past years, the marginalized populations occupying this area suddenly became undesirable in the eyes of many of these new wealthy residents. Moreover, condo owner associations have tended to successfully lobby municipal authorities to ensure that the SPVM's "fight against incivilities" would target first and foremost those "incivilities" committed by marginalized populations deemed socially unfit, such as the homeless, prostitutes, street youth, and squeegee kids. In fact, the spokespersons of these associations regularly show up to borough city council meetings to voice their complaints regarding homeless people's alleged misconducts.[62] Similarly, many business owner associations have representatives sitting on decision making and advisory bodies at the municipal level. By doing so, they gain the power to induce police forces to "clean up" the downtown area, that is, to remove from it poor and marginalized populations whose mere presence is deemed detrimental to business. Over the past fifteen years, the many revitalization projects of downtown Montréal (the Quartier des spectacles, the CHUM project, etc.), as well as the city's numerous summer festivals that have sprung up — resulting in substantial economic spin-offs — have turned the downtown area into a rather inhospitable place for homeless people. SPVM officials confirmed to the Commission that the complaints and grievances voiced by downtown condo and business owners were one of the main catalysts for police intervention against homeless persons.

For the Commission, the fact that lobbying groups are pressuring politicians and police officials into "clamping down" on homelessness cannot be used as a justification by the SPVM for profiling homeless people as part of their "fight against incivilities," no matter how politically influential these lobby groups are. Accepting such a rationale would be tantamount to endorsing a two-tier justice system whereby the interests and expectations of citizens endowed with high economic, social, and political capital would be given preference by law enforcement authorities over the interests and expectations of the most underprivileged

62 Sylvestre, 2010, *ibid*.

1 2 3 4 5 6 7 8 9 10 11 12 13 14

and vulnerable segments of society. According to the Commission, the SPVM seemed to overlook the fact that homeless persons, although socially disempowered compared with business owners and downtown residents, are nonetheless equally entitled, as citizens, to access and occupy the public domain. Such a discriminatory preference, stated the Commission, clearly encroaches upon homeless persons' equal right to the safeguard of their dignity.

Of course condominium and business owners' expectations as regards law enforcement priorities ought to be considered as worthy of attention by the SPVM as those expressed by any other group (including homeless people and marginalized groups). However, as discussed above, the problem is that these expectations are often derived from perceptions which, as such, are not reliable indicators of public safety breaches or risks. Thus, it has been argued that the very notion of "public disorder" is not neutral, as its meaning tends to vary drastically depending on which individual or social group sets the standard against which the notion of order is defined. This is not to deny that homeless persons in urban areas are sometimes likely to encroach upon other citizens' rights or to cause public nuisance. However, police officers would be better advised to determine based on neutral behavioural criteria the extent to which the alleged misconduct poses an actual risk to public safety or represents an actual nuisance for other citizens. In any case, police discretion ought to be used in a non-discriminatory manner and, to do so, police officers need to be cognizant of the stereotypes and prejudices (whether their own or others') interfering with the exercise of their independent judgment.

D. CONCLUSION

The concept of social profiling has thus proven to be highly useful to capture the kind of biased policing that homeless people experience on a regular basis, mostly by being specifically targeted by law enforcement authorities as part of their efforts to crack down on minor misconducts and incivilities. It should be also kept in mind that social profiling is often carried out within a broader social and legal framework characterized by systemic discrimination. Thus, in Montréal, the Commission observed that biased policing was fuelled by police-made standards and policies explicitly construing homelessness as a law and order issue to be dealt with accordingly. Upon carefully analyzing these standards and policies, it also appeared that the rationales put forward by the SPVM to justify such discriminatory targeting were not rationally connected to the objectives underlying its commitment to fight public disorders. More specifically, neither the alleged sense of insecurity generated by homeless people, nor the criticisms voiced against them by condominium and business owners or ordinary citizens, are sufficient grounds for justifying any discriminatory distinction against them in police standards and policies and, correlatively, in the treatment they get from law enforcement officers.

Although it was beyond the limited scope of this paper to elaborate on this issue, the Commission also stressed in its report that social profiling was sustained by certain laws and bylaws which, although displaying *prima facie* neutrality, contributed to compounding the overrepresentation of homeless people in the judicial system. At least two bylaws enacted by the Ville-Marie borough (located in Montréal's downtown) fell into this category, including one prohibiting the presence of dogs in a park that was known to attract many homeless dog owners, and another one closing during night time the last downtown parks where the homeless could still stay overnight for sleeping purposes. The Commission also argued that the provisions of the *Code of Penal Procedure*[63] enabling a judge to order imprisonment for unpaid fines regardless of one's ability to pay was infringing upon the right of the disadvantaged to exercise their *Charter* protected right to dignity (section 4) and personal freedom and inviolability (section 1) without discrimination based on social condition. Furthermore, the Commission emphasized that, in the case of homeless people, imprisonment may often result in aggravating any mental health or addiction problem they might have had prior to incarceration and, what's more, in seriously jeopardizing their social reintegration prospects once released from prison.

Though the main focus of this paper was social profiling, it must be reminded that in the last chapter of its 2009 report, the Commission, invoking the right to adequate housing recognized under international law, urged governments to deal with the root causes of homelessness. To do so, a paradigm shift is needed so that all levels of government start prioritizing prevention over repression, for example by extending the

63 CPP, above note 14, ss 237, 346, & 347.

1 2 3 4 5 6 7 8 9 10 11 12 13 14

current supply of social and affordable housing, by making psychosocial and mental health services more accessible to homeless people, and by supporting their gradual labour market integration when possible, etc. In short, in this neoliberal era of growing class inequalities and socio-economic exclusion, governments need to move away from the punitive approach to poverty to progressive policy making aimed at counteracting the disruptive effects of social insecurity.[64]

To conclude, it can be said that Québec's Human Rights Commission greatly contributed to raise public awareness regarding the over-judicialization of homeless people and, above all, to help construe the problem as a discrimination issue. The Commission's leadership in this matter consisted of going beyond a narrowly-defined case-by-case approach in order to grasp the problem from a systemic angle. As mentioned in the introduction, prior to conducting its investigation, the Commission's attempts to initiate a constructive dialogue between all the stakeholders in this matter eventually reached an impasse because Montréal's police forces, as well as elected officials, refused to recognize the role played by discrimination in the over-judicialization of homeless people in Montréal. However, after the Commission's report was released and publicized in November 2009, the SPVM started to cooperate with the Commission and NGOs in order to find ways to prevent and eradicate biased law enforcement practices directed at Montréal's homeless and other socially marginalized populations. In its 2011 annual action plan, the SPVM stopped referring to homelessness as a "security" problem and, in 2012, it released a three-year strategic plan laying out its policy orientations with respect to racial and social profiling. Although this is good news, it must be kept in mind that, according to recent data, the over-judicialization of homeless people continues on the ground without any sign of slowing down. But at least, social profiling is now acknowledged and taken seriously by the SPVM, and the Commission is certainly no stranger to this sudden change of direction.

64 Loïc Wacquant, *Punir les pauvres. Le nouveau gouvernement de l'insécurité sociale* (Marseille: Agone, 2004).

PART 5

The Future of Human Rights Institutions in Canada: Interdisciplinary and Interinstitutional Collaboration

CHAPTER 13

THE ONTARIO HUMAN RIGHTS COMMISSION AND THE FRAMEWORK FOR MAPPING AND ADDRESSING COMPETING HUMAN RIGHTS[1]

Lorne Foster & Lesley Jacobs[2]

A. INTRODUCTION

The Ontario Human Rights Commission (OHRC) has been a leader in Canada and internationally in its efforts to address competing human rights through education and policy development. The OHRC released its *Policy on Competing Human Rights*[3] in April 2012, culminating a six-year program of research and consultation focused on detailing effective ways to address competing human rights claims. In general, competing human rights claims are situations in which legally codified human rights are claimed by two or more parties to a dispute, thus complicating the normal approach to resolving a human rights dispute where only one side claims a human right in relation to an alleged violator

1 This chapter draws in part on Shaheen Amzi, Lorne Foster, & Lesley Jacobs, eds, *Balancing Competing Human Rights Claims in Diverse Societies: Institutions, Policy, Principles* (Toronto: Irwin Law, 2012), especially the Introduction and cc 2 and 8.

2 Lorne Foster is the director of the graduate program in Public Policy Administration and Law (MPPAL), and a professor in the School of Public Policy and Administration (SPPA) and the Department of Equity Studies (DES) at York University.

Lesley Jacobs is professor of law & society and political science as well as director of the Institute for Social Research at York University. He is also executive director of the Canadian Forum on Civil Justice.

3 Ontario Human Rights Commission, *Policy on Competing Human Rights* (Toronto: OHRC, 2012) [OHRC, *Policy*], online: OHRC www.ohrc.on.ca/sites/default/files/policy%20on%20competing%20human%20rights_accessible_2.pdf.

of rights. This chapter is designed to both explain the OHRC's policy and contextualize the role of the OHRC in the formulation of Canada's first competing rights policy. It stresses in particular the importance of social constructionism for making sense of how human rights policy in Canada is developed and implemented as a response to increasing diversity.

B. COMPETING HUMAN RIGHTS IN THE FACE OF DIVERSITY

In the context of globalization, diversity has become an increasingly valued characteristic of contemporary societies. Diverse societies are viewed as remarkable for their variety in terms of religious practices, spoken languages, ethnicities, sexualities, and expressions of multiculturalisms. Such societies are said to allow for a measure of openness and adaptability that enable them to meet efficiently and effectively the ever changing needs and demands of a global economy.

Yet, as societies have embraced and indeed aspire towards diversity, certain challenges and tensions have become visible that were not fully anticipated. With increased diversity comes the ordeal of more visible conflicts between different beliefs about how people should best lead their lives and what sorts of accommodations should be made for persons with different beliefs out of respect for human dignity and mutual recognition. Competing human rights claims are one reflection of this ordeal.

Our point is that the practice of human rights has taken on increasing complexity in Canada and other diverse societies because more and more often around the world the claim to a right of one individual or group directly affects the claim to the human rights of another group. Such competing human rights claims can be played out in many places, from the classroom to workplaces, from the public square to the international stage, where ever individuals or groups actively claim the recognition of rights that may interfere with the access to rights of others.

Examples of these sorts of competing human rights should be familiar to all of us. Think about religious organizations that object on the grounds of the right to religious practice to prohibitions against discrimination against gays and lesbians or measures that promote the inclusion of women. Imagine, for example, a barber who refuses to cut the hair of a woman as a matter of religious conscience or a pharmacist who refuses to dispense birth control for similar reasons. The rights of parents to excuse their children from exposure to topics like world religions or evolutionary biology in schools provide other examples. Imagine likewise a situation where an individual with a Seeing Eye dog seeks to enter the taxi of a driver who is allergic to dog hair. The rights of one person with a disability are here in competition with the rights of someone else with a different sort of disability. The rights of individuals to wear certain types of religious dress or carry symbolic weapons in public places such as schools or courts compete with the rights of others to security or a fair trial. Claims from immigrant groups to be protected from expressions of racism or hate can compete with the rights of journalists or academics to express critical or controversial views about immigration policy or practices.

Recognition that human rights claims can come into conflict or be in competition with each other is not new. Among rights theorists, the potential for conflict between rights claims has been an important theme in philosophical debates throughout the twentieth century. But the conflict was conceived of in a particular way, that is to say, between the right to liberty and the right to equality, or the right to private property and the right to equality. These debates yielded innovative approaches to thinking about these conflicts. Some philosophers such as John Rawls[4] argued that in the case of conflicts, some rights to basic liberties should have lexical priority over others. Legal theorist Ronald Dworkin[5] argued on the contrary that equality should always have priority. Others argued that these conflicts should be resolved in favour of a calculation about what rights serve the greatest overall good for society.[6] Others still such as Isaiah Berlin[7] believed that there is no single principle for resolving conflicting rights claims and that we should draw on our intuitions in particular instances to decide what to do.

Competing human rights claims in diverse societies are, in our view, not best thought of abstractly in terms of a conflict between the demands of equality and liberty but rather as arising from different beliefs about

---

4 John Rawls, *A Theory of Justice* (Cambridge, MA: Harvard University Press, 1971).

5 Ronald Dworkin, *Taking Rights Seriously, New Edition* (Cambridge, MA: Harvard University Press, 1977).

6 LW Sumner, *The Moral Foundation of Rights* (Oxford: Oxford University Press, 1987).

7 Isaiah Berlin, *Four Essays on Liberty* (Oxford: Oxford University Press, 1969).

how people should best lead their lives and what sorts of accommodations should be made for persons with different beliefs out of respect for human dignity and mutual recognition. These sorts of differences are not new but in diverse societies people with these differences live together in close proximity, which brings the possibilities for conflicts and competing human rights claims to the forefront.

Unlike the conflict between equality and liberty, balancing or reconciling competing human rights claims in diverse societies has received scant systematic academic attention nor has it been the site for significant policy development and innovation. Instead, until recently, the popular media and the courts have been the major sites for discussing how to balance competing human rights claims in diverse societies. Those discussions have rarely been careful nor probed deeply into what it means for human rights claims to be in competition nor how best to balance them in a diverse society.

C. SOCIAL CONSTRUCTIONIST MAPPING OF COMPETING HUMAN RIGHTS

The institutions at the core of the Canadian human rights system — the courts and human rights commissions — are currently struggling to respond to the challenges presented by competing human rights claims in Canada. These challenges for human rights commissions in particular are multi-dimensional, involving deep philosophical questions about the nature of human rights, juridical questions about how cases involving competing human rights should be judged and decided, and policy questions about how in principle and practice issues involving competing human rights should be framed and approached in Canadian society.

Human rights commissions in Canada assume a *social constructionist* engagement with human rights. In our view, social constructionism is integral for making sense of how Canadian human rights commissions are mapping the phenomena of competing human rights claims that arise from diversity and the vision of inclusive citizenship that underpins how they address this phenomena. Social constructionism is a sociological theory of knowledge that considers how social phenomena develop in social contexts, and seeks to explore rigorously the nuances, contingencies, contestations, and meanings that are part and parcel of the social construction of reality. Within constructionist thought, rights are considered as a construct or "artifact" that is dependent on contingent variables of our social selves. There is now a substantive body of literature examining various aspects of the social practice of human rights. Here, rights are not simply given as divine will, or as transhistorical being, or as universal ontology — but are considered products of human social interaction with all its imbalances and imperfections. From this perspective, human rights are invariably the product of the balance of power between normatively-oriented social actors in social-historical context. Practically, human rights commissions in Canada and the codes that guide them are all the products of legislation. They are, in other words, the outcome of political processes, not idealized instruments of social justice.

The idea of the "universality" of rights, argued Malcolm Waters, "is itself a human construct."[8] The social constructionist approach examines what actors actually do with human rights in everyday life, in institutional settings, and in other specific fields of political contestation. In developing a framework for understanding the social construction of rights, research has begun a move toward foreclosing on the age-old philosophical and ontological status debates, and focusing on the investigation of their meaning, use, and mobilization. Moreover, by declaring an interest in the "indeterminacy" of rights, social constructionist research is well placed to investigate the shifting dynamics of rights disputes, or *competing human rights claims*, which are becoming increasing prevalent in our transnational and diverse world. By investigating the social relationships, practices, and struggles that mobilize rights claims and rights talk, and animate rights disputes, the social constructionist approach can "bracket" the prevailing dominant discourses and provide a more dynamic and textured understanding of rights.

From a social constructionist perspective, human rights claims should be seen as the product of a particular place and time, and in this respect historically and socially contingent. This observation is significant in a number of ways. First, rights are not simply inalienable or natural; and they are not necessarily beneficial for the rights holder to exercise. Second, human rights were invented in the modern age both as a product of the exercise of a particular type of political power and as

8 Malcolm Waters, "Human Rights and the Universalisation of Interests: Towards a Social Constructionist Approach" (1996) 30:3 Sociology 593 at 593.

a response to a particular form of power.[9] Contrary to Lockean political philosophy, "rights" and "freedom" were not in existence before "power," but rather are the distinctive products of the "new mode of life" that is modern global capitalism.[10] They have a paradoxical nature in that they allow us to challenge inequalities whilst contributing to the production of social divisions. Third, although human rights typically find expression in law, they have a life in society outside the law and do not rely solely on the juridical sphere to dictate their meaning. For this reason, the doctrine of human rights can go beyond law and form a fundamental moral basis for regulating contemporary social order.

Viewed through the lens of a social constructionist perspective, competing rights in Canada are best understood as a product of broad structural factors related to the imbalance of power between marginalized and dominant cultures. The tensions between the power, beliefs, norms, and values of marginalized minorities and the dominant majority culture in Canada act as push and pull factors that continue to increasingly challenge Canada's human rights regime along national and international lines, and in terms of legislative and public policy safeguards. For instance, allegations of competing human rights scenarios in which legally codified human rights are claimed by two or more parties to a dispute have been identified in Ontario's new competing human rights policy to include:[11]

- *Code* right v *Code* right: For example, a blind college professor's guide dog is affecting one of her students who has a severe allergy to dogs. Both individuals might make *Code*-based human rights claims on the ground of "disability."
- *Code* right v *Code*/legal defence: For example, a religious organization, providing supportive group living to persons with disabilities of any denomination, requires staff to abide by a religious code of behaviour and dismisses a support worker once it becomes aware she was in a same-sex relationship. The dismissed worker might claim *Code*-based discrimination on the ground of sexual orientation

9 See Lynn Hunt, *Inventing Human Rights* (New York: WW Norton, 2007).

10 Anthony Woodiwiss, *Human Rights* (New York: Routledge, 2005) at 32.

11 See OHRC, *Policy*, above note 3. In the following, *Code* refers to the Ontario *Human Rights Code*, RSO 1990, c H.19 and *Charter* refers to the *Canadian Charter of Rights and Freedoms*, Part I of the *Constitution Act, 1982*, being Schedule B to the *Canada Act 1982* (UK), 1982, c 11.

while the religious organization might claim a *Code* defence that allows restrictions on terms of employment for religious and other fraternal types of organizations with conditions.

- *Code* right *v* other legislated right: For example, school curriculum: Some parents want the Ministry of Education to modify sex education curriculum so as not to interfere with their beliefs; some for religious-based reasons, some for personal reasons. Other parents support the new curriculum changes; some based on the *Code* ground of family status and sexual orientation. Others want the new curriculum based on the legislated right to public education. Parents opposed to some types of sex education because of their beliefs might claim *Code*-based discrimination on the ground of creed. Other parents might claim a *Code* right based on family status, sexual orientation, and a legislated right to the curriculum based on the broader purpose and requirements of the *Education Act*.[12]

- *Code* right *v* *Charter* right: For example, a Muslim woman observes the niqab (a face veil) and is required to act as a witness against an accused in a court. The woman might claim a right to accommodation of religious observance based on the *Code* ground of creed while the accused might claim the right to observe the woman's face while she provides witness in the court based on *Charter* rights to full answer and defence.

- *Code* right *v* common law right: For example, a Jewish family is asked to remove a temporary sukkah hut placed on their balcony for religious celebration because it does not comply with the condominium's bylaws and is interfering with the neighbours' enjoyment of their balcony. The Jewish family might claim *Code*-based discrimination on the ground of creed while the condominium might claim a right to peaceful enjoyment of property for its members based on both common law and Ontario's *Residential Tenancies Act*.[13]

- International treaty right *v* *Code*/*Charter* defence: For example, non-Catholic religious school users claim a right to non-discriminatory religious school funding based on provisions of the United Nations

12 RSO 1990, c E.2.
13 SO 2006, c 17.

International Covenant on Economic, Social and Civil Rights.[14] The UN treaty body responsible for the Covenant found Ontario's public funding of the Catholic school system to the exclusion of all other religions to be discriminatory. The government claimed provisions of the *Education Act*, an exemption in the *Code*, the *Charter*, and related caselaw in its defence.

- *Charter* right v *Charter* right: For example, an accuser in a sexual harassment criminal proceeding wishes to testify wearing her niqab in accordance with her section 15 *Charter* religious equality rights. The accused claims this would violate his section 7 *Charter* right to make full answer and defence. Both sides claim *Charter* rights.

This social constructionist mapping of competing human rights claims in Ontario opens up possibilities to expand the protections of the *Code*, address new and emerging human rights issues and trends, incorporate international perspectives on human rights, and provide a broad understanding of the social and economic aspects of human rights. Fundamentally, this mapping exercise is designed to provide clear policy direction in new unexplored areas or in areas of ambiguity for a wide variety of citizens concerned with competing human rights claims.

D. SOCIAL CITIZENSHIP AND HUMAN RIGHTS CLAIMS

Although in diverse societies there is a high degree of fragmentation and potential for conflict, members of these societies share a common citizenship.[15] Citizenship means, for our purposes, "the collection of public claims and duties bestowed on people by the political order."[16] Social citizenship is at base a form of community membership, as opposed to a legal status bestowed by the state. (On this definition, even undocumented immigrants or unsuccessful refugee applicants are social citizens.) From a social constructionist perspective, the public claims and duties that define citizenship are not changeless but rather socially

14 16 December 1966, 993 UNTS 3, 6 ILM 368 (entered into force 3 January 1976).

15 Will Kymlicka, *Multicultural Citizenship* (Oxford: Oxford University Press, 1996).

16 Lawrence Mead, "Citizenship and Social Policy: TH Marshall and Poverty" (1997) 14(2) Social Philosophy and Policy 197 at 198.

contingent. In countries like Canada, the public is more than just the state; there is no doubt that the public nature of the claims and duties of citizenship regulate the relations between citizens. In other words, shared citizenship defines in part what we owe each other.

Human rights in a society that values and aspires to diversity should be, in our view, a constitutive component of full citizenship, and standing on human rights claims is an expression of that shared citizenship. In a social constructionist ideal world, social actors go through human rights discourses to get to citizenship. In this ideal world, the mutual recognition of others as human rights bearers is a function of shared citizenship, which shifts the terms of debate from the problems of balancing or reconciling competing human rights claims to their democratic citizenship potential. Here, competitive practice and conflicting rights claims at the individual and collective level are conceived as disciplinary threads in weaving the social fabric of a fulsome and expanded "social citizenship." This social ideal is an emergent reality that extends the meaning of citizenship rights beyond conventional notions of legal and political equality to encompass rights of inclusion. These social citizenship rights of inclusion refer to guarantees of equal opportunity, equity, and non-discrimination for socially disadvantaged groups, such as women, Aboriginal peoples, and other people of colour, to participate fully in the public as well as economic life and to expect a reasonable level of respect and recognition from others. In this ideal social constructionist world, the task of state and institutional social actors, the courts, and human rights commissions is to increase the access points to justice. Shared citizenship provides, in other words, the context for these actors to advance competing human rights claims against each other and the state.

This idea that shared citizenship frames competing human rights claims differs from how too often parties in these disputes as well as the media and other interpretative communities frame competing human rights. Rather than identify shared citizenship, these conflicts are framed often in terms of the rights of "others." "Others" are precisely not people with whom we share anything other than perhaps a common humanity. This language of the rights of others is exemplified in the cases of the human rights claims of refugees or recent immigrants.[17] And the most often cited examples of disputes involving competing human

---

17 Seyla Benhabib, *The Rights of Others: Aliens, Residents and Citizens* (Cambridge: Cambridge University Press, 2004).

rights claims in Canada revolve around immigrants or refugees with their "foreign" cultural practices. Framed in terms of the rights of others, there is unfortunately little promise of striking a fair balance between competing human rights claims, for there is no common ground. Framing these disputes instead as ones involving parties who share a social citizenship means that there is some common ground between them, for citizenship defines in part what the parties owe each other. What do these parties owe each other? At minimum, they owe each other mutual respect and recognition, which is in most cases enough to sway the parties to join a process where the competing human rights claims are balanced against each other.

The modern concept of citizenship, as we noted, entails recognition of a full and inclusive membership in society. The extent of this membership is the outcome of political contestation. Following the Second World War, the British sociologist TH Marshall offered an important analysis of citizenship that concerns the content of mutual recognition and empowerment and how they may be realized in the context of market-based inequalities.[18] Marshall divided citizenship into three elements: civil, political, and social. Civil rights include "liberty of person, freedom of speech, thought and faith, the right to own property . . . and the right to justice." Political rights for Marshall included the right to vote and the right to run for political office. The institutions he associated most closely with these first two elements were the courts and Parliament.[19] But Marshall was also concerned with social rights — "the right to a modicum of economic welfare and security . . . according to the standards prevailing in society" — and he viewed the welfare state as the institutional mechanism for the distribution of these rights.[20] Through the welfare state, provisions are made for public education, universal health care, and public housing and income security programs. Thus, social rights make possible a fuller expression of citizenship for those groups who would be disadvantaged in terms of resources and power and, hence, would suffer most acutely from insecurities generated by a market economy. Without

18 See TH Marshall, "Citizenship and Social Class" in TH Marshall & Tom Bottomore, eds, *Citizenship and Class* (London: Pluto Press, 1991) 18 [Marshall].

19 *Ibid* at 8.

20 *Ibid*.

the provision of social rights, gross inequalities would undermine the equality of political and civil rights inherent in the idea of citizenship.[21]

Marshall's argument for social citizenship can be read as a dynamic account of the social-historical development of citizenship in Western society, and as a relentless struggle between the extension of political equality and social rights on the one hand, and the capitalist market and social class on the other hand.[22] In this account, civil citizenship becomes the arena for this struggle with each side trying to limit the reach of the other by defining the scope of civil rights in terms favourable to its side. And this struggle is then deflected back into the political arena. That is, Marshall provides a picture of a dynamic struggle in which the proponents of the market are continually seeking to reign in the spread of social rights by redefining civil protections in individualist terms while seeking to confine political equality to the sphere of the state. The proponents of social citizenship, by contrast, are seeking to expand not just a steadily higher level of social services rendering money income less relevant, but, more significantly, forging within civil society a sphere of "citizenship" that complements political citizenship in the state. Thus, the struggle for social rights against the market and social class becomes a struggle for the very definition of civil society itself.[23]

In Marshall's view, through this historical struggle of equity-seeking groups, the meaning of citizenship rights in capitalist societies has been expanded beyond formal legal and political equality to encompass social equality rights, including the right to a minimum level of economic security and social welfare assured by the state. Here is contained Marshall's notion of an emergent universal dictate that all members of the political community ought to have a fundamental claim to certain social services and programs such as food security, health care, education, unemployment insurance, environmental safety, and so on. The degree of universality of these reforms is the degree to which the concept has been realized. Social citizenship implies an equality of status in

21 Ruth Lister, *Citizenship: Feminist Perspectives* (London: Macmillan Press, 1997).

22 Peter Breiner, "Is Social Citizenship Really Outdated? TH Marshall Revisited" (Paper delivered at the annual meeting of the Western Political Science Association, Hyatt Regency Albuquerque, Albuquerque, New Mexico, 17 March 2006), online: All Academic Research http://citation.allacademic.com/meta/p_mla_apa_research_citation/0/9/7/5/7/pages97572/p97572-1.php.

23 *Ibid.*

the social realm, in the same way that contemporary or prevailing versions of citizenship denote equality in the political realm: just as there is universal enfranchisement, there ought to be universal entitlement to certain social security guarantees within civil society and the contemporary global order.

The dynamic vision we are advancing sees shared social citizenship being extended from a form of membership that is a response to the challenges of class inequality in a capitalist economy to one that addresses the challenges of increased diversity in Canadian society. Human rights institutions grounded on shared citizenship are invaluable for the recognition, protection, and promotion of rights of inclusion and developing policy for balancing competing human rights claims that arise from that diversity.

E. THE NEW MANDATE OF THE ONTARIO HUMAN RIGHTS COMMISSION

The OHRC developed its new policy on competing human rights claims in the wake of historic changes in its role and mandate. The fact that the role and mandate of the OHRC has been reinvented[24] enforces our point above that its actions can be best understood in terms of social constructionism. Until July 2008, the OHRC mandate included the responsibility to take and process human rights complaints. This included mediation, investigation, and referral of complaints to the Ontario Human Rights Tribunal (OHRT) and litigation of complaints before the OHRT and the courts. Changes to the *Code* in 2008 resulted in the responsibility for processing complaints being passed to the OHRT, providing the public with direct access to a formal hearing, and leaving the OHRC to focus on the promotion of human rights. Promotion methods include: establishing human rights policy, conducting research and inquiry, intervening in legal proceedings, and providing public education. The OHRC is the only human rights commission in Canada that no longer receives and processes human rights complaints.[25]

---

24 *Human Rights Code Amendment Act*, SO 2006, c 30 [*HRC Amendment Act*].

25 Andrew Pinto, Ontario Human Rights Commission, *Report of the Ontario Human Rights Review 2012* (Toronto: Ministry of the Attorney General of Ontario, 2012) [Pinto Report], online: Ministry of the Attorney General

The establishment of a direct access to the OHRT combined with relieving the OHRC of its historical compliance and enforcement functions is consistent with the current forces of neoliberalism and the trend toward downloading responsibility for anti-discrimination and social justice from the state to the individual. It is now well established that "the politics of neoliberalism"[26] in the age of the global economy involves "processes of privatization" which act to shift the construction of the public and private spheres and (re)conceive state and citizen duties accordingly.[27] In an attempt to transform all forms of state intervention into market functions, that which was once considered a public responsibility of the state is now constructed as the responsibility of individual citizens, under the auspices of the privatization of justice.

Hence, many critics have charged Ontario's *direct access* human rights system with off-loading of the public mandate to combat discrimination onto the marginalized minority communities who are the usual victims of human rights violations and the under-resourced not-for-profit sector in the area of legal supports. In this regard, it has been recently observed[28] that while the new legislation promised speedy tribunal hearings and free access to lawyers for every Ontarian, in reality the tribunal system is based on a "stage-by-stage approach to litigation and case management" that has been far from expeditious, free, and all-inclusive, and is often financially prohibitive and bureaucratically daunting for claimants from vulnerable minority groups. Financial support for claims brought forward is reassessed at every stage in the

---

www.attorneygeneral.jus.gov.on.ca/english/about/pubs/human_rights/Pinto_human_rights_report_2012-ENG.pdf.

26 See Fiona MacDonald, "(Re)conceiving Citizenship: the Welfare-Multiculturalism Dynamic" (Paper delivered at the Annual Meeting of the American Political Science Association, University of Manitoba, 30 August–2 September 2007).

27 Paul Starr, "The Meaning of Privatization" in Sheila Kamerman & Alfred Kahn, eds, *Privatization and the Welfare State* (Princeton: Princeton University Press, 1989).

28 See, for example, Neil Stammers, "Social Movements and the Social Construction of Human Rights" (1999) 21:4 Hum Rts Q 980; Ken Plummer, "Rights Work: Constructing Lesbian, Gay and Sexual Rights in Late Modern Times" in Lydia Morris, ed, *Rights: Sociological Perspectives* (New York: Routledge, 2006); Lydia Morris, ed, *Rights: Sociological Perspectives, ibid*; Bryan S Turner, *Vulnerability and Human Rights* (University Park, PA: The Pennsylvania State University Press, 2006); Mark Goodale & Sally Engle Merry, *The Practice of Human Rights: Tracking Law Between the Global and Local* (Cambridge, NY: Cambridge University Press, 2007).

process. Here, the progressive privatization of the complaint carriage is actually a challenge to access, absent to power imbalances between parties, and represents a distinct move away from the progressive formalization of human rights complaints.

Meanwhile, there seems to be growing evidence (distinguished by the dearth of public interest cases brought forward by the OHRC to date) that decoupling of the individual complaint from its other functions results in undermining public interest goals by encouraging a privatized view of wrongs (which impact not only the individual, but also the social environment and the public atmosphere more broadly). Most importantly, there seems to be clear evidence today that those equity-seeking minorities that are most impacted by the human rights system have the least influence on its development and direction. The preponderance of white people in the new system seems troubling. It seems most senior decision-maker positions in the new system are held by white people; it also seems that appointments in the new system fail to represent the people they are expected to serve — ergo, this accounts for it being dubbed by some as "The Human Whites System."[29]

These historic changes have surprisingly also presented the OHRC with some new opportunities to be innovative and take on a leadership role on emerging human rights issues in Canada.[30] The redrawing of the administrative boundaries of the human rights system in Ontario has by coincidence allowed the OHRC to consolidate its own organizational energies and gain an agility and dexterity in its human rights promotion and public education role that it formerly did not have. The new challenge of the OHRC living under reduced circumstances has also afforded a unique opportunity to refine current promotional methods and policy instruments, and ensure that they are responding to today's problems.

Comprehending the history of human rights protection in Ontario through the lens of social constructionism provides a fruitful vocabulary for situating the new role of the OHRC. In more concrete terms, this approach to competing human rights claims can be shown to fit well

---

29 See Accessibility for Ontarians with Disabilities Act Alliance, *Supplemental Brief To The Andrew Pinto Ontario Human Rights Code Review* (Toronto: AODA, 2012), online: AODA www.aodaalliance.org/strong-effective-aoda/04122012.asp; African Canadian Legal Clinic, *Written Submissions to the Ontario Human Rights Review* (Toronto: ACLC, 2012); Federation of Asian Canadian Lawyers, *FACL Submissions: Ontario Human Rights Review 2011–2012* (Toronto: FACL, 2012).

30 Pinto Report, above note 25.

with the new mandate of the OHRC given by the 2006 *HRC Amendment Act*.[31] The new mandate requires the OHRC to bridge the gap between public policy and justice administration. Thereby, the OHRC is now responsible for developing public policy as well as addressing tension and conflict in the province, in order to bring people and communities together to help resolve differences. This new mandate bestows the unique capacity to address multi-faceted social issues with a broad range of processes — those both rule and policy-based, and those left to discretionary decision makers.

Section 30 of the *Code* authorizes the OHRC to prepare, approve, and publish human rights policies and to provide guidance on interpreting its provisions. The power to develop policies is part of the OHRC's broader responsibility under section 29 to promote, protect, and advance respect for human rights in Ontario, to protect the public interest, and to eliminate discriminatory practices. Section 45.5 of the *Code* states that the OHRT may consider policies approved by the OHRC in its proceedings. Where a party or an intervenor in a proceeding requests it, the OHRT *shall* consider an OHRC policy. Where an OHRC policy is relevant to the subject matter of a human rights application, parties and intervenors are encouraged to bring the policy to the OHRT's attention for consideration. Section 45.6 of the *Code* states that if a final decision or order of the OHRT is not consistent with an OHRC policy, in a case where the OHRC was either a party or an intervenor, the OHRC may apply to have the OHRT state a case to the Divisional Court to address this inconsistency.

Although OHRC policies and guidelines are not binding on the OHRT or on courts, they are often given great deference and applied to the facts of human rights cases before courts or tribunals, and are quoted in the decisions of these bodies. In addition, the OHRC's policies contain practical guidance relevant to the everyday lives of Ontarians. They aim to influence social behaviour to prevent human rights violations before they occur and to promote social change. They set standards for how individuals, employers, housing providers, service providers, and policy makers should act to ensure compliance with the *Code*. OHRC policies are widely used as a source of guidance by those responsible for applying the *Code*, such as lawyers, unions, human resource managers, and others. They are perceived as useful and instructive because they respond to day-to-day human rights issues.

---

31 *HRC Amendment Act*, above note 24.

The OHRC has become a leader in the development of human rights policy in the country. There are currently twenty-one OHRC-approved policies that are accessible through its website.[32] The first of these was the *Policy on Height and Weight Requirements*,[33] which was released in 1996. One of the most recent is the *Policy on Human Rights and Rental Housing*[34] released in 2009. These policies range in style from short, focused policy positions on issues such as drug and alcohol testing,[35] to comprehensive and detailed policy documents addressing multiple issues and positions related to major *Code* grounds like "race" or "disability," or significant social areas such as "employment."[36] These more substantive policies typically contain sections on historical, legal, and social context, linguistic and conceptual clarification, identification of specific types of discrimination, and detailing of best practices and approaches to addressing these types of discrimination. The most widely used OHRC policies such as the *Policy and Guidelines on Disability and the Duty to Accommodate*[37] (2000), the *Policy and Guidelines on Racism and Racial Discrimination*[38] (2005), and *Human Rights at Work*[39] (2008) are more substantive in nature.

---

32 "Policies and guidelines," online: OHRC www.ohrc.on.ca/en/our_work/policies_guidelines.

33 Ontario Human Rights Commission, *Policy on Height and Weight Requirements* (Toronto: OHRC, 1996), online: OHRC www.ohrc.on.ca/sites/default/files/attachments/Policy_on_height_and_weight_requirements.pdf.

34 Ontario Human Rights Commission, *Policy on Human Rights and Rental Housing* (Toronto: OHRC, 2009), online OHRC www.ohrc.on.ca/sites/default/files/attachments/Policy_on_human_rights_and_rental_housing.pdf.

35 See, for example, Ontario Human Rights Commission, *Policy on Drug and Alcohol Testing* (Toronto: OHRC, 2000), online: OHRC www.ohrc.on.ca/sites/default/files/attachments/Policy_on_drug_and_alcohol_testing.pdf.

36 See, for example, Ontario Human Rights Commission, *Policy on Employment-Related Medical Information* (Toronto: OHRC, 1996), online: OHRC www.ohrc.on.ca/sites/default/files/attachments/Policy_on_employment-related_medical_information.pdf.

37 Ontario Human Rights Commission, *Policy and Guidelines on Disability and the Duty to Accommodate* (Toronto: OHRC, 2000), online: OHRC www.ohrc.on.ca/sites/default/files/attachments/Policy_and_guidelines_on_disability_and_the_duty_to_accommodate.pdf.

38 Ontario Human Rights Commission, *Policy and Guidelines on Racism and Racial Discrimination* (Toronto: OHRC, 2005), online: OHRC www.ohrc.on.ca/sites/default/files/attachments/Policy_and_guidelines_on_racism_and_racial_discrimination.pdf.

39 Ontario Human Rights Commission, *Human Rights at Work 2008*, 3d ed (Toronto: OHRC, 2008), online: OHRC www.ohrc.on.ca/en/human-rights-work-2008-third-edition.

Under the mandate of the *HRC Amendment Act*,[40] the OHRC is responsible for monitoring the state of human rights and reporting directly to the people of Ontario. It has been given the power to:

- expand its work in promoting a culture of human rights in the province;
- conduct public inquiries;
- initiate applications (formerly called "complaints");
- intervene in proceedings at the HRTO; and
- focus on engaging in proactive measures to prevent discrimination using public education, policy development, research, and analysis.

The interpretive principles governing the *Code* have been left to the courts and tribunals. But the new mandate shifts the institutional focus of the OHRC from a more legalistic to a more social policy approach. In the words of the Attorney General of Ontario,

> the Ontario Human Rights Commission works to promote, protect and advance human rights. Its main focus is to address the root causes of discrimination. Activities include research and monitoring, policy development, and education and training. The Commission also conducts human rights inquiries and may initiate human rights applications or intervene in important cases before the Tribunal. Through outreach, cooperation and partnership the Commission aims to advance Ontario's human rights culture.[41]

In the old human rights structure, the issues of Commission gatekeeping and delay certainly reveal the limitations of the system. The challenge for the new Commission is affecting social policy by bringing people and communities together to help resolve differences, while being at risk of becoming an object of the tension and conflict they seek to resolve. Yet it must be said that, as sophisticated articulations of constitutionally-protected rights emanate from the courts and laypersons perceive a broad spectrum of wrong treatment as at least potentially actionable discrimination or harassment, the commission system cannot be expected to bear the full weight of responsibility for achieving

---

40 Above note 24.

41 Ministry of the Attorney General of Ontario, *Human Rights in Ontario* (Toronto: Ministry of the Attorney General, 2008), online: Ministry of the Attorney General www.attorneygeneral.jus.gov.on.ca/english/news/2008/20080630-ohrc-brochure-en.pdf.

anti-discrimination social goals. Rosanna Langer[42] has argued that government-sponsored anti-discrimination enforcement must be situated within a broader set of common practices such as municipal accessibility plans, for example those stipulated under the *Accessibility for Ontarians with Disabilities Act*,[43] progressive employment legislation, in-house corporate and employer anti-discrimination and anti-harassment "best practices," and community-based educational initiatives. The new mandate of the OHRC can constructively be situated within a broader human rights system grounded in the belief that a healthy network of anti-discrimination practices is the best insurance of a vital normative fabric of human rights protections.

Meanwhile, the pragmatism of seeking social policy solutions, as opposed to judicial ones, fits comfortably within the new mandate of the OHRC. Its new flexibility can also mean increasing the range and repertoire of remedies for fulfilling social justice goals. This includes, and also opens up, the possibility of incorporating Alternative Dispute Resolution (ADR) and "win-win approaches," rights-based mediation, and the collaborative problem-solving techniques that integrate practical experience with theoretical knowledge.

ADR, for example, has experienced increasing acceptance and utilization primarily because of a perception of greater flexibility, costs below those of traditional litigation, and speedy resolution of disputes. In recent years there has been more discussion about taking a systems approach in order to offer different kinds of options to people who are in conflict, and to foster appropriate and effective dispute resolution. Some cases and some complaints are viewed to be appropriate for formal grievance or for referral to court or to the police or to a tribunal and the like. Other conflicts could be settled by the parties if they had enough support and coaching, and yet other cases need third-party mediation or arbitration. Thus, alternative dispute resolution usually means a method that is not the courts, and involves processes and techniques that act as a means for disagreeing parties to come to an agreement short of litigation. Dispute resolution considers all the possible responsible options for conflict resolution that are relevant for a given issue.

---

42 Rosanna Langer, "Publics and Counter-Publics: Exploring the Contested Nature of the Public Interest in Domestic Human Rights Administration" in *Symposium Proceedings, Values, Ethics and the Public Sector: How to Serve the Public Interest?* (Ottawa: St. Paul University Centre for Ethics, 2006).

43 SO 2005, c 11.

There is indeed serious consideration of making mediation mandatory for all complaints brought to the OHRT.[44]

Ultimately, the social justice mandate of the OHRC is configured by the assurance of neutral (non-advocate, non-adversarial) communicative interactions, which open up the possibility for contextual problem solving for the mutual empowerment of human rights bearers. In this world, access to justice ought not to require formal processes for its assurance. The ideal OHRC would be responsible for engaging the public interest goals in anti-discrimination beyond a formulaic rigidity of law, by broadening the constellation of remedies, and preventing the premature legalization of individual and social harms.

F. THE OHRC'S 2012 POLICY ON COMPETING HUMAN RIGHTS

At the core of the OHRC's new policy on competing human rights[45] is a multi-step approach for balancing competing rights claims. Development of the policy in effect involved identifying possible types of competing rights claims and then mapping out a process for approaching different scenarios. These scenarios derive from human rights principles, Canadian and international caselaw, research in the social sciences, and input from community organizations and other stakeholders. The policy framework is summarized in the table below, which identifies three stages and five steps in the OHRC process for recognizing and reconciling competing human rights claims.

44 Pinto Report, above note 25.

45 OHRC, *Policy*, above note 3.

PROCESS FOR ADDRESSING COMPETING HUMAN RIGHTS SITUATIONS

Stage One: Recognizing competing rights claims

Step 1: What are the claims about?

Step 2: Do claims connect to legitimate rights?

(a) Do claims involve individuals or groups rather than operational interests?

(b) Do claims connect to human rights, other legal entitlements or *bona fide* reasonable interests?

(c) Do claims fall within the scope of the right when defined in context?

Step 3: Do claims amount to more than minimal interference with rights?

Stage Two: Reconciling competing rights claims?

Step 4: Is there a solution that allows enjoyment of each right?

Step 5: If not, is there a "next best" solution?

Stage Three: Making decisions

- Decisions must be consistent with human rights and other laws, court decisions, human rights principles, and have regard for OHRC policy.
- At least one claim must fall under the Ontario *Human Rights Code* to be actionable at the Human Rights Tribunal of Ontario.

This policy framework is designed to guide organizations facing competing human rights claims such as schools and workplaces. It is intended to provide those facing competing claims with a step-by-step process for moving forward. It is also designed to inform decision making by the OHRT when it addresses applications that involve competing human rights claims.

G. MAKING SENSE OF THE COMPETING HUMAN RIGHTS POLICY

Under section 29 of the *Code*, the OHRC has been designated the broad responsibility to promote, protect, and advance respect for human rights in Ontario, to protect the public interest, and to eliminate discriminatory practices. As we noted above, section 30 authorizes the OHRC to prepare, approve, and publish human rights policies to provide guidance on interpreting its provisions. These powers to both promote a culture of human rights and develop anti-discrimination policy do not "beef-up" the province's human rights administration system so much as simplify its focus making it less cumbersome organizationally than the old enforcement and compliance model, and potentially more responsive in addressing an increasingly diverse population and more complex rights scenarios. The new discrimination prevention model provides the necessary administrative space from which to undertake more robust and progressive intervention into the ever-increasing intricacies of modern rights claims and growing intractability of rights conflicts and disputes.

In a discrimination prevention model, the OHRC can assume a role as the instrument of the positive state, facilitating the realization of human potential by developing human rights policies that provide cutting-edge and innovative interpretations of human rights law, opening up possibilities for expanding the protections of the *Code* in order to address new and emerging human rights issues and trends, incorporating international understandings of human rights, and breaking down social and economic barriers to the exercise of positive freedom. In this regard, the discrimination prevention model should be understood as an authorization to deal in areas of new and more inclusive citizenship. The OHRC's role in dealing with "tension and conflict" and bringing people and communities together to help resolve differences recommends a foundation for mutual recognition and empowerment of human rights claimants, consistent with the remedial objectives of the *Code*. This model has to have the capacity to effectively address human rights scenarios and disputes by building on a pattern of practices, and creating the necessary social space for rights parties with rights claims and disputes to engage in interpersonal responsiveness and constructive interaction. In a discrimination prevention model, the norm of human rights administration shifts to a more inclusive and respectful approach to marginalized and historically disadvantaged persons with the goal to give people a voice and diminish any power imbalances.

How does the idea of shared social citizenship in a diverse society help us to make sense of the OHRC's new mandate? For Marshall and social constructionist thought, citizenship is a dynamic phenomenon that flexes the dimensions of political, social, and civil life. In a human rights context, it is a logical extension of inclusive citizenship for legal rights to be reinforced and further developed in civil society through self-reflective social policy initiatives that create opportunities for empowerment and recognition. The discrimination prevention model affords the opportunity for the new OHRC to use its mandate to promote rights of inclusion in diverse Ontario by resolving human rights claims and disputes in a manner that is respectful, efficient, transparent, and more in-line with anti-oppression principles and transformative approaches than the former process. More than simply enforcing the provisions of the *Code*, the OHRC is now mandated as a positive state actor exposing the dimensions of power embedded in historical, social, and political contexts, and making more room for power considerations when balancing competing human rights claims.

H. CONCLUSION

Issues of competing human rights claims arising from diversity have become in Canada one of the most important and pressing challenges for the human rights system. Different provinces have responded in different ways to this challenge. In Québec, for example, the provincial government mandated in 2007 the Bouchard-Taylor *Consultation Commission on Accommodation Practices Related to Cultural Differences* to hear from the public on "reasonable accommodations" of religious and ethnic minorities and issue a report of their findings and recommendations. The Commission reported back to the Québec government in 2008[46] but few of its recommendations have been followed. In Ontario, in contrast, the OHRC has taken the lead to develop and implement the first policy in Canada to address competing human rights claims. This

46 Gérard Bouchard & Charles Taylor, *Commission de consultation sur les pratiques d'accommodement reliées aux différences culturelles, Building the Future: A Time for Reconciliation* (Québec: Gouvernement du Québec, 2008).

policy development included extensive consultation with the public, academics, human rights commissions elsewhere in the country, and stakeholders in the human rights community in Ontario. It also included significant efforts to map the nature of competing human rights in Ontario. These efforts by the OHRC resulted in a policy for Ontario, released in April 2012. We are now just beginning to witness the implementation of this policy.

1 2 3 4 5 6 7 8 9 10 11 12 13 14

CHAPTER 14

EMERGING HUMAN RIGHTS INSTITUTIONS: THE CASE OF MUSEUMS IN A HUMAN RIGHTS CULTURE

Jennifer Carter & Jennifer A Orange[1]

> *"One thing to remember is to talk to the animals. If you do, they will talk back to you. But if you don't talk to the animals, they won't talk back to you, then you won't understand, and when you don't understand you will fear, and when you fear you will destroy the animals, and if you destroy the animals, you will destroy yourself."*
>
> — *Chief Dan George*[2]

A. INTRODUCTION

When we debate the idea of human rights, we often hear the voices of two seemingly opposite groups. The first praises laws that enable the realization of the dignity of all people, flourishing to their human potential and experiencing the beauty of our rich and diverse societies. The other is more cynical, or perhaps, realistic. The second notes the historical and ongoing violations of human rights by oppressive states,

1 Jennifer Carter, PhD, is Professor of new museologies, intangible heritage, and cultural objects in the Department of Art History at the Université du Québec à Montréal (UQÀM).

Jennifer A Orange, B.A., LL.B., LL.M., Barrister and Solicitor (Ontario), is an adjunct professor and SJD candidate at the University of Toronto, Faculty of Law where she teaches International Human Rights Law and the Law of Armed Conflict.

2 "Chief Dan George," online: California Indian Education www.californiaindianeducation.org/famous_indian_chiefs/dan_george/.

organizations, and individuals despite both the post-Second World War founding of the United Nations (UN) to safeguard the "equal rights of men and women and nations large and small"[3] and the subsequent conclusion of numerous international human rights treaties intended to enforce this commitment.

This chapter addresses the potential of cultural institutions to bridge the gap in civil society between the inspiration and cynicism that prevail in human rights discourses and, more specifically, to enrich the important work of national human rights institutions. It proposes a *new* form of human rights institution to promote human rights within the fabric of civil society. Our focus is the potential of museums to contribute purposefully to a human rights culture, although we do not mean to limit the discussion to the museum. We leave open the possibility for some new and unique form of institution that combines human rights law and culture in a yet undiscovered way. While a number of social institutions, such as human rights commissions, are discussed at length in this book, it is worth dwelling on the distinct roles of cultural institutions such as museums, libraries, and archives to raise awareness about human rights and to perform as catalysts for social transformation in the important arena of human rights.

Our essay is divided into three sections. We begin by imagining what a culture of human rights looks like by defining its terms and goals. We then review the mandates and work of National Human Rights Institutions (NHRIs), within the UN's mechanisms, for the purpose of comparing their goals and methods with the work of museums. Lastly, we examine how cultural institutions support the development and sustenance of such a culture, using examples of museums as institutions that communicate and educate about, and now increasingly across the globe advocate for, human rights. We conclude this section with an analysis of the founding ideas of the Canadian Museum for Human Rights (CMHR). We assess the work that has already been done to establish the CMHR, as well as its potential to promote a human rights culture in Canada and beyond.

---

3 *Charter of the United Nations*, 26 June 1945, Can TS 1945 No 7, Preamble [*UN Charter*].

B. DEVELOPING A HUMAN RIGHTS CULTURE

Before we discuss how a museum can contribute to the project of creating a human rights culture, it is necessary to define this particular culture and its goals. The definition of human rights in itself is complex. Human rights scholar Jack Donnelly describes human rights as "literally the rights one has simply because one is a human being."[4] Amnesty International elaborates that:

> Human rights are basic rights and freedoms that all people are entitled to regardless of nationality, sex, national or ethnic origin, race, religion, language, or other status.
>
> Human rights include civil and political rights, such as the right to life, liberty and freedom of expression; and social, cultural and economic rights including the right to participate in culture, the right to food, and the right to work and receive an education. Human rights are protected and upheld by international and national laws and treaties.[5]

It is important to note that this definition puts human rights within the boundaries and protection of the law. We recognize the often persuasive critiques of law as an agent of social change, and the tense relationship between the lawmaker (the state) and the individuals who are the "beneficiaries" of legal protection.[6] Further, the letter or enforcement of the law may fall behind the global community's conception of a human right so that a right, such as the right of equality for women, may not yet be legally protected in one or more states. Despite the fallibility of law, we see human rights law and culture in a necessary dialogue. While they may not walk together in lockstep, their interaction can support the realization of human rights, whether law leads cultural norms or vice-versa.[7]

---

4 Jack Donnelly, *Universal Human Rights in Theory and Practice* (Ithaca: Cornell University Press, 1989) at 9.

5 Amnesty International, USA, "Human Rights Basics," online: Amnesty International (USA) www.amnestyusa.org/research/human-rights-basics. See also Office of the High Commissioner for Human Rights, "What are Human Rights?," online: OHCHR www.ohchr.org/EN/Issues/Pages/WhatareHumanRights.aspx.

6 See, for example, "The Limits of Rights Discourse" in Makau wa Mutua, *Human Rights: A Political and Cultural Critique* (Philadelphia: University of Pennsylvania Press, 2002) 126.

7 An interesting example is the realization of same-sex rights in North America. Cultural acceptance of gay marriage, for example, was prevalent

We must also understand human rights culture beyond the law and recognize the roles of individual activists, social movements, grassroots organizations, advocacy groups, and political leaders in shaping this culture. Amartya Sen envisions this culture widely, grounding his definition of human rights within a moral and ethical framework defined by freedom. He writes that:

> Human rights can serve as the motivation for many different activities, from legislation and implementation of appropriate laws to enabling help from other people and public agitation against rights violations. The different activities can contribute — separately and together — to advancing the realization of important human freedoms. It is perhaps important to emphasize that not only are there several ways of safeguarding and promoting human rights other than legislation, these different routes have considerable complementarity; for example, for effective enforcement of new human rights laws, public monitoring and pressure can make a considerable difference. The ethics of human rights can be made more effective through a variety of interrelated instruments and a versatility of ways and means. This is one of the reasons why it is important to give the general ethical status of human rights its due, rather than locking up the concept of human rights prematurely within the narrow box of legislation — real or ideal.[8]

The pre-eminence Sen gives to ethics within his conception of human rights is indeed the foundation of both human rights law and culture, while his emphasis on the need for complementarity in how we collectively promote and safeguard human rights in society provides a useful starting point for thinking about the role of museums within this culture.

---

in some segments of Canadian society, but certainly not all. The Supreme Court of Canada's decision in *Re Same-Sex Marriage*, 2004 SCC 79, requiring legal amendments to allow same-sex marriage pushed forward cultural acceptance. A 2012 poll found that since 2004 "the numbers of those approving full recognition of same-sex marriage have skyrocketed, to more than sixty per cent from about forty per cent." See Michael Den Tandt, "Polls Show Canada Actually More Progressive after Six Years of Tory Rule" *National Post* (3 July 2012), online: National Post http://fullcomment.nationalpost.com/2012/07/03/canada-progressive/. A similar process may now be unfolding in the United States.

8 Amartya Sen, *The Idea of Justice* (Cambridge, MA: Belknap Press of Harvard University Press, 2009) at 366.

As we attempt to define human rights, it is important to recognize the continual evolution of societal views of rights norms. As our global community evolves, so do our concepts of human rights, such that the rights enshrined in legal instruments may not sufficiently describe all of the human rights that are identified today, or for that matter, rights that will emerge in our future consciousness. For example, while children's rights were included in the *Universal Declaration of Human Rights*[9] (*UDHR*) (for example, article 26 right to education), the rights of children have significantly expanded in scope since 1948. The 1989 *Convention on the Rights of the Child* requires state parties to ensure that the "best interests of the child" be a primary consideration in *all* "actions concerning children, whether undertaken by public or private social welfare institutions, courts of law, administrative authorities or legislative bodies."[10]

Our conception of human rights and the laws that protect them change over time. The process of evolution of law and culture gives museums a special opportunity to be on the cutting edge of human rights in a way that may not be fully recognized in law or respected by cultures. This is because museums as civil society institutions are capable of addressing human rights issues as these evolve at grassroots levels, to diverse audiences in non-specialized language through exhibitions, public programming, and collecting initiatives, and in so doing they provide a dialogical space for these issues to be debated and critically examined by any and all interested members of civil society.

Culture is widely considered to be more than material goods and traditional practices; it also includes the way that we perceive our environment and relate to our fellow human beings.[11] The UNESCO *Universal Declaration on Cultural Diversity* defines culture as "the set of distinctive spiritual, material, intellectual and emotional features of society or a social group, and that it encompasses, in addition to art and literature, lifestyles, ways of living together, value systems, traditions

---

9 *Universal Declaration of Human Rights*, GA Res 217(III), UNGAOR, 3d Sess, Supp No 13, UN Doc A/810, (1948) 71 [*UDHR*].

10 *Convention on the Rights of the Child*, 20 November 1989, 1577 UNTS 3 (entered into force 2 September 1990), article 3.

11 Mahnaz Afkhami, "Identity and Culture: Women as Subjects and Agents of Cultural Change" in Margaret A Schuler, ed, *From Basic Needs to Basic Rights: Women's Claim to Human Rights* (Washington, DC: The Institute for Women, Law, and Development, 1996).

and beliefs."[12] Human rights discourses manifest what many anthropologists consider to be "cultural" features: "Rights — understood as rights talk, rights thinking, rights practices — entail certain constructions of self and sociality, and specific modes of agency."[13] For example, a human rights culture in a workplace may be manifested by employees using gender-neutral language, in the way management constructs its hiring practices, or in attempts by employees and management to combat structural inequities in the work environment.

Human rights have become a global value system, a tradition, and a belief, and they are increasingly ingrained in all aspects of how we relate to one another as human beings. Living in a human rights culture requires people to respect and protect human rights in their ways of living together, that is, in the way they talk, think, and act in their everyday lives. Joseph Wronka would refer to this as having a "*lived* awareness" of human rights principles, such that these principles are not only understood cognitively, they are implemented in active practice as well. This particular understanding of a human rights culture, with its insistence on the individual's role in realizing this culture, nevertheless relies on "human rights instruments [that] can serve as tools to 'till the soil' and create a foundation from which human needs can flourish."[14] Not unlike Wronka, Joong-Seop Kim usefully reminds us that achieving a human rights culture is a matter of social practice:

> . . . we pay attention to the promotion of a human rights culture that contributes to spreading the core values of human rights into members' daily lives and every stage of social practice in the local community . . . . Thus, a human rights culture provides a social plat-

12 UN Educational, Scientific and Cultural Organisation, *Universal Declaration on Cultural Diversity* (2 November 2001). This definition is in line with the conclusions of the World Conference on Cultural Policies (MONDIACULT) (*Mexico City Declaration on Cultural Policies*, 1982), of the World Commission on Culture and Development (*Our Creative Diversity*, Paris, 1995), and of the Intergovernmental Conference on Cultural Policies for Development (*The Stockholm Conference*, 1998).

13 Jane K Cowan, Marie-Bénédicte Dembour, & Richard A Wilson, *Introduction in Culture and Rights: Anthropological Perspectives* (Cambridge: Cambridge University Press, 2001) at 11–12.

14 Joseph Wronka, *Human Rights and Social Justice* (Los Angeles: Sage Publications, 2008) at 35–36.

> form to transform all social conventions and institutions into ones that are sensitive and favorable to human rights.[15]

Human rights institutions that are dedicated to education and the dissemination of knowledge about human rights issues and transgressions constitute one such social platform, still others interpret this mandate legally and politically.

These ideals of a human rights culture rely on a wide conception of human rights. Robust laws, an enlightened judiciary, a committed enforcement system, and an engaged international community of non-governmental organizations (NGOs), grassroots organizations, and individual citizens are required to promote and to protect human rights around the globe, but so too must social, cultural, educational, and political institutions be used to grow and nurture this culture, to achieve, recalling Wronka's expression, the requisite awareness of human rights. When human rights are viewed within this broader framework, in which civil society institutions are actively solicited to advance the cause of human rights, both individual citizens and society at large benefit.

C. NATIONAL HUMAN RIGHTS INSTITUTIONS

1) Human Rights within the UN System

Since its origins in 1945, the UN has become the world's key organization dedicated to promoting and maintaining international peace and security. It was founded by fifty-one countries (today it has grown to 193 member states)[16] in response to the devastating effects of two massive world wars and as a safeguard for preventing further wars of similar scale. Its internal structure, built upon the mutually reinforcing endeavours of supporting and facilitating peace and security, conflict resolution, development, and human rights, demonstrates this commitment. In this regard, the UN occupies a unique and essential global leadership position that requires of it ongoing vigilance and active international

---

15 Kim Joong-Seop, "Toward Human Rights in the Local Community: Multiple Approaches for Implementation" (2010) 39:1 Development and Society 119 at 129 & 130.

16 United Nations, "Growth in United Nations Membership, 1945 to present," online: United Nations www.un.org/en/members/growth.shtml.

engagement to ensure the sustenance of, in the words of Secretary-General Ban Ki-moon, the "global collective good."[17] In partnership with states, NGOs, and a wide range of civil society organizations (CSOs), the UN system fuels the collective drive for international peace, security, prosperity, and the realization of human rights.

Of the many issues with which UN bodies are actively engaged, human rights are core to achieving the vision that has guided UN activities since its inception. The first session of the UN General Assembly in 1946 reviewed a draft of the document that would become the *UDHR*, widely considered a complement to the *UN Charter*[18] and a "road map" to guaranteeing individual rights around the globe. Adopted in 1948, this seminal document constitutes the foundation of modern international human rights law, and has since inspired a large number of international human rights treaties in addition to domestic bills and constitutional amendments that bolster the fight against oppression, repression, and social injustice in countries around the world. With its affirmation of the inherent inalienability of fundamental rights and freedoms of all human beings, the *UDHR* sets the benchmark for everyone's right to life, equality before the law, freedom of expression, and education, among others.[19]

2) The Mandates of NHRIs

While the *UDHR* aims to be universal in scope and application, it is an aspirational and non-binding document that relies on a large number of international bodies and specialized agencies, as well as state governments, to achieve its goals.[20] There are several *UN Charter*-based human rights mechanisms and treaty-based bodies responsible for monitoring, promoting, and protecting human rights within the UN member states. The UN has also encouraged these states to establish local human rights

---

17 Secretary-General Ban Ki-moon (Address delivered at the World Economic Forum, Davos, Switzerland, 29 January 2009), online: United Nations www.un.org/en/civilsociety/index.shtml.

18 *UN Charter*, above note 3.

19 See, for example, *UDHR*, above note 9, art 3 (life), art 7 (equality), art 19 (freedom of expression), and art 26 (education).

20 While the *UDHR* was initially accepted by the General Assembly as a non-binding declaration, there are good arguments to support the assertion that the *UDHR* is binding today as international customary law. For more, see Hurst Hannum, "The *UDHR* in National and International Law" (1998) 3:2 Health & Hum Rts 144 at 148.

institutions to bring international legal standards into domestic practice. Over the past six decades, member states have created over 100 national institutions, such as human rights commissions and ombudsmen, to act as independent public bodies with very specific responsibilities to protect and promote human rights at arm's length from their governments.[21] In other words, by definition they are pillars of a nation's human rights system, and in practice they are capable of criticizing the very governments that fund them as part of the larger state apparatus, when human rights violations occur under their watch.[22] These organizations, known as National Human Rights Institutions (NHRIs), have functioned with mixed reviews owing to their limited resources and to their statutory mandates that limit these institutions' enforcement powers.[23]

In spite of their status as national institutions, international standards guiding the work of NHRIs have existed since 1978 when the UN Commission on Human Rights held a seminar resulting in draft guidelines for the structure and functions of these institutions.[24] Finessing these guidelines became the focus of the first International Workshop on National Institutions for the Promotion and Protection of Human Rights in Paris in 1991. The workshop drafted the *Principles Relating to the Status of National Institutions*, better known as the Paris Principles,[25] producing the document that today comprehensively outlines the role, composition, methods, status, and functions of NHRIs. A measure of its significance, this document has been endorsed by the 1993 World Conference on Human Rights in Vienna[26] and by the Commission on Human Rights in 2005.[27] In December 2011, the notion of providing human rights education received renewed impetus when the General Assembly adopted the *UN Declaration on Human Rights Education and Training*,

---

21 International Coordinating Committee of National Institutions for the Promotion and Protection of Human Rights, "A Brief History of NHRIs," online: NHRI http://nhri.ohchr.org/EN/AboutUs/Pages/HistoryNHRIs.aspx.

22 United Nations Office of the High Commissioner, *National Human Rights Institutions: History, Principles, Roles and Responsibilities* (New York: United Nations, 2010) at 13 [OHCHR].

23 See ch 7.

24 OHCHR, above note 22 at 7.

25 *Principles Relating to the Status of National Institutions*, annex to *National Institutions for the Promotion and Protection of Human Rights*, CHR Res 54, UNESCOR, Supp No 2, UN Doc E/1992/22, (1992); GA Res 48/134, UNGAOR, 48th Sess, (1993) Annex [Paris Principles].

26 *Vienna Declaration and Programme of Action*, UNGAOR, 1993, UN Doc A/Conf.157/23 at Part I, para 36.

27 *National Institutions for the Promotion and Protection of Human Rights*, UNCHROR, 2005, UN Doc A/HRC/RES/20/14.

1 2 3 4 5 6 7 8 9 10 11 12 13 14

which not only reinforced the role of NHRIs in education and training, this declaration also defined the very nature of this education and the manner it should be delivered.[28]

The Paris Principles provide benchmarks for NHRIs. They also articulate the twofold mandate of NHRIs to protect and promote human rights. Protection functions include receiving, investigating, and resolving human rights complaints, as well as mediating conflicts and monitoring activities. Promotion functions include education, outreach, media, publishing, training, and capacity building for both civil society and governments.[29]

On an institutional level, the Paris Principles establish six main criteria that fully functioning NHRIs should meet:

1) have a broad mandate based on universal human rights standards;
2) be autonomous from government;
3) be independent as guaranteed by statute or constitution;
4) embrace pluralism in its membership and/or effective cooperation with the variety of social forces in the state;
5) have adequate resources; and
6) have adequate powers of investigation.[30]

All of these functions are important for any institution to effectively promote and protect human rights. As international human rights treaties leave the responsibility for addressing human rights violations with the state, any institution that aims to promote and protect human rights must be able to freely criticize the state and hold it accountable. With independence comes credibility.[31]

There are now six recognized models of NHRIs: human rights commissions, human rights ombudsman institutions, hybrid institutions, consultative and advisory bodies, and — of particular interest to us here — institutes and centres.[32] In 2009, human rights commissions consti-

---

28 *United Nations Declaration on Human Rights Education and Training*, GA Res 66-137, UNGAOR, 66th Sess, UN Doc A/RES/66/137, (2011), art 9.

29 OHCHR, above note 22 at 31.

30 *Ibid*.

31 Office of the High Commissioner for Human Rights, "Survey on National Human Rights Institutions: Report on the Findings and Recommendations of a Questionnaire Addressed to NHRIs Worldwide" (Geneva: OHCHR, July 2009) at 15 [OHCHR, *Survey*], online: NHRI http://www.nhri.net/2009/Questionnaire%20-%20Complete%20Report%20FINAL-edited.pdf.

32 International Coordinating Committee of National Institutions for the Promotion and Protection of Human Rights, "Roles and Types of NHRIs,"

tuted more than half of NHRIs, with ombudsmen making up about one-third.[33] It is important to note that most states have only one NHRI and the most common forms appear to spend more resources on protection than on promotional functions. In a 2009 survey of NHRIs,

> [r]espondents were asked to comment on the main challenges their institution faces in promoting human rights education. The most frequent challenge noted by respondents was the lack of resources available to the institution.[34]

Numerous human rights commissions focus their core functions on investigating violations and complaints and making recommendations. The decisions of some commissions are subject to the review of the courts, which can lead to delays and higher costs required to bring any one complaint to a final result.

3) NHRIs and the Work of Developing a Human Rights Culture

As described above, NHRIs are mandated to both protect and promote human rights. While protecting human rights through investigation, adjudication, making recommendations or enforcement orders is critical for supporting a human rights culture, these functions generally fall outside of the core competencies of cultural institutions.[35] However,

---

online: NHRI http://nhri.ohchr.org/EN/AboutUs/Pages/RolesTypesNHRIs.aspx.

33 OHCHR, above note 22 at 15.

34 OHCRH, *Survey*, above note 31 at 35.

35 Although we note that some museums have used their archival expertise to support international criminal tribunals, or have been founded as a direct result of a recommendation made by a nation's truth and reconciliation commission. The Tuol Sleng Museum and former S-21 Prison of the Khmer Rouge regime in Cambodia, for example, houses records of Khmer Rouge activities and abuses of human rights. These records have been used as evidence in a hybrid tribunal overseen by the Royal Government of Cambodia and the United Nations, a tribunal known as the Extraordinary Chambers in the Courts of Cambodia. See Michelle Caswell "Khmer Rouge Archives: Accountability, Truth, and Memory in Cambodia" (2010) 10 Archival Science 25 at 26. The Museo de la Memoria y Los Derechos Humanos in Santiago, Chile, was created as a result of a recommendation made by the Valech Commission's Report, that was conducted as a result of Chile's second Truth and Reconciliation Commission (2003–05). See United States Institute of Peace, "Commission of Inquiry: Chile 03: Truth Commissions Digital Collection," online: USIP www.usip.org/publications/commission-inquiry-chile-03.

1 2 3 4 5 6 7 8 9 10 11 12 13 **14**

many of the activities in which NHRIs are engaged to promote human rights are in areas where museums have long-standing expertise and museums are taking on these activities in the name of human rights promotion. Recalling the promotional functions of NHRIs (outreach, publishing, training, etc.), three examples demonstrate the breadth and scope of their work and reveal methods that are integral to museum work as well.

In 2010, the Scottish Human Rights Commission developed training and awareness raising resources titled *Care about Rights?* dedicated to the care and support of older people. The project contains interactive resources to increase awareness of (1) human rights in care settings, (2) how human rights balance risks and rights in decision making, and (3) how human rights can support the delivery of person-centred care.[36] The resources include a training course of films, educational information, and case study scenarios, all available online. The project also includes an outreach network that has partnered with various community organizations across Scotland with the goal of both bringing education of a human rights framework to older people and their caregivers, and also ensuring that the *Care about Rights?* project hears the views of older people who have direct experience with care services.[37] Stepping into the political realm, the project was involved with a lunchtime reception for Members of the Scottish Parliament (MSP) that led to MSPs publicizing their support for *Care about Rights?* in the media.[38]

Engaging in a partnership with a human rights museum would provide this valued social initiative with additional material and human resources, as well as specialized skills, in support of the application of human rights principles to the care of the elderly. By combining the expertise of professionals at both the Scottish Human Rights Commission and the museum, such programming would expand its potential audience base to the constituencies of both institutions. Museum professionals have expertise in developing exhibitions, seminars, and workshops, among other forms of mediation, and attend to a variety of learning

---

36 Scottish Human Rights Commission, "Welcome to Care about Rights," online: SHRC www.scottishhumanrights.com/careaboutrights.

37 Scottish Human Rights Commission, "Outreach Network," online: SHRC www.scottishhumanrights.com/careaboutrights/welcome-outreach.

38 Scottish Human Rights Commission, "MSPs Support Care about Rights," online: SHRC www.scottishhumanrights.com/careaboutrights/welcome-msps.

styles, which can be useful toward deepening the impact of the Commission's educational programs.

In a second example, the Human Rights Commission of Sri Lanka recognized the need for a program to support the human rights of the country's over one million internally displaced persons after two decades of war. In 2002, the Commission founded a program now known as the *National Protection and Durable Solutions for Internally Displaced Persons Project*. While part of the project's work is focused on complaints and violations of civil and political rights, the program also looks to enhance Sri Lankans' understanding of the role of human rights in their everyday lives.[39] The project has a number of thematic services, including those regarding children's rights, gender-based violence, human rights defenders, and security forces.

There are many opportunities that a partnership between the Human Rights Commission of Sri Lanka and a local museum dedicated to human rights can bring toward developing programming to aid displaced persons with societal reintegration or regaining basic life necessities and skills. Bernadette Lynch describes one such initiative shared by a diaspora Somali community and the Manchester Museum in the United Kingdom, the *Telling Our Lives* project, in which women used objects from the Museum's collection as catalysts for retrieving and telling stories about home and the homeland as a means to adjust to new life situations.[40] The program enabled these women to personally work through the challenges associated with displacement and life-altering situations — a process that Brison refers to as a "remaking" of the self.[41]

The Human Rights Commission of Sri Lanka has already successfully initiated a program to support the child survivors of Sri Lanka's ethnic conflict toward reclaiming their self-identity. The "Pulse of the Displaced" – Children's Day Programme organized a children's art exhibition to give war-affected children a chance to "illustrate their aspirations,

---

39 Human Rights Commission of Sri Lanka, "National Protection and Durable Solutions for Internally Displaced Persons Project: About Us," online: Human Rights Commission of Sri Lanka www.idpsrilanka.lk/html/npdsproject.php.

40 Bernadette Lynch, "The Amenable Object: Working with Diaspora Communities through a Psychoanalysis of Touch" in Helen J Chatterjee, ed, *Touch in Museums: Policy and Practice in Object Handling* (Oxford: Berg, 2008) 261 at 264 [Lynch].

41 Brison, cited in *ibid* at 265.

hope and dreams as well as their anticipations and frustrations."[42] The program brought art material to approximately 3,000 children aged ten to eighteen years old and then selected 100 drawings for the exhibit. Those 100 children were then brought to the capital and attended an awards ceremony. Concurrently, the project retained a child psychiatrist to conduct a psychological study of the children and make recommendations on what different branches of government should do to support these children going forward. The report recommended counselling for the children, quality and sustainable education, vocational training for school dropouts, and work to prevent incidents of child labour.[43]

The Canadian Human Rights Commission created a program to support the integration of human rights values into the workplace. The *Human Rights Maturity Model* is a "voluntary, proactive and incremental business management tool that stimulates real change. The Model provides an online tool to support businesses and organizations in their work towards a sustainable and progressive human rights culture."[44] The tool helps businesses evaluate their business practices in a human rights framework in successive steps until they reach "maturity." The evaluation looks at five areas: (1) leadership and accountability; (2) communication and consultation; (3) alignment of policies and processes; (4) capacity building and resources; and (5) evaluation for performance measurement and continuous improvement.[45] If the business so chooses, the Commission will also make recommendations and collaborate with the business on an action plan. Furthermore, the Commission offers an official designation to those businesses that have their self-assessment validated.[46]

Tailoring such specific programming to the needs of citizens is precisely the type of work that innovative museums have been engaged in for over a generation. In Washington, DC, the Anacostia Neighbourhood Museum — a bold new museum type that emerged during the new museology movement of the 1970s and 1980s when museums quite literally

---

42 Human Rights Commission of Sri Lanka, "Child Rights Programmes," online: Human Rights Commission of Sri Lanka www.idpsrilanka.lk/html/SpecialProgrammes/ChildrenRights.html.

43 *Ibid.*

44 Canadian Human Rights Commission, "Human Rights Maturity Model," online: CHRC www.hrmm-mmdp.ca/index-eng.aspx.

45 Canadian Human Rights Commission, "The Model — How it Works," online: CHRC www.hrmm-mmdp.ca/unsec/mod/model1-eng.aspx.

46 *Ibid.*

sought to reinvent themselves as tools of social development — offered similar skills-building workshops and socially relevant exhibitions to its local constituencies. The key to Anacostia's success was that it developed this programming based on the needs of its community, rather than waiting for communities to discover their "need" of the museum.[47]

Curating exhibitions and developing programming is by no means the strict purview of museological institutions. However, as museums increasingly diversify their work and their relationships with different constituencies and demonstrate their commitment to developing socially responsible programming, we require increased collaborative initiatives and partnerships with other civil society organizations.

D. CULTURAL INSTITUTIONS IN THE SERVICE OF HUMAN RIGHTS CULTURE

1) Museums as Evolving Institutions

Museums have a long history as cultural institutions. Several writers, the Greek historian and geographer Strabo among them, have described the first instances of the *mouseion*[48] in antiquity as places of philosophical enquiry and discussion. Their descriptions dwell not on the iconic architectures and material collections by which we have come to know the public museum since the late eighteenth century, but rather on the idea of the museum as a place of reflection and scholarly debate. We liken these early museums to the models of Aristotle's Lyceum and Plato's Academy — places of research where the activities of philosophers are core to the purpose of the museum project. As sites of dialogue, these early museums centred on human interactions rather than on the relationship between humans and things as François Mairesse has observed.[49]

Museums have evolved significantly, and their development in the modern era has been characterized by the centrality of material (and more recently non-material) collections to the institution's professional

47 John Kinard, "The Smithsonian's Anacostia Neighbourhood Museum" (1968) 11:3 Curator 190.

48 Or "temple of the muses," the term from which the Latin derivation of museum has evolved.

49 François Mairesse, *Le musée, temple spectaculaire : Une histoire du projet muséal* (Lyon: Presses Universitaires de Lyon, 2002) at 14–19.

identity, in addition to the museum's pedagogical function as a site of informal learning. By virtue of this twofold dynamic, museums have become intensely complex institutions, whose polyvalent purposes the academic and writer David Carr has described as "places created *to hold* and preserve objects and texts, *to expand* the boundaries of public knowledge associated with those artifacts and words, and *to open* the possibilities of learning in the contexts of everyday life."[50] Carr's account underscores that museums are one among several important social institutions dedicated to knowledge, learning, and exploration within everyday life, and moreover that as organized knowledge structures museums have the important capacity to encourage and enhance a culture of enquiry.

Carr's description of the purposes and programs of cultural institutions provides not only an excellent starting point for considering how museums perform differently from other social institutions dedicated to knowledge and its dissemination, but equally to how the original conception of the museum as a space of enquiry and debate is undergoing a contemporary resurgence in museums dedicated to issues of social responsibility. While one can argue that museums have always been dedicated to exploring ideas, a different kind of cultural space has taken shape since the late twentieth century, one that is challenging two centuries of object-centred museology. Rethinking the museological practices of programming, exhibitions, and display, these issues-based museums have cast new roles for museums as sites premised on the engagement of social, cultural, and political issues. Such museums — dedicated to memorial history, immigration, and now human rights — assume significant responsibilities as civil society institutions in their ability to address those values most at risk today — and to make a difference in doing so.

As an increasing number of museums around the globe are taking up issues of human rights and social justice in their exhibition, education, and programming initiatives, many museums are now introducing activist practices into the fold of the more traditional museological functions of collecting, conserving, and exhibiting. As a manifestation of a broader human rights culture, this change has been precipitated by calls for greater social accountability and agency from within and beyond the museological sector, and out of a growing recognition of the range

---

50 David Carr, *The Promise of Cultural Institutions* (Lanham, MD: Rowan Altamira, 2003) at xiii.

of public responsibilities inherent in museum work.[51] However, as museums rethink the terms of their modes of social and civic engagement, an attendant level of moral and ethical responsibility necessarily accompanies the way these institutions engage with publics about social justice, and its intersection with genocide, war, and discrimination, among other human rights transgressions. This responsibility is negotiated on multiple levels, from the curatorial (what is told and how), to the educational (the nature and aim of programming initiatives), and the institutional (what is actually implemented). In this, attentiveness to not only *how* the museum's narratives are constructed and how audiences experience them, but moreover to how these experiences are taken *forward* and make a difference in society, is of critical concern for a new generation of museum professionals.

One area where this shift is most apparent is in the globalized human rights movement that has altered dominant discourses from citizenship formation to universal human rights and that is manifest in museums foregrounding a human rights and social justice agenda. Museums such as the Canadian Museum for Human Rights in Winnipeg, Manitoba, the Museo de la Memoria y los Derechos Humanos in Santiago, Chile, and the Osaka Human Rights Museum (Liberty Osaka) in Japan have taken up human rights as the subject of their mission, exhibitions, and programming initiatives, with the effect that human rights as a subject and practice are increasingly debated within museum institutions worldwide.

Human rights museums may seem to cohere through their aims to make human rights a museological phenomenon; however, the nature of the institution's investiture in the subject is anything but universal. Addressing genocide, civil rights, war, and slavery, in addition to peace, memory, and tolerance through the lens of a human rights framework, human rights museums are growing in number and diversity of approaches. Their discourses interrogate these subjects widely, and vary from the celebration or protection of rights, to community experiences of fundamental rights transgressed.

This new role of the museum as a human rights institution comes with many challenges but equally with enormous potential for contributing not only to a culture of enquiry, as Carr has envisioned, but more proactively still for fostering the culture of human rights that has also

51 Eithne Nightingale & Richard Sandell, "Introduction" in Richard Sandell & Eithne Nightingale, eds, *Museums, Equality and Social Justice* (London: Routledge, 2012) at 2.

galvanized NHRIs and grassroots, citizenship-based movements around the globe.

2) Imagining Museums in Support of National Human Rights Institutions

There is a strong case to be made for thinking about museums as a new form of NHRI. Like the broader mandate of NHRIs that work to promote and educate about human rights, we might say that museums also inherently fulfill this function through their educational mandates. Trends in museums taking up human rights also point to the increasing tendency to apply human rights pedagogy to museum programming and a new awareness of the impact of exhibitions on critical thinking about human rights around the world. Increasingly aware of their important role in nurturing a civil society that is politically engaged and informed, museums on several continents have brought their skills to bear on human rights work and are endeavouring to perform as catalysts for social transformation in the arena of human rights.

Museums work in fundamentally different ways from legal, NGO, and educational institutions dedicated to human rights. If we consider what is in essence the purview of museological practice — that of research, collecting, and display — the potential contributions of a cultural institution dedicated to human rights become apparent. Public museums are institutions that specialize in rendering information accessible to a variety of communities — be these communities composed of adults or children, specialists or neophytes — in order to provide opportunities for informal learning on a broad array of subjects in the context of the everyday. They do so having acquired specialized knowledge as to the diverse learning styles and needs of their visiting publics, in addition to the requisite skill sets for the realization of the exhibition and programming practices that distinguish these institutions. As such, museums are important exercises in social, cultural, and visual literacy.

We will discuss three ways in which museums dedicated to human rights directly benefit the framework of a human rights culture: as sites for knowledge production and transfer, as sites of informal learning and free enquiry, and more recently, as sites that encourage activism in the arena of human rights. When we consider the public work of museums, the two most important functions of these institutions are their exhibition and programming initiatives. In a museum dedicated to human rights, what, exactly, does this entail?

Museums dedicated to human rights offer a unique perspective on the field and practices of human rights as sites for knowledge production and transfer. Their presentation of human rights can be historical or contemporary, of local or international remit, and they have the benefit of addressing potentially contentious issues from several competing perspectives. Museums are aptly equipped to expand on any one singular disciplinarian treatment of the subject by thoughtfully examining human rights in relation to other useful concepts such as identity, culture, political action, social movements, and the law. This means that exhibitions and programming initiatives within the museum setting have the capacity to be polyvalent and forward-looking in their scope, and self-reflexive in their approach. Museums house collections of reference materials related to the subjects of their display. As such, their libraries, archives, and collections constitute important research material for communities of researchers, more so when museums establish research centres in order to support ongoing research as part of their institutional mission.

Museums dedicated to human rights are sites of informal learning and free enquiry that provide accessible education and a public forum for research undertaken in the field. As alternatives to academic institutions, human rights museums reach socially diverse audiences, and deploy a broad range of media in their treatment of human rights subjects. Museums are themselves complex media that rely on multiple modes of communication from films, oral histories, and digital technologies, to object-based presentations and textual narratives, lecture series and contemporary art as a means of probing subjects of enquiry from a diversity of perspectives. A museum dedicated to addressing social issues through a human rights lens will necessarily reach out to a variety of communities. In many instances, one can expect these museums to serve the needs of communities whose rights have been violated, by bringing public attention to these violations and an opportunity to project the voices of those previously silenced by socially unjust behaviours. In a more general way, however, human rights museums can also nurture the development of a human rights consciousness by the diversity and effectiveness of its presentations and practices.

Yet another significant feature of human rights museums is the manner they mobilize publics through various forms of social media

1 2 3 4 5 6 7 8 9 10 11 12 13 **14**

and activist interventions. One of the ways that museums are engaging in the work of human rights borrows from contemporary human rights practices and discourses themselves. Increasingly, the pedagogies of human rights organizations can be useful to museum work: a human rights education perspective instructs on methods of advocacy, public outreach, and mobilization, in addition to capacity building, facilitating, and conflict prevention and resolution. These skills provide models for thinking through how other institutions, human rights museums in particular, approach the field of human rights advocacy in society while contributing to a socially conscious and engaged citizenry. Inspired by the pedagogies of human rights education and the campaign mechanisms of non-governmental organizations such as Anti-Slavery International and the Environmental Justice Foundation, museums dedicated to taking up human rights abuses such as the US Holocaust Memorial Museum in Washington, DC, and the International Slavery Museum in Liverpool, UK, have recently begun to incorporate interventionist strategies in their exhibitions and programming initiatives, providing visitors with the means to become further engaged upon leaving the museum.

In this sense, these institutions are broadening the outreach of other NHRIs such as human rights commissions (which typically *react* to human rights abuses in order to provide redress and prevent recurrences of such abuses in future) by taking proactive measures to encourage citizen involvement in social and political issues. The use of new technologies and social networking allows museums to mobilize publics differently, while responding to human rights situations as they are arising. This agility is a welcome counterpart to the didacticism of exhibitions that can typically take several years to plan and produce, and gives museums the potential to move on human rights ahead of the law.

There has also been a philosophical change in historical consciousness in museum work. In the manner they have relied not only on relating historical injustices, but moreover on examining the legacies of these injustices as a catalyst for future action, the International Coalition of Sites of Conscience has been groundbreaking in developing programming that brings museological and human rights fields closer together. Yet another manifestation is the innovative creation of human rights departments within museum complexes, a move embraced by the Montréal Memorial Holocaust Foundation and the South African Holocaust and Genocide Foundation in Cape Town.

If we return to these three fundamental ideas of what museums as cultural institutions can bring to the table as human rights institutions — as sites for knowledge production and transfer, as sites for informal learning that provide important alternatives to other educational outlets of NHRIs, and as sites to politicize publics, we note that museums offer vastly different modes of entry to the subject than other human rights institutions.

3) The Canadian Museum for Human Rights: The Makings of a New Human Rights Institution

The Canadian Museum for Human Rights (CMHR) is poised to support the work of NHRIs as a major player in human rights museology. While other museums dedicated to human rights exist in cities around the globe, the CMHR proclaims itself the first of its kind in scale and national stature and it has the potential to occupy a central place in the landscape of Canada's human rights institutions.

The CMHR is one of Canada's newest human rights institutions. Conceived in the early millennium[52] by the late media baron, politician, lawyer, and philanthropist Israel (Izzy) Asper,[53] the CMHR was subsequently established as a national institution in 2008 and as the first of Canada's national museums to be located outside of the nation's capital, Ottawa. The CMHR's purpose, articulated in Canada's *Museums Act*,[54] is to "explore the subject of human rights, with special but not exclusive reference to Canada, in order to enhance the public's understanding of human rights, to promote respect for others and to encourage reflection and dialogue."[55] This Act provides Canadian federal museums with a

---

52 Canadian Museum for Human Rights Content Advisory Committee, *Content Advisory Committee Final Report to the Canadian Museum for Human Rights, May 25, 2010* (Winnipeg: Canadian Museum for Human Rights, 2010) at iii [*Final Report to the CMHR*, 2010].

53 Israel Asper (who died in 2003) was founder of the now-dissolved Canwest Global Communications Corporation, a major Canadian media company headquartered in Winnipeg, MB, and with radio, television, and publishing assets in countries around the world. He was leader of the Manitoba Liberal Party from 1970–75.

54 *Museums Act*, SC 1990, c 3 [*Museums Act*].

55 Canadian Museum for Human Rights, *Report to the Minister of Canadian Heritage on the Canadian Museum for Human Rights* (Winnipeg: Canadian Museum for Human Rights, 2008), Section I at 5 [2008 *Report*]. See also, *Museums Act*, above note 54, s 15.2.

certain — though not total — distance from political influence or interference, a distance that is of justifiable concern given the subject matter, with its broad ties to global political landscapes, to which the CMHR is dedicated.

The CMHR differs from a growing number of other museums dedicated to human rights around the world, such as Chile's post-Pinochet era Museo de la Memoria y los Derechos Humanos in Santiago (inaugurated in 2010) or the Liberty Osaka Museum dedicated to the themes of prejudice and discrimination in Japanese society, for its insistence on situating the subject of human rights within a larger framework than one defined strictly by geography and a national history. Rather, it intends to draw on international content as part of its remit, while recognizing the importance of situating human rights discourses in broader historical and societal context. Thus, the CMHR will not focus strictly on Canada's own track record in human rights — with its treatment of First Nations communities across the country, Japanese Canadians during their internment in Canadian camps during the Second World War, or of immigrant Jews fleeing Europe. It will, it appears, endeavour to strike a happy medium, by balancing a wide range of topics transcending national and political borders and including the subjects of First Nations communities, genocides, war and conflicts, and sexual orientation.

Widely recognized as a new kind of institution, the CMHR intends to transcend traditional museum practice by envisioning new models and identifying new learning objectives for achieving social relevance. The CMHR appears to draw inspiration from a number of other museums who share the CMHR's activist objectives, the International Coalition of Sites of Conscience among them.[56] Collectively, these museums, with their socially responsible agendas, are re-conceptualizing not only the core missions and functions of contemporary museums, but their programming initiatives and partnerships as well. In the words of the authors of the *Report to the Minister of Canadian Heritage on the Canadian Museum for Human Rights* (2008 *Report*), the authors suggested that the CMHR should seek to fulfill its roles by engaging publics simultaneously as a centre of

---

56 2008 *Report*, above note 55 at 7–9. The Report identifies the following institutions: the Lower East Side Tenement Museum in New York City; the District Six Museum in Cape Town, South Africa; the Museum of Tolerance in Los Angeles; the United States Holocaust Memorial Museum in Washington, DC; the Museum of New Zealand's Te Papa Tongarewa in Wellington; as well as the International Coalition of Sites of Conscience as sites for further study.

education, research, and exhibition, as a place of exploration and reflection, and moreover, as a call to action.[57] This appeal to personal action is in fact the first of a long list of recommendations assembled by the 2008 *Report*, which urged the CMHR to consider itself more than a "passive presenter of objects and ideas" — rather, it espoused the idea that the CMHR should and must "offer visitors the opportunity to experience personal transformation and a personal call to action" should it wish to realize its potential as a leader of human rights and a catalyst for change in the human rights arena.[58] It is this rhetoric, this call to action, this imperative to perform not as a repository but as an "advocate for the principles of human rights"[59] that distinguishes this issues-based institution from traditional object-based museums.

4) Best Practices

The CMHR is scheduled to open its doors to the public in September 2014.[60] While it is obviously too early to comment on the Museum's work, here we will explore the ways that other museums are advancing a human rights culture in order to make recommendations for the future and how the CMHR can support the mandate of NHRIs in three key areas: research activities, public education programs, and exhibition practices.

a) Research Activities

In the 2008 *Report*,[61] the authors recommended that the CMHR "take a leadership role in contributing to national and international dialogue on the future of human rights in an informed and apolitical manner" (Point 31). It also advised that the CMHR actively contribute to public debate while serving "as a leader and role model on the human rights landscape" by engaging in issues ranging from individual and collective rights to environmental rights and responsibilities, sustainable development, privacy, and security (Point 51). The 2008 *Report* also advocated that the CMHR present human rights history and not restrict itself to contemporary human rights issues. It called for the Museum to adopt a flexible approach to presenting the subject of human rights such that the

57 2008 *Report*, *ibid* at 5.
58 *Ibid* at 4.
59 *Final Report to the CMHR*, 2010, above note 52 at 60.
60 As cited on the CMHR website (as of 12 December 2013), online: CMHR http://humanrightsmuseum.ca/home.
61 2008 *Report*, above note 55.

traditional permanent and temporary structures of museum exhibitions be rethought in light of core and supplementary categories, allowing the CMHR to adapt quickly to changes in global human rights issues as these evolve on an ongoing basis.

While these recommendations may appear to be articulated in light of the CMHR's exhibitionary functions, they are also very useful when considering other institutional divisions that can serve the dual purposes of generating content for exhibitions and producing research for the benefit of the larger field of human rights. While most museums house collections that serve as the sites of ongoing research and future exhibition material, fewer institutions have the in-house facilities and financial resources to fully capitalize on the research possibilities that their collections provide by systematically opening these to a broad community of scholars. The CMHR has an exceptional opportunity to act upon the recommendations of the 2008 *Report* and to develop a cutting-edge research centre as Dominique Clément has argued, to attract visiting scholars, local professionals, school groups, and other specialized interest groups that would not only utilize the archival, bibliographic, and material collections of the CMHR as a site for ongoing research, but also nurture a diverse international community of researchers and scholars in-residence whose research platforms and outcomes could further inform the CMHR's exhibition mandates and programming needs.[62]

Several models of this institutional type exist, for example at the US Holocaust Memorial Museum's Center for Advanced Holocaust Studies in Washington, DC, where visiting scholar programs host researchers from numerous academic disciplines to pursue studies related to the Museum's collection — some of which has not yet been examined by scholars. Likewise, the Canadian Centre for Architecture (CCA) in Montréal, Canada, is an institution that proclaims itself first an international research centre to advance ideas about the history, theory, practice, and role of architecture in society, and only secondly describes itself as a museum. While the CCA is rich in material collections, its exhibitions have clearly demonstrated the effect of the issues-based turn on museography.

62 An excellent summary, prepared by academic and human rights scholar Dominique Clément, outlines a number of possibilities to enhance the CMHR as a hub of human rights-based research. See Dominique Clément, *New Scholars, Historians and the Canadian Museum for Human Rights: Brief Submitted to the Content Advisory Committee at the Canadian Museum for Human Rights* (2009), online: History of Rights www.historyofrights.com/PDF/CMHR_brief.pdf.

Its exhibitions are ideas-rich, and many are not explicitly focused on material collections, a condition it could well share with the CMHR. Much like the CMHR has done throughout its formative years, when the CCA was founded by architect and philanthropist Phyllis Lambert in 1979, it too proclaimed its intention as a new kind of cultural institution, and like the CMHR, did so out of the conviction that architecture — read now human rights — should be positioned as a public concern.

In thinking itself an international reference and resource centre of human rights, the CMHR benefits from partnerships with other local human rights initiatives in Winnipeg, notably the University of Manitoba's Centre for Human Rights Research and this Centre's network of more than 150 scholars. In 2011, the CMHR signed a memorandum of understanding with the University of Manitoba to co-operate on human rights education and research, and towards this end *Critical Conversations: The Idea of a Human Rights Museum* was launched as a lecture series that brought together academics and CMHR professionals to engage the idea of a human rights museum from multidisciplinary perspectives. This university-museum partnership can continue to be an extremely fruitful one, and one which requires nurturing in order to draw upon the expertise of professionals in both arenas, while expanding upon the intended publics that these milieus serve as distinct social institutions. But the CMHR's partnership need not stop at the University's doors. Establishing partnerships with territorial, provincial, and federal human rights commissions, national truth and reconciliation commissions, as well as international organizations, such as Amnesty International and Human Rights Watch, would also enable research conducted at the CMHR to serve the needs of other civil society organizations.[63]

b) Public Education Programs

The 2008 *Report* linked the importance of the CMHR as a research centre to its educational mandate. The *2010 CMHR Content Advisory Committee Report* (2010 *Report*) also emphasized that the CMHR should "conduct its public education programs and design its exhibits so as to add to the global store of understanding and acceptance, and promote respect for

63 At the time of writing, the CMHR had also recently signed a Memorandum of Understanding with the Canadian Association of Statutory Human Rights Associations (CASHRA) aimed at facilitating collaboration and education about human rights between the CMHR and the CASHRA.

human rights."[64] Our review of existing museum public education programs dedicated to human rights reveals a focus on three main areas: awareness, substantive knowledge, and capacity building. In other words, participants in a human rights culture need to be able to recognize their rights and the rights of others, know the content and scope of their rights, and identify actions they can take to enhance the dignity and freedoms of all.

The District Six Museum in Cape Town, South Africa, does all three, in part by framing its public education programs through a dialogue between the Museum and its visitors:

> The Programme attempts to go beyond presenting knowledge in a one-directional way, and instead engage the public in such a way that they are empowered to generate knowledge. The museum has always acknowledged that knowledge not be confined to the literary or the traditionally academic. It thus encourages the recognition and preservation of the diverse knowledge of Cape Town's cultural practices generated in the public. By engaging with public in this way, the programme hopes to go beyond documentation, and is a crucial part of the vitality of a Museum, which places as much emphasis on the present and future as it does on the past.[65]

Among their offerings, which include film screenings in addition to musical and theatre performances, staff at the District Six Museum train young people to conduct oral history interviews which will themselves become part of the Museum's collection. These staff also teach grade eleven students to give presentations about the museum as part of the Heritage Ambassadors Program. In addition to the knowledge and public speaking skills the program aims to develop, it empowers youth to be leaders, aims to improve self-esteem, and provides role models for elementary school students who then see the Museum as "a cool place to be."[66] The District Six Museum uses dialogue and leadership training to impart and create knowledge for the benefit of the learners and the Museum. As the 2008 *Report* suggested that the CMHR's educational programs should be targeted, although not exclusively, at youth, we can

---

64 *Final Report to the CMHR*, 2010, above note 52.

65 District Six Museum, "Public Education Programme," online: District Six www.districtsix.co.za/public%20education.htm.

66 District Six Museum, "Heritage Ambassadors Programme," online: District Six www.districtsix.co.za/ambassadors.htm.

imagine a program for elementary and high school students that imparts substantive knowledge while building Canadians who are ready to lead in the field of human rights.

A further advantage is that museums can target their initiatives to certain sectors of society in order to reach societal groups that are not participating in the conventional education process on emerging topics in human rights. In this vein, the US Holocaust Memorial Museum created a program aimed at educating societal leaders in genocide prevention:

> Who are our "leaders"? We have defined them as those holding leadership positions in professions that hold the public trust. This includes law enforcement, civil servants, judges, medical professionals, military — basically — those professionals in positions to safeguard the ideals of a democratic society . . . those roles come with responsibility.[67]

One part of this program focuses on military officers-in-training and active duty officers. The substance of the program aims to teach that genocide is a process that begins long before the actual killing and to highlight some early warning signs that can lead to preventative action. It further questions the roles and complicity of professional institutions in the genocidal process, as well as those of individual professionals.[68]

Each of these examples demonstrates educational programs that are contributing to the formation of a human rights culture. The programs improve awareness of how rights are at issue in our everyday lives and encourage participants, as well as increasing their capacity, to act in a manner that protects and respects human rights. The CMHR could position its programs to complement the curriculum of Canadian educational institutions and human rights commissions in order to reach broader audiences and challenge the boundaries of human rights norms. In this way, the CMHR has an opportunity to impact Canada's human rights culture in a formative way.

---

67 Jennifer A Ciardelli, "Can A Museum Prevent Genocide?: Educational Training for Military Professionals at the United States Holocaust Memorial Museum" (Paper delivered at the Federation of International Human Rights Museums Conference, 2011) at 6, online: FIHRM www.fihrm.org/conference/conference2011.html#papers.

68 *Ibid* at 12–20.

c) Exhibition Practices

The 2010 Content Advisory Committee recommended that the CMHR's exhibitions demonstrate an understanding of the colonial experience of Canadian Indigenous Peoples and demonstrate respect for their culture, experience, and language. One of the challenges of representing the First Nations experience is presenting it in a way that does not oversimplify or essentialize culture. Furthermore, the legacies of an oppressive colonial past are ongoing, such as discrimination, poor health, and inadequate water supplies on reserves.[69] The 2010 *Report* recommends that the CMHR work to build a relationship of trust with Indigenous Peoples and ensure that Indigenous Peoples "are available within the Museum to contribute to all aspects of exhibit development, communication, and programming, including at senior levels."[70]

The International Slavery Museum of the National Museums Liverpool in the United Kingdom shows respect and empathy for enslaved Africans in its comprehensive exhibition on the trans-Atlantic slave trade. The exhibition space is divided into three sections, "Life in West Africa," "Enslavement and the Middle Passage," and "Legacies of Slavery." By starting with depicting life in West Africa, the gallery grounds the visitor's experience in the rich cultures and lives of the victims of slavery before engaging in the histories of the human rights abuses they suffered. This helps the visitor identify with the experiences of the slaves,

---

69 At the time of writing, Canada's recognition of the right to water is in flux. In 2010, Canada abstained on a UN General Assembly resolution titled "The Human Right to Water and Sanitation" GA Res 64/292, UNGAOR, 2010, UN Doc A/RES/64/292. In 2002, Canada refused to support *Comment 15 of the UN Committee on Economic, Social and Cultural Rights*, UNCESCOR, UN Doc E/C.12/2002/11, (2003) which confirmed that the right to water is implicitly contained in the *International Covenant on Economic, Social and Cultural Rights*. However, in June 2012 at the Rio+20 UN Conference on Sustainable Development, Minister of the Environment, Peter Kent, stated: "With regard to the reaffirmation of the human right to safe drinking water and basic sanitation, Canada's understanding is that this right is an essential component of the right to an adequate standard of living under Article 11 of the *International Covenant on Economic, Social and Cultural Rights*. It is also Canada's understanding that this right is to be progressively realized and does not encompass transboundary water issues including bulk water trade, nor any mandatory allocation of international development assistance," online: Environment Canada www.ec.gc.ca/default.asp?lang=En&n=6F2DE1CA-1&news=B9CDF026-DABF-45D7-B447-9040A6CDFD3C. The right to water would be a fascinating topic for a CMHR exhibition.

70 *Final Report to the CMHR*, 2010, above note 52 at 28.

recognizing that these victims are fellow human beings. The third section reminds the visitor that discriminatory practices live on in our societies, but that in spite of the challenges posed by ongoing discrimination, survivors of the African Diaspora continue to achieve as leaders in the West.[71] At the end of the "Legacies of Slavery" gallery, the visitor finds the "Campaign Zone." This zone goes one step further and encourages the visitor to take action against modern forms of slavery. At the time of writing this essay, for example, the highlighted issue is adult and child forced labour in cotton production in Uzbekistan.[72]

The trans-Atlantic slave trade exhibition provides several helpful examples of modes of display practice that move society towards a human rights culture. Levin refers to the first as "unpacking assumptions." In her work on feminist and queer theory in museum practice, she asks museum professionals to be self-reflective on gender-based biases and urges them to "ask what unexamined gender assumptions continue to be unpacked every time we mount an exhibition or greet a visitor in our galleries."[73] The International Slavery Museum demonstrates a self-reflective practice by challenging museum professionals and visitors to respect the enslaved, not only for their suffering, but for their rich culture and modes of resistance. The CMHR should make certain that it has a system to ensure continual self-reflection, which would include committing to employ diverse staff who can critically assess the various representations the Museum makes in its displays.

The campaign zone within the trans-Atlantic slave trade exhibition challenges our own complicity in modern forms of slavery as we support enforced labour by purchasing cotton clothes made by forced labourers. It would be too simple to merely create a hatred of those who made a living from the historical trans-Atlantic slave trade. The campaign zone helps the visitor recognize his or her own responsibility for ongoing slavery, and, even more critically, provides visitors with the capability to engage in different practices going forward. The Museum seeks not only to engage with visitors during the time spent at the museum, but to actively transform these visitors so that they will continue to dialogue with

---

71 International Slavery Museum, "Museum Highlights," online: International Slavery Museum www.liverpoolmuseums.org.uk/ism/collections/.

72 International Slavery Museum, "Uzbekistan: Cotton and the Crushing of a Nation," online: International Slavery Museum www.liverpoolmuseums.org.uk/ism/exhibitions/whitegold/uzbekistan.aspx.

73 Amy K Levin, "Unpacking Gender: Creating Complex Models for Gender Inclusivity in Museums," in Sandell & Nightingale, above note 51 at 159.

others and engage in their own self-reflection long after the visit is over. In this way, an exhibition can support the creation of a human rights culture by changing the way visitors talk, think, and act regarding human rights abuses. The CMHR could use this precedent in its own exhibitions in order to support the transformation of visitors into leaders who both recognize human rights violations as they are occurring and are empowered to take action against them.

E. CONCLUSION

Cultural institutions committed to social justice and societal development demonstrate that by encouraging cutting-edge research that builds into and across museum practices, by creating educational programs that lead to the realization of rights both in the manner in which lessons are taught and in the substantive building of knowledge and skills, and by deploying self-reflexive strategies in curating exhibitions, museums can be powerful forces in the promotion of human rights culture.

The idea that the emergent genre of human rights museums should ally itself with other national human rights institutions initiates an important conversation on the relationship of human rights and museums as conduits to achieving human freedoms. Like national human rights institutions, museums are implicated in their own positioning as state-funded institutions that are open to, and designed in support of, public needs. Yet, precisely because of this unique position, there is an innate opportunity for museums to fill an existing gap in the work of NHRIs by demonstrating in their practices the very routes of complementarity such as public monitoring and campaigning that Amartya Sen argues are essential to advancing the realization of humanity's ethical claims to freedom. Museums can broaden the human rights lens by addressing a wider range of historical and contemporary issues than many of the NHRIs whose focus is limited by legislative mandates to discrimination and equity. Museums also provide a different public forum by enabling valuable dialogical engagement to occur amongst a diverse range of community members and interest groups.

Issues-based museums are most effective when they take up a complex idea in complex terms, in other words, when human rights museums address their subject matter from a broad human rights perspective that acknowledges the expertise of a wide array of societal forces and academic disciplines. This approach transcends human rights law and, as Sen suggests, renders explicit the many activities required to advance human freedoms as a social practice. Many museums have already done this, whether by implementing innovative programming that instructs on human rights pedagogies, or by facilitating networking between museum visitors and established human rights organizations.

With the extensive range of their institutional expertise, museums are well equipped to assume the promotional and educational aspects of human rights that NHRIs are mandated to provide. They also have much to gain in collaborative opportunities and infrastructural and institutional support by this association. Museums have a growing opportunity as they increasingly affirm their roles in the arenas of human rights and human rights museology, thereby contributing to the culture of human rights.

1 2 3 4 5 6 7 8 9 10 11 12 13 **14**

SELECTED READINGS

A. BOOKS

Azmi, Shaheen, Lorne Foster, & Lesley Jacobs, eds. *Balancing Competing Human Rights Claims in Diverse Societies: Institutions, Policy, Principles* (Toronto: Irwin Law, 2012).

Backhouse, Constance, & Leah Cohen. *The Secret Oppression: Sexual Harassment of Working Women* (Toronto: Macmillan, 1978).

Cornish, Mary, Fay Faraday, & Jo-Anne Pickel. *Enforcing Human Rights in Ontario* (Aurora, ON: Canada Law Book, 2009).

Howe, R Brian & David Johnson. *Restraining Equality: Human Rights Commissions in Canada* (Toronto: University of Toronto Press, 2000).

Langer, Rosanna. "Publics and Counter-Publics: Exploring the Contested Nature of the Public Interest in Domestic Human Rights Administration" in *Symposium Proceedings, Values, Ethics and the Public Sector: How to Serve the Public Interest?* (Ottawa: St. Paul University Centre for Ethics, 2006).

MacKinnon, Catharine A. *Sexual Harassment of Working Women* (New Haven, CT: Yale University Press, 1979).

Nightingale, Eithne, & Richard Sandell, eds. *Museums, Equality and Social Justice* (London: Routledge, 2012).

Tarnopolsky, Walter Surma. *The Canadian Bill of Rights* (Toronto, Carswell, 1966).

Yalden, Maxwell. *Transforming Rights* (Toronto: University of Toronto Press, 2009).

B. PERIODICALS

Castel, J-G. "International Year for Human Rights 1968" (1968) 46 Can Bar Rev 545.

Cox, Rachel. "Psychological Harassment Legislation in Québec: The First Five Years" (2010) 32 International Comparative Labor Law and Policy Journal 55.

Howe, R Brian, & Malcolm J Andrade. "The Reputations of Human Rights Commissions in Canada" (Fall/automne 1994) 9:2 CJLS/RCDS 1.

Joong-Seop, Kim. "Toward Human Rights in the Local Community: Multiple Approaches for Implementation" (2010) 39:1 Development and Society 119.

Murray, Rachel. "National Human Rights Institutions — Criteria and Factors for Assessing their Effectiveness" (2007) 25:2 Nethl QHR 189.

Tarnopolsky, Walter Surma. "The Iron Hand in the Velvet Glove" (1968) 46 Can Bar Rev 565.

Wacquant, Loïc. "The Penalization of Poverty and the Rise of Neo-liberalism" (2001) 9 Eur J Crim Pol'y & Research 401.

C. REPORTS

Alberta, Human Rights Commission. *Equal in Dignity and Rights — A Review of Human Rights in Alberta by the Alberta Human Rights Review Panel* (Edmonton: AHRC, 1994).

Black, William. *Report Concerning Internal Procedure of the B.C. Council of Human Rights and Related Agencies* (November 1993).

Black, William, & Kathryn Thomson. *Report on Legal Representation Models under the British Columbia Human Rights Code* (British Columbia, 1998).

Canada, Parliament House of Commons Special Committee on Hate Propaganda in Canada. *Report to the Minister of Justice of the Special Committee on Hate Propaganda in Canada* (Ottawa: Roger Duhamel, 1966).

Canadian Human Rights Act Review Panel. *Promoting Equality: A New Vision* (Ottawa: Minister of Justice, 2000).

Eid, Paul, & Me Christine Campbell, Québec, Commission des droits de la personne et des droits de la jeunesse. *La judiciarisation des personnes itinérantes à Montréal: un profilage social* (Québec: CDPDJ, 2009).

Moon, Richard. *Report to the Canadian Human Rights Commission Concerning Section 13 of the* Canadian Human Rights Act *and the Regulation of Hate Speech on the Internet* (October 2008), online: CHRC www.chrc-ccdp.ca/pdf/moon_report_en.pdf.

Ontario Human Rights Commission. *Paying the Price: The Human Cost of Racial Profiling: Inquiry Report* (Toronto: OHRC, 2003).

Pinto, Andrew. *Report of the Ontario Human Rights Review 2012* (Toronto: OAG, 2012), online: OAG www.attorneygeneral.jus.gov.on.ca/english/about/pubs/human_rights/Pinto_human_rights_report_2012-ENG.pdf.

D. OTHER

Canadian Human Rights Reporter, online: www.cdn-hr-reporter.ca/.

Ministry of the Attorney General of Ontario. "Human Rights in Ontario" (Toronto: Ministry of the Attorney General, 2008), online: Ministry of the Attorney General www.attorneygeneral.jus.gov.on.ca/english/news/2008/20080630-ohrc-brochure-en.pdf.

Principles Relating to the Status of National Institutions, annex to *National Institutions for the Promotion and Protection of Human Rights*, CHR Res 54, UNESCOR, Supp No 2, UN Doc E/1992/22, (1992); GA Res 48/134, UNGAOR, 48th Sess, (1993) Annex.

1 2 3 4 5 6 7 8 9 10 11 12 13 14

INDEX

ABOUT THE EDITORS

Shelagh Day is an expert on human rights with many years of experience working with governments and non-governmental organizations, the President and Senior Editor of the Canadian Human Rights Reporter, as well as a Director of the Poverty and Human Rights Centre in Vancouver.

Lucie Lamarche is a professor of law at the Université du Québec à Montréal (UQÀM). She is the former Gordon F Henderson Chair in Human Rights and the former Research Director of the Human Rights Research and Education Centre of the University of Ottawa.

Ken Norman is a professor of Law at the University of Saskatchewan.

Kolibri 360 GmbH
Ferdinand-Jühlke-Straße 7
99095 Erfurt, Deutschland
produktsicherheit@kolibri360.de